International Corporate Finance
FIN 4920

Madura

THOMSON
SOUTH-WESTERN

Australia · Canada · Mexico · Singapore · Spain · United Kingdom · United States

THOMSON

SOUTH-WESTERN

International Corporate Finance
Madura

Executive Editors:
Michele Baird, Maureen Staudt &
Michael Stranz

Project Development Manager:
Linda deStefano

Sr. Marketing Coordinators:
Lindsay Annett and Sara Mercurio

Production/Manufacturing Manager:
Donna M. Brown

Production Editorial Manager:
Dan Plofchan

Pre-Media Services Supervisor:
Becki Walker

Rights and Permissions Specialist:
Kalina Ingham Hintz

Cover Image
Getty Images*

The Adaptable Courseware Program consists of products and additions to existing Thomson products that are produced from camera-ready copy. Peer review, class testing, and accuracy are primarily the responsibility of the author(s).

For more information, please contact Thomson Custom Solutions, 5191 Natorp Boulevard, Mason, OH 45040. Or you can visit our Internet site at http://www.thomsoncustom.com

For permission to use material from this text or product, contact us by:
Tel (800) 730-2214
Fax (800) 730 2215
www.thomsonrights.com

ISBN-13: 978-0-324-60707-9
ISBN-10: 0-324-60707-5

International Divisions List

Asia (Including India):
Thomson Learning
(a division of Thomson Asia Pte Ltd)
5 Shenton Way #01-01
UIC Building
Singapore 068808
Tel: (65) 6410-1200
Fax: (65) 6410-1208

Australia/New Zealand:
Thomson Learning Australia
102 Dodds Street
Southbank, Victoria 3006
Australia

Latin America:
Thomson Learning
Seneca 53
Colonia Polano
11560 Mexico, D.F., Mexico
Tel (525) 281-2906
Fax (525) 281-2656

Canada:
Thomson Nelson
1120 Birchmount Road
Toronto, Ontario
Canada M1K 5G4
Tel (416) 752-9100
Fax (416) 752-8102

UK/Europe/Middle East/Africa:
Thomson Learning
High Holborn House
50-51 Bedford Row
London, WC1R 4LS
United Kingdom
Tel 44 (020) 7067-2500
Fax 44 (020) 7067-2600

Spain (Includes Portugal):
Thomson Paraninfo
Calle Magallanes 25
28015 Madrid
España
Tel 34 (0)91 446-3350
Fax 34 (0)91 445-6218

Acknowledgements

The content of this text has been adapted from the following product(s):

International Financial Management
Madura ISBN-10: (0-324-16551-X)
ISBN-13: (978-0-324-16551-7)

Table Of Contents

1

MULTINATIONAL FINANCIAL MANAGEMENT: AN OVERVIEW

Firms continually devise strategies to improve their cash flows and therefore enhance shareholder wealth. Some strategies involve the penetration of foreign markets. Since foreign markets can be distinctly different from local markets, they create opportunities for improving the firm's cash flows. Many barriers to entry into foreign markets have been reduced or removed recently, thereby encouraging firms to pursue international business (producing and/or selling goods in foreign countries). Consequently, many firms have evolved into multinational corporations (MNCs), which are defined as firms that engage in some form of international business.

Initially, firms may merely attempt to export products to a particular country or import supplies from a foreign manufacturer. Over time, however, many of them recognize additional foreign opportunities and eventually establish subsidiaries in foreign countries. Some businesses, such as Dow Chemical, ExxonMobil, American Brands, and Colgate-Palmolive, commonly generate more than half of their sales in foreign countries. A prime example is the Coca-Cola Co., which distributes its products in more than 160 countries and uses 40 different currencies. Over 60 percent of its total annual operating income is typically generated outside the United States.

An understanding of international financial management is crucial not only for the largest MNCs with numerous foreign subsidiaries but also for other firms that conduct international business. Even smaller U.S. firms commonly generate more than 20 percent of their sales in foreign markets, including AMSCO International (Pennsylvania), Ferro (Ohio), Interlake (Illinois), Medtronic (Minnesota), Sybron (Wisconsin), and Synoptics (California). These U.S. firms that conduct international business tend to focus on the niches that have made them successful in the United States. They tend to penetrate specialty markets where they will not have to compete with large firms that could capitalize on economies of scale. While some small firms have established subsidiaries, many of them penetrate foreign markets through exports.

Seventy-five percent of U.S. firms that export have fewer than 100 employees.

International financial management is important even to companies that have no international business, since these companies must recognize how their foreign competitors will be affected by movements in exchange rates, foreign interest rates, labor costs, and inflation. Such economic characteristics can affect the foreign competitors' costs of production and pricing policies.

Companies must also recognize how domestic competitors that obtain foreign supplies or foreign financing will be affected by economic conditions in foreign countries. If these domestic competitors are able to reduce their costs by capitalizing on opportunities in international markets, they may be able to reduce their prices without reducing their profit margins. This could allow them to increase market share at the expense of the purely domestic companies.

This chapter provides a background on the goals of an MNC and the potential risk and returns from engaging in international business.

The specific objectives of this chapter are to:
- identify the main goal of the MNC and potential conflicts with that goal,
- describe the key theories that justify international business, and
- explain the common methods used to conduct international business.

GOAL OF THE MNC

The commonly accepted goal of an MNC is to maximize shareholder wealth. Developing a goal is necessary because all decisions should contribute to its accomplishment. Thus, if the objective were to maximize earnings in the near future, rather than to maximize shareholder wealth, the firm's policies would be different.

Some MNCs based outside the United States tend to focus more on satisfying the respective goals of their governments, banks, or employees than on maximizing shareholder wealth.

The focus of this text is also on MNCs whose parents wholly own any foreign subsidiaries, which means that the U.S. parent is the sole owner of the subsidiaries. This is the most common form of ownership of U.S.-based MNCs, and it enables financial managers throughout the MNC to have a single goal of maximizing the value of the entire MNC instead of maximizing the value of any particular foreign subsidiary.

Conflicts with the MNC Goal

It has often been argued that managers of a firm may make decisions that conflict with the firm's goal to maximize shareholder wealth. For example, a decision to establish a subsidiary in one location versus another may be based on the location's appeal to a particular manager rather than on its potential benefits to shareholders. A decision to expand may be determined by a manager's desire to make the division grow in order to receive more responsibility and compensation. When a firm has only one owner who is also the sole manager, such a conflict of goals does not occur. However, for corporations with shareholders who differ from their managers, a conflict of goals can exist. This conflict is often referred to as the **agency problem**.

The costs of ensuring that managers maximize shareholder wealth (referred to as *agency costs*) are normally larger for MNCs than for purely domestic firms for several reasons. First, MNCs with subsidiaries scattered around the world may experience larger agency problems because monitoring managers of distant subsidiaries in foreign countries is more difficult. Second, foreign subsidiary managers raised in different cultures may not follow uniform goals. Third, the sheer size of the larger MNCs can also create large agency problems. Fourth, some non-U.S. managers tend to downplay the short-term effects of decisions, which may result in decisions for foreign subsidiaries of the U.S.-based MNCs that are inconsistent with maximizing shareholder wealth.

Financial managers of an MNC with several subsidiaries may be tempted to make decisions that maximize the values of their respective subsidiaries. This objective will not necessarily coincide with maximizing the value of the overall MNC.

Example A subsidiary manager obtained financing from the parent firm (headquarters) to develop and sell a new product. The manager estimated the costs and benefits of the project from the subsidiary's perspective and determined that the project was feasible. However, the manager neglected to realize that any earnings from this project remitted to the parent would be heavily taxed by the host government. The estimated after-tax benefits received by the parent were more than offset by the cost of financing the project. While the subsidiary's individual value was enhanced, the MNC's overall value was reduced.

If financial managers are to maximize the wealth of their MNC's shareholders, they must implement policies that maximize the value of the overall MNC rather than the value of their respective subsidiaries. Many MNCs require major decisions by subsidiary managers to be approved by the parent. However, it is difficult for the parent to monitor all decisions made by subsidiary managers.

Impact of Management Control

The magnitude of agency costs can vary with the management style of the MNC. A centralized management style, as illustrated in the top section of Exhibit 1.1, can reduce agency costs because it allows managers of the parent to control foreign subsidiaries and therefore reduces the power of subsidiary managers. However, the parent's managers may make poor decisions for the subsidiary if they are not as informed as subsidiary managers about financial characteristics of the subsidiary.

The alternative style of organizing an MNC's management is a decentralized management style, as illustrated in the bottom section of Exhibit 1.1. This style is more likely to result in higher agency costs because subsidiary managers may make decisions that do not focus on maximizing the value of the entire MNC. Yet, this style gives more control to those managers who are closer to the subsidiary's operations and environment. To the extent that subsidiary managers recognize the goal of maximizing the value of the overall MNC and are compensated in accordance with that goal, the decentralized management style may be more effective.

Given the obvious tradeoff between centralized and decentralized management styles, some MNCs attempt to achieve the advantages of both styles. That is, they allow subsidiary managers to make the key decisions about their respective

Exhibit 1.1
Management Styles of MNCs

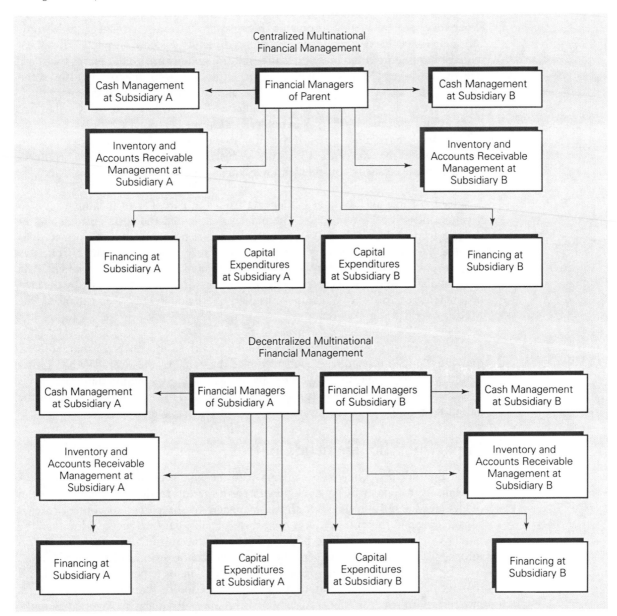

operations, but the parent's management monitors the decisions to ensure that they are in the best interests of the entire MNC.

How the Internet Facilitates Management Control. The Internet is making it easier for the parent to monitor the actions and performance of its foreign subsidiaries.

Example The parent of Jersey, Inc., has subsidiaries in Australia and Italy. The subsidiaries are in different time zones, so communicating frequently by phone is inconvenient and expensive. In addition, financial reports and designs of new products or plant sites cannot be easily communicated over the phone. The Internet allows the foreign subsidiaries to e-mail updated information in a standardized format to avoid language problems and to send images of financial reports and product designs. The parent can easily track inventory, sales, expenses, and earnings of each subsidiary on a weekly or monthly basis. Thus, the use of the Internet can reduce agency costs due to international business.

Impact of Corporate Control

An MNC is subject to various forms of corporate control that can be used to reduce agency problems. First, an MNC may partially compensate its board members and its executives with its stock, which can encourage them to make decisions that maximize the MNC's stock price. However, this strategy may effectively control only decisions by managers and board members who receive stock as compensation. In addition, some managers may still make decisions that conflict with the MNC's goal if they do not expect their decisions to have much of an impact on the stock price.

A second form of corporate control is the threat of a hostile takeover if the MNC is inefficiently managed. In theory, this threat is supposed to encourage managers to make decisions that enhance the MNC's value, since other types of decisions would cause the MNC's stock price to decline. Another firm might then acquire the MNC at a low price and terminate the existing managers. In the past, this threat was not very imposing for managers of subsidiaries in foreign countries because foreign governments commonly protected employees; therefore, the potential benefits from a takeover were effectively eliminated. However, governments have recently recognized that such protectionism may promote inefficiencies, and they are now more willing to accept takeovers and the subsequent layoffs that occur.

A third form of corporate control is monitoring by large shareholders. U.S.-based MNCs are commonly monitored by mutual funds and pension funds because a large proportion of their outstanding shares are held by these institutions. Their monitoring tends to focus on broad issues to ensure that the MNC uses a compensation system that motivates managers or board members to make decisions to maximize the MNC's value; to use excess cash for repurchasing shares of stock rather than investing in questionable projects; and to ensure that the MNC does not insulate itself from the threat of a takeover (by implementing anti-takeover amendments, for example). An MNC whose decisions appear inconsistent with maximizing shareholder wealth will be subjected to shareholder activism as pension funds and other large institutional shareholders lobby for management changes or other changes. MNCs that have been subjected to various forms of shareholder activism include Eastman Kodak, IBM, and Sears Roebuck.

Like U.S. mutual funds and pension funds, foreign-owned banks also maintain large stock portfolios (unlike U.S. commercial banks, which do not use deposited funds to purchase stocks). The foreign banks are large and hold a sufficient proportion of shares of numerous firms (including some U.S.-based MNCs) to have some influence on key corporate policies. Their additional role as a lender to many of these firms enhances their ability to monitor corporate policies. To date, however, these banks have not played a major role in corporate control. In general, they do not attempt to intervene unless a particular firm is experiencing major financial problems.

Corporate control on MNCs based in the United States has increased and is sometimes cited as the reason for the unusually strong stock price performance of U.S. firms during the 1990s. Corporate policies are now undertaken with more awareness of their impact on the stock price.

Historically, other countries accepted a broad goal for managers to satisfy not just shareholders, but also the employees, the government, and the local community. In recent years, however, as the use of stock to finance business has become more common in other countries, there is an increasing focus on maximizing shareholder wealth. Furthermore, other countries are adopting U.S. corporate control practices as a means of forcing local firms to make decisions that satisfy their shareholders.

Constraints Interfering with the MNC's Goal

When financial managers of MNCs attempt to maximize their firm's value, they are confronted with various constraints that can be classified as environmental, regulatory, or ethical in nature.

Environmental Constraints. Each country enforces its own environmental constraints. Some countries may enforce more of these restrictions on a subsidiary whose parent is based in a different country. Building codes, disposal of production waste materials, and pollution controls are examples of restrictions that force subsidiaries to incur additional costs. Many European countries have recently imposed tougher antipollution laws as a result of severe pollution problems.

Regulatory Constraints. Each country also enforces its own regulatory constraints pertaining to taxes, currency convertibility rules, earnings remittance restrictions, and other regulations that can affect cash flows of a subsidiary established there. Because these regulations can influence cash flows, financial managers must consider them when assessing policies. Also, any change in these regulations may require revision of existing financial policies, so financial managers should monitor the regulations for any potential changes over time.

Ethical Constraints. There is no consensus standard of business conduct that applies to all countries. A business practice that is perceived to be unethical in one country may be totally ethical in another. For example, U.S.-based MNCs are well aware that certain business practices that are accepted in some less developed countries would be declared illegal in the United States. Bribes to governments in order to receive special tax breaks or other favors are common in some countries. A recent report presented to Congress estimated that U.S. firms lost out on at least $36 billion of international business transactions because of bribes paid by foreign competitors. The MNCs face a dilemma. If they do not participate in such practices, they may be at a competitive disadvantage. Yet, if they do participate, their reputations will suffer in countries that do not approve of such practices. Some U.S.-based MNCs have made the costly choice to refrain from business practices that are legal in certain foreign countries but not legal in the United States. Thus, they follow a worldwide code of ethics. This may enhance their worldwide credibility, which can increase global demand for their products.

THEORIES OF INTERNATIONAL BUSINESS

The commonly held theories as to why firms become motivated to expand their business internationally are (1) the theory of comparative advantage, (2) the imperfect markets theory, and (3) the product cycle theory. The three theories overlap to a degree and can complement each other in developing a rationale for the evolution of international business.

Theory of Comparative Advantage

Multinational business has generally increased over time. Part of this growth is due to the heightened realization that specialization by countries can increase production efficiency. Some countries, such as Japan and the United States, have a technology advantage, while other countries, such as Jamaica, Mexico, and South Korea, have an advantage in the cost of basic labor. Since these advantages cannot be easily transported, countries tend to use their advantages to specialize in the production of goods that can be produced with relative efficiency. This explains why countries such as Japan and the United States are large producers of computer components, while countries such as Jamaica and Mexico are large producers of agricultural and handmade goods.

Specialization in some products may result in no production of other products, so that trade between countries is essential. This is the argument made by the classical theory of **comparative advantage**. Comparative advantages allow firms to penetrate foreign markets. Many of the Virgin Islands, for example, specialize in tourism and rely completely on international trade for most products. Although producing some goods would be possible on these islands, it is more efficient to specialize in tourism. That is, the islands are better off using some revenues earned from tourism to import products rather than attempting to produce all the products that they need.

Imperfect Markets Theory

Countries differ with respect to resources available for the production of goods. Yet, even with such comparative advantages, the volume of international business would be limited if all resources could be easily transferred among countries. If markets were perfect, factors of production (except land) would be mobile and freely transferable. The unrestricted mobility of factors would create equality in costs and returns and remove the comparative cost advantage, the rationale for international trade and investment. However, the real world suffers from **imperfect market** conditions where factors of production are somewhat immobile. There are costs and often restrictions related to the transfer of labor and other resources used for production. There may also be restrictions on transferring funds and other resources among countries. Because markets for the various resources used in production are "imperfect," firms often capitalize on a foreign country's resources. Imperfect markets provide an incentive for firms to seek out foreign opportunities.

Product Cycle Theory

One of the more popular explanations as to why firms evolve into MNCs is introduced in the **product cycle theory**. According to this theory, firms become established in the home market as a result of some perceived advantage over existing competitors, such as a need by the market for at least one more supplier of the product. Because information about markets and competition is more readily available at home, a firm is likely to establish itself first in its home country. Foreign demand for the firm's product will initially be accommodated by exporting. As time passes, the firm may feel the only way to retain its advantage over competition in foreign countries is to produce the product in foreign markets, thereby reducing its transportation costs. Over time, the competition in the foreign markets may increase as other producers become more familiar with the firm's product. Then, the firm may develop strategies to prolong the foreign demand for its product. A common approach is to attempt to differentiate the product so that other competitors cannot offer exactly the same product. These phases of the cycle are illustrated in Exhibit 1.2. As an example, 3M Co. uses one new product to penetrate foreign markets. After entering the market, it expands its product line.

There is more to the product cycle theory than is summarized here. This discussion merely suggests that, as a firm matures, it may recognize additional opportunities outside its home country. Whether the firm's foreign business diminishes or expands over time will depend on how successful it is at maintaining some advantage over its competition. The advantage could represent an edge in its production or financing approach that reduces costs or an edge in its marketing approach that generates and maintains a strong demand for its product.

Exhibit 1.2
International Product
Life Cycle

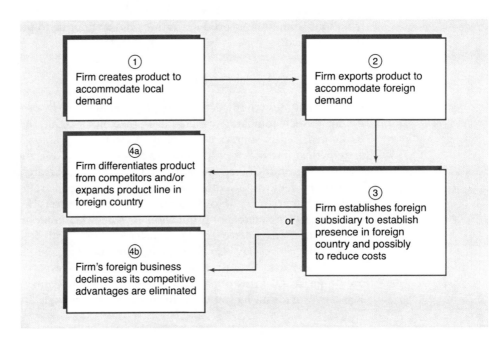

INTERNATIONAL BUSINESS METHODS

Firms use several methods to conduct international business. The most common methods are these:

- International trade
- Licensing
- Franchising
- Joint ventures
- Acquisitions of existing operations
- Establishing new foreign subsidiaries

Each method is discussed in turn, with some emphasis on its risk and return characteristics.

International Trade

International trade is a relatively conservative approach that can be used by firms to penetrate markets (by exporting) or to obtain supplies at a low cost (by importing). This approach entails minimal risk because the firm does not place any of its capital at risk. If the firm experiences a decline in its exporting or importing, it can normally reduce or discontinue this part of its business at a low cost.

HTTP:// USING THE WEB

Trade Conditions for Industries An outlook of international trade conditions for each of several industries is provided at http://www.ita.doc.gov/td/industry/otea.

Many large U.S.-based MNCs, including Boeing, DuPont, General Electric, and IBM, generate more than $4 billion in annual sales from exporting. Yet, more than 20 percent of the value of all U.S. exports is provided by small businesses.

How the Internet Facilitates International Trade. Many firms use their website to list the products that they sell, along with the price for each product. This allows them to easily advertise their products to potential importers anywhere in the world without mailing brochures to various countries. In addition, a firm can add to its product line or change prices by simply revising its website. Thus, importers need only monitor an exporter's website periodically to keep abreast of its product information.

Firms can also use their websites to accept orders online. Some products such as software can be delivered directly to the importer over the Internet in the form of a file that lands in the importer's computer. Other products must be shipped, but the Internet makes it easier to track the shipping process. An importer can transmit its order for products via e-mail to the exporter. The exporter's warehouse fills orders. When the warehouse ships the products, it can send an e-mail message to the importer and to the exporter's headquarters. The warehouse may even use technology to monitor its inventory of products so that suppliers are automatically notified to send more supplies once the inventory is reduced to a specific level. If the exporter uses multiple warehouses, the Internet allows them to work as a network so that if one warehouse can not fill an order, another warehouse will.

Licensing

Licensing obligates a firm to provide its technology (copyrights, patents, trademarks, or trade names) in exchange for fees or some other specified benefits. For example, AT&T and Verizon Communications have licensing agreements to build and operate parts of India's telephone system. Sprint Corp. has a licensing agreement to develop telecommunications services in the United Kingdom. Eli Lilly & Co. has a licensing agreement to produce drugs for Hungary and other countries. IGA, Inc., which operates more than 3,000 supermarkets in the United States, has a licensing agreement to operate supermarkets in China and Singapore. Licensing allows firms to use their technology in foreign markets without a major investment in foreign countries and without the transportation costs that result from exporting. A major disadvantage of licensing is that it is difficult for the firm providing the technology to ensure quality control in the foreign production process.

How the Internet Facilitates Licensing. Some firms with an international reputation use their brand name to advertise products over the Internet. They may use manufacturers in foreign countries to produce some of their products subject to their specifications.

Example | Springs, Inc., has set up a licensing agreement with a manufacturer in the Czech Republic. When Springs receive orders for its products from customers in Eastern Europe, it relies on this manufacturer to produce and deliver the products ordered. This expedites the delivery process and may even allow Springs to have the products manufactured at a lower cost than if it produced them itself.

Franchising

Franchising obligates a firm to provide a specialized sales or service strategy, support assistance, and possibly an initial investment in the franchise in exchange for periodic fees. For example, McDonald's, Pizza Hut, Subway Sandwiches, Blockbuster Video, and Dairy Queen have franchises that are owned and managed by local residents in many foreign countries. Like licensing, franchising allows firms to penetrate foreign markets without a major investment in foreign countries. The recent relaxation of barriers in foreign countries throughout Eastern Europe and South America has resulted in numerous franchising arrangements.

Joint Ventures

A **joint venture** is a venture that is jointly owned and operated by two or more firms. Many firms penetrate foreign markets by engaging in a joint venture with firms that reside in those markets. Most joint ventures allow two firms to apply their respective comparative advantages in a given project. For example, General Mills, Inc., joined in a venture with Nestlé SA, so that the cereals produced by General Mills could be sold through the overseas sales distribution network established by Nestlé.

Xerox Corp. and Fuji Co. (of Japan) engaged in a joint venture that allowed Xerox Corp. to penetrate the Japanese market and allowed Fuji to enter the photocopying business. Sara Lee Corp. and SBC Communications have engaged in joint ventures with Mexican firms to gain entry to Mexico's markets. Joint ventures between automobile manufacturers are numerous, as each manufacturer can offer its technological advantages. General Motors has ongoing joint ventures with automobile manufacturers in several different countries, including Hungary and the former Soviet states.

Acquisitions of Existing Operations

Firms frequently acquire other firms in foreign countries as a means of penetrating foreign markets. For example, American Express recently acquired offices in London, while Procter & Gamble purchased a bleach company in Panama. Acquisitions allow firms to have full control over their foreign businesses and to quickly obtain a large portion of foreign market share.

Example In 2001, Home Depot acquired the second largest home improvement business in Mexico. This acquisition was Home Depot's first in Mexico, but allowed the firm to expand its business after establishing name recognition there. Home Depot plans to expand in Mexico over time, just as it did in Canada throughout the 1990s.

An acquisition of an existing corporation is normally riskier than the other methods previously mentioned because of the large investment required. In addition, if the foreign operations perform poorly, it may be difficult to sell the operations at a reasonable price.

Some firms engage in partial international acquisitions in order to obtain a stake in foreign operations. This requires a smaller investment than full international acquisitions and therefore exposes the firm to less risk. On the other hand, the firm will not have complete control over foreign operations that are only partially acquired.

Establishing New Foreign Subsidiaries

Firms can also penetrate foreign markets by establishing new operations in foreign countries to produce and sell their products. Like a foreign acquisition, this method requires a large investment. Establishing new subsidiaries may be preferred to foreign acquisitions because the operations can be tailored exactly to the firm's needs. In addition, a smaller investment may be required than would be needed to purchase existing operations. However, the firm will not reap any rewards from the investment until the subsidiary is built and a customer base established.

Summary of Methods

The methods of increasing international business extend from the relatively simple approach of international trade to the more complex approach of acquiring foreign firms or establishing new subsidiaries. Any method of increasing international business that requires a direct investment in foreign operations normally is referred to as a **direct foreign investment (DFI)**. International trade and licensing usually are not considered to be DFI because they do not involve direct investment in foreign operations. Franchising and joint ventures tend to require some investment in foreign operations, but to a limited degree. Foreign acquisitions and the establish-

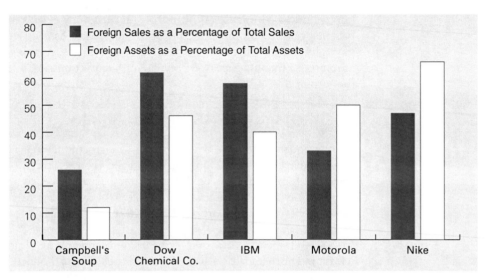

ment of new foreign subsidiaries require substantial investment in foreign operations and represent the largest portion of DFI.

The optimal method for increasing international business may depend on the characteristics of the MNC. Exhibit 1.3 provides a sampling of U.S.-based MNCs with substantial international business. Some MNCs, such as Dow Chemical Co. and IBM, generate the majority of their revenue from outside the United States. Other MNCs, such as Motorola and Nike, have substantial foreign assets so that they can produce products at lower costs than is possible in the United States. Some of the products they sell in the United States were produced in foreign countries. Some MNCs, such as Motorola and IBM, derive some of their foreign revenue from various licensing agreements. Such agreements do not require as much direct foreign investment to generate foreign revenue.

INTERNATIONAL OPPORTUNITIES

Visit lcweb2.loc.gov/frd/cs/ cshome.html, a page of the Library of Congress's website, for detailed studies of 85 countries.

Because of possible cost advantages from producing in foreign countries or possible revenue opportunities from demand by foreign markets, the growth potential becomes much greater for firms that consider international business. Exhibit 1.4 illustrates how a firm's growth can be affected by foreign investment and financing opportunities.

Investment Opportunities

Exhibit 1.4 shows hypothetical investment opportunities for both a purely domestic firm and an MNC with similar operating characteristics. Each horizontal step represents a specific project. Each project is expected to generate a marginal return to the firm.

Moving from left to right in Exhibit 1.4, the projects are prioritized according to marginal return. Assume that these projects are independent of each other and that their expected returns as shown have been adjusted to account for risk. With

Exhibit 1.4

Cost-Benefit
Evaluation for Purely
Domestic Firms
versus MNCs

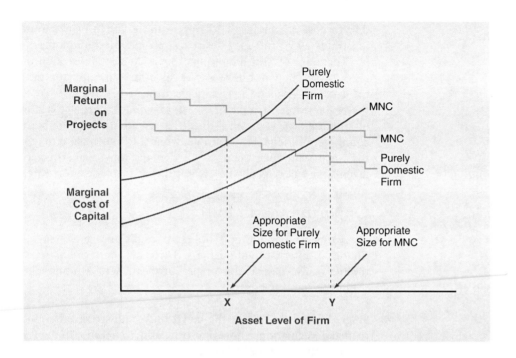

these assumptions, a firm would select the project with the highest marginal return as the most feasible and would undertake this project. Then, it would undertake the proposed project with the next highest marginal return, and so on. The marginal returns on projects for the MNC are above those of the purely domestic firm because the MNC has an expanded opportunity set of possible projects from which to select.

Financing Opportunities

Exhibit 1.4 also displays cost-of-capital curves for the MNC and the purely domestic firm. The exhibit shows the cost of capital increasing with asset size for either type of firm. This is based on the premise that creditors or shareholders require a higher rate of return as the firm grows. Growth in asset size requires increased debt, which forces the firm to increase its periodic interest payments to creditors. Consequently, the firm has a greater probability of being unable to meet its debt obligations. To the extent that creditors and shareholders require a higher return for a more highly indebted firm, the cost of capital to the firm rises with its volume of assets. The MNC is shown to have an advantage in obtaining capital funding at a lower cost than can the purely domestic firm. This is due to its larger opportunity set of funding sources around the world.

Once the marginal cost of financing projects exceeds the marginal return on projects, the firm should not pursue such projects. As shown in Exhibit 1.4, a purely domestic firm will continue to accept projects up to point X. After that point, the marginal cost of additional projects exceeds the expected benefits.

When foreign resources, funds, and potential projects are considered, the firm's volume of feasible projects is greater. The MNC's projects become unacceptable after point Y. This optimal level of assets exceeds that of the purely domestic firm due to cost advantages and opportunities in foreign countries. This comparison illustrates why firms may desire to become internationalized.

There are several limitations to the concept illustrated in Exhibit 1.4. In some cases, a firm may not have any feasible foreign opportunities. In addition, an argument could be made that foreign projects are riskier than domestic projects and therefore result in a higher cost of capital. Firms that diversify their business internationally, however, reduce the sensitivity of their performance to the home country conditions. For example, while a U.S. recession may lower the U.S. demand for a firm's product, the non-U.S. demand may be unaffected. The optimal size of a given firm will typically be greater if that firm considers foreign opportunities.

Opportunities in Europe

Over time, economic and political conditions can change, creating new opportunities in international business. Three events have had a major impact on opportunities in Europe: (1) the Single European Act, (2) removal of the Berlin wall, and (3) inception of the euro.

Single European Act. In the late 1980s, industrialized countries in Europe agreed to make regulations more uniform and to remove many taxes on goods traded between these countries. This agreement, supported by the Single European Act of 1987, was followed by a series of negotiations among countries to begin phasing in policies that achieved uniformity by 1992. The act allows firms in a given European country greater access to supplies from firms in other European countries.

Many firms, including European subsidiaries of U.S.-based MNCs, have capitalized on the agreement by attempting to penetrate markets in border countries. Before the Single European Act, some subsidiaries conducted business only in their host countries because opportunities in border countries were discouraged by taxes and other barriers. As these barriers were reduced in the late 1980s, firms began to enter new markets. By producing more of the same product and distributing it across European countries, firms are now better able to achieve economies of scale. Best Foods (now part of Unilever) was one of many MNCs that was able to increase efficiency by streamlining manufacturing operations as a result of the reduction in barriers.

Removal of the Berlin Wall. In 1989, another historic event occurred in Europe when the Berlin Wall separating East Germany from West Germany was torn down. This was symbolic of new relations between East Germany and West Germany and was followed by the reunification of the two countries. In addition, it encouraged free enterprise in all Eastern European countries and the privatization of businesses that were owned by the government. A key motive for pursuing opportunities in Eastern Europe was the lack of products available there. Coca-Cola Co., Reynolds Metals Co., General Motors, and numerous other MNCs aggressively pursued expansion in Eastern Europe as a result of the momentum toward free enterprise.

While the Single European Act of 1987 and the move toward free enterprise in Eastern Europe offered new opportunities to MNCs, they also posed new risks. As the Single European Act removed cross-border barriers, it exposed firms to additional competition. As in other historical examples of deregulation, the more efficient firms have benefited at the expense of less efficient firms.

Inception of the Euro. In 1999, several European countries adopted the euro as their currency for business transactions between these countries. The euro was phased in as a currency for other transactions during 2001 and completely replaced the currencies of the participating countries on January 1, 2002. The creation of the euro allowed firms (including European subsidiaries of U.S.-based MNCs) to use only one currency in international transactions and thus eliminated transactions costs resulting from exchanging currencies. It also eliminated concerns about potential effects of exchange rate fluctuations on the cash flows resulting from this type of international business. Though the full effects are not yet known, the single currency system in Europe should definitely encourage more trade among European countries. In addition, the use of a single currency in most of Europe allows for a single monetary policy in Europe. Therefore, in assessing the economic growth in Europe, MNCs can focus on only one monetary policy rather than the country-specific monetary policies that were prevalent before 1999.

HTTP:// USING THE WEB

Updated Euro Information An update of information on the euro is provided at http://europa.eu.int/euro/html/entry.html.

Opportunities in Latin America

Like Europe, Latin America offers more business opportunities now because of a reduction in restrictions.

NAFTA. As a result of the North American Free Trade Agreement (NAFTA) of 1993, trade barriers between the United States and Mexico were eliminated. Some U.S. firms attempted to capitalize on this by exporting goods that had previously been restricted by barriers to Mexico. Other firms established subsidiaries in Mexico to produce their goods at a lower cost than was possible in the United States and then sell the goods in the United States. The removal of trade barriers essentially allowed U.S. firms to penetrate product and labor markets that previously had not been accessible.

The removal of trade barriers between the United States and Mexico allows Mexican firms to export some products to the United States that were previously restricted. Thus, U.S. firms that produce these goods are now subject to competition from Mexican exporters. Given the low cost of labor in Mexico, some U.S. firms have lost some of their market share. The effects are most pronounced in the labor-intensive industries.

Within a month after the NAFTA accord, the momentum for free trade continued with a GATT (General Agreement on Tariffs and Trade) accord. This accord was the conclusion of trade negotiations from the so-called Uruguay Round that had begun seven years earlier. It called for the reduction or elimination of trade restrictions on specified imported goods over a ten-year period across 117 countries. The accord has generated more international business for firms that had previously been unable to penetrate foreign markets because of trade restrictions.

Removal of Investment Restrictions. Many Latin American countries have made it easier for MNCs to engage in direct foreign investment there by allowing MNCs more ownership rights if they acquire a local company. MNCs with technological advantages are now able to capitalize on their comparative advantages in Latin America. The flow of direct foreign investment into Latin America has not only been beneficial to MNCs, but has also improved the level of technology there.

Opportunities in Asia

MNCs have commonly identified Asia as having tremendous business potential because of its large population base. Yet, MNCs had difficulty pursuing growth opportunities in Asia because of excessive restrictions on investment there. Some of the restrictions were explicit, while others were implicit (major bureaucratic delays).

Removal of Investment Restrictions. During the 1990s, many Asian countries reduced the restrictions imposed on investment by MNCs based in other countries. Consequently, MNCs can now acquire companies in Asia more easily, or create licensing agreements with Asian companies without government interference.

Since the reduction in restrictions, U.S. firms such as PepsiCo, Coca-Cola Co., Apple Computer, and International Paper have increased their international business in Asia. Many U.S. firms view China as the country with the most potential for growth. General Motors, Ford Motor Co., Procter & Gamble, and AT&T have invested billions of dollars in China to capitalize on the expected growth.

Many U.S. breweries have expanded into China to capitalize on the large increase in the demand for beer in that market. Pabst Blue Ribbon, which has lost much of its market share in the United States, has been very successful in China. Heilman Brewing has also had success with its Lone Star Beer, as the American cowboy image has been a useful marketing tool in China. Miller High Life has expanded into China through a licensing agreement, while Anheuser-Busch (producer of Budweiser) has partially acquired a Chinese beer company.

Impact of the Asian Crisis. In 1997, several Asian countries including Indonesia, Malaysia, and Thailand experienced severe economic problems. Many local companies went bankrupt, and concerns about the countries caused financial outflows of funds. These outflows left limited funds to support the economy. Interest rates increased because of the outflow of funds; this placed even more strain on firms that needed to borrow money. This so-called Asian crisis lingered into 1998 and adversely affected numerous U.S.-based MNCs that conducted business in these countries.

Yet, the crisis also created international business opportunities. The values of local firms were depressed, and Asian governments reduced restrictions on acquisitions, which allowed MNCs from the United States and other countries to pursue acquisitions in the Asian countries. Some U.S.-based MNCs were able to purchase local companies at a relatively low cost, improve the efficiency of the firms, and benefit from future economic growth. For example, during the Asian crisis in 1997–1998, South Korea's large conglomerate firms (called *chaebols*) experienced financial problems and began to sell many of their business units to obtain cash. General Electric, Procter & Gamble, and Coca-Cola Co. were among the U.S.-based MNCs that acquired business units in Asia during this period.

EXPOSURE TO INTERNATIONAL RISK

Although international business can reduce an MNC's exposure to its home country's economic conditions, it usually increases an MNC's exposure to (1) exchange rate movements, (2) foreign economic conditions, and (3) political risk. Each of these forms of exposure is briefly described here and is discussed in more detail in later sections of the text. MNCs that plan to pursue international business should consider these potential risks.

Exposure to Exchange Rate Movements

Most international business results in the exchange of one currency for another to make payment. Since exchange rates fluctuate over time, the cash outflows required to make payments change accordingly. Consequently, the number of units of a firm's home currency needed to purchase foreign supplies can change even if the suppliers have not adjusted their prices.

Exchange rate fluctuations also affect the value of cash flows received by firms that accept foreign currencies for their exported products. This effect is illustrated in Exhibit 1.5. The top graph shows the value of the British pound over time. The

---

Financial Markets Perspective

Impact of the Asian Crisis on Currency Values

MNCs can be affected by conditions in various international financial markets, including the foreign exchange market (where currencies are traded) and securities markets. When the prices of currencies or securities change, MNCs holding those currencies or securities experience a gain or a loss. A classic example is the Asian crisis of 1997–1998, which had a dramatic effect on the values of Asian currencies in the foreign exchange market. Currencies of some Asian countries (such as South Korea) depreciated by more than 20 percent against the dollar within a week. As a result, the dollar value of earnings remitted by Asian subsidiaries also fell by more than 20 percent. Over a nine-month period ending in April 1998, the Indonesian rupiah depreciated by about 80 percent against the dollar. Thus, the U.S. dollars received by a U.S. parent from a given amount of remitted earnings by an Indonesian subsidiary were about 80 percent less in April 1998 than they had been nine months earlier.

As Asian currencies weakened, the amount of remitted dollars declined.

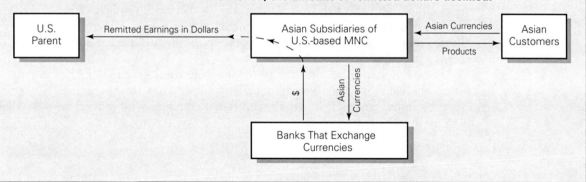

Exhibit 1.5

Impact of Exchange Rates on Cash Flows

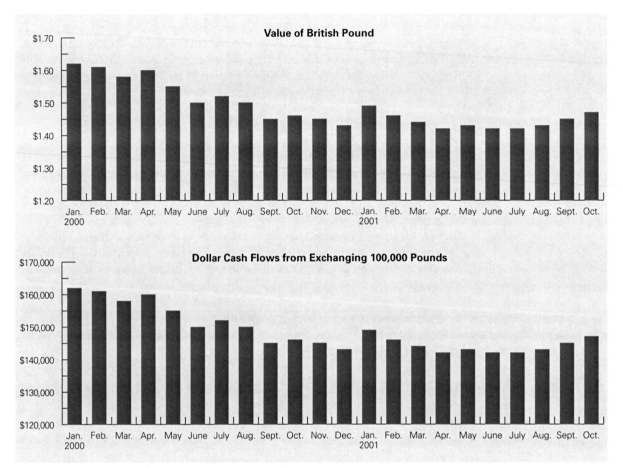

lower graph shows the dollar cash inflows to a U.S. firm that exports products denominated in 100,000 British pounds each month. Notice how the cash inflows are $162,000 in January 2000, when the pound's value was relatively high. Yet, in July 2001, the cash inflows are only $142,000 because the pound's value had declined by then.

Even if an exporter denominates its exports in its own currency, exchange rate fluctuations may affect the foreign demand for the firm's product. When the home currency strengthens, products denominated in that currency become more expensive to foreign customers, which may cause a decline in demand and, therefore, a decline in cash inflows.

For MNCs with subsidiaries in foreign countries, exchange rate fluctuations affect the value of cash flows remitted by subsidiaries to the parent. When the parent's home currency is strong, the remitted funds will convert to a smaller amount of the home currency.

Exposure to Foreign Economies

http://

Visit the Fed's data bank at www.stls.frb.org/fred for numerous economic and financial time series, e.g., on balance of payment statistics, interest rates, and foreign exchange rates.

When MNCs enter foreign markets to sell products, the demand for these products is dependent on the economic conditions in those markets. Thus, the cash flows of the MNC are subject to foreign economic conditions. For example, U.S. firms such as DuPont and Nike experienced lower-than-expected cash flows because of weak European economies in the 1992–1993 period and again in the 2000–2001 period. U.S.-based MNCs such as Nike and 3M Co. that conducted business in Asia were adversely affected by the Asian crisis in 1998, as the weak Asian economies reduced the Asian demand for products. Mirage Resorts was adversely affected when gambling by its Asian customers declined.

Exposure to Political Risk

When MNCs establish subsidiaries in foreign countries, they become exposed to **political risk**, which arises because the host government or the public may take actions that affect the MNC's cash flows (political risk is often viewed as a subset of **country risk**, which is explained later). For example, the host government may impose higher taxes on U.S.-based subsidiaries in retaliation for actions by the U.S. government. Alternatively, the host government may decide to buy out a subsidiary at whatever price it decides is fair. One form of an exposure to political risk is terrorism. A terrorist attack can affect a firm's operations or its employees. The September 11, 2001 terrorist attack on the World Trade Center reminded MNCs around the world of the exposure to terrorism. MNCs from more than 50 countries were directly affected because they occupied space in the World Trade Center. In addition, other MNCs were also affected because they engage in trade or have direct foreign investment in foreign countries that may also experience an increase in terrorism. Milder forms of risk include actions by the host government that place foreign firms at a disadvantage. For example, the Mexican government was slow to respond to the request of United Parcel Service (UPS) to use its large vehicles for providing delivery services.

Nike Problem

International Business Opportunities and Risk

In every chapter, some of the key concepts discussed in the chapter are applied to Nike, Inc., a firm known for its growth through penetration of foreign markets.

The evolution of Nike began in 1962, when Phil Knight, a business student in Stanford's business school, wrote a paper on how a U.S. firm could use Japanese technology to break the German dominance of the athletic shoe industry in the United States. After graduation, Knight visited the Unitsuka Tiger shoe company in Japan. He subcontracted that company to produce a shoe that he sold in the United States under the name Blue Ribbon Sports (BRS). During the 1960s, Knight focused his business in the United States. In 1972, he experimented with international business by exporting his shoes to Canada. In 1974, he opened his first U.S. factory (in New Hampshire) and also expanded his operations into Australia. At that time, the firm's annual revenues were $4.8 million. In 1977, the firm subcontracted factories in Taiwan and Korea to produce athletic shoes and then sold the shoes in Asian countries. In 1978, BRS became Nike, Inc., and began to export shoes to Europe and South America. Nike expanded internationally as it developed a global image through its name recognition at the Olympics and other sporting events. Its image represents a comparative advantage in many countries. As a result of its exporting and its direct foreign investment, Nike's international sales reached $1 billion by 1992 and were about $4 billion by 2000.

Even with substantial international growth, Nike is not near the end of its product cycle. It has focused most of its European sales in five countries, with 70 percent of European sales attributed to the United Kingdom. Thus, Nike has much potential for growth in other European countries, including Eastern Europe. In addition, though sales in Asia declined during the Asian crisis, sales should increase over time as Asian economies rebound. Furthermore, there is still much room for growth in South American countries. Nike not only has many opportunities to expand its athletic shoe business internationally, but it could also expand its product line and sell new athletic products internationally as well.

Discussion: What factors do you think Nike considers about each country when deciding where to expand next?

Overview of an MNC's Cash Flows

Most U.S.-based MNCs have some local business within the United States, similar to other purely domestic firms. Because of the MNCs' international operations, however, their cash flow streams differ from those of purely domestic firms. Exhibit 1.6 shows cash flow diagrams for three common profiles of MNCs. Profile A in this exhibit reflects an MNC whose only international business is international trade. Thus, its international cash flows result from either paying for imported supplies or receiving payment in exchange for products that it exports.

Profile B reflects an MNC that engages in both international trade and some international arrangements (which can include international licensing, franchising, or joint ventures). Any of these international arrangements can require cash outflows by the MNC in foreign countries to comply with the arrangement, such as the expenses incurred from transferring technology or offering partial investment in a franchise or joint venture. These arrangements generate cash flows to the MNC in the form of fees for services (such as technology or support assistance) it provides.

Profile C reflects an MNC that engages in international trade, international arrangements, and direct foreign investment. This type of MNC has one or more foreign subsidiaries. There can be cash outflows from the U.S. parent to its foreign subsidiaries in the form of invested funds to help finance the operations of the foreign subsidiaries. There are also cash flows from the foreign subsidiaries to the U.S. parent in the form of remitted earnings and fees for services provided by the parent, which can all be classified as remitted funds from the foreign subsidiaries. In general, the cash outflows associated with international business by the U.S. parent are to pay for imports, to comply with its international arrangements, or to support the creation or expansion of foreign subsidiaries. Conversely, it will receive cash flows in the form of payment for its exports, fees for the services it provides within its international arrangements, and remitted funds from the foreign subsidiaries.

Many MNCs initially conduct international business in the manner illustrated by Profile A. Some of these MNCs develop international arrangements and foreign subsidiaries over time; others are content to focus on exporting or importing as their only method of international business. Although the three profiles vary, they all show how international business generates cash flows. These cash flows represent the cash inflows received by the MNC minus the cash outflows.

Exhibit 1.6

Cash Flow Diagrams
for MNCs

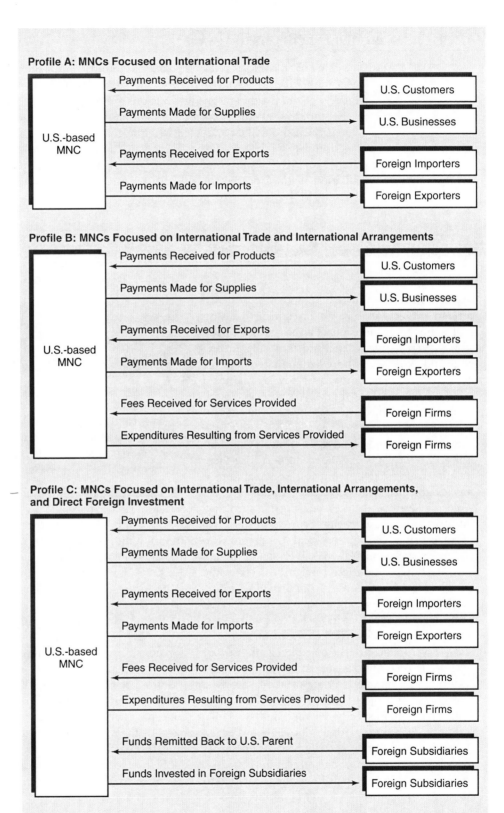

VALUATION MODEL FOR AN MNC

The value of an MNC is relevant to its shareholders and its debtholders. When managers make decisions that maximize the value of the firm, they maximize shareholder wealth (assuming that the decisions are not intended to maximize the wealth of debtholders at the expense of shareholders). Since international financial management should be conducted with the goal of increasing the value of the MNC, it is useful to review some basics of valuation. There are numerous methods of valuing an MNC, and some methods will lead to the same valuation. The one valuation method described here can be used to understand the key factors that affect an MNC's value in a general sense.

Managing for Value: Yahoo!'s Decision to Expand Internationally

Many U.S.-based MNCs have penetrated foreign markets in recent years. Like domestic projects, foreign projects involve an investment decision and a financing decision. The investment decision to engage in a foreign project results in revenue and expenses that are denominated in a foreign currency. The decision of how to finance a foreign project affects the MNC's cost of capital. Most foreign projects are assessed on the basis of their potential to attract new demand and therefore generate additional cash flows. Consider Yahoo!, which has expanded its portal services in numerous foreign countries. For example, it has established main pages in Canada, Latin America, Europe, and Asia. It generates cash inflows from these foreign projects in the form of advertising fees paid by local merchants who purchase space on Yahoo!'s website. It incurs cash outflows from these foreign projects in the form of expenses incurred from providing information. It needs funding to finance these foreign projects and hopes that its cash flows will generate a return that exceeds the cost of financing.

Every foreign project considered by Yahoo! is subject to conditions specific to that country, resulting in a unique estimate of net cash flows. Every foreign project is also subject to a cost of financing that is specific to the country. Thus, Yahoo!'s decision regarding a possible project in Argentina may not necessarily be the same as its decision regarding a similar project in Australia.

Once an MNC such as Yahoo! has decided to pursue a foreign project, it must continually consider a set of multinational finance decisions, such as:

- how to forecast exchange rates of the currencies it uses,
- how to assess its exposure to exchange rate movements,
- whether and how to hedge its exposure to exchange rate movements,
- how to pursue additional foreign expansion,
- how to finance its foreign expansion, and
- how to manage its international cash and liquidity.

These are the key multinational finance decisions that are made by Yahoo! and other MNCs, and they are therefore given much attention in this text. To the extent that Yahoo!'s managers can make multinational finance decisions that increase the overall present value of its future cash flows, they can maximize the firm's value.

Before financial managers of Yahoo! and other MNCs make these multinational finance decisions, they need to understand how international financial markets can facilitate their business and must recognize the forces that affect exchange rates. These macroeconomic concepts, which are discussed in the first two parts of the text, set the stage for understanding how the performance of any business is influenced by local country conditions. Then, in the last three parts of the text, multinational finance decisions are examined.

Domestic Model

Before modeling an MNC's value, consider the valuation of a purely domestic firm that does not engage in any foreign transactions. The value (V) of a purely domestic firm in the United States is commonly specified as the present value of its expected cash flows, where the discount rate used reflects the weighted average cost of capital and represents the required rate of return by investors:

$$V = \sum_{t=1}^{n} \left\{ \frac{[E(CF_{\$,t})]}{(1+k)^t} \right\}$$

where $E(CF_{\$,t})$ represents expected cash flows to be received at the end of period t, n represents the number of periods into the future in which cash flows are received, and k represents the required rate of return by investors. The dollar cash flows in period t represent funds received by the firm minus funds needed to pay expenses or taxes, or to reinvest in the firm (such as an investment to replace old computers or machinery). The expected cash flows are estimated from knowledge about various existing projects as well as other projects that will be implemented in the future. A firm's decisions about how it should invest funds to expand its business can affect its expected future cash flows and therefore can affect the firm's value. Holding other factors constant, an increase in expected cash flows over time should increase the value of the firm.

The required rate of return (k) in the denominator of the valuation equation represents the cost of capital (including both the cost of debt and the cost of equity) to the firm and is essentially a weighted average of the cost of capital based on all of the firm's projects. As the firm makes decisions that affect its cost of debt or its cost of equity for one or more projects, it affects the weighted average of its cost of capital and therefore affects the required rate of return. For example, if the firm's credit rating is suddenly lowered, its cost of capital will probably increase and so will its required rate of return. Holding other factors constant, an increase in the firm's required rate of return will reduce the value of the firm, because expected cash flows must be discounted at a higher interest rate. Conversely, a decrease in the firm's required rate of return will increase the value of the firm because expected cash flows are discounted at a lower required rate of return.

Valuing International Cash Flows

An MNC's value can be specified in the same manner as a purely domestic firm's. However, consider that the expected cash flows generated by a U.S.-based MNC's parent in the period t may be coming from various countries and may therefore be denominated in different foreign currencies. The foreign currency cash flows will be converted into dollars. Thus, the expected dollar cash flows to be received at the end of period t are equal to the sum of the products of cash flows denominated in each currency j times the expected exchange rate at which currency j could be converted into dollars by the MNC at the end of period t.

$$E(CF_{\$,t}) = \sum_{j=1}^{m} [E(CF_{j,t}) \times E(ER_{j,t})]$$

where $CF_{j,t}$ represents the amount of cash flow denominated in a particular foreign currency j at the end of period t, and $ER_{j,t}$ represents the exchange rate at which the foreign currency (measured in dollars per unit of the foreign currency) can be converted to dollars at the end of period t.

For example, an MNC that does business in two currencies could measure its expected dollar cash flows in any period by multiplying the expected cash flow in each currency times the expected exchange rate at which that currency could be converted to dollars and then summing those two products. If the firm does not use various techniques (discussed later in the text) to hedge its transactions in foreign currencies, the expected exchange rate in a given period would be used in the valuation equation to estimate the corresponding expected exchange rate at which the foreign currency can be converted into dollars in that period. Conversely, if the MNC hedges these transactions, the exchange rate at which it can hedge would be used in the valuation equation.

It may help to think of an MNC as a portfolio of currency cash flows, one for each currency in which it conducts business. The expected dollar cash flows derived from each of those currencies can be combined to determine the total expected dollar cash flows in each future period. The present value of those cash flows serves as the estimate of the MNC's value. It is easier to derive an expected dollar cash flow value for each currency before combining the cash flows among currencies within a given period, because each currency's cash flow amount must be converted to a common unit (the dollar) before combining the amounts.

Example

To illustrate how the dollar cash flows of an MNC can be measured, consider a U.S. firm that had expected cash flows of $100,000 from local business and 1,000,000 Mexican pesos from business in Mexico at the end of period t. Assuming that the peso's value is expected to be $.09, the expected dollar cash flows are:

$$
\begin{aligned}
E(CF_{\$,t}) &= [E(CF_{j,t}) \times E(ER_{j,t})] \\
&= [\$100,000] + [1,000,000 \text{ pesos} \times (\$.09)] \\
&= [\$100,000] + \$[90,000] \\
&= \$190,000.
\end{aligned}
$$

The cash flows of $100,000 from U.S. business were already denominated in U.S. dollars and therefore did not have to be converted.

The MNC's dollar cash flows at the end of every period in the future can be estimated in the same manner. Then, the MNC's value can be measured by determining the present value of the expected dollar cash flows, which is the sum of the discounted dollar cash flows that are expected in all future periods. This example uses only two currencies, but if the MNC had transactions involving 40 currencies, the same process could be used. The expected dollar cash flows for each of the 40 currencies would be estimated separately for each future period. The expected dollar cash flows for each of the 40 currencies within each period could then be combined to derive the total dollar cash flows per period. Finally, the cash flows in each period would be discounted to derive the value of the MNC.

The general formula for the dollar cash flows received by an MNC in any particular period can be written as:

$$
E(CF_{\$,t}) = \sum_{j=1}^{m} [E(CF_{j,t}) \times E(ER_{j,t})]
$$

The value of an MNC can be more clearly differentiated from the value of a purely domestic firm by substituting the expression $[E(CF_{j,t}) \times E(ER_{j,t})]$ for $E(CF_{\$,t})$ in the valuation model, as shown here:

$$V = \sum_{t=1}^{n} \left\{ \frac{\sum_{j=1}^{m} [E(CF_{j,t}) \times E(ER_{j,t})]}{(1+k)^t} \right\}$$

where $CF_{j,t}$ represents the cash flow denominated in a particular currency (including dollars), and $ER_{j,t}$ represents the exchange rate at which the MNC can convert the foreign currency at the end of period t. Thus, the value of an MNC can be affected by a change in expectations about $CF_{j,t}$ or $ER_{j,t}$. Only those cash flows that are to be received by the MNC's parent in the period of concern should be counted. To avoid double-counting, cash flows of the MNC's subsidiaries are considered in the valuation model only when they reflect transactions with the U.S. parent. Thus, any expected cash flows received by foreign subsidiaries should not be counted in the valuation equation until they are expected to be remitted to the parent.

The denominator of the valuation model for the MNC remains unchanged from the original valuation model for the purely domestic firm. However, recognize that the weighted average cost of capital for the MNC is based on funding some projects that reflect business in different countries. Thus, any decision by the MNC's parent that affects the cost of its capital supporting projects in a specific country can affect its weighted average cost of capital (and its required rate of return) and therefore can affect its value.

In general, the valuation model shows that an MNC's value can be affected by forces that influence the amount of its cash flows in a particular currency (CF_j), the exchange rate at which that currency is converted into dollars (ER_j), or the MNC's weighted average cost of capital (k).

Impact of Financial Management and International Conditions on Value

U.S.-based MNCs recognize that they may increase their value by increasing their dollar cash flows or by reducing their cost of capital. Hence, their challenge is to make decisions that will accomplish one or both of these objectives. An MNC's financial decisions include how much business to conduct in each country and how much financing to obtain in each currency. Its financial decisions determine its exposure to the international environment. If it conducts very little international business, its potential for enhancing its value is limited, but so is its vulnerability to changes in exchange rate movements or other international conditions. Conversely, if an MNC pursues substantial international business in markets where there are opportunities, it may be able to substantially increase its dollar cash flows and therefore increase its value, but it will be highly exposed to exchange rate effects, economic conditions, and political conditions in these markets.

The uncertainty surrounding a U.S.-based MNC's dollar cash flows is influenced by the composition of its international business, as well as by the amount of that business. Exchange rates, economic conditions, and political conditions are much more volatile in some countries than in others. Therefore, two MNCs of the same size and in the same industry may have the same volume of foreign business, but one of them might be less risky because it conducts business in more stable countries.

Though an MNC does not have control over a country's exchange rate, economic conditions, or political conditions, it can control its degree of exposure to those conditions with its financial management. Two MNCs of the same size and in the same industry could have the exact same composition of international business, but one of them might be less risky because it makes financial decisions that reduce its exposure to exchange rates, economic conditions, or political conditions.

How Chapters Relate to Valuation

The international opportunities described in this chapter can affect the valuation of an MNC, as illustrated in Exhibit 1.7. New international opportunities can enhance the expected currency cash flows and therefore enhance the value of the firm. However, this potential advantage must be weighed against the exposure to foreign economies, exchange rate risk, and political risk, which can cause a reduction in cash flows or a higher cost of capital, and could reduce the value of the firm. MNCs that focus primarily on importing are exposed to exchange rate movements but are not heavily exposed to foreign economies or political risk. MNCs that are engaged in international arrangements such as licensing or joint ventures have more exposure to foreign economies and to political risk than importers but not as much exposure as MNCs with foreign subsidiaries.

Exhibit 1.7

Impact of New International Opportunities on an MNC's Value

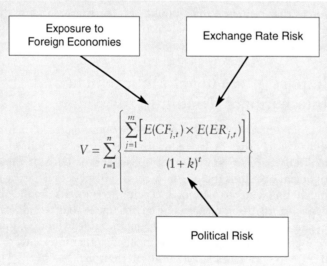

$$V = \sum_{t=1}^{n} \left\{ \frac{\sum_{j=1}^{m} \left[E(CF_{j,t}) \times E(ER_{j,t}) \right]}{(1+k)^t} \right\}$$

V = value of the U.S.-based MNC
$E(CF_{j,t})$ = expected cash flows denominated in currency j to be received by the U.S. parent in period t
$E(ER_{j,t})$ = expected exchange rate at which currency j can be converted to dollars at the end of period t
k = weighted average cost of capital of the U.S. parent company
m = number of currencies
n = number of periods

Near the end of each chapter, the main concepts explained in that chapter are related to the valuation model to illustrate how they are relevant to the valuation of an MNC. Thus, the potential impact of these concepts on MNCs becomes more obvious.

The organization of the chapters in this text is shown in Exhibit 1.8. Chapters 2 through 8 discuss international markets and conditions from a macroeconomic perspective, focusing on external forces that can affect the value of an MNC. Though financial managers may not have control over these forces, they do have some control over their degree of exposure to these forces. These macroeconomic chapters provide the background necessary to make financial decisions.

Chapters 9 through 21 take a microeconomic perspective and focus on how the financial management of an MNC can affect its value. Financial decisions by MNCs are commonly classified as either investing decisions or financing decisions. In general, investing decisions by an MNC tend to affect the numerator of the valuation model because such decisions affect expected cash flows. Yet, investing decisions by the MNC's parent may also affect the denominator of the valuation model if they alter the firm's weighted average cost of capital. Long-term financing decisions by an MNC's parent tend to affect the denominator of the valuation model because they affect the MNC's cost of capital.

Exhibit 1.8

Organization of Chapters

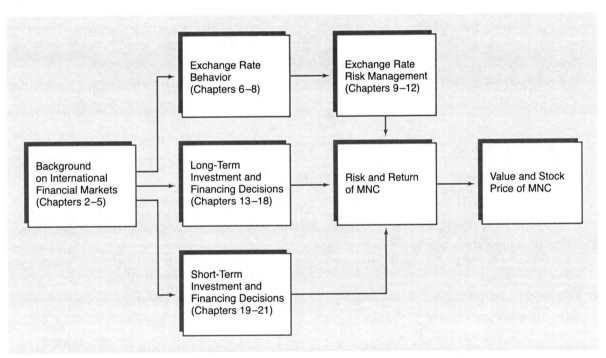

SUMMARY

- The main goal of an MNC is to maximize shareholder wealth. When managers are tempted to serve their own interests instead of those of shareholders, an agency problem exists. Managers also face environmental, regulatory, and ethical constraints that can conflict with the goal of maximizing shareholder wealth.

- International business is justified by three key theories. The theory of comparative advantage suggests that each country should use its comparative advantage to specialize in its production and rely on other countries to meet other needs. The imperfect markets theory suggests that because of imperfect markets, factors of production are immobile, which encourages countries to specialize based on the resources they have. The product cycle theory suggests that after firms are established in their home countries, they commonly expand their product specialization in foreign countries.

- The most common methods by which firms conduct international business are international trade, licensing, franchising, joint ventures, acquisitions of foreign firms, and formation of foreign subsidiaries. Methods such as licensing and franchising involve little or low capital investment but distribute some of the profits to other parties. Acquisition of foreign firms and formation of foreign subsidiaries require substantial capital investments but offer the potential for large returns.

SELF TEST

Answers are provided in Appendix A at the back of the text.

1. What are typical reasons why MNCs expand internationally?

2. Describe the changes in Europe and Mexico that have created new opportunities for U.S.-based MNCs.

3. Identify the more obvious risks faced by MNCs that expand internationally.

QUESTIONS AND APPLICATIONS

1. Explain the agency problem of MNCs. Why might agency costs be larger for an MNC than for a purely domestic firm?

2. Explain how the theory of comparative advantage relates to the need for international business.

3. Explain how the existence of imperfect markets has led to the establishment of subsidiaries in foreign markets.

4. If perfect markets existed, would wages, prices, and interest rates among countries be more similar or less similar than under conditions of imperfect markets? Why?

5. Explain how the product cycle theory relates to the growth of an MNC.

6. How does access to international opportunities affect the size of corporations? Describe a scenario in which the size of a corporation is not affected by access to international opportunities.

7. What factors cause some firms to become more internationalized than others?

8. Offer your opinion on why the Internet may result in more international business.

9. Explain how the adoption of the euro as the single currency by European countries could be beneficial to MNCs based in Europe and to MNCs based in the United States.

10. As an overall review of this chapter, identify possible reasons for growth in international business. Then, list the various disadvantages that may discourage international business.

11. Describe constraints that interfere with an MNC's objective.

12. The managers of Loyola Corp. recently had a meeting to discuss new opportunities in Europe as a result of the recent integration among European countries. They decided not to penetrate new markets because of their present focus on expanding market share in the United States. Loyola's financial managers have developed forecasts for earnings based on the 12 percent market share (defined here as its percentage of total European sales) that Loyola currently has in Europe. Is 12 percent an appropriate estimate for next year's European market share? If not, does it likely overestimate or underestimate the actual European market share next year?

13. Would the agency problem be more pronounced for Berkeley Corp., which has its parent company make most major decisions for its foreign subsidiaries, or Oakland Corp., which uses a decentralized approach?

14. Explain why more standardized product specifications across countries can increase global competition.

15. How were German subsidiaries of U.S.-based MNCs able to capitalize on the removal of the Berlin Wall that separated East and West Germany?

16. McCanna Corp. has a French subsidiary that produces wine and exports to various European countries. Explain how the subsidiary's business may have been affected since the conversion of many European currencies into a single currency (the euro) in 1999.

17. Review the table of contents and indicate whether each of the chapters from Chapter 2 through Chapter 21 has a macro- or microperspective.

18. Explain why MNCs such as Coca-Cola and PepsiCo, Inc., still have numerous opportunities for international expansion.

19. Duve, Inc., desires to penetrate a foreign market by entering a licensing agreement with a foreign firm or by acquiring a foreign firm. Explain the differences in potential risk and return between a licensing agreement with a foreign firm and the acquisition of a foreign firm.

20. Anheuser-Busch, the producer of Budweiser and other beers, has recently expanded into Japan by engaging in a joint venture with Kirin Brewery, the largest brewery in Japan. The joint venture enables Anheuser-Busch to have its beer distributed through Kirin's distribution channels in Japan. In addition, it can utilize Kirin's facilities to produce beer that will be sold locally. In return, Anheuser-Busch provides information about the American beer market to Kirin.

    a. Explain how the joint venture can enable Anheuser-Busch to achieve its objective of maximizing shareholder wealth.

    b. Explain how the joint venture can limit the risk of international business.

    c. Many international joint ventures are intended to circumvent barriers that normally prevent foreign competition. What barrier in Japan is Anheuser-Busch circumventing as a result of the joint venture? What barrier in the United States is Kirin circumventing as a result of the joint venture?

    d. Explain how Anheuser-Busch could lose some of its market share in countries outside Japan as a result of this particular joint venture.

21. Explain why political risk may discourage international business.

Impact of 9/11/01

22. Following the September 2001 terrorist attack on the United States, the valuations of many MNCs declined by more than 10 percent. Explain why the expected cash

flows of MNCs were reduced, even if they were not directly hit by the terrorist attacks.

Internet Application

Assessing Direct Foreign Investment Trends

23. The website address of the Bureau of Economic Analysis is: **www.bea.doc.gov**

    a. Use this website to assess recent trends in direct foreign investment (DFI) abroad by U.S. firms. Compare the DFI in the United Kingdom with the DFI in France.

Offer a possible reason for the large difference.

    b. Based on the recent trends in DFI, are U.S.-based MNCs pursuing opportunities in Asia? In Eastern Europe? In Latin America?

Running Your Own MNC

This exercise can be found on the Student CD-ROM.

Blades, Inc. Case

Decision to Expand Internationally

Blades, Inc., is a U.S.-based company that has been incorporated in the United States for three years. Blades is a relatively small company, with total assets of only $200 million. The company produces a single type of product, roller blades. Due to the booming roller blade market in the United States at the time of the company's establishment, Blades has been quite successful. For example, in its first year of operation, it reported a net income of $3.5 million. Recently, however, the demand for Blades' "Speedos," the company's primary product in the United States, has been slowly tapering off, and Blades has not been performing well. Last year, it reported a return on assets of only 7 percent. In response to the company's annual report for its most recent year of operations, Blades' shareholders have been pressuring the company to improve its performance; its stock price has fallen from a high of $20 per share three years ago to $12 last year. Blades produces high-quality roller blades and employs a unique production process, but the prices it charges are among the top 5 percent in the industry.

In light of these circumstances, Ben Holt, the company's chief financial officer (CFO), is contemplating his alternatives for Blades' future. There are no other cost-cutting measures that Blades can implement in the United States without affecting the quality of its product. Also, production of alternative products would require

major modifications to the existing plant setup. Furthermore, and because of these limitations, expansion within the United States at this time seems pointless.

Ben Holt is considering the following: If Blades cannot penetrate the U.S. market further or reduce costs here, why not import some parts from overseas and/or expand the company's sales to foreign countries? Similar strategies have proved successful for numerous companies that expanded into Asia in recent years to increase their profit margins. The CFO's initial focus is on Thailand. Thailand has recently experienced weak economic conditions, and Blades could purchase components there at a low cost. Ben Holt is aware that many of Blades' competitors have begun importing production components from Thailand.

Not only would Blades be able to reduce costs by importing rubber and/or plastic from Thailand due to the low costs of these inputs, but it might also be able to augment weak U.S. sales by exporting to Thailand, an economy still in its infancy and just beginning to appreciate leisure products such as roller blades. While several of Blades' competitors import components from Thailand, few are exporting to the country. Long-term decisions would also eventually have to be made; maybe Blades, Inc., could establish a subsidiary in Thailand and gradually shift its focus away from the United States if its U.S. sales do not rebound. Establishing a subsidiary in Thailand would also make sense for Blades due to its superior production process. Ben Holt is reasonably sure that Thai firms could not duplicate the high-quality production process employed by Blades. Furthermore, if the company's initial approach of exporting works well, establishing a subsidiary in Thailand would preserve Blades' sales before Thai competitors are able to penetrate the Thai market.

As a financial analyst for Blades, Inc., you are assigned to analyze international opportunities and risk resulting from international business. Your initial assessment should focus on the barriers and opportunities that international trade may offer. Ben Holt has never been involved in international business in any form and is unfamiliar with any constraints that may inhibit his plan to export to and import from a foreign country. Mr. Holt has presented you with a list of initial questions you should answer.

1. What are the advantages Blades could gain from importing from and/or exporting to a foreign country such as Thailand?

2. What are some of the disadvantages Blades could face as a result of foreign trade in the short run? In the long run?

3. Which theories of international business described in this chapter apply to Blades, Inc., in the short run? In the long run?

4. What long-range plans other than establishment of a subsidiary in Thailand are options for Blades and may be more suitable for the company?

Small Business Dilemma

Developing a Multinational Sporting Goods Corporation

In every chapter of this text, some of the key concepts are illustrated with an application to a small sporting goods firm that conducts international business. These "Small Business Dilemma" features allow students to recognize the dilemmas and possible decisions that firms (such as this sporting goods firm) may face in a global environment. For this chapter, the application is on the development of the sporting goods firm that would conduct international business.

Last month, Jim Logan completed his undergraduate degree in finance and decided to pursue his dream of managing his own sporting goods business. Jim had worked in a sporting goods shop while going to college, and he had noticed that many customers wanted to purchase a low-priced football. However, the sporting goods store where he worked, like many others, sold only top-of-the-line footballs. From his experience, Jim was aware that top-of-the-line footballs had a high markup and that a low-cost football could possibly penetrate the U.S. market. He also knew how to produce footballs. His goal was to create a firm that would produce low-priced footballs and sell them on a wholesale basis to various sporting goods stores in the United States. Unfortunately, many sporting goods stores began to sell low-priced footballs just before Jim was about to start his business. The firm that began to produce the low-cost footballs already provided many other products to sporting goods stores in the United States and therefore had already established a business relationship with these stores. Jim did not believe that he could compete with this firm in the U.S. market.

Rather than pursue a different business, Jim decided to implement his idea on a global basis. While football (as it is played in the United States) has not been a traditional sport in foreign countries, it has become more popular in some foreign countries in recent years. Furthermore, the expansion of cable networks in foreign countries would allow for much more exposure to U.S. football games in those countries in the future. To the extent that this would increase the popularity of football (U.S. style) as a hobby in the foreign countries, it would result in a demand for footballs in foreign countries. Jim asked many of his foreign friends from college days if they recalled seeing footballs sold in their home countries. Most of them said they rarely noticed footballs being sold in sporting goods stores but that they expected the demand for footballs to increase in their home countries. Consequently, Jim decided to start a business of producing low-priced footballs and exporting them to sporting goods distributors in foreign countries. Those distributors would then sell the footballs at the retail level. Jim planned to expand his product line over time once he identified other sports products that he might sell to foreign sporting goods stores. He decided to call his business "Sports Exports Company." To avoid any rent and labor expenses, Jim planned to produce the footballs in his garage and to perform the work himself. Thus, his main business expenses were the cost of the material used to produce footballs and expenses associated with finding distributors in foreign countries who would attempt to sell the footballs to sporting goods stores.

1. Is Sports Exports Company a multinational corporation?

2. Why are the agency costs lower for Sports Exports Company than for most MNCs?

3. Does Sports Exports Company have any comparative advantage over potential competitors in foreign countries that could produce and sell footballs there?

4. How would Jim Logan decide which foreign markets he would attempt to enter? Should he initially focus on one or many foreign markets?

5. The Sports Exports Company has no immediate plans to conduct direct foreign investment. However, it might consider other less costly methods of establishing its business in foreign markets. What methods might the Sports Exports Company use to increase its presence in foreign markets by working with one or more foreign companies?

2

Measuring Exposure to Exchange Rate Fluctuations

Exchange rate risk can be broadly defined as the risk that a company's performance will be affected by exchange rate movements. Multinational corporations (MNCs) closely monitor their operations to determine how they are exposed to various forms of exchange rate risk. Financial managers must understand how to measure the exposure of their MNCs to exchange rate fluctuations so that they can determine whether and how to protect their companies from that exposure.

The specific objectives of this chapter are to:
- Discuss the relevance of an MNC's exposure to exchange rate risk.
- Explain how transaction exposure can be measured.
- Explain how economic exposure can be measured.
- Explain how translation exposure can be measured.

Is Exchange Rate Risk Relevant?

Some have argued that exchange rate risk is irrelevant. These contentions, in turn, have resulted in counterarguments, as summarized here.

Purchasing Power Parity Argument

One argument for exchange rate irrelevance is that, according to purchasing power parity (PPP) theory, exchange rate movements are just a response to differentials in price changes between countries. Therefore, the exchange rate effect is offset by the change in prices.

Example

Office Import Co., a U.S. importer of office supplies, distributes these supplies throughout the country. It currently competes against several U.S. companies that produce their own office supplies. If the dollar depreciates, Office Import Co. will need more dollars to cover its import payments. Yet, according to PPP, a decline in the dollar will be associated with relatively high inflation in the United States. Thus, while Office Import's competitors would not be affected by the dollar's decline, their cost of producing supplies would increase as a result of inflation. And although Office Import would be adversely affected by the dollar's decline, it would avoid the higher production costs in the United States. It can therefore be argued that this offsetting effect makes exchange rate risk irrelevant.

PPP does not necessarily hold, however, so the exchange rate will not necessarily change in accordance with the inflation differential between the two countries. Since a perfect offsetting effect is unlikely, the firm's competitive capabilities may indeed be influenced by exchange rate movements. Even if PPP did hold over a very long period of time, this would not comfort managers of MNCs that are focusing on the next year or even the next five years.

The Investor Hedge Argument

A second argument for exchange rate irrelevance is that investors in MNCs can hedge this risk on their own.

Example

If investors in Office Import Co. are aware that its performance may be affected by exchange rate fluctuations, they may choose to take positions (in futures contracts or options contracts) to offset any adverse impact of dollar depreciation on the company. Hence, one can argue that exchange rate risk is not relevant to corporations because shareholders can deal with this risk individually.

The investor hedge argument assumes that investors have complete information on corporate exposure to exchange rate fluctuations as well as the capabilities to correctly insulate their individual exposure. To the extent that investors prefer that corporations perform the hedging for them, exchange rate exposure is relevant to corporations.

Currency Diversification Argument

Another argument is that if a U.S.-based MNC is well diversified across numerous countries, its value will not be affected by exchange rate movements because of offsetting effects. It is naive, however, to presume that exchange rate effects will offset each other just because an MNC has transactions in many different currencies.

Stakeholder Diversification Argument

Some critics also argue that if stakeholders (such as creditors or stockholders) are well diversified, they will be somewhat insulated against losses experienced by an MNC due to exchange rate risk. However, several MNCs in which they have a stake could be affected in the same way because of exchange rate risk. In 1998, for example, numerous U.S.-based MNCs were adversely affected by the depreciation of Asian currencies against the dollar. In 2000, some MNCs were adversely affected by the depreciation of European currencies against the dollar.

Because creditors can experience large losses if the MNCs to which they have extended loans experience financial problems, they may prefer that the MNCs maintain low exposure to exchange rate risk. Consequently, MNCs that hedge their exposure to risk may be able to borrow funds at a lower cost.

Response from MNCs

To the extent that MNCs can stabilize their earnings over time by hedging their exchange rate risk, they may also reduce their general operating expenses over time (by avoiding costs of downsizing and restructuring). Many MNCs, including Colgate-Palmolive, Eastman Kodak, and Merck, have attempted to stabilize their earnings with hedging strategies—an indication that they believe exchange rate risk is relevant. Further evidence that MNCs consider exchange rate risk to be relevant can be found in annual reports. The following comments from annual reports of MNCs are typical:

The primary purpose of the Company's foreign currency hedging program is to manage the volatility associated with foreign currency purchases of materials and other assets and liabilities created in the normal course of business. Corporate policy prescribes a range of allowable hedging activity.

Procter & Gamble Co.

The Company enters into foreign exchange contracts and options to hedge various currency exposures . . . . the primary business objective of the activity is to optimize the U.S. dollar value off the Company's assets, liabilities, and future cash flows with respect to exchange rate fluctuations.

Dow Chemical Co.

TYPES OF EXPOSURE

As mentioned in the previous chapter, exchange rates cannot be forecasted with perfect accuracy, but the firm can at least measure its exposure to exchange rate fluctuations. If the firm is highly exposed to exchange rate fluctuations, it can consider techniques to reduce its exposure. Such techniques are identified in the following chapter. Before choosing among them, the firm should first measure its degree of exposure.

Exposure to exchange rate fluctuations comes in three forms:

- Transaction exposure
- Economic exposure
- Translation exposure

Each type of exposure will be discussed in turn.

TRANSACTION EXPOSURE

The value of a firm's cash inflows received in various currencies will be affected by the respective exchange rates of these currencies when they are converted into the currency desired. Similarly, the value of a firm's cash outflows in various currencies will be dependent on the respective exchange rates of these currencies. The degree to which the value of future cash transactions can be affected by exchange rate fluctuations is referred to as **transaction exposure.**

Example   Consider those U.S. exporters that sold products to Asian countries during the 1997–1998 Asian crisis, when some Asian currencies depreciated by 80 percent. If the products were invoiced in Asian currencies, the exporters' cash flows may have been 80 percent less than they anticipated. If the products were invoiced in dollars, the exporters would have not been subject to the transaction exposure, but the Asian importing companies would have faced it. The impact of large swings in currency values can be devastating to a firm that relies heavily on international trade for its business.

Measuring transaction exposure involves two steps: (1) determine the projected net amount of inflows or outflows in each foreign currency and (2) determine the overall risk of exposure to those currencies. Each of these steps is discussed in turn.

Transaction Exposure to "Net" Cash Flows

MNCs tend to focus on transaction exposure over an upcoming short-term period (such as the next month or the next quarter) for which they can anticipate foreign currency cash flows with reasonable accuracy. Since MNCs commonly have foreign subsidiaries spread around the world, they need an information system that can track their currency positions. The Internet enables all subsidiaries to tap into the same network and provide information on their existing and expected future currency positions.

To measure its transaction exposure, an MNC needs to project the consolidated net amount in currency inflows or outflows for all its subsidiaries, categorized by currency. One foreign subsidiary may have inflows of a foreign currency while another has outflows of that same currency. In that case, the MNC's net cash flows of that currency overall may be negligible. If most of the MNC's subsidiaries have future inflows in another currency, however, the net cash flows in that currency could be substantial. Estimating the consolidated net cash flows per currency is a useful first step when assessing an MNC's exposure because it helps to determine the MNC's overall position in each currency.

Example   Miami Co. conducts its international business in four currencies. Its objective is to first measure its exposure in each currency in the next quarter and then estimate its consolidated cash flows for one quarter ahead, as shown in Exhibit 10.1. For example, Miami expects Canadian dollar inflows of C$12,000,000 and outflows of C$2,000,000 over the next quarter. Thus, Miami expects net inflows of C$10,000,000. Given an expected exchange rate of $.80 at the end of the quarter, it can convert the expected net inflow of Canadian dollars into an expected net inflow of $8,000,000 (estimated as C$10,000,000 × $.80).

Exhibit 10.1

Consolidated Net Cash Flow Assessment of Miami Co.

Currency	Total Inflow	Total Outflow	Net Inflow or Outflow	Expected Exchange Rate at End of Quarter	Net Inflow or Outflow as Measured in U.S. Dollars
British pounds	£17,000,000	£7,000,000	+£10,000,000	$1.50	+$15,000,000
Canadian dollars	C$12,000,000	C$2,000,000	+C$10,000,000	$ .80	+$ 8,000,000
Swedish kronar	SK20,000,000	SK120,000,000	−SK100,000,000	$ .15	−$15,000,000
Mexican pesos	MXP90,000,000	MXP10,000,000	+MXP80,000,000	$ .10	+$ 8,000,000

The same process is used to determine the net cash flows of each of the other three currencies. Notice from the last column of Exhibit 10.1 that the expected net cash flows in three of the currencies are positive, while the net cash flows in Swedish kronar are negative (reflecting cash outflows).

The information in Exhibit 10.1 needs to be converted into dollars so that Miami Co. can assess the exposure of each currency by using a standardized measure. For each currency, the net cash flows are converted into dollars to determine the dollar amount of exposure. Notice that Miami has a smaller dollar amount of exposure in Mexican pesos and Canadian dollars than in the other currencies. However, this does not necessarily mean that Miami will be less affected by these exposures, as will be explained shortly.

Recognize that the net inflows or outflows in each foreign currency and the exchange rates at the end of the period are uncertain. Thus, Miami might develop a range of possible exchange rates for each currency, as shown in Exhibit 10.2, instead of a point estimate. In this case, there is a range of net cash flows in dollars rather than a point estimate. Notice that the range of dollar cash flows resulting from Miami's peso transactions is wide, reflecting the high degree of uncertainty surrounding the peso's value over the next quarter. In contrast, the range of dollar cash flows resulting from the Canadian dollar transactions is narrow because the Canadian dollar is expected to be relatively stable over the next quarter.

Exhibit 10.2

Estimating the Range of Net Inflows or Outflows for Miami Co.

Currency	Net Inflow or Outflow	Range of Possible Exchange Rates at End of Quarter	Range of Possible Net Inflows or Outflows in U.S. Dollars (Based on Range of Possible Exchange Rates)
British pound	+£10,000,000	$1.40 to $1.60	+$14,000,000 to +$16,000,000
Canadian dollar	+C$10,000,000	$.79 to $.81	+$ 7,900,000 to +$ 8,100,000
Swedish krona	−SK100,000,000	$.14 to $.16	−$14,000,000 to −$16,000,000
Mexican peso	+MXP80,000,000	$.06 to $.11	+$ 4,800,000 to +$ 8,800,000

In the example, Miami Co. assessed its net cash flow situation for only one quarter. The company could also derive its expected net cash flows for other periods, such as a week or a month. Some MNCs assess their transaction exposure during several periods by applying the methods just described to each period. The further into the future an MNC attempts to measure its transaction exposure, the less accurate will be the measurement due to the greater uncertainty about inflows or outflows in each foreign currency, as well as future exchange rates, over periods further into the future. An MNC's overall exposure can be assessed only after considering each currency's variability and the correlations among currencies. The overall exposure of Miami Co. will be assessed after the following discussion of currency variability and correlations.

Transaction Exposure Based on Currency Variability

In the previous example, the expected exchange rates for the end of the period were given without any explanation as to how they were derived. Each MNC may have its own method for developing exchange rate projections. Some methods have been described in the previous chapter. Although it is difficult to predict future currency values with much accuracy, an MNC can evaluate historical data to at least assess the potential degree of movement for each currency.

http://

See www.ny.frb.org/pihome/ mktrates for current and historic exchange rates and implied currency option volatilities.

Measurement of Currency Variability. The standard deviation statistic is one possible way to measure the degree of movement for each currency. Exhibit 10.3 shows the standard deviations of several foreign currencies (based on monthly data) over two separate periods. Notice that within each period, some currencies clearly fluctuate much more than others. For example, the standard deviations of the monthly movements in the Japanese yen and the Swiss franc are more than twice that of the Canadian dollar. Based on this information, the potential for substantial deviations from the projected future values is greater for the yen and the Swiss franc than for the Canadian dollar (from the U.S. firm's perspective). Some currencies in emerging markets are much more volatile than those shown here. For example, the standard deviation of the Mexican peso was more than twice that of any currency shown in Exhibit 10.3 over the 1994–1998 period.

Exhibit 10.3
Standard Deviations of Exchange Rate Movements (Based on Monthly Data)

	Time Period	
Currency	1981–1993	1994–1998
British pound	0.0309	0.0148
Canadian dollar	0.0100	0.0110
Indian rupee	0.0219	0.0168
Japanese yen	0.0279	0.0298
New Zealand dollar	0.0289	0.0190
Swedish krona	0.0287	0.0195
Swiss franc	0.0330	0.0246
Singapore dollar	0.0111	0.0174

Currency Variability over Time. The variability of a currency will not necessarily remain consistent from one time period to another. Exhibit 10.3 illustrates how standard deviations can change over time. For example, the British pound's value became less volatile.

Since currency variability levels change over time, an MNC's assessment of a currency's future variability will not be perfect when a previous time period is used as the indicator. Nevertheless, the MNC can benefit from information such as that in Exhibit 10.3 if it is used wisely. Although the MNC may not be able to predict a currency's future variability with perfect accuracy, it can identify currencies whose values are *most likely* to be stable or highly variable in the future. For example, the Canadian dollar consistently exhibits lower variability than the other currencies. This explains the findings in the previous chapter that the forecast errors when forecasting the value of the Canadian dollar are consistently smaller than when forecasting values of other currencies.

HTTP:// ONLINE APPLICATION **Historical Exchange Rates** Exchange rate volatility based on historical exchange rate movements is provided at http://www.oanda.com.

Click on FXHistory to review daily exchange rates for a currency that you specify over a period of time that you specify. Identify the two currencies whose exchange rates you want to view and the period for which you want data. The website provides the data that you request.

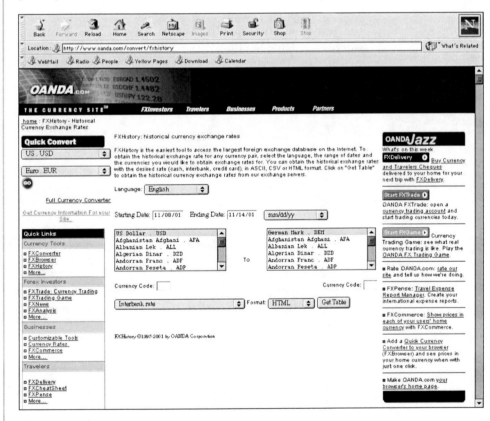

Transaction Exposure Based on Currency Correlations

To illustrate how MNCs assess exposure based on currency movements, consider the historical exchange rate fluctuations shown in Exhibit 10.4 for Currencies X, Y, and Z. Assume you are the treasurer of a U.S.-based MNC as you consider the following two examples.

Example 1

You expect that one year from now your company will need $10 million to purchase Currency X and another $20 million to purchase Currency Y. You also expect to receive about $30 million from converting inflows of Currency Z one year from now. This situation involves considerable transaction exposure, as explained next.

Exhibit 10.4 indicates that Currencies X and Y are highly correlated with each other but negatively correlated with Currency Z. If Currencies X and Y appreciate against the U.S. dollar, more dollars will be needed to purchase them. And if they appreciate against the dollar, Currency Z will likely depreciate against the dollar, based on its historical co-movements with Currencies X and Y. Since the MNC expects to receive Currency Z in the future, this cash inflow will convert to fewer U.S. dollars if the currency does depreciate. Thus, the MNC could end up receiving fewer dollars and paying out more dollars than it currently expects.

Example 2

You expect that one year from now your company will need $10 million to purchase Currency X and another $20 million to purchase Currency Y (as in Example 1). Also assume that you expect to need another $30 million to purchase Currency Z one year from now. Finally, assume that you have no projected inflows in foreign currencies. This situation does not involve much transaction risk, when you consider all the currencies simultaneously. Based on the correlations shown in

Exhibit 10.4

Illustration of Currency Movements for Examples

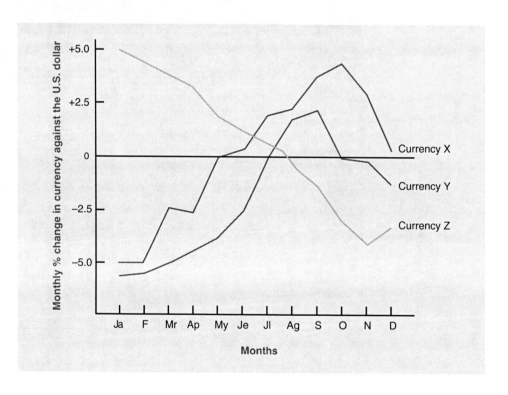

Exhibit 10.4, the changes in values of Currencies X and Y will be somewhat offset by opposite movements in Currency Z. For example, if Currencies X and Y appreciate by 20 percent, the MNC will need $36 million instead of $30 million to buy these currencies. Yet, Currency Z will likely depreciate under this scenario. A perfect offset will occur if Currency Z depreciates by 20 percent. In that case, only $24 million will be needed to purchase the necessary amount of Currency Z. Thus, the additional $6 million needed to purchase Currencies X and Y will be offset by the $6 million saved due to depreciation of Currency Z. A perfect offset is not likely to occur, but the point here is to be able to detect positions that can somewhat offset each other.

In summary, the first step when assessing transaction exposure is to determine the size of the position in each currency. The second step is to determine how each individual currency position could affect the firm by assessing the standard deviations and correlations of the currencies. Even if a particular currency is perceived as risky, its impact on the firm's overall exposure will not be severe if the firm has taken only a minor position in that currency. For this reason, both of these steps must be considered when developing an overall assessment of the firm's transaction risk.

Measurement of Currency Correlations. The correlations among currency movements can be measured by their *correlation coefficients*, which indicate the degree to which two currencies move in relation to each other. Thus, MNCs can use such information when determining their degree of transaction exposure. The extreme case is perfect positive correlation, which is represented by a correlation coefficient equal to 1.00. Correlations can also be negative, reflecting an inverse relationship between individual movements, the extreme case being –1.00.

Exhibit 10.5 shows the correlation coefficients (based on quarterly data) for currency pairs in three different periods. It is clear that some currency pairs exhibit a much higher correlation than others. At the other extreme, the Canadian dollar has a very low correlation with other currencies. Currency correlations are generally positive; this implies that currencies tend to move in the same direction against the U.S. dollar (though by different degrees). The positive correlation may not always occur on a day-to-day basis, but it appears to hold over longer periods of time for most currencies.

Exhibit 10.5

Correlations among Exchange Rate Movements

	British Pound	Canadian Dollar	Japanese Yen	New Zealand Dollar	Swedish Krona	Swiss Franc
British pound	1.00					
Canadian dollar	.18	1.00				
Japanese yen	.45	.06	1.00			
New Zealand dollar	.39	.20	.33	1.00		
Swedish krona	.62	.16	.46	.33	1.00	
Swiss franc	.63	.12	.61	.37	.70	1.00

Applying Currency Correlations to Net Cash Flows. The implications of currency correlations for a particular MNC depend on the cash flow characteristics of that MNC.

The concept of currency correlations can be applied to the earlier example of Miami Co.'s net cash flows, as displayed in Exhibit 10.2. Since movements in the British pound and the Swedish krona are highly correlated, the exposures of the cash inflows and outflows to these currencies will offset each other to a degree.

Miami Co. anticipates cash inflows in British pounds equivalent to $15 million and cash outflows in Swedish kronar equivalent to $15 million. Thus, if a weak-dollar cycle occurs, Miami will be adversely affected by its exposure to kronar, but favorably affected by its pound exposure. During a strong-dollar cycle, it will be adversely affected by the pound exposure but favorably affected by its kronar exposure. If Miami expects that these two currencies will move in the same direction and by about the same degree over the next period, its exposures to these two currencies are partially offset.

Miami may not be too concerned about its exposure to the Canadian dollar's movements because the Canadian dollar is somewhat stable with respect to the U.S. dollar over time; risk of substantial depreciation of the Canadian dollar is low. However, the company should be concerned about its exposure to the Mexican peso's movements because the peso is quite volatile and could depreciate substantially within a short period of time. Therefore, Miami Co. should seriously consider whether to hedge its expected net cash flow position in pesos.

Currency Correlations over Time. Exhibit 10.6 show the trends of exchange rate movements of various currencies against the dollar. Notice how correlations and volatility levels of currencies vary among currencies and over time. The Chinese yuan's value has been stable because it has been pegged to the dollar since 1994. The value of the Indian rupee has declined consistently while the value of other currencies has increased in some periods and declined in others.

An MNC cannot use previous correlations to predict future correlations with perfect accuracy. Nevertheless, some general relationships tend to hold over time. For example, movements in the values of the pound, the euro, and other European currencies against the dollar tend to be positively correlated. In addition, the Canadian dollar consistently moves almost independently of the other currencies, based on its continued low correlations with them.

Transaction Exposure Based on Value-at-Risk

http://
See
pacific.commerce.ubc.ca/xr/
data.html for a foreign
exchange series for over
60 countries that can be
customized with respect to
period and base currency.

A related method for assessing exposure is the value-at-risk (VAR) method, which incorporates volatility and currency correlations to determine the potential maximum one-day loss on the value of positions of an MNC that is exposed to exchange rate movements.

Exhibit 10.6

Movements of Major Currencies against the Dollar

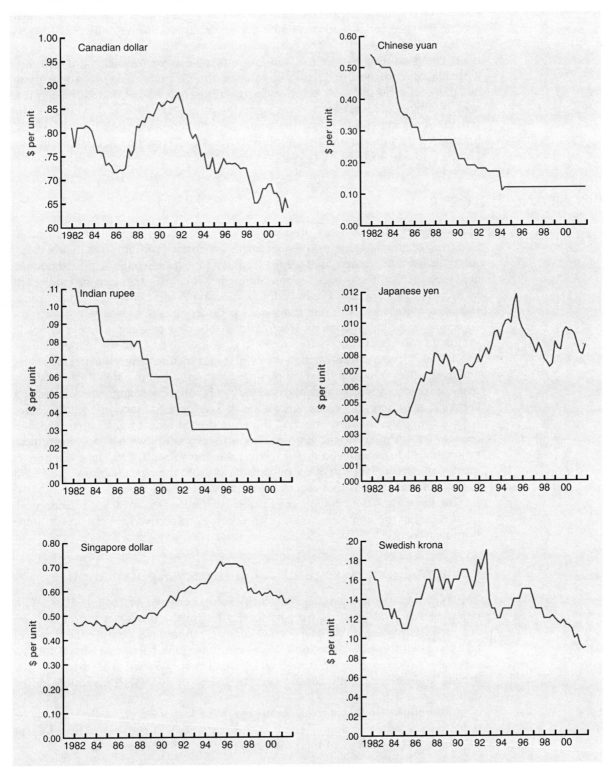

Example   Pitt, Inc., a U.S.-based-MNC, typically has receivables in Japanese yen. It first determines the maximum potential one-day decline in the yen that would be likely using a recent historical period such as 90 days. Pitt then applies that potential decline to its receivables to determine the potential loss in the dollar value of its receivables if that decline in the yen does occur.

Now Pitt has other positions in yen (such as a Japanese subsidiary), it will also determine the potential reduction in value of those positions due to a maximum one-day decline in the yen's value. By aggregating these effects, Pitt can determine how its value could be affected by a maximum one-day loss in the value of the yen. By repeating this process, the company can determine how its value could be affected by a maximum loss in the yen over a different time horizon, such as a 7-day or 30-day horizon.

ECONOMIC EXPOSURE

The degree to which a firm's present value of future cash flows can be influenced by exchange rate fluctuations is referred to as **economic exposure** to exchange rates. All types of transactions that cause transaction exposure also cause economic exposure because these transactions represent cash flows that can be influenced by exchange rate fluctuations. In addition, other types of business that do not cause transaction exposure can cause economic exposure.

Some of the more common international business transactions that typically subject an MNC's cash flows to economic exposure are listed in the first column of Exhibit 10.7. Transactions listed in the exhibit that require conversion of currencies, and thus reflect transaction exposure, include exports denominated in foreign currency, interest received from foreign investments, imports denominated in foreign currency, and interest owed on foreign loans. The other transactions, which do not require conversion of currencies and therefore do not reflect transaction exposure, are also a form of economic exposure because the cash flows resulting from these transactions can be influenced by exchange rate movements. Exchange rate movements can have as large an effect on cash flows from these transactions as on cash flows from transactions that require currency conversion.

The second and third columns of Exhibit 10.7 indicate how each transaction can be affected by the appreciation and depreciation, respectively, of the firm's home (local) currency. The next sections discuss these effects in turn.

Economic Exposure to Local Currency Appreciation

The following discussion is related to the second column of Exhibit 10.7. With regard to the firm's cash inflows, its local sales (in the firm's home country) are expected to decrease if the local (home) currency appreciates because the firm will face increased foreign competition. Local customers will be able to obtain foreign substitute products cheaply with their strengthened currency. The extent of the decline in local sales will depend on the degree of foreign competition in the domestic market.

Cash inflows from exports denominated in the local currency will also likely be reduced as a result of appreciation in that currency. The reason is that foreign importers will need more of their own currency to pay for these products.

Exhibit 10.7
Economic Exposure to Exchange Rate Fluctuations

Transactions That Influence the Firm's Local Currency Inflows	Impact of Local Currency Appreciation on Transactions	Impact of Local Currency Depreciation on Transactions
Local sales (relative to foreign competition in local markets)	Decrease	Increase
Firm's exports denominated in local currency	Decrease	Increase
Firm's exports denominated in foreign currency	Decrease	Increase
Interest received from foreign investments	Decrease	Increase
Transactions That Influence the Firm's Local Currency Outflows		
Firm's imported supplies denominated in local currency	No change	No change
Firm's imported supplies denominated in foreign currency	Decrease	Increase
Interest owed on foreign funds borrowed	Decrease	Increase

Example

General Corp. arranged to sell software to Mexican customers in the early 1980s. Later, however, the Mexican peso was devalued by 40 percent against the dollar, substantially increasing the price of the software to Mexican customers. Consequently, General Corp.'s sales to Mexico declined.

In 1997 and 1998, many U.S.-based MNCs were adversely affected by exchange rates because of their economic exposure to Asian currencies (such as the Indonesian rupiah, Thail baht, and Korean won). First, the weakening of Asian currencies raised the prices of the MNCs' exports to Asia from the perspective of Asian importers (because the exports were usually denominated in dollars). Thus, even though these exporters were not affected by transaction exposure in this case, they were affected by economic exposure. Second, many U.S. exporters also experienced a decline in demand for their products in other countries, as some importers shifted to Asian exports because the weak Asian currencies caused the prices of those products to be lower than the prices charged by U.S. exporters from the importers' perspective.

Exports and investment income denominated in the foreign currency also will likely result in reduced cash inflows, but for a different reason. Foreign importers' demand for the firm's product will not change because they can use their own currency and do not need to obtain the firm's local currency. When the firm receives the foreign currency inflows, however, it will convert them to its local currency. If the local currency has appreciated, these inflows will convert to a reduced amount. Finally, any interest or dividends received from foreign investments will also convert to a reduced amount if the local currency has strengthened.

With regard to the firm's cash outflows, the cost of imported supplies denominated in the local currency will not be directly affected by changes in exchange rates. If the local currency appreciates, however, the cost of imported supplies denominated in the foreign currency will be reduced. In addition, any interest to be paid on financing in foreign currencies will be reduced (in terms of the local currency) if the local currency appreciates because the strengthened local currency will be exchanged for the foreign currency to make the interest payments.

Overall, appreciation in the firm's local currency causes a reduction in both cash inflows and outflows. Thus, it is difficult to generalize whether net cash flows will increase or decrease when the local currency's appreciates. The impact on a firm's net cash flows will depend on whether the inflow transactions are affected more or less than the outflow transactions. If, for example, the firm is in the exporting business but obtains its supplies and borrowed funds locally, its inflow transactions will be reduced by a greater degree than its outflow transactions. In this case, net cash flows will be reduced. Conversely, cash inflows of a firm concentrating its sales locally with little foreign competition will not be severely reduced by appreciation of the local currency. If such a firm obtains supplies and borrowed funds overseas, its outflows will be reduced. Overall, this firm's net cash flows will be enhanced by the appreciation of its local currency.

Economic Exposure to Local Currency Depreciation

If the firm's local currency depreciates (see the third column of Exhibit 10.7), its transactions will be affected in a manner opposite to the way they are influenced by appreciation. Local sales should increase due to reduced foreign competition, because prices denominated in strong foreign currencies will seem high to the local customers. The firm's exports denominated in the local currency will appear cheap to importers, thereby increasing foreign demand for those products. Even exports denominated in the foreign currency can increase cash flows because a given amount in foreign currency inflows to the firm will convert to a larger amount of the local currency. In addition, interest or dividends from foreign investments will now convert to more of the local currency.

With regard to cash outflows, imported supplies denominated in the local currency will not be directly affected by any change in exchange rates. The cost of imported supplies denominated in the foreign currency will rise, however, because

---

Managing for Value: Caterpillar's Exposure to Exchange Rate Risk

Caterpillar, Inc., relies heavily on exports for a large portion of its sales. The weakening of the dollar reduces the price importers must pay for Caterpillar's products. When the dollar is relatively weak, the demand for Caterpillar's exports increases, and so does Caterpillar's performance. Caterpillar's exposure to exchange rates works in both directions, however. When the dollar is strong, importers incur a higher cost of importing from Caterpillar because it takes more of their currency to obtain the dollars to purchase Caterpillar's products. Caterpillar is especially vulnerable to the value of the dollar because its key competitor is Komatsu of Japan, whose exports are denominated in Japanese yen.

Thus, when the dollar is expensive, Caterpillar's customers can switch to a competitor whose prices are not denominated in dollars.

During the 1999–2000 period, many currencies weakened against the dollar but strengthened against the yen. Consequently, Caterpillar's performance declined in response to the decline in the foreign demand for its product, and its stock price fell. Just as Caterpillar's value may be enhanced by a weak dollar, it is adversely affected by a strong dollar. Other U.S. firms that rely heavily on exports typically have the same type of exposure, especially when their competitors are based outside the United States.

more of the weakened local currency will be required to obtain the foreign currency needed. Any interest payments paid on financing in foreign currencies will increase.

In general, depreciation of the firm's local currency causes an increase in both cash inflows and outflows. Because a partial offsetting effect is likely, it is difficult to generalize as to whether net cash flows will increase or decrease due to the local currency's depreciation. The end result depends on whether inflow variables are affected more than outflow variables. A firm that concentrates on exporting and obtains supplies and borrowed funds locally will likely benefit from a depreciated local currency. This is the case for Caterpillar, Ford, and General Motors in periods when the dollar weakens substantially against most major currencies. Conversely, a firm that concentrates on local sales, has very little foreign competition, and obtains foreign supplies (denominated in foreign currencies) will likely be hurt by a depreciated local currency.

Economic Exposure of Domestic Firms

Although our focus is on the financial management of MNCs, even purely domestic firms are affected by economic exposure.

Example

Burlington, Inc., is a U.S. manufacturer of steel that purchases all of its supplies locally and sells all of its steel locally. Because its transactions are solely in the local currency, Burlington is not subject to transaction exposure. It is subject to economic exposure, however, because it faces foreign competition in its local markets. If the exchange rate of the foreign competitor's invoice currency depreciates against the dollar, customers interested in steel products will shift their purchases toward the foreign steel producer. Consequently, demand for Burlington's steel will likely decrease, and so will net cash inflows. Thus, Burlington is subject to economic exposure even though it is not subject to transaction exposure.

Economic Exposure of MNCs

Even though purely domestic firms can be subject to economic exposure, the degree of exposure is likely to be much greater for a firm involved in international business. The impact of the U.S. dollar's movements varies across U.S.-based MNCs because of their different operating characteristics. Even those U.S.-based MNCs that are heavy exporters may be affected differently, depending on how their competitors react to exchange rate movements. A U.S. exporter whose foreign competitors are willing to reduce their prices during a weak-dollar period may not necessarily benefit from the exchange rate movements.

The effects of exchange rate movements on MNCs can also vary with the currency of concern, since exchange rates can change by varying degrees.

Managing for Value: Honda's Exposure to the Euro

Some European countries including Denmark, Switzerland, and the United Kingdom have decided to continue using their own currency rather than participate in the euro. Their decision to use their own currency enables them to determine their own monetary policy. Nevertheless, MNCs that produce products in the United Kingdom and export those products to other European countries are still affected by movements in the euro's value. In 2000, the euro weakened against the British pound, which caused the European demand for British exports to decline, dampening the United Kingdom's economy.

In 1999, Honda, a large Japanese producer of automobiles, had drawn up plans to expand its production facilities in the United Kingdom so that it could produce more cars for export throughout Europe. In 2000, however, when the European demand for its cars built in the United Kingdom declined in response to the weak euro, Honda postponed those plans. It was concerned that the future European demand for its U.K.-produced cars would be weak because consumers in euro-zone countries would choose

alternative cars. If the United Kingdom participated in the euro, Honda would not face this type of exchange rate exposure because European consumers could use euros (rather than British pounds) to purchase British products. Notice, however, that in a period when the euro strengthens against the pound, Honda could be positioned to benefit because its cars produced in the United Kingdom and denominated in pounds will be cheap to consumers in the euro-zone countries.

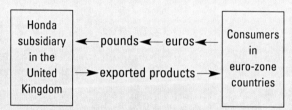

Honda's managers are well aware that its value is highly susceptible to movements in the euro. As the euro's value changes, so does the demand for Honda's vehicles, which affects its value. Awareness of exposure to exchange rate fluctuations is the first step in deciding whether that exposure should be hedged.

Measuring Economic Exposure

Since MNCs are affected by economic exposure, they should assess the potential degree of exposure that exists and then determine whether to insulate themselves against it. Assessing the economic exposure of an MNC with subsidiaries scattered across countries is difficult, due to the interaction of cash flows denominated in various currencies into, out of, and within the MNC. The overall impact of a given currency's fluctuation on all of the subsidiaries is extremely complex.

Sensitivity of Earnings to Exchange Rates. One method of measuring an MNC's economic exposure is to classify the cash flows into different income statement items and subjectively predict each income statement item based on a forecast of exchange rates. Then an alternative exchange rate scenario can be considered and the forecasts for the income statement items revised. By reviewing how the earnings forecast in the income statement changes in response to alternative exchange rate scenarios, the firm can assess the influence of currency movements on its earnings and cash flows. This procedure is especially useful for firms that have more expenses than revenue in a particular foreign currency as illustrated next.

Example

Madison, Inc., is a U.S.-based MNC that conducts a portion of its business in Canada. Its U.S. sales are denominated in U.S. dollars, while its Canadian sales are denominated in Canadian dollars. Its pro forma income statement for next year is shown in Exhibit 10.8. The income statement items are segmented into those for the United States and for Canada. Assume that Madison, Inc., desires to assess how its income statement items would be affected by three possible exchange rate scenarios for the Canadian dollar over the period of concern: (1) $.75, (2) $.80, and (3) $.85. These scenarios are separately analyzed in the second, third, and fourth columns of Exhibit 10.9.

If the U.S. sales are unaffected by the possible exchange rates, the impact of exchange rates on all income statement items can be assessed from the information contained in Exhibit 10.8. However, Madison's sales in the United States are higher when the Canadian dollar (C$) is stronger because Canadian competitors are priced out of the U.S. market. To be specific, assume the following forecasts for U.S. sales corresponding to each possible exchange rate scenario:

Possible Exchange Rate of C$	Forecasted U.S. Sales (in Millions)
$.75	$300
.80	304
.85	307

The impact of an exchange rate on local sales for any firm will depend on the foreign competition of concern. Historical data can be used to assess how local sales were affected by exchange rates in the past. For our example, the impact of the exchange rate on local sales is given, so there is no need to assess historical data.

Given this information, Madison, Inc., can determine how its pro forma statement would be affected by each exchange rate scenario, as shown in Exhibit 10.9. The assumed impact of exchange rates on U.S. sales is shown in row 1. Row 2 shows the amount in U.S. dollars to be received as a result of Canadian sales (after converting the forecasted C$4 million of Canadian sales into U.S. dollars). Row 3 shows the estimated U.S. dollars to be received from total sales, which is determined by combining rows 1 and 2. Row 4 shows the cost of goods sold in the United States. Row 5 converts the estimated C$200 million cost of goods sold into U.S.

Exhibit 10.8

Revenue and Cost Estimates: Madison, Inc. (in Millions of U.S. Dollars and Canadian Dollars)

	U.S. Business	Canadian Business
Sales	$304.00	C$ 4
Cost of goods sold	50.00	200
Gross profit	$254.00	C$–196
Operating expenses:		
Fixed	$ 30.00	—
Variable	30.72	—
Total	$ 60.72	—
Earnings before interest and taxes	$193.28	C$–196
Interest expense	3.00	10
Earnings before taxes (EBT)	$190.28	C$–206

Exhibit 10.9

Impact of Possible Exchange Rate Movements on Earnings of Madison, Inc. (in Millions)

	Exchange Rate Scenario		
	C$ = $.75	C$ = $.80	C$ = $.85
Sales:			
(1) U.S.	$300.0	$304.00	$307.00
(2) Canadian	C$4 = 3.0	C$4 = 3.20	C$4 = 3.40
(3) Total	$303.0	$307.20	$310.40
Cost of goods sold:			
(4) U.S.	$ 50.0	$ 50.00	$ 50.00
(5) Canadian	C$200 = 150.0	C$200 = 160.00	C$200 = 170.00
(6) Total	$200.0	$210.00	$220.00
(7) Gross profit	$103.0	$ 97.20	$ 90.40
Operating expenses:			
(8) U.S.: Fixed	$ 30.0	$ 30.00	$ 30.00
(9) U.S.: Variable (10% of total sales)	30.3	30.72	31.04
(10) Total	$ 60.3	$ 60.72	$ 61.04
(11) EBIT	$ 42.7	$ 36.48	$ 29.36
Interest expense:			
(12) U.S.	$ 3.0	$ 3.00	$ 3.00
(13) Canadian	C$10 = 7.5	C$10 = 8.00	C$10 = 8.50
(14) Total	$ 10.5	$ 11.00	$ 11.50
(15) EBT	$ 32.2	$ 25.48	$ 17.86

dollars for each exchange rate scenario. Row 6 measures the estimated U.S. dollars needed to cover the total cost of goods sold, which is determined by combining rows 4 and 5. Row 7 estimates the gross profit in U.S. dollars, determined by subtracting row 6 from row 3. Rows 8 through 10 show estimated operating expenses, and row 11 subtracts total operating expenses from gross profit to determine earnings before interest and taxes (EBIT). Row 12 estimates the interest expenses paid in the United States, while row 13 estimates the U.S. dollars needed to make interest payments in Canada. Row 14 combines rows 12 and 13 to estimate total U.S. dollars needed to make all interest payments. Row 15 shows earnings before taxes (EBT), estimated by subtracting row 14 from row 11.

The effect of exchange rates on Madison's revenues and costs can now be reviewed. Exhibit 10.9 illustrates how both U.S. sales and the dollar value of Canadian sales would increase as a result of a stronger Canadian dollar. Because Madison's Canadian cost of goods sold exposure (C$200 million) is much greater than its Canadian sales exposure (C$4 million), a strong Canadian dollar has a negative overall impact on gross profit. The total amount in U.S. dollars needed to make interest payments is also higher when the Canadian dollar is stronger. In general, Madison, Inc., would be adversely affected by a stronger Canadian dollar. It would be favorably affected by a weaker Canadian dollar because the reduced value of total revenue would be more than offset by the reduced cost of goods sold and interest expenses.

A general conclusion from this example is that firms with more (less) in foreign costs than in foreign revenue will be unfavorably (favorably) affected by a stronger foreign currency. The precise anticipated impact, however, can be determined only by utilizing the procedure described here or some alternative procedure. The example is based on a one-period time horizon. If firms have developed forecasts of sales, expenses, and exchange rates for several periods ahead, they can assess their economic exposure over time. Their economic exposure will be affected by any change in operating characteristics over time.

Sensitivity of Cash Flows to Exchange Rates. A firm's economic exposure to currency movements can also be assessed by applying regression analysis to historical cash flow and exchange rate data as follows:

$$PCF_t = a_0 + a_1 e_t + \mu_t$$

where

PCF_t = percentage change in inflation-adjusted cash flows measured in the firm's home currency over period t

e_t = percentage change in the exchange rate of the currency over period t

μ_t = random error term

a_0 = intercept

a_1 = slope coefficient

The regression coefficient a_1, estimated by regression analysis, indicates the sensitivity of PCF_t to e_t. If the firm anticipates no major adjustments in its operating structure, it will expect the sensitivity detected from regression analysis to be somewhat similar in the future.

This regression model can be revised to handle more complex situations. For example, if additional currencies are to be assessed, they can be included in the model as additional independent variables. Each currency's impact is measured by estimating its respective regression coefficient. If an MNC is influenced by numerous currencies, it can measure the sensitivity of PCF_t to an index (or composite) of currencies.

The analysis just described for a single currency can also be extended over separate subperiods, as the sensitivity of a firm's cash flows to a currency's movements may change over time. This would be indicated by a shift in the regression coefficient, which may occur if the firm's exposure to exchange rate movements changes.

Some MNCs may prefer to use their stock price as a proxy for the firm's value and then assess how their stock price changes in response to currency movements. Regression analysis could also be applied to this situation by replacing PCF_t with the percentage change in stock price in the model specified here.

Some researchers, including Adler and Dumas,[1] suggest the use of regression analysis for this purpose. By assigning stock returns as the dependent variable, regression analysis can indicate how the firm's value is sensitive to exchange rate fluctuations.

[1]Michael Adler and Bernard Dumas, "Exposure to Currency Risk: Definition and Measurement," *Financial Management*, 13, no. 2 (Summer 1984): 41–50.

Some companies may assess the impact of exchange rates on particular corporate characteristics, such as earnings, exports, or sales.

Example | Toyota Motor Corp. measures the sensitivity of its exports to the yen exchange rate (relative to the U.S. dollar). Consequently, it can determine how the level of exports may change in response to potential changes in the value of the yen. This information is useful when Toyota determines its production level and manages its inventory.

TRANSLATION EXPOSURE

An MNC creates its financial statements by consolidating all of its individual subsidiaries' financial statements. A subsidiary's financial statement is normally measured in its local currency. To be consolidated, each subsidiary's financial statement must be translated into the currency of the MNC's parent. Since exchange rates change over time, the translation of the subsidiary's financial statement into a different currency is affected by exchange rate movements. The exposure of the MNC's consolidated financial statements to exchange rate fluctuations is known as **translation exposure**. In particular, subsidiary earnings translated into the reporting currency on the consolidated income statement are subject to changing exchange rates.

Does Translation Exposure Matter?

The relevance of translation exposure can be argued based on a cash flow perspective or a stock price perspective.

Cash Flow Perspective. Translation of financial statements for consolidated reporting purposes does not by itself affect an MNC's cash flows. For this reason, some analysts suggest that translation exposure is not relevant. MNCs could argue that the subsidiary earnings do not actually have to be converted into the parent's currency. Therefore, if a subsidiary's local currency is currently weak, the earnings could be retained rather than converted and sent to the parent. The earnings could be reinvested in the subsidiary's country if feasible opportunities exist.

If an MNC's subsidiary remits a portion of the earnings to its parent, however, a weak foreign currency adversely affects cash flows. Even if the subsidiary does not plan to remit any earnings today, it will remit earnings at some point in the future. To the extent that today's spot rate serves as a forecast of the spot rate that will exist when earnings are remitted, a weak foreign currency today results in a forecast of a weak exchange rate at the time that the earnings are remitted. In this case, the expected future cash flows are affected by the prevailing weakness of the foreign currency.

Stock Price Perspective. Many investors tend to use earnings when valuing firms, either by deriving estimates of expected cash flows from previous earnings or by applying a price-earnings (P/E) ratio to expected annual earnings to derive a value per share of stock. Since an MNC's translation exposure affects its consolidated earnings, it can affect the MNC's valuation.

Example   In 1996, the chief financial officer of IBM announced that the second quarter's earnings would be reduced by $.25 per share simply because of the impact of exchange rates on the foreign earnings when they were translated into dollars to consolidate all of IBM's earnings. If this decline in earnings was not important to investors because it affected only reported earnings and did not affect cash flow, then investors should not have reacted to the announcement. Yet, investors did react by selling their shares of IBM stock, which caused an immediate decline in IBM's stock at the time of the announcement.

Conclusion about the Relevance of Translation Exposure. Translation exposure is relevant for three reasons: (1) some MNC subsidiaries may want to remit a portion of their earnings to their respective parents now, (2) the prevailing exchange rates may be used to forecast the expected cash flows that will result from future remittances by subsidiaries, and (3) many investors use consolidated earnings to value MNCs.

Determinants of Translation Exposure

Some MNCs are subject to a greater degree of translation exposure than others. An MNC's degree of translation exposure is dependent on the following:

- The proportion of its business conducted by foreign subsidiaries
- The locations of its foreign subsidiaries
- The accounting methods that it uses

Proportion of Its Business Conducted by Foreign Subsidiaries. The greater the percentage of an MNC's business conducted by its foreign subsidiaries, the larger the percentage of a given financial statement item that is susceptible to translation exposure.

Example   Locus Co. and Zeuss Co. each generate about 30 percent of their sales from foreign countries. However, Locus Co. generates all of its international business by exporting, whereas Zeuss Co. has a large Mexican subsidiary that generates all of its international business. Locus Co. is not subject to translation exposure (although it is subject to economic exposure), while Zeuss has substantial translation exposure.

Locations of Foreign Subsidiaries. The locations of the subsidiaries can also influence the degree of translation exposure because the financial statement items of each subsidiary are typically measured by the home currency of the subsidiary's country.

Example   Zeuss Co. and Canton Co. each have one large foreign subsidiary that generates about 30 percent of their respective sales. However, Zeuss Co. is subject to a much higher degree of tranlslation exposure because its subsidiary is based in Mexico, and the peso's value is subject to a large decline. In contrast, Canton's subsidiary is based in Canada, and the Canadian dollar is very stable against the U.S. dollar.

Accounting Methods. An MNC's degree of translation exposure can be greatly affected by the accounting procedures it uses to translate when consolidating financial statement data. Many of the important consolidated accounting rules for U.S.-based MNCs are based on the Financial Accounting Standards Board No. 52 (FASB-52):

1. The functional currency of an entity is the currency of the economic environment in which the entity operates.
2. The current exchange rate as of the reporting date is used to translate the assets and liabilities of a foreign entity from its functional currency into the reporting currency.
3. The weighted average exchange rate is used to translate revenue, expenses, and gains and losses of a foreign entity from its functional currency into the reporting currency.
4. Translated income gains or losses due to changes in foreign currency values are not recognized in current net income but are reported as a second component of stockholder's equity; an exception to this rule is a foreign entity located in a country with high inflation.
5. Realized income gains or losses due to foreign currency transactions are recorded in current net income, although there are some exceptions.

Under FASB-52, consolidated earnings are sensitive to the functional currency's weighted average exchange rate.

Example

A British subsidiary of Providence, Inc., earned £10,000,000 in Year 1 and £10,000,000 in Year 2. When these earnings are consolidated along with other subsidiary earnings, they are translated into dollars at the weighted average exchange rate in that year. Assume the weighted average exchange rate is $1.90 in Year 1 and $1.50 in Year 2. The translated earnings for each reporting period in U.S. dollars are determined as follows:

Reporting Period	Local Earnings of British Subsidiary	Weighted Average Exchange Rate of Pound over the Reporting Period	Translated U.S. Dollar Earnings of British Subsidiary
Year 1	£10,000,000	$1.90	$19,000,000
Year 2	£10,000,000	$1.50	$15,000,000

Notice that even though the subsidiary's earnings in pounds were the same each year, the translated consolidated dollar earnings were reduced by $4 million in Year 2. The discrepancy here is due to the change in the weighted average of the British pound exchange rate. Although financial analysts may give the MNC a poor evaluation due to its British subsidiary's reduced earnings (when measured in dollars) in Year 2, the drop in earnings is not the fault of the subsidiary, but rather of the weakened British pound that makes its Year 2 earnings look small (when measured in U.S. dollars). During the 1990s, the pound's exchange rate varied by the amount shown in the example which partially explains the variability in earnings of MNCs over time.

Examples of Translation Exposure

Consolidated earnings of Black & Decker, The Coca-Cola Company, and other MNCs are very sensitive to exchange rates because more than a third of their assets and sales are overseas. Their earnings in foreign countries are reduced when foreign currencies depreciate against the dollar.

The earnings of numerous U.S.-based MNCs were favorably affected by the weakened dollar over the 1994–1996 period. The boost in earnings was primarily attributed to the foreign subsidiary earnings that were translated into dollars at a higher exchange rate. During the 1997–1998 Asian crisis, currencies of some Asian countries depreciated by more than 50 percent against the dollar, causing the translated dollar value of earnings of Asian subsidiaries of U.S.-based MNCs to also fall by more than 50 percent. Although much attention has focused on how foreign subsidiaries based in Asia experienced lower earnings because of the crisis, the translation effect caused additional adverse effects because it forced Asian earnings (which were lower than normal for most subsidiaries during the crisis) to be translated at very low exchange rates, which had a negative effect on the consolidated earnings of the U.S.-based MNCs. According to World Research Advisory estimates, translated earnings of U.S.-based MNCs in aggregate were reduced by $20 billion in the third quarter of 1998 alone simply because of the depreciation of Asian currencies against the dollar.

The impact of the Asian crisis on translation exposure was not limited to MNCs that had subsidiaries in countries such as Thailand, Malaysia, and Indonesia, although those countries were affected the most. The substantial depreciation of these currencies also encouraged Japan to weaken its currency (the yen) so that its export prices would still be competitive. Thus, the earnings of Japanese subsidiaries of U.S.-based MNCs translated into relatively small amounts of dollar earnings because of the weakness of the yen over the period that the earnings occurred.

Nike Problem

Nike's Translation Exposure

Nike has foreign subsidiaries that facilitate its international business. Its consolidated earnings are partially attributed to earnings generated by these foreign subsidiaries. Since the foreign earnings must be translated into U.S. dollars, the consolidated statements are subject to translation exposure; that is, the exchange rates at which the earnings are translated into dollars to derive the consolidated earnings are dependent on exchange rates over the time period of concern. In those years (such as 1997) when the local currencies of the foreign subsidiaries depreciate against the dollar, the earnings of those subsidiaries are reduced because of translation exposure. Nike noted in its annual report that any little earnings blip can have a significant impact on the stock price. Thus, the decline in Nike's stock price during 1997 was at least partially due to its translation exposure. Even though translation exposure does not directly affect cash flows, it can affect Nike's value through its effect on consolidated earnings.

Discussion: Should Nike be concerned about its translation exposure, or will the effects even out over time?

Financial Markets Perspective

Integrating Translation Exposure with Economic Exposure

The degree to which an MNC can be affected by currency fluctuations is dependent on its economic exposure and translation exposure and on conditions in the foreign exchange market. Consider the case of Minnesota Mining & Manufacturing (3M) Co., which experienced significantly lower earnings in 1998 during the Asian crisis because of its exposure to exchange rate movements of Asian currencies against the dollar. 3M normally relies on Asia for about 17 percent of its total worldwide revenue. First, 3M has receivables in some Asian currencies that are converted to dollars (transaction exposure, which is a subset of economic exposure), and the substantial depreciation of the Asian currencies in the foreign exchange market caused 3M's receivables to be converted to a smaller amount of dollars. Second, 3M was subject to economic exposure beyond its transaction exposure because the Asian demand for 3M's products that are denominated in dollars declined as the Asian currencies weakened.

Third, 3M suffered from its translation exposure because its Asian subsidiaries' earnings were translated into the reported consolidated earnings at weak exchange rates, which reduced the level of reported earnings. In June 1998, 3M announced that its earnings were significantly below the level that was expected, which caused its stock price to decline by more than 6 percent in a single day. Overall, the valuation of 3M in the stock market was affected by conditions in the foreign exchange market.

In the 2000–2001 period, the weakness of the euro caused several U.S.-based MNCs to report lower earnings than they expected. In September 2000, when DuPont announced that its consolidated earnings would be affected by its translation exposure to the euro, investors responded quickly by dumping DuPont's shares. The stock price of DuPont declined 10 percent on that day. Other MNCs including Colgate-Palmolive, Gillette, Goodyear, and McDonald's followed with similar announcements.

IMPACT OF EXCHANGE RATE MOVEMENTS ON AN MNC'S VALUE

An MNC's exposure to exchange rate movements can affect its value, as shown in Exhibit 10.10. The foreign currency cash flows generated by the foreign subsidiaries are subject to transaction exposure if those subsidiaries had transactions with foreign countries that involved the exchange of the local currency for other currencies. Transaction exposure definitely affects the dollar cash flows that are ultimately received when exchanging foreign currency cash flows because the future exchange rates at which the foreign currency cash flows are converted to dollars will change over time.

The foreign currency cash flows generated by the foreign subsidiaries may be subject to economic exposure even before those cash flows are converted into dollars. For example, the subsidiaries may compete with firms in other countries, and the demand for their products (and therefore foreign currency cash flows received) are dependent on the exchange rates of the currencies denominating the competitors' products.

Exhibit 10.10
Impact of Exposure on an MNC's Value

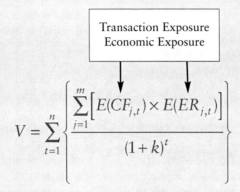

$$V = \sum_{t=1}^{n} \left\{ \frac{\sum_{j=1}^{m} \left[E(CF_{j,t}) \times E(ER_{j,t}) \right]}{(1+k)^t} \right\}$$

V = value of the U.S.-based MNC
$E(CF_{j,t})$ = expected cash flows denominated in currency j to be received by the U.S. parent in period t
$E(ER_{j,t})$ = expected exchange rate at which currency j can be converted to dollars at the end of period t
k = weighted average cost of capital of the U.S. parent company
m = number of currencies
n = number of periods

Although the diagram does not show any effect of exposure on the parent's cost of capital, an effect is possible in some cases. If the foreign subsidiaries are subject to a very high degree of economic exposure, their cost of capital (and therefore the required return on their investment) may be affected, which also influences the MNC's value.

SUMMARY

- MNCs with less risk can obtain funds at lower financing costs. Since they may experience more volatile cash flows because of exchange rate movements, exchange rate risk can affect their financing costs. Thus, MNCs may benefit from hedging exchange rate risk.

- Transaction exposure is the exposure of an MNC's future cash transactions to exchange rate movements. MNCs can measure their transaction exposure by determining their future payables and receivables positions in various currencies, along with the variability levels and correlations of these currencies. From this information, they can assess how their revenue and costs may change in response to various exchange rate scenarios.

- Economic exposure is any exposure of an MNC's cash flows (direct or indirect) to exchange rate movements. MNCs can attempt to measure their economic exposure by determining the extent to which their cash flows will be affected by their exposure to each foreign currency.

- Translation exposure is the exposure of an MNC's consolidated financial statements to exchange rate movements. To measure translation exposure, MNCs can forecast their earnings in each foreign currency and then determine the potential exchange rate movements of each currency relative to their home currency.

SELF TEST

Answers are provided in Appendix A at the back of the text.

1. Given that shareholders can diversify away an individual firm's exchange rate risk by investing in a variety of firms, why are firms concerned about exchange rate risk?

2. Bradley, Inc., considers importing its supplies from either Canada (denominated in C$) or Mexico (denominated in pesos) on a monthly basis. The quality is the same for both sources. Once the firm completes the agreement with a supplier, it will be obligated to continue using that supplier for at least three years. Based on existing exchange rates, the dollar amount to be paid (including transportation costs) will be the same. The firm has no other exposure to exchange rate movements. Given that the firm prefers to have less exchange rate risk, which alternative is preferable? Explain.

3. Assume your U.S. firm currently exports to Mexico on a monthly basis. The goods are priced in pesos. Once material is received from a source, it is quickly used to produce the product in the United States, and then the product is exported. Currently, there is no other exposure to exchange rate risk. You have a choice of purchasing the material from Canada (denominated in C$), from Mexico (denominated in pesos), or from within the United States (denominated in U.S. dollars). The quality and your expected cost are similar across the three sources. Which source is preferable, given that you prefer minimal exchange rate risk?

4. Using the information in the previous question, consider the proposal to price the exports to Mexico in dollars and to use the U.S. source for material. Would this proposal eliminate the exchange rate risk?

5. Assume that the dollar is expected to strengthen against the euro over the next several years. Explain how this will affect the consolidated earnings of U.S.-based MNCs with subsidiaries in Europe.

QUESTIONS AND APPLICATIONS

1. Why would an MNC consider examining only its "net" cash flows in each currency when assessing its transaction exposure?

2. Your employer, a large MNC, has asked you to assess its transaction exposure. Its projected cash flows are as follows for the next year:

Currency	Total Inflow	Total Outflow	Current Exchange Rate in U.S. Dollars
Danish krone	(DK) DK50,000,000	DK40,000,000	$ .15
British pound	(£) £2,000,000	£1,000,000	$1.50

Assume that the movements in the Danish krona and the pound are highly correlated. Provide your assessment as to your firm's degree of transaction exposure (as to whether the exposure is high or low). Substantiate your answer.

3. What factors affect a firm's degree of transaction exposure in a particular currency? For each factor, explain the desirable characteristics that would reduce transaction exposure.

4. Are currency correlations perfectly stable over time? What does your answer imply about using past data on correlations as an indicator for the future?

5. Kopetsky Co. has net receivables in several currencies that are highly correlated with

each other, What does this imply about the firm's overall degree of transaction exposure?

6. Compare and contrast transaction exposure and economic exposure.

7. How should appreciation of a firm's home currency generally affect its cash inflows? Why?

8. How should depreciation of a firm's home currency generally affect its cash inflows? Why?

9. Fischer, Inc., exports products from Florida to Europe. It obtains its supplies and borrows funds locally. How would appreciation of the euro likely affect its net cash flows? Why?

10. Why are the cash flows of a purely domestic firm exposed to exchange rate fluctuations?

11. Memphis Co. hires you as a consultant to assess its degree of economic exposure to exchange rate fluctuations. How would you handle this task? Be specific.

12. a. In using regression analysis to assess the sensitivity of cash flows to exchange rate movements, what is the purpose of breaking the database into subperiods?

   b. Assume the regression coefficient based on assessing economic exposure was much higher in this second subperiod than in the first subperiod. What does this tell you about the firm's degree of economic exposure over time? Why might such results occur?

13. a. Present an argument for why translation exposure is relevant to an MNC.

   b. Present an argument for why translation exposure is not relevant to an MNC.

14. What factors affect a firm's degree of translation exposure? Explain how each factor influences translation exposure.

15. How can a U.S. company use regression analysis to assess its economic exposure to fluctuations in the British pound?

16. Consider a period in which the U.S. dollar weakens against the euro. How will this affect the reported earnings of a U.S.-based MNC with European subsidiaries?

17. Consider a period in which the U.S. dollar strengthens against most foreign currencies. How will this affect the reported earnings of a U.S.-based MNC with subsidiaries all over the world?

18. Walt Disney World built an amusement park in France that opened in 1992. How do you think this project has affected Disney's overall economic exposure to exchange rate movements? Explain.

19. Using the cost and revenue information shown for DeKalb, Inc., determine how the costs, revenue, and earnings items would be affected by three possible exchange rate scenarios for the New Zealand dollar (NZ$): (1) NZ$ = $.50, (2) NZ$ = $.55, and (3) NZ$ = $.60. (Assume U.S. sales will be unaffected by the exchange rate.) Assume that NZ$ earnings will be remitted to the U.S. parent at the end of the period.

Revenue and Cost Estimates: DeKalb, Inc.
(in millions of U.S. dollars and New Zealand dollars)

	U.S. Business	New Zealand Business
Sales	$ 800	NZ$ 800
Cost of goods sold	500	100
Gross profit	$ 300	NZ$ 700
Operating expenses	300	0
Earnings before interest and taxes	$0	NZ$ 700
Interest expenses	100	0
Earnings before taxes	$–100	NZ$ 700

20. Aggie Co. produces chemicals. It is a major exporter to Europe, where its main competition is from other U.S. exporters. All of these companies invoice the products in U.S. dollars. Is Aggie's transaction exposure likely to be significantly affected if the euro strengthens or weakens? Explain. If the euro weakens for several years, can you think of

any change that might occur in the global chemicals market?

21. Longhorn Co. produces hospital equipment. Most of its revenues are in the United States. About half of its expenses require outflows in Philippine pesos (to pay for Philippine materials). Most of Longhorn's competition is from U.S. firms that have no international business at all. How will Longhorn Co. be affected if the peso strengthens?

22. Lubbock, Inc., produces furniture and has no international business. Its major competitors import most of their furniture from Brazil and then sell it out of retail stores in the United States. How will Lubbock, Inc., be affected if Brazil's currency (the real) strengthens over time?

23. Sooner Co. is a U.S. wholesale company that imports expensive high-quality luggage and sells it to retail stores around the United States. Its main competitors also import high-quality luggage and sell it to retail stores. None of these competitors hedge their exposure to exchange rate movements. The treasurer of Sooner Co. told the board of directors that the firm's performance would be more volatile over time if it hedged its exchange rate exposure. How could a firm's cash flows be more stable as a result of such high exposure to exchange rate fluctuations?

24. Boulder, Inc., exports chairs to Europe (invoiced in U.S. dollars) and competes against local European companies. If purchasing power parity exists, why would Boulder not benefit from a stronger euro?

25. Toyota Motor Corp. measures the sensitivity of exports to the yen exchange rate (relative to the U.S. dollar). Explain how regression analysis could be used for such a task. Identify the expected sign of the regression coefficient if Toyota primarily exported to the United States. If Toyota established plants in the United States, how might the regression coefficient on the exchange rate variable change?

26. Cornhusker Co. is an exporter of products to Singapore. It wants to know how its stock price is affected by changes in the Singapore dollar's exchange rate. It believes that the impact may occur with a lag of one to three quarters. How could regression analysis be used to assess the impact?

27. Vegas Corp. is a U.S. firm that exports most of its products to Canada. It historically invoiced its products in Canadian dollars to accommodate the importers. However, it was adversely affected when the Canadian dollar weakened against the U.S. dollar. Since Vegas did not hedge, its Canadian dollar receivables were converted into a relatively small amount of U.S. dollars. After a few more years of continual concern about possible exchange rate movements, Vegas called its customers and requested that they pay for future orders with U.S. dollars instead of Canadian dollars. At this time, the Canadian dollar was valued at \$.81. The customers decided to oblige, since the number of Canadian dollars to be converted into U.S. dollars when importing the goods from Vegas was still slightly smaller than the number of Canadian dollars that would be needed to buy the product from a Canadian manufacturer. Based on this situation, has transaction exposure changed for Vegas Corp.? Has economic exposure changed? Explain.

28. Cieplak, Inc., is a U.S.-based MNC that has recently expanded into Asia. Its U.S. parent exports to some Asian countries, with its exports denominated in the Asian currencies. It also has a large subsidiary in Malaysia that serves that market. Offer at least two reasons related to exposure to exchange rates why Cieplak's earnings were reduced during the Asian crisis.

29. During the Asian crisis in 1998, there were rumors that China would weaken its currency (the yuan) against many currencies in the United States and in Europe. This caused investors to sell stocks in Asian countries such as Japan, Taiwan, and Singapore. Offer an intuitive explanation for such an effect. What types of Asian firms would be affected the most?

Impact of 9/11/01

30. Explain how the September 11, 2001, terrorist attack on the United States could adversely affect MNCs that are subject to transaction exposure. Based on your expectations, would U.S. exporters or importers be more adversely affected?

Internet Application

31. The following website provides daily exchange rate data for several currencies over the last few months: **http://pacific.commerce.ubc.ca/xr/data.html**.

    a. Use this website to assess the volatility of recent daily exchange rates of the Canadian dollar and Australian dollar over the last two months. Which currency appears to be more volatile? What are the implications for U.S. firms that recently had cash flows denominated in Australian dollars versus Canadian dollars?

    b. The following website contains annual reports of many MNCs: **http://www.reportgallery.com**. Review the annual report of your choice. Look for any comments in the report that describe the MNC's transaction exposure, economic exposure, or translation exposure. Summarize the MNC's exposure based on the comments in the annual report.

Running Your Own MNC

 This exercise can be found on the Student CD-ROM.

Blades, Inc. Case

Assessment of Exchange Rate Exposure

Blades, Inc., is currently exporting roller blades to Thailand and importing certain components needed to manufacture roller blades from that country. Under a fixed contractual agreement, Blades' primary customer in Thailand has committed itself to purchase 180,000 pairs of roller blades annually at a fixed price of 4,594 Thai baht (THB) per pair. Blades is importing rubber and plastic components from various suppliers in Thailand at a cost of approximately THB2,871 per pair, although the exact price (in baht) depends on current market prices. Blades imports materials sufficient to manufacture 72,000 pairs of roller blades from Thailand each year. The decision to import materials from Thailand was reached because rubber and plastic components needed to manufacture Blades' products are inexpensive, yet high quality, in Thailand.

Blades has also conducted business with a Japanese supplier in the past. Although Blades' analysis indicates that the Japanese components are of a lower quality than the Thai components, Blades has occasionally imported components from Japan when the prices were low enough. Currently, Ben Holt, Blades' chief financial officer (CFO), is considering importing components from Japan more frequently. Specifically, he would like to reduce Blades' baht exposure by taking advantage of the recently high correlation between the baht and the yen. Since Blades has net inflows denominated in baht and would have outflows denominated in yen, its net transaction exposure would be reduced if these two currencies were highly correlated. If Blades decides to import components from Japan, it would probably import materials sufficient to manufacture 1,700 pairs of roller blades annually at a price of ¥7,440 per pair.

Holt is also contemplating further expansion into foreign countries. Although he would eventually like to establish a subsidiary or acquire an existing business overseas, his immediate focus is on increasing Blades' foreign sales. Holt's primary reason for this plan is that the profit margin from Blades' imports and exports exceeds 25 percent, while the profit margin from Blades' domestic production is below 15 percent. Consequently, he believes that further foreign expansion will be beneficial to the company's future.

Though Blades' current exporting and importing practices have been profitable, Ben Holt is contemplating extending Blades' trade relationships to countries in different regions of the world. One reason for this decision is that various Thai roller blade manufacturers have recently established subsidiaries in the United States. Furthermore, various Thai roller blade manufacturers have recently targeted the U.S. market by advertising their products over the Internet. As a result of this increased competition from Thailand, Blades is uncertain whether its primary customer in Thailand will renew the current commitment to purchase a fixed number of roller blades annually. The current agreement will terminate in two years. Another reason for engaging in transactions with other, non-Asian, countries is that the Thai baht has depreciated substantially recently, which has somewhat reduced Blades' profit margins. The sale of roller blades to other countries with more stable currencies may increase Blades' profit margins.

While Blades will continue exporting to Thailand under the current agreement for the next two years, it may also export roller blades to Jogs, Ltd., a British retailer. Preliminary negotiations indicate that Jogs would be willing to commit itself to purchase 200,000 pairs of "Speedos," Blades' primary product, for a fixed price of £80 per pair.

Holt is aware that further expansion would increase Blades' exposure to exchange rate fluctuations, but he believes that Blades can supplement its profit margins by expanding. He is vaguely familiar with the different types of exchange rate exposure but has asked you, a financial analyst at Blades, Inc., to help him assess how the contemplated changes would affect Blades' financial position. Among other concerns, Holt is aware that recent economic problems in Thailand have had an effect on Thailand and other Asian countries. Whereas the correlation between Asian currencies such as the Japanese yen and the Thai baht is generally not very high and very unstable, these recent problems have increased the correlation among most Asian currencies. Conversely, the correlation

between the British pound and the Asian currencies is quite low.

To aid you in your analysis, Holt has provided you with the following data:

Currency	Expected Exchange Rate	Range of Possible Exchange Rates
British pound	$1.50	$1.47 to $1.53
Japanese yen	$0.0083	$0.0079 to $0.0087
Thai baht	$0.024	$0.020 to $0.028

Holt has asked you to answer the following questons:

1. What type(s) of exposure (i.e., transaction, economic, or translation exposure) is Blades subject to? Why?

2. Using a spreadsheet, conduct a consolidated net cash flow assessment of Blades, Inc., and estimate the range of net inflows and outflows for Blades for the coming year. Assume that Blades enters into the agreement with Jogs, Ltd.

3. If Blades does not enter into the agreement with the British firm and continues to export to Thailand and import from Thailand and Japan, do you think the increased correlations between the Japanese yen and the Thai baht will increase or reduce Blades' transaction exposure?

4. Do you think Blades should import components from Japan to reduce its net transaction exposure in the long run? Why or why not?

5. Assuming Blades enters into the agreement with Jogs, Ltd., how will its overall transaction exposure be affected?

6. Given that Thai roller blade manufacturers located in Thailand have begun targeting the U.S. roller blade market, how do you think Blades' U.S. sales were affected by the depreciation of the Thai baht? How do you think its exports to Thailand and its imports from Thailand and Japan were affected by the depreciation?

Small Business Dilemma

Assessment of Exchange Rate Exposure by the Sports Exports Company

At the current time, the Sports Exports Company is willing to receive payments in British pounds for the monthly exports it sends to the United Kingdom. While all of its receivables are denominated in pounds, it has no payables in pounds or in any other foreign currency. Jim Logan, owner of the Sports Exports Company, wants to assess his firm's exposure to exchange rate risk.

1. Would you describe the exposure of the Sports Exports Company to exchange rate risk as transaction exposure? Economic exposure? Translation exposure?

2. Jim Logan is considering a change in the pricing policy in which the importer must pay in dollars, so that Jim will not have to worry about converting pounds to dollars every month. If implemented, would this policy eliminate the transaction exposure of the Sports Exports Company? Would it eliminate Sports Exports' economic exposure? Explain.

3. If Jim decides to implement the policy described in the previous question, how would the Sports Exports Company be affected (if at all) by appreciation of the pound? By depreciation of the pound? Would these effects on Sports Exports differ if Jim retained his original policy of pricing the exports in British pounds?

APPENDIX 10

ESTIMATING THE VARIABILITY OF A CURRENCY PORTFOLIO

To illustrate how the variability of foreign currency cash flows is affected by correlations, consider a simplified example in which an MNC has only two foreign currencies. Fifty percent of the MNC's funds are expected to come from Currency A, and the remaining funds from Currency B. Assume that over an annual period, the standard deviation of exchange rate movements is 4 percent for Currency A and 4 percent for Currency B. Also assume that these two currencies are perfectly positively correlated so that their correlation coefficient is 1.00. The standard deviation of this two-currency portfolio (σ_p) can be determined from the following equation:

$$\sigma_p = \sqrt{W_A^2 \sigma_A^2 + W_B^2 \sigma_B^2 + 2W_A W_B \sigma_A \sigma_B CORR_{AB}}$$

where

W_A = percentage of funds to be received from receivables in Currency A
W_B = percentage of funds to be received from receivables in Currency B
σ_A = standard deviation of exchange rate movements for Currency A
σ_B = standard deviation of exchange rate movements for Currency B
$CORR_{AB}$ = correlation coefficient of exchange rate movements between Currencies A and B

Using the information provided, the variability of the combined (portfolio) cash flows of Currencies A and B can be estimated as

$$\sigma_p = \sqrt{.5^2(.04)^2 + .5^2(.04)^2 + 2(.5)(.5)(.04)(.04)(1.0)}$$
$$= \sqrt{.0004 + .0004 + .0008}$$
$$= \sqrt{.0016}$$
$$= .04, \text{ or } 4\%$$

Notice that the standard deviation in the portfolio is as high as the standard deviation of either individual currency. The diversification between these two currencies does not reduce variability because the currency movements are perfectly positively correlated. Diversification between currencies with a low correlation could substantially reduce the variability of the portfolio of inflow currencies. For example, if the two currencies had a correlation coefficient of .2, the portfolio variability (assuming 50 percent weight to each currency) would be

$$\sigma_p = \sqrt{.5^2(.04)^2 + .5^2(.04)^2 + 2(.5)(.5)(.04)(.04)(0.2)}$$
$$= \sqrt{.0004 + .0004 + .0016}$$
$$= \sqrt{.0096}$$
$$= \text{about } .031, \text{ or } 3.1\%$$

A negative correlation coefficient between Currencies A and B would reduce the portfolio variability to an even greater degree. For example, consider an extreme example in which Currencies A and B are perfectly negatively correlated, as represented by a correlation coefficient of −1.00. The portfolio variability (assuming 50 percent weight to each currency) would be

$$\sigma_p = \sqrt{.5^2(.04)^2 + .5^2(.04)^2 + 2(.5)(.5)(.04)(.04)(-1.0)}$$
$$= \sqrt{.0004 + .0004 + (-.0008)}$$
$$= \sqrt{.0}$$
$$= 0$$

The portfolio's exchange rate movements against the dollar would be stable because of the offsetting effects between Currencies A and B, if they are perfectly negatively correlated. Such a situation would normally be favorably perceived by an MNC, since the home currency value of the portfolio of foreign currencies could be virtually insulated from movements in these currencies.

It is unlikely that the MNC will be able to structure its foreign cash flows so that it is totally insulated against exchange rate movements. However, the examples given here demonstrate that a set of foreign currency cash inflows is less volatile if the correlations are low. The cash flows would also be less volatile if the standard deviations of the individual currencies were lower. This can be verified by assuming a standard deviation of less than 4 percent for each currency in the preceding examples and recomputing the portfolio's standard deviation.

3

MANAGING TRANSACTION EXPOSURE

Recall from the previous chapter that a multinational corporation (MNC) is exposed to exchange rate fluctuations in three ways: (1) transaction exposure, (2) economic exposure, and (3) translation exposure. This chapter focuses on the management of transaction exposure, while the following chapter focuses on the management of economic and translation exposure. By managing transaction exposure, financial managers may be able to increase cash flows and enhance the value of their MNCs.

The specific objectives of this chapter are to
- Identify the commonly used techniques for hedging transaction exposure.
- Explain how each technique can be used to hedge future payables and receivables.
- Compare the advantages and disadvantages among hedging techniques.
- Suggest other methods of reducing exchange rate risk when hedging techniques are not available.

TRANSACTION EXPOSURE

Transaction exposure exists when the future cash transactions of a firm are affected by exchange rate fluctuations. A U.S. firm that purchases Mexican goods may need pesos to buy the goods. Though it may know exactly how many pesos it will need, it doesn't know how many dollars will be needed to be exchanged for those pesos. This uncertainty occurs because the exchange rate between pesos and dollars fluctuates over time. A U.S.-based MNC that will be receiving a foreign currency is exposed because it does not know how many dollars it will obtain when it exchanges the foreign currency for dollars.

If transaction exposure exists, the firm faces three major tasks. First, it must identify its degree of transaction exposure. Second, it must decide whether to hedge this exposure. Finally, if it decides to hedge part or all of the exposure, it must choose among the various hedging techniques available. Each of these tasks is discussed in turn.

Identifying Net Transaction Exposure

Before an MNC makes any decisions related to hedging, it should identify the individual **net transaction exposure** on a currency-by-currency basis. The term *net* here refers to the consolidation of all expected inflows and outflows for a particular time and currency. The management at each subsidiary plays a vital role in reporting its expected inflows and outflows. Then a centralized group consolidates the subsidiary reports to identify, for the MNC as a whole, the expected net positions in each foreign currency during several upcoming periods.

The MNC can identify its exposure by reviewing this consolidation of subsidiary positions. For example, one subsidiary may have net receivables in Mexican pesos three months from now, while a different subsidiary has net payables in pesos. If the peso appreciates, this will be favorable to the first subsidiary and unfavorable to the second subsidiary. However, the impact on the MNC as a whole is at least partially offset. Each subsidiary may desire to hedge its net currency position in order to avoid the possible adverse impacts on its performance due to fluctuation in

Managing for Value: Centralization by MNCs

Eastman Kodak Co. uses a centralized currency management approach to manage its transaction exposure. Kodak bills its subsidiaries in their local currencies. The rationale behind this strategy is to shift the foreign exchange exposure from the subsidiaries to the parent company. When the parent was reorganized to concentrate its resources and expert personnel, it centralized its currency exposure management. The parent receives foreign currencies from its subsidiaries overseas and converts them to U.S. dollars. It can maintain the currencies as foreign deposits if it believes the currencies will strengthen against the U.S. dollar in the near future.

Borg-Warner Corp. has set up a central clearinghouse system that also reflects a centralized management approach. Thus, the company assesses and manages its currency exposure on the entire portfolio of all subsidiaries, rather than on each subsidiary individually.

Fiat, the Italian auto manufacturer, implemented a centralized system to monitor 421 sub-

sidiaries dispersed among 55 countries. It uses a comprehensive reporting system that keeps track of its aggregate cash flows in each currency. The net inflow or outflow position for each currency can then be assessed to determine whether and how the position should be balanced out.

DuPont Co. uses a centralized approach to determine its net inflow or outflow in each currecny. Using this approach, it recently anticipated a net inflow position of more than 1 billion British pounds. It used hedging techniques to hedge almost all of its net exposure in pounds. The hedge generated substantial savings for DuPont because the pound's value declined by the time the pounds were received.

The important point here is that a hedging decision cannot be made until the firm has determined its exposure to a particular currency. The centralized approach enables the MNC to determine its net transaction exposure in each currency so that it can decide whether to hedge these positions.

the currency's value. The overall performance of the MNC, however, may already be insulated by the offsetting positions between subsidiaries. Therefore, hedging the position of each individual subsidiary may not be necessary.

Adjusting the Invoice Policy to Manage Exposure

In some circumstances, the U.S. firm may be able to modify its pricing policy to hedge against transaction exposure. That is, the firm may be able to invoice (price) its exports in the same currency that will be needed to pay for imports.

Example

Clarkson, Inc., has continual payables in Mexican pesos because a Mexican exporter sends goods to Clarkson under the condition that the goods be invoiced in Mexican pesos. Clarkson also exports products (invoiced in U.S. dollars) to other corporations in Mexico. If Clarkson changes its invoicing policy from U.S. dollars to pesos, it can use the peso receivables from its exports to pay off its future payables in pesos. It is unlikely, however, that Clarkson would be able to (1) invoice the precise amount of peso receivables to match the peso payables and (2) perfectly time the inflows and outflows to match each other.

Because the matching of inflows and outflows in foreign currencies does have its limitations, an MNC will normally be exposed to some degree of exchange rate risk and, therefore, should consider the various hedging techniques identified next.

TECHNIQUES TO ELIMINATE TRANSACTION EXPOSURE

If an MNC decides to hedge part or all of its transaction exposure, it may select from the following hedging techniques:

- Futures hedge
- Forward hedge
- Money market hedge
- Currency option hedge

Before selecting a hedging technique, MNCs normally compare the cash flows that would be expected from each technique. The proper hedging technique can vary over time, as the relative advantages of the various techniques may change over time. Each technique is discussed in turn, with examples provided. After all techniques have been discussed, a comprehensive example illustrates how all the techniques can be compared to determine the appropriate technique to hedge a particular position.

Futures Hedge

Currency futures can be used by firms that desire to hedge transaction exposure.

Purchasing Currency Futures. A firm that buys a currency futures contract is entitled to receive a specified amount in a specified currency for a stated price on a specified date. To hedge a payment on future payables in a foreign currency, the firm may purchase a currency futures contract for the currency it will need in the near future. By holding this contract, it locks in the amount of its home currency needed to make the payment.

Selling Currency Futures. A firm that sells a currency futures contract is entitled to sell a specified amount in a specified currency for a stated price on a specified date. To hedge the home currency value of future receivables in a foreign currency, the firm may sell a currency futures contract for the currency it will be receiving. Therefore, the firm knows how much of its home currency it will receive after converting the foreign currency receivables into its home currency. By locking in the exchange rate at which it will be able to exchange the foreign currency for its home currency, the firm insulates the value of its future receivables from the fluctuations in the foreign currency's spot rate over time.

Forward Hedge

Like futures contracts, forward contracts can be used to lock in the future exchange rate at which a MNC can buy or sell a currency. A forward contract hedge is very similar to a futures contract hedge, except that forward contracts are commonly used for large transactions, whereas futures contracts tend to be used for smaller amounts. Also, MNCs can request forward contracts that specify the exact number of units that they desire, whereas futures contracts represent a standardized number of units for each currency.

Forward contracts are commonly used by large corporations that desire to hedge. For example, DuPont Co. often has the equivalent of $300 million to $500 million in forward contracts at any one time to cover open currency positions. To recognize the uses of forward contracts, consider the following quotations from the annual reports of U.S.-based MNCs:

Outstanding foreign currency forward contracts used as a means of offsetting earnings fluctuations from anticipated foreign currency cash flows totaled $182 million.

Union Carbide

The Company enters into forward currency exchange contracts to hedge its equity investments in certain foreign subsidiaries and to manage its exposure against fluctuations in foreign currency rates. . . The Company has entered into forward currency exchange contracts to reduce its exposure to currency fluctuations on the proceeds of its sale of its investment in Asahi Fiber Glass Company, Ltd. . . . . The Company entered into forward currency exchange contracts to reduce its exposure to currency fluctuations on earnings of certain European subsidiaries.

Owens Corning Co.

USX uses forward currency contracts to reduce exposure to currency price fluctuations when transactions require settlement in a foreign currency.

USX Corp.

Forward Contracts. Recall that forward contracts are negotiated between the firm and a commercial bank and specify the currency, the exchange rate, and the date of the forward transaction. MNCs that need a foreign currency in the future can negotiate a forward contract to purchase the currency forward, thereby locking in the exchange rate at which they will obtain the currency on a future date. MNCs that wish to sell a foreign currency in the future can negotiate a forward contract to sell the currency forward, thereby locking in the exchange rate at which they sell the currecny on a future date.

Forward Hedge versus No Hedge on Payables. Although forward contracts are easy to use for hedging, that does not mean that every exposure to exchange rate movements should be hedged. In some cases, an MNC may prefer not to hedge its exposure to exchange rate movements.

HTTP:// **USING THE WEB**

Forward Rates for Hedging Forward rates are available for the euro, British pound, Canadian dollar, and Japanese yen for 1-month, 3-month, 6-month, and 12-month maturities at http://www.bmo.com/economic/regular/fxrates.html.

These forward rates indicate the exchange rates at which positions in these currencies can be hedged for specific time periods.

The decision as to whether to hedge a position with a forward contract or to keep it unhedged can be made by comparing the known result of hedging to the possible results of remaining unhedged.

Example Durham Co. will need £100,000 in 90 days to pay for British imports. Today's 90-day forward rate of the British pound is $1.40. To assess the future value of the British pound, Durham Co. may develop a probability distribution, as shown in Exhibit 11.1. This is graphically illustrated in Exhibit 11.2, which breaks down the probability distribution. Both exhibits can be used to determine the probability that a forward hedge will be more costly than no hedge. This is achieved by estimating the **real cost of hedging** payables (RCH_p). The real cost of hedging measures the additional expenses beyond those incurred without hedging. The real cost of hedging payables is measured as

$$RCH_p = NCH_p - NC_p$$

where

$$NCH_p = \text{nominal cost of hedging payables}$$
$$NC_p = \text{nominal cost of payables without hedging}$$

Exhibit 11.1

Feasibility Analysis for Hedging

Possible Spot Rate of £ in 90 Days	Probability	Nominal Cost of Hedging £100,000	Amount in $ Needed to Buy £100,000 if Firm Remains Unhedged	Real Cost of Hedging £100,000
$1.30	5%	$140,000	$1.30 × 100,000 = $130,000	$10,000
1.32	10	140,000	1.32 × 100,000 = 132,000	8,000
1.34	15	140,000	1.34 × 100,000 = 134,000	6,000
1.36	20	140,000	1.36 × 100,000 = 136,000	4,000
1.38	20	140,000	1.38 × 100,000 = 138,000	2,000
1.40	15	140,000	1.40 × 100,000 = 140,000	0
1.42	10	140,000	1.42 × 100,000 = 142,000	− 2,000
1.45	5	140,000	1.45 × 100,000 = 145,000	− 5,000

Exhibit 11.2

Comparison of Costs
of Hedging versus
No Hedge

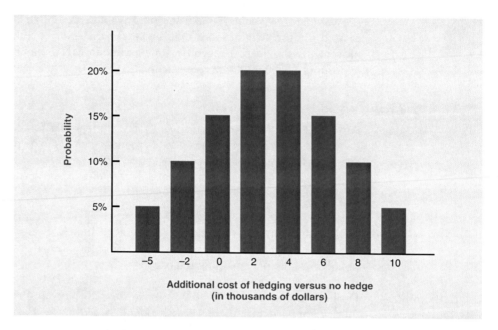

When the real cost of hedging is negative, this implies that hedging is more favorable than not hedging. The RCH_p is estimated for each scenario in Column 5 of Exhibit 11.1. While NCH_p is certain, NC_p is uncertain, causing RCH_p to be uncertain.

Though Durham Co. doesn't know RCH_p in advance, it can at least use the information in Exhibits 11.1 and 11.2 to decide whether a hedge is feasible. First, it can estimate the expected value of the RCH_p. This expected value is determined by

$$\text{Expected value of } RCH_p = \Sigma P_i RCH_i$$

where P_i represents the probability that the ith outcome will occur. In our example, the expected value of the RCH_p can be computed as

$$
\begin{aligned}
E(RCH_p) &= \Sigma P_i RCH_i \\
&= 5\%(\$10,000) + 10\%(\$8,000) + 15\%(\$6,000) \\
&\quad + 20\%(\$4,000) + 20\%(\$2,000) + 15\%(0) \\
&\quad + 10\%(-\$2,000) + 5\%(-\$5,000) \\
&= \$500 + \$800 + \$900 \\
&\quad + \$800 + \$400 + 0 \\
&\quad - \$200 - \$250 \\
&= \$2,950
\end{aligned}
$$

Although this expected value is useful in assessing RCH_p, it does not clearly indicate the overall probability that hedging will be more costly. A review of Exhibit 11.1 or 11.2. reveals that probability. The data indicate there is a 15 percent chance that the RCH_p will be negative (that the nominal cost of hedging will be lower than remaining unhedged). The probability of incurring a lower cost when remaining unhedged is 85 percent, so Durham decides not to hedge.

The hedge-versus-no-hedge decision is based on the firm's degree of risk aversion. Firms with a greater desire to avoid risk will hedge their open positions in foreign currencies more often than firms that are less concerned with risk.

If the forward rate is an accurate predictor of the future spot rate, the RCH_p will be zero. Because the forward rate often underestimates or overestimates the future spot rate, RCH_p differs from zero. If, however, the forward rate is an unbiased predictor of the future spot rate, RCH_p will be zero on average, as the differences between the forward rate and future spot rate will offset each other over time. If a firm believes that the forward rate is an unbiased predictor of the future spot rate, it will consider hedging its payables, since the forecasted RCH_p is zero, and the transaction exposure can be eliminated.

Forward Hedge versus No Hedge on Receivables. For firms with exposure in receivables, the real cost of hedging receivables (RCH_r) can be estimated as

$$RCH_r = NR_r - NRH_r$$

where

NR_r = nominal home currency revenues received without hedging
NRH_r = nominal home currency revenues received from hedging

This equation is structured so that the real cost of hedging receivables is positive when hedging results in lower revenue than not hedging. This allows for consistency between RCH_p and RCH_r, in that a negative (positive) value of either indicates that hedging results in a more (less) favorable outcome than not hedging.

As with payable positions, firms can determine whether to hedge receivable positions by first developing a probability distribution for the future spot rate and then using it to develop a probability distribution of RCH_r. If the RCH_r is likely to be negative, hedging is preferred. If the RCH_r is likely to be positive, the firm needs to evaluate whether the potential benefits from remaining unhedged are worth the risk. If the forward rate is believed to be an unbiased predictor of the future spot rate, firms will consider hedging their receivables positions at an expected real cost of zero (ignoring transaction costs).

Measuring the Real Cost of Hedging with Forward Contracts. The RCH has been defined here in terms of the MNC's home currency (U.S. dollars, in our example). It can also be expressed as a percentage of the nominal hedged amount. This may be a useful measurement when comparing the RCHs for various currencies.

If a U.S. firm is hedging various currencies in different amounts, a comparison of the dollar amount of RCH among currencies would be distorted by the dollar amount of payables or receivables hedged. For this reason, the RCH for each currency should be measured as a percentage of its respective hedged amount if the RCHs are to be compared.

The RCH cannot be determined until the payables or receivables period is over. When firms hedge, they should be pleased if the RCH turns out to be very low, and especially pleased if it is negative. Conservative firms, however, may feel hedging is worthwhile even if the RCH turns out to be high.

Exhibit 11.3

Real Cost of Hedging British Pounds over Time

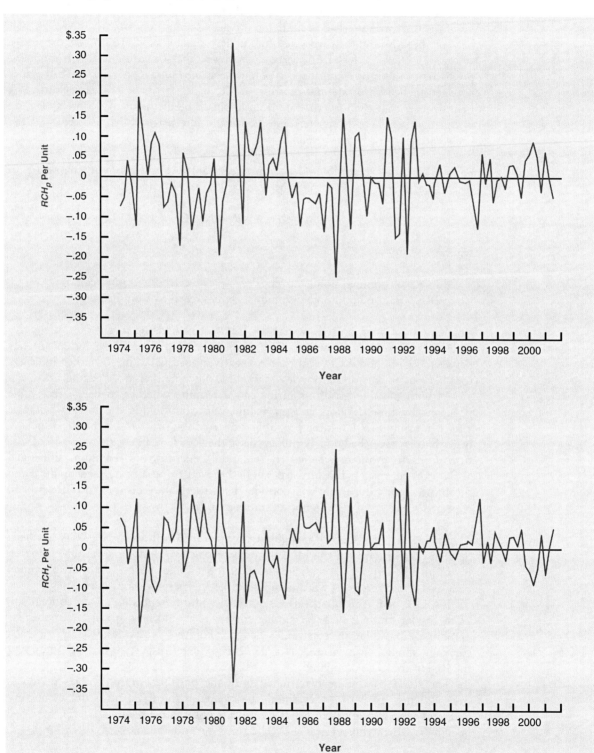

Actual Real Cost of Hedging British Pounds. The real cost of hedging British pounds over time (from a U.S. firm's perspective) is displayed in Exhibit 11.3. The top graph shows the real cost of hedging payables, and the lower graph shows the real cost of hedging receivables. Ninety-day periods were used to measure the real costs of hedging. The costs were measured on a per-unit basis. The real cost of hedging pound payables (shown in the top graph of Exhibit 11.3) was high in the early 1980s, when the pound was weakening. Thus, the existing spot rate at the time payables were due was typically below the forward rate available at the beginning of each corresponding 90-day period. The real cost of hedging pound payables was often negative in the late 1970s, late 1980s, and early 1990s, when the pound was strengthening. In the mid- and late 1990s, the real cost of hedging was closer to zero, as the pound's value was not as volatile over that period. The real cost of hedging was high in 2000 and part of 2001 because of the pound's weakness at the time.

The real cost of hedging receivables is shown in the bottom graph of Exhibit 11.3. Since transaction costs were ignored when measuring the real costs of hedging in the exhibit, the real cost of hedging receivables is the exact opposite of the real cost of hedging payables.

Money Market Hedge

A **money market hedge** involves taking a money market position to cover a future payables or receivables position. Money market hedges on payables and receivables will be discussed separately.

Money Market Hedge on Payables. If a firm has excess cash, it can create a short-term deposit in the foreign currency that it will need in the future. The first example illustrates a simplified money market hedge, in which the firm has excess cash. Even if a firm does not have excess cash, it can use a money market hedge to hedge payables, as the second example shows.

Example   Ashland, Inc., needs $1,000,000 in New Zealand dollars (NZ$) in 30 days, and it can earn 6 percent annualized (.5 percent for 30 days) on a New Zealand security over this period. In this case, the amount needed to purchase a New Zealand one-month security is

$$\text{Deposit amount to hedge NZ\$ payables} = \frac{\text{NZ\$1,000,000}}{1+.005}$$
$$= \text{NZ\$995,025}$$

Assuming that the New Zealand dollar's spot rate is $.65, then $646,766 is needed to purchase the New Zealand security (computed as NZ$995,025 × $.65). In 30 days, the security will mature and provide NZ$1,000,000 to Ashland, Inc., which can then use this money to cover its payables. Regardless of how the New Zealand dollar exchange rate changes over this period, Ashland's investment in the New Zealand security will be able to cover its payables position.

In many cases, MNCs prefer to hedge payables without using their cash balances. A money market hedge can still be used in this situation, but it requires two money market positions: (1) borrowed funds in the home currency and (2) a short-term investment in the foreign currency.

Example

Reconsider the previous example, in which Ashland, Inc., needs NZ$1,000,000 in 30 days. Recall that $646,766 is needed to obtain the investment of NZ$995,025, which in turn will accumulate to the NZ$1,000,000 needed in 30 days. If Ashland has no excess cash, it can borrow $646,766 from a U.S. bank and exchange those dollars for New Zealand dollars in order to purchase the New Zealand security.

Because the New Zealand investment will cover Ashland's future payables position, the firm needs to be concerned only about the dollars owed back on the loan in 30 days. The firm's money market hedge used to hedge payables can be summarized as follows:

Step 1. Borrow $646,766 from a U.S. bank; assume a .7 percent interest rate over the 30-day loan period.

Step 2. Convert the $646,766 to NZ$995,025, given the exchange rate of $.65 per New Zealand dollar.

Step 3. Use the New Zealand dollar to purchase a New Zealand security that offers .5 percent over one month.

Step 4. Repay the U.S. loan in 30 days, plus interest; the amount owed is $651,293 (computed as $646,766 × 1.007).

Money Market Hedge on Receivables. If a firm expects receivables in a foreign currency, it can hedge this position by borrowing the currency now and converting it to dollars. The receivables will be used to pay off the loan.

Example

Bakersfield Co. is a U.S. firm that transports goods to Singapore and expects to receive 400,000 Singapore dollars (S$) in 90 days. A simplified money market hedge can be implemented if Bakersfield needs to borrow U.S. funds for 90 days anyway. Instead of borrowing U.S. dollars, it can borrow Singapore dollars and convert them into U.S. dollars for use. Assuming an annualized interest rate of 8 percent, or 2 percent over the 90-day period, the amount of Singapore dollars to be borrowed to hedge the future receivables is

$$\text{Borrowed amount to hedge S\$ receivables} = \frac{\text{S\$400,000}}{1+.02}$$
$$= \text{S\$392,157}$$

If Bakersfield borrows S$392,157 and converts those Singapore dollars to U.S. dollars, then it can use the receivables to pay off the Singapore dollar loan in 90 days. Meanwhile, the proceeds of the loan can be used for whatever purpose Bakersfield Co. desires.

In some cases, MNCs may not need to borrow funds for a 90-day period. In these situations, a money market hedge can still be used to hedge receivables if the firm takes two positions in the money markets: (1) borrow the foreign currency representing future receivables and (2) invest in the home currency.

Example

Reconsider the previous example. Even if Bakersfield Co. does not have a use for the S$392,157 borrowed, it can invest the funds in a 90-day U.S. security. Assuming that a Singapore dollar is worth $.55, the Singapore dollars borrowed can be converted to $215,686. Assuming an annualized U.S. interest rate of 7.2 percent (1.8 percent over 90 days) on 90-day securities, the U.S. investment will be worth $219,568 (computed as $215,686 × 1.018) in 90 days. Since the receivables can cover the existing loan, Bakersfield will have $219,568 as a result of enacting the money market hedge.

Hedging with a Money Market Hedge versus a Forward Hedge. Should an MNC implement a forward contract hedge or a money market hedge ? The forward hedge and the money market hedge are directly comparable. Since the results of both hedges are known beforehand, the firm can implement the one that is more feasible. Of course, the firm cannot determine whether either hedge will outperform an unhedged strategy until the period of concern has elapsed.

Implications of IRP for the Money Market Hedge. If interest rate parity (IRP) exists, and transaction costs do not exist, the money market hedge will yield the same results as the forward hedge. This is so because the forward premium on the forward rate reflects the interest rate differential between the two currencies. The hedging of future payables with a forward purchase will be similar to borrowing at the home interest rate and investing at the foreign interest rate.

The hedging of future receivables with a forward sale is similar to borrowing at the foreign interest rate and investing at the home interest rate. Even if the forward premium generally reflects the interest rate differential between countries, the existence of transaction costs may cause the results from a forward hedge to differ from those of the money market hedge.

Currency Option Hedge

Firms recognize that hedging techniques such as the forward hedge and money market hedge can backfire when a payables currency depreciates or a receivables currency appreciates over the hedged period. In these situations, an unhedged strategy would likely outperform the forward hedge or money market hedge. The ideal type of hedge would insulate the firm from adverse exchange rate movements but allow the firm to benefit from favorable exchange rate movements. Currency options exhibit these attributes. However, a firm must assess whether the advantages of a currency option hedge are worth the price (premium) paid for it. Details on currency options are provided in Chapter 5. The following discussion illustrates how they can be used in hedging.

http://
See
www.futures.com/library/
contents.html, the website
of *Futures* magazine, for
coverage of various aspects
of derivatives trading such
as new products, strategies,
and market analyses.

Hedging Payables with Currency Call Options. A currency call option provides the right to buy a specified amount of a particular currency at a specified price (the exercise price) within a given period of time. Yet, unlike a futures or forward contract, the currency call option *does not obligate* its owner to buy the currency at that price. If the spot rate of the currency remains lower than the exercise price throughout the life of the option, the firm can let the option expire and simply purchase the currency at the existing spot rate. On the other hand, if the spot rate of the currency appreciates over time, the call option allows the firm to purchase the currency at the exercise price. That is, the firm owning a call option has locked in a maximum price (the exercise price) to pay for the currency. It also has the flexibility, though, to let the option expire and obtain the currency at the existing spot rate when the currency is to be sent for payment.

Example   Clemson Corp. has payables of £100,000, 90 days from now. Assume there is a call option available with an exercise price of $1.60. Assume that the option premium is $.04 per unit. For options that cover the 100,000 units, the total premium is $4,000 (100,000 × $.04). Clemson doesn't have to exercise its call option if it can obtain pounds at a lower spot rate.

Clemson expects the spot rate of the pound to be either $1.58, $1.62, or $1.66 when the payables are due. The effect of each of these scenarios on Clemson's cost of payables is shown in Exhibit 11.4. Columns 1 and 2 simply identify the scenario to be analyzed. Column 3 shows the premium per unit paid on the option, which is the same regardless of the spot rate that occurs when payables are due. Column 4 shows the amount that Clemson would pay per pound for the payables under each scenario, assuming that it owned call options. If Scenario 1 occurs, Clemson will let the options expire and purchase pounds in the spot market for $1.58 each. If Scenario 2 or 3 occurs, Clemson will exercise the options and therefore purchase pounds for $1.60 per unit, and it will use the pounds to make its payment. Column 5, which is the sum of Columns 3 and 4, shows the amount paid per unit when the premium paid on the call option is included. Column 6 converts Column 5 into a total dollar cost, based on the £100,000 hedged.

Hedging Receivables with Currency Put Options. Like currency call options, currency put options can be a valuable hedging device. A currency put option provides the right to sell a specified amount in a particular currency at a specified price (the exercise price) within a given period of time. Firms can use a currency put option to hedge future receivables in foreign currencies, since it guarantees a certain price (the exercise price) at which the future receivables can be sold. The currency put option *does not obligate* its owner to sell the currency at a specified price. If the existing spot rate of the foreign currency is above the exercise price when the firm receives the foreign currency, the firm can sell the currency received at the spot rate and let the put option expire.

Exhibit 11.4

Use of Currency Call Options for Hedging British Pound Payables (Exercise Price = $1.60; Premium = $.04)

(1)	(2)	(3)	(4)	(5) = (4) + (3)	(6)
Scenario	Spot Rate When Payables Are Due	Premium per Unit Paid on Call Options	Amount Paid per Unit When Owning Call Options	Total Amount Paid per Unit (Including the Premium) When Owning Call Options	$ Amount Paid for £100,000 When Owning Call Options
1	$1.58	$.04	$1.58	$1.62	$162,000
2	1.62	.04	1.60	1.64	164,000
3	1.66	.04	1.60	1.64	164,000

Exhibit 11.5

Use of Currency Put Options for Hedging New Zealand Dollar Receivables (Exercise Price = $.50; Premium = $.03)

(1) Scenario	(2) Spot Rate When Payment on Receivables Is Received	(3) Premium per Unit on Put Options	(4) Amount Received per Unit When Owning Put Options	(5) = (4) – (3) Net Amount Received per Unit (after Accounting for Premium Paid)	(6) Dollar Amount Received from Hedging NZ$600,000 Receivables with Put Options
1	$.44	$.03	$.50	$.47	$282,000
2	.46	.03	.50	.47	282,000
3	.51	.03	.51	.48	288,000

Example

Knoxville, Inc., transports goods to New Zealand and expects to receive NZ$600,000 in about 90 days. Because it is concerned that the New Zealand dollar may depreciate against the U.S. dollar, Knoxville is considering purchasing put options to cover its receivables. The New Zealand dollar put options considered here have an exercise price of $.50 and a premium of $.03 per unit. Knoxville anticipates that the spot rate in 90 days will be either $.44, $.46, or $.51. The amount to be received as a result of owning currency put options is shown in Exhibit 11.5. Columns 2 through 5 are on a per-unit basis. Column 6 is determined by multiplying the per-unit amount received in Column 5 by 600,000 units.

HTTP:// USING THE WEB

Implied Volatilities Implied volatilities of major currencies as of today are provided at http://www.ny.frb.org/pihome/statistics/.

These implied volatilities may be used to understand why the premiums on options vary across currencies. For example, the Canadian dollar's option premium is less than those of other options because its implied volatility is lower, as shown on this website.

Comparison of Hedging Techniques

Each of the hedging techniques is briefly summarized in Exhibit 11.6. When using a futures hedge, forward hedge, or money market hedge, the firm can estimate the funds (denominated in its home currency) that it will need for future payables, or the funds that it will receive after converting foreign currency receivables. Thus, it can compare the costs or revenue and determine which of these hedging techniques is appropriate. However, the cash flow associated with the currency option hedge cannot be determined with certainty because the costs of purchasing payables and the revenue generated from receivables are not known ahead of time.

Comparison of Techniques to Hedge Payables. A comparison of hedging techniques should focus on obtaining a foreign currency at the lowest possible cost. To reinforce an understanding of the hedging techniques, a comprehensive example is provided here.

Exhibit 11.6

Review of Techniques for Hedging Transaction Exposure

Hedging Technique	To Hedge Payables	To Hedge Receivables
1. Futures hedge	Purchase a currency futures contract (or contracts) representing the currency and amount related to the payables.	Sell a currency futures contract (or contracts) representing the currency and amount related to the receivables.
2. Forward hedge	Negotiate a forward contract to purchase the amount of foreign currency needed to cover the payables.	Negotiate a forward contract to sell the amount of foreign currency that will be received as a result of the receivables.
3. Money market hedge	Borrow local currency and convert to currency denominating payables. Invest these funds until they are needed to cover the payables.	Borrow the currency denominating the receivables, convert it to the local currency, and invest it. Then pay off the loan with cash inflows from the receivables.
4. Currency option hedge	Purchase a currency call option (or options) representing the currency and amount related to the payables.	Purchase a currency put option (or options) representing the currency and amount related to the receivables.

Example

Assume that Fresno Corp. will need £200,000 in 180 days. It considers using (1) a forward hedge, (2) a money market hedge, (3) an option hedge, or (4) no hedge. Its analysts develop the following information, which can be used to assess the alternative solutions:

- Spot rate of pound as of today = $1.50
- 180-day forward rate of pound as of today = $1.47

Interest rates are as follows:

	U.K.	U.S.
180-day deposit rate	4.5%	4.5%
180-day borrowing rate	5.0%	5.0%

- A call option on pounds that expires in 180 days has an exercise price of $1.48 and a premium of $.03.
- A put option on pounds that expires in 180 days has an exercise price of $1.49 and a premium of $.02.

Fresno Corp. forecasted the future spot rate in 180 days as follows:

Possible Outcome	Probability
$1.43	20%
1.46	70
1.52	10

Fresno Corp. then assesses the alternative solutions, as shown in Exhibit 11.7. Each alternative is analyzed to estimate the nominal dollar cost of paying for the payables denominated in pounds. The cost is known with certainty for the forward rate hedge and money market hedge. When using the call option or remaining unhedged, however, the cost is dependent on the spot rate 180 days from now. The costs of the four alternatives are also compared with the use of probability

Exhibit 11.7

Comparison of Hedging Alternatives for Fresno Corp.

Forward Hedge

Purchase pounds 180 days forward.

$$\text{Dollars needed in 180 days} = \text{payables in £} \times \text{forward rate of £}$$
$$= £200,000 \times \$1.47$$
$$= \$294,000$$

Money Market Hedge

Borrow $, convert to £, invest £, repay $ loan in 180 days.

$$\text{Amount in £ to be invested} = \frac{£200,000}{(1 + .045)}$$
$$= £191,388$$

$$\text{Amount in \$ needed to convert into £ for deposit} = £191,388 \times \$1.50$$
$$= \$287,082$$

$$\text{Interest and principal owed on \$ loan after 180 days} = \$287,082 \times (1 + .05)$$
$$= \$301,436$$

Call Option

Purchase call option (the following computations assume that the option is to be exercised on the day pounds are needed, or not at all. Exercise price = $1.48, premium = $.03.)

Possible Spot Rate in 180 days	Premium per Unit Paid for Option	Exercise Option?	Total Price (Including Option Premium) Paid per Unit	Total Price Paid for £200,000	Probability
$1.43	$.03	No	$1.46	$292,000	20%
1.46	.03	No	1.49	298,000	70
1.52	.03	Yes	1.51	302,000	10

Remain Unhedged

Purchase £200,000 in the spot market 180 days from now.

Future Spot Rate Expected in 180 Days	Dollars Needed to Purchase £200,000	Probability
$1.43	$286,000	20%
1.46	292,000	70
1.52	304,000	10

Exhibit 11.8
Nominal Dollar
Cost of Pound-
Denominated
Payables

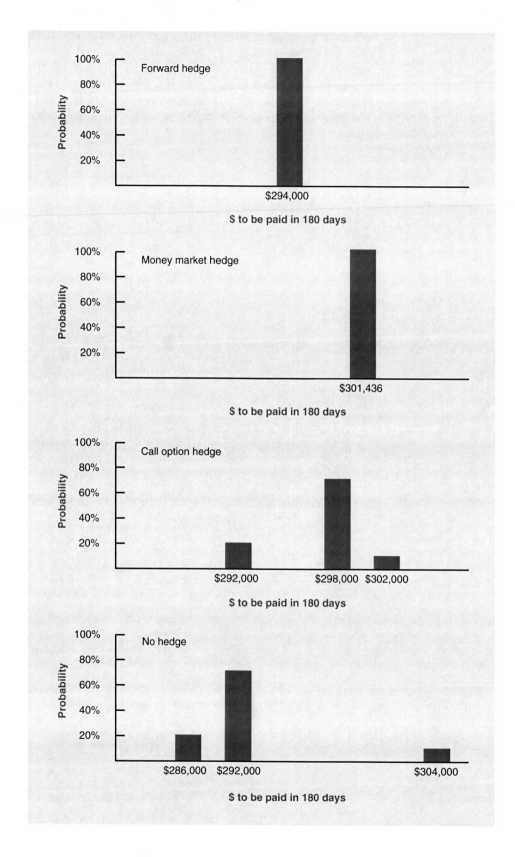

distributions, as shown in Exhibit 11.8. A review of this exhibit shows that the forward hedge is superior to the money market hedge, since the dollar cost is definitely less. A comparison of the forward hedge to the call option hedge shows that there is an 80 percent chance that the call option hedge will be more expensive. Thus, the forward hedge appears to be the optimal hedge for Fresno Corp.

The probability distribution of outcomes for the no-hedge strategy appears to be more favorable than that for the forward hedge. Thus, Fresno Corp. is likely to perform best if it remains unhedged, but if it prefers to hedge, it should choose the forward hedge. If Fresno does not hedge, it should periodically reassess its hedging decision. For example, after 60 days it should repeat the analysis shown here, based on the applicable spot rate, forward rate, interest rates, call option information, and forecasts of the spot rate 120 days into the future (when the payables are due).

Comparison of Techniques to Hedge Receivables. If a firm desires to hedge receivables, it will conduct a similar analysis of transaction exposure. From a U.S. firm's perspective, the comparison should focus on selecting a technique that will maximize the dollars to be received as a result of hedging.

Example

Gator Corp. anticipates no payables in pounds, but it will receive £300,000 in 180 days. The same information on the spot, forward, and options prices is used to compare hedging techniques and an unhedged strategy in Exhibit 11.9. The dollar amounts to be received from each of the four alternatives are compared in Exhibit 11.10. It appears that the money market hedge is the optimal hedge for Gator.

Managing for Value: Merck's Hedging Strategy

DuPont, IBM, Merck, and most other MNCs do not use one type of hedging technique exclusively, but determine which technique is optimal on a case-by-case basis. The optimal hedging technique is dependent on exchange rate projections. If the projections cause the firm to believe that it will definitely be adversely affected by its transaction exposure, a forward hedge or money market hedge is normally appropriate. Conversely, if the firm believes that it may benefit from its exposure, the currency option hedge is more appropriate (if any hedge is used at all).

Consider the case of Merck, with worldwide sales of over $6 billion per year. Merck has substantial receivables denominated in foreign currencies as a result of exporting. It could use forward or futures contracts to lock in the rate at which those currencies will be converted to dollars. However, it recognizes that hedging with forward or futures contracts could result in an opportunity cost, measured as the amount of funds forgone if the foreign currencies denominating the receivables appreciate by the time the receivables are converted to dollars. Since Merck wants to capitalize on the possible appreciaition of these foreign currencies (weakening of the dollar), it uses put options to hedge its receivables denominated in foreign currencies. If the dollar weakens, Merck lets the put options expire, and the receivables are worth more at the prevailing spot rate. Meanwhile, the put options provide insurance in case the dollar strengthens. If Merck feels very confident that the dollar will strengthen, it uses forward or futures contracts instead of put options, because a premium must be paid for the put options. Yet, when it is unsure of the future movements in the foreign currencies, put options are attractive. By making a hedging decision that is consistent with its perceptions of future exchange rate movements, Merck maximizes its value.

Although the no-hedge strategy would outperform the money market hedge if the spot rate of the pound in 180 days is $1.52, there is only a 10 percent probability of that outcome. Therefore, Gator Corp. will likely decide to hedge its receivables position.

Exhibit 11.9

Comparison of Hedging Alternatives for Gator Corp.

Forward Hedge

Sell pounds 180 days forward.

$$\text{Dollars to be received in 180 days} = \text{receivables in £} \times \text{forward rate of £}$$
$$= £300,000 \times \$1.47$$
$$= \$441,000$$

Money Market Hedge

Borrow £, convert to $, invest $, use receivables to pay off loan in 180 days.

$$\text{Amount in £ borrowed} = \frac{£300,000}{(1 + .05)}$$
$$= £285,714$$

$$\$ \text{ received from converting £} = £285,714 \times \$1.50 \text{ per £}$$
$$= \$428,571$$

$$\$ \text{ accumulated after 180 days} = \$428,571 \times (1 + .045)$$
$$= \$447,857$$

Put Option Hedge

Purchase put option (assume the options are to be exercised on the day pounds are to be received, or not at all. Exercise price = $1.49; premium = $.02.)

Possible Spot Rate in 180 days	Premium per Unit Paid for Option	Exercise Option?	Total Dollars Received per Unit (after Accounting for the Premium)	Total Dollars Received from Converting £300,000	Probability
$1.43	$.02	Yes	$1.47	$441,000	20%
1.46	.02	Yes	1.47	441,000	70
1.52	.02	No	1.50	450,000	10

Remain Unhedged

Possible Spot Rate in 180 Days	Total Dollars Received from Converting £300,000	Probability
$1.43	$429,000	20%
1.46	438,000	70
1.52	456,000	10

Exhibit 11.10
Dollars Received
from Pound-
Denominated
Receivables

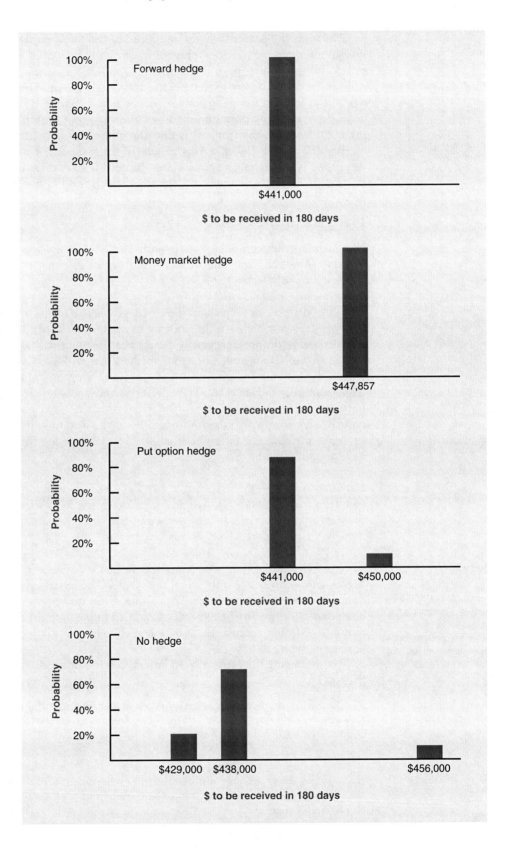

Although the preceding example assessed only one particular currency option, several alternative currency options are normally available with different exercise prices. When hedging payables, a firm can reduce the premium paid by choosing a call option with a higher exercise price. Of course, the tradeoff is that the maximum amount to be paid for the payables will be higher. Similarly, a firm hedging receivables can reduce the premium paid by choosing a put option with a lower exercise price. In this case, the tradeoff is that the minimum amount to be received for the receivables will be lower. Firms generally compare the available options first to determine which is most appropriate. Then, this particular option is compared to the other hedging techniques to determine which technique (if any) should be used.

Hedging Policies of MNCs

In general, hedging policies vary with the MNC management's degree of risk aversion. An MNC may choose to hedge most of its exposure, to hedge none of its exposure, or to selectively hedge.

Hedging Most of the Exposure. Some MNCs hedge most of their exposure so that their value is not highly influenced by exchange rates. MNCs that hedge most of their exposure do not necessarily expect that hedging will always be beneficial. In fact, such MNCs may even use some hedges that will likely result in slightly worse outcomes than no hedges at all, just to avoid the possibility of a major adverse movement in exchange rates. They prefer to know what their future cash inflows or outflows in terms of their home currency will be in each period because this improves corporate planning. A hedge allows the firm to know the future cash flows (in terms of the home currency) that will result from any foreign transactions that have already been negotiated.

Hedging None of the Exposure. MNCs that are well diversified across many countries may consider not hedging their exposure. This strategy may be driven by the view that a diversified set of exposures will limit the actual impact that exchange rates will have on the MNC during any period.

See www.ibm.com as an example of an MNC's website. The websites of various MNCs make financial statements such as annual reports available that disclose the use of financial derivatives for the purpose of hedging interest rate risk and foreign exchange rate risk.

Selective Hedging. Many MNCs, such as Black & Decker, Eastman Kodak, and Merck choose to hedge only when they expect the currency to move in a direction that will make hedging feasible. For example, Zenith hedges its imports of Japanese components only when it expects the yen to appreciate. In addition, these MNCs may hedge future receivables if they foresee depreciation in the currency denominating the receivables.

The following quotations from annual reports illustrate the strategy of selective hedging:

The purpose of the Company's foreign currency hedging activities is to reduce the risk that the eventual dollar net cash inflows resulting from sales outside the U.S. will be adversely affected by exchange rates.

The Coca-Cola Co.

Decisions regarding whether or not to hedge a given commitment are made on a case-by-case basis by taking into consideration the amount and duration of the exposure, market volatility, and economic trends.

DuPont Co.

We selectively hedge the potential effect of the foreign currency fluctuations related to operating activities.

General Mills Co.

Selective hedging implies that the MNC prefers to exercise some control over its exposure and makes decisions based on conditions that may affect the currency's future value.

LIMITATIONS OF HEDGING

Although hedging transaction exposure can be effective, there are some limitations that deserve to be mentioned here.

Limitation of Hedging an Uncertain Amount

Some international transactions involve an uncertain amount of goods ordered and therefore involve an uncertain transaction amount in a foreign currency. Consequently, an MNC may create a hedge for a larger number of units than it will acutally need, which causes the opposite form of exposure.

Example

Recall the previous example on hedging receivables, which assumed that Gator Corp. will receive £300,000 in 180 days. Now assume that the receivables amount could actually be much lower. If Gator uses the money market hedge on £300,000 and the receivables amount to only £200,000, it will have to make up the difference by purchasing £100,000 in the spot market to achieve the £300,000 needed to pay off the loan. If the pound appreciates over the 180-day period, will need a large amount in dollars to obtain the £100,000.

This example shows how **overhedging** (hedging a larger amount in a currency than the actual transaction amount) can adversely affect a firm. A solution to avoid overhedging is to hedge only the minimum known amount in the future transaction. In our example, if the future receivables could be as low as £200,000, Gator could hedge this amount. Under these conditions, however, the firm may not have completely hedged its position. If the actual transaction amount turns out to be £300,000 as expected, Gator will be only partially hedged and will need to sell the extra £100,000 in the spot market.

Firms commonly face this dilemma because the precise amount to be received in a foreign currency at the end of a period can be uncertain, especially for firms heavily involved in exporting. Based on this example, it should be clear that most MNCs cannot completely hedge all of their transactions. Nevertheless, by hedging a portion of those transactions that affect them, they can reduce the sensitivity of their cash flows to exchange rate movements.

Limitation of Repeated Short-Term Hedging

The continual hedging of repeated transactions that are expected to occur in the near future has limited effectiveness over the long run.

Exhibit 11.11

Illustration of
Repeated Hedging
of Foreign Payables
When the Foreign
Currency Is
Appreciating

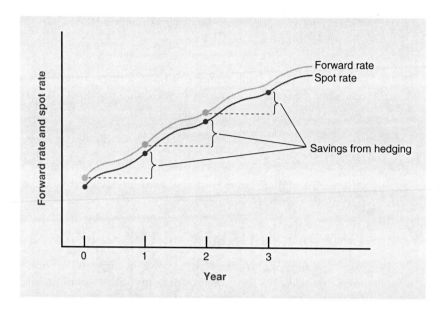

Example

Winthrop Co. is a U.S. importer that specializes in importing particular CD players in one large shipment per year and then selling them to retail stores throughout the year. Assume that today's exchange rate of the Japanese yen is $.005 and that the CD players are worth ¥60,000, or $300. The forward rate of the yen generally exhibits a premium of 2 percent. Exhibit 11.11 shows the dollar/yen exchange rate to be paid by the importer over time. As the spot rate changes, the forward rate will often change by a similar amount. Thus, if the spot rate increases by 10 percent over the year, the forward rate may increase by about the same amount, and the importer will pay 10 percent more for next year's shipment (assuming no change in the yen price quoted by the Japanese exporter). The use of a one-year forward contract during a strong-yen cycle is preferable to no hedge in this case but will still result in

Exhibit 11.12

Long-Term Hedging
of Payables When the
Foreign Currency Is
Appreciating

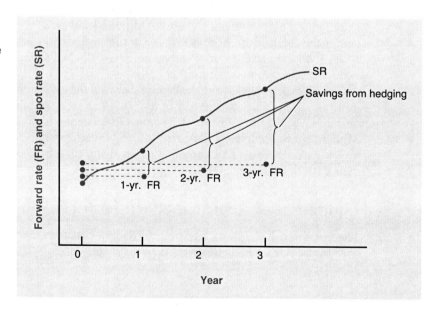

subsequent increases in prices paid by the importer each year. This illustrates that the use of short-term hedging techniques does not completely insulate a firm from exchange rate exposure, even if the hedges are repeatedly used over time.

If the hedging techniques can be applied to longer-term periods, they can more effectively insulate the firm from exchange rate risk over the long run. That is, Winthrop Co. could, as of Time 0, create a hedge for shipments to arrive at the end of each of the next several years. The forward rate for each hedge would be based on the spot rate as of today, as shown in Exhibit 11.12. During a strong-yen cycle, such a strategy would save a substantial amount of money.

This strategy faces a limitation, however, in that the amount in yen to be hedged further into the future is more uncertain because the shipment size will be dependent on economic conditions or other factors at that time. If a recession occurs, Winthrop Co. may reduce the number of CD players ordered, but the amount in yen to be received by the importer is dictated by the forward contract that was created. If the CD player manufacturer goes bankrupt, or simply experiences stockouts, Winthrop Co. is still obligated to purchase the yen, even if a shipment is not forthcoming.

HEDGING LONG-TERM TRANSACTION EXPOSURE

Some MNCs are certain of having cash flows denominated in foreign currencies for several years and attempt to use long-term hedging. For example, Walt Disney Co. has hedged its Japanese yen cash flows that will be remitted to the United States (from its Japanese theme park) 20 years ahead. Eastman Kodak Co. and General Electric Co. incorporate foreign exchange management into their long-term corporate planning. Thus, techniques for hedging long-term exchange rate exposure are needed.

Nike Problem

Nike's Management of Transaction Exposure

Since Nike conducts business across many countries, it can be exposed to exchange rate movements. It commonly hedges its transaction exposure. In a recent annual report, Nike stated that its foreign currency hedging activities are intended to protect the company from the risk that the eventual dollar cash flows resulting from the sale and purchase of products in foreign currencies will be adversely affected by changes in exchange rates. The annual report also said that Nike nets its foreign exchange exposures to capitalize on natural offsets that occur through intracompany transactions and other business transactions. In those cases where there is not a natural offset, it commonly hedges by negotiating forward contracts and currency options contracts with high-quality financial institutions.

Discussion: Since Nike conducts much business in Japan, it is likely to have cash flows in yen that will periodically be remitted by its Japanese subsidiary to the U.S. parent. What are the limitations of hedging these remittances one year in advance over each of the next 20 years? What are the limitations of creating a hedge today that will hedge these remittances over each of the next 20 years?

Firms that can accurately estimate foreign currency payables or receivables that will occur several years from now commonly use three techniques to hedge such long-term transaction exposure:

- Long-term forward contract
- Currency swap
- Parallel loan

Each technique is discussed in turn.

Long-Term Forward Contract

Until recently, **long-term forward contracts**, or long forwards, were seldom used. Today, the long forward is quite popular. Most large international banks routinely quote forward rates for terms of up to five years for British pounds, Canadian dollars, Japanese yen, and Swiss francs. Long forwards are especially attractive to firms that have set up fixed-price exporting or importing contracts over a long period of time and want to protect their cash flow from exchange rate fluctuations.

Like a short-term forward contract, the long forward can be tailored to accommodate the specific needs of the firm. Maturities of up to 10 years or more can sometimes be set up for the major currencies. Because a bank is trusting that the firm will fulfill its long-term obligation specified in the forward contract, it will consider only very creditworthy customers.

Currency Swap

A **currency swap** is a second technique for hedging long-term transaction exposure to exchange rate fluctuations. It can take many forms. One type of currency swap accommodates two firms that have different long-term needs.

Example

Bellevue, Inc., a U.S. firm, is hired to build an oil pipeline in the United Kingdom. It expects to receive payment in British pounds in five years when the job is completed. At the same time, a British firm is hired by a U.S. bank for a long-term consulting project. Assume that this British firm will be paid in U.S. dollars and that much of the payment will occur in five years. Thus, Bellevue, Inc., will be receiving British pounds in five years, and the British firm will be receiving U.S. dollars in five years. These two firms could arrange a currency swap that allows for an exchange of pounds for dollars in five years at some negotiated exchange rate. In this way, Bellevue can lock in the number of U.S. dollars the British pound payment will convert to in five years. Likewise, the British firm can lock in the number of British pounds the U.S. dollar payment will convert to in five years.

To create a currency swap, firms rely on financial intermediaries who can accommodate their needs. Large banks and investment firms employ brokers who act as intermediaries for swaps. Corporations that want to eliminate transaction exposure to specific currencies at certain future dates contact a broker, who then finds one firm that needs the currency another firm wants to dispose of (and vice versa) and matches them up. The broker receives a fee for the service.

Over time, the currency swap obligation may become undesirable to one of the parties involved. Using our example, if the British pound appreciates substantially over time, Bellevue, Inc., will be worse off than if it had been able to obtain its dollars in the spot market. Of course, it did not know this when it engaged in a swap agreement. The swap agreement may require periodic payments from one party to the other to account for exchange rate movements, so as to reduce the possibility that one party will not fulfill its obligation by the time the exchange of currencies is supposed to occur.

Parallel Loan

A **parallel loan** (or "back-to-back loan") involves an exchange of currencies between two parties, with a promise to reexchange currencies at a specified exchange rate and future date. It represents two swaps of currencies, one swap at the inception of the loan contract and another swap at the specified future date. A parallel loan is interpreted by accountants as a loan and is therefore recorded on financial statements.

ALTERNATIVE HEDGING TECHNIQUES

When a perfect hedge is not available (or is too expensive) to eliminate transaction exposure, the firm should consider methods to at least reduce exposure. Such methods include the following:

- Leading and lagging
- Cross-hedging
- Currency diversification

Each method is discussed in turn.

Leading and Lagging

The act of leading and lagging involves an adjustment in the timing of a payment request or disbursement to reflect expectations about future currency movements.

Example Corvalis Co. is based in the United States and has subsidiaries dispersed around the world. The focus here will be on a subsidiary in the United Kingdom that purchases some of its supplies from a subsidiary in Hungary. These supplies are denominated in Hungary's currency (the forint). If Corvalis Co. expects that the pound will soon depreciate against the forint, it may attempt to expedite the payment to Hungary before the pound depreciates. This strategy is referred to as **leading**.

As a second scenario, assume that the British subsidiary expects the pound to appreciate against the forint soon. In this case, the British subsidiary may attempt to stall its payment until after the pound appreciates. In this way it could use fewer pounds to obtain the forint needed for payment. This strategy is referred to as **lagging**.

General Electric and other well-known MNCs commonly use leading and lagging strategies in countries that allow them. In some countries, the government limits the length of time involved in leading and lagging strategies so that the flow of funds into or out of the country is not disrupted. Consequently, an MNC must be aware of government restrictions in any countries where it conducts business before using these strategies.

Cross-Hedging

Cross-hedging is a common method of reducing transaction exposure when the currency cannot be hedged.

Example Greeley Co., a U.S. firm, has payables in zloty (Poland's currency) 90 days from now. Because it is worried that the zloty may appreciate against the U.S. dollar, it may desire to hedge this position. If forward contracts and other hedging techniques are not possible for the zloty, Greeley may consider cross-hedging. In this case, it needs to first identify a currency that can be hedged and is highly correlated with the zloty. Greeley notices that the euro has recently been moving in tandem with the zloty and decides to set up a 90-day forward contract on the euro. If the movements in the zloty and euro continue to be highly correlated relative to the U.S. dollar (that is, they move in a similar direction and degree against the U.S. dollar), then the exchange rate between these two currencies should be somewhat stable over time. By purchasing euros 90 days forward, Greeley Co. can then exchange euros for the zloty. The effectiveness of this strategy depends on the degree to which these two currencies are positively correlated. The stronger the positive correlation, the more effective will be the cross-hedging strategy.

Currency Diversification

A third method for reducing transaction exposure is **currency diversification**, which can limit the potential effect of any single currency's movements on the value of an MNC. Some MNCs, such as The Coca-Cola Co., PepsiCo, and Philip Morris, claim that their exposure to exchange rate movements is significantly reduced because they diversify their business among numerous countries.

The dollar value of future inflows in foreign currencies will be more stable if the foreign currencies received are *not* highly positively correlated. The reason is that lower positive correlations or negative correlations can reduce the variability of the dollar value of all foreign currency inflows. If the foreign currencies were highly correlated with each other, diversifying among them would not be a very effective way to reduce risk. If one of the currencies substantially depreciated, the others would do so as well, given that all these currencies move in tandem.

How Transaction Exposure Management Affects an MNC's Value

An MNC's management of transaction exposure can affect its value, as shown in Exhibit 11.13. If the MNC's foreign subsidiaries exchange their local currencies when conducting normal business, their expected foreign currency cash flows are dependent on whether they hedge those transactions or remain unhedged. Whether hedging each transaction results in higher or lower cash flows to those subsidiaries is not known until the transaction occurs.

Regardless of whether the business transactions of the foreign subsidiaries are hedged, the expected dollar value of the foreign currency cash flows remitted by the

Exhibit 11.13

Impact of Hedging Transaction Exposure on an MNC's Value

$$V = \sum_{t=1}^{n} \left\{ \frac{\sum_{j=1}^{m} \left[E(CF_{j,t}) \times E(ER_{j,t}) \right]}{(1+k)^t} \right\}$$

Hedging Decisions on Transaction Exposure

V = value of the U.S.-based MNC
$E(CF_{j,t})$ = expected cash flows denominated in currency j to be received by the U.S. parent in period t
$E(ER_{j,t})$ = expected exchange rate at which currency j can be converted to dollars at the end of period t
k = weighted average cost of capital of the U.S. parent
m = number of currencies
n = number of periods

foreign subsidiaries is dependent on whether those remitted cash flows are hedged. Hedging decisions on remitted funds affect the expected value of the exchange rate at which the funds are converted to dollars and therefore affect the dollar cash flows that are ultimately received by the U.S. parent.

SUMMARY

- MNCs use the following techniques to hedge transaction exposure: (1) futures hedge, (2) forward hedge, (3) money market hedge, and (4) currency options hedge.

- To hedge payables, a futures or forward contract on the foreign currency can be purchased. Alternatively, a money market hedge strategy can be used; in this case, the MNC borrows its home currency and converts the proceeds into the foreign currency that will be needed in the future. Finally, call options on the foreign currency can be purchased.

- To hedge receivables, a futures or forward contract on the foreign currency can be sold. Alternatively, a money market hedge strategy can be used. In this case, the MNC borrows the foreign currency to be received and converts the funds into its home currency; the loan is to be repaid by the receivables. Finally, put options on the foreign currency can be purchased.

- Futures contracts and forward contracts normally yield similar results. Forward contracts are more flexible because they are not standardized. The money market hedge yields results similar to those of the forward hedge if interest rate parity exists. The currency options hedge has an advantage over the other hedging techniques in that it does not have to be exercised if the MNC would be better off unhedged. A premium must be paid to purchase the currency options, however, so there is a cost for the flexibility they provide.

- When hedging techniques are not available, there are still some methods of reducing transaction exposure, such as leading and lagging, cross-hedging, and currency diversification.

SELF TEST

Answers are provided in Appendix A at the back of the text.

1. Montclair Co., a U.S. firm, plans to use a money market hedge to hedge its payment of 3,000,000 Australian dollars for Australian goods in one year. The U.S. interest rate is 7 percent, while the Australian interest rate is 12 percent. The spot rate of the Australian dollar is $.85, while the one-year forward rate is $.81. Determine the amount of U.S. dollars needed in one year if a money market hedge is used.

2. Using the information in the previous question, would Montclair Co. be better off hedging the payables with a money market hedge or with a forward hedge?

3. Using the information about Montclair from the first question, explain the possible advantage of a currency option hedge over a money market hedge for Montclair Co. What is a possible disadvantage of the currency option hedge?

4. Sanibel Co. purchases British goods (denominated in pounds) every month. It negotiates a one-month forward contract at the beginning of every month to hedge its payables. Assume the British pound appreciates consistently over the next five years. Will Sanibel be affected? Explain.

5. Using the information from question 4, suggest how Sanibel Co. could more effectively insulate itself from the possible long-term appreciation of the British pound.

6. Hopkins Co. transported goods to Switzerland and will receive 2,000,000 Swiss francs in three months. It believes the three-month forward rate will be an accurate forecast of the future spot rate. The three-month forward rate of the Swiss franc is $.68. A put option is available with an exercise price of $.69 and a premium of $.03. Would Hopkins prefer a put option hedge to no hedge? Explain.

QUESTIONS AND APPLICATIONS

1. Quincy Corp. estimates the following cash flows in 90 days at its subsidiaries as follows:

Net Position in Each Currency Measured in the Parent's Currency (in 1000s of Units)			
Subsidiary	Currency 1	Currency 2	Currency 3
A	+200	−300	−100
B	+100	− 40	− 10
C	−180	+200	− 40

Determine the consolidated net exposure of the MNC to each currency.

2. Assume that Stevens Point Co. has net receivables of 100,000 Singapore dollars in 90 days. The spot rate of the S$ is $.50, and the Singapore interest rate is 2 percent over 90 days. Suggest how the U.S. firm could implement a money market hedge. Be precise.

3. Assume that Vermont Co. has net payables of 200,000 Mexican pesos in 180 days. The Mexican interest rate is 7 percent over 180 days, and the spot rate of the peso is $.10. Suggest how the U.S. firm could implement a money market hedge. Be precise.

4. Assume that Citadel Co. purchases some goods in Chile that are denominated in Chilean pesos. It also sells goods denominated in U.S. dollars to some firms in Chile. At the end of each month, it has a large net payables position in Chilean pesos. How can this U.S. firm use an invoicing strategy to reduce this transaction exposure? List any limitations on the effectiveness of this strategy.

5. Explain how a U.S. corporation could hedge net receivables in euros with futures contracts.

6. Explain how a U.S. corporation could hedge net payables in Japanese yen with futures contracts.

7. Explain how a U.S. corporation could hedge net receivables in Malaysian ringgit with a forward contract.

8. Explain how a U.S. corporation could hedge payables in Canadian dollars with a forward contract.

9. Assume that Loras Corp. imported goods from New Zealand and needs 100,000 New Zealand dollars 180 days from now. It is trying to determine whether to hedge this position. Loras has developed the following probability distribution for the New Zealand dollar:

Possible Value of New Zealand Dollar in 180 days	Probability
$.40	5%
.45	10
.48	30
.50	30
.53	20
.55	5

The 180-day forward rate of the New Zealand dollar is $.52. The spot rate of the New Zealand dollar is $.49. Develop a table showing a feasibility analysis for hedging. That is, determine the possible differences between the costs of hedging and those of not hedging. What is the probability that hedging will be more costly to the firm than not hedging?

10. Using the information from question 9, determine the expected value of the additional cost of hedging.

11. If hedging is expected to be more costly than not hedging, why would a firm even consider hedging?

12. Assume that Suffolk Co. negotiated a forward contract to purchase 200,000 British pounds in 90 days. The 90-day forward rate was $1.40 per British pound. The pounds to be purchased were to be used to purchase British supplies. On the day the pounds were delivered in accordance with the forward contract, the spot rate of the British pound was $1.44. What was the real cost of hedging the payables for this U.S. firm?

13. Repeat question 12, except assume that the spot rate of the British pound was $1.34 on the day the pounds were delivered in accordance with the forward contract. What was the real cost of hedging the payables in this example?

14. Assume that Bentley Co. negotiated a forward contract to sell 100,000 Canadian dollars in one year. The one-year forward rate on the Canadian dollar was $.80. This strategy was designed to hedge receivables in Canadian dollars. On the day the Canadian dollars were to be sold off in accordance with the forward contract, the spot rate of the Canadian dollar was $.83. What was the real cost of hedging receivables for this U.S. firm?

15. Repeat question 14, except assume that the spot rate of the Canadian dollar was $.75 on the day the Canadian dollars were to be sold off in accordance with the forward contract. What was the real cost of hedging receivables in this example?

16. Assume the following information:

90-day U.S. interest rate	4%
90-day Malaysian interest rate	3%
90-day forward rate of Malaysian ringgit	$.400
Spot rate of Malaysian ringgit	$.404

Assume that Santa Barbara Co. in the United States will need 300,000 ringgit in 90 days. It wishes to hedge this payables position. Would it be better off using a forward hedge or a money market hedge? Substantiate your answer with estimated costs for each type of hedge.

17. Assume the following information:

180-day U.S. interest rate	8%
180-day British interest rate	9%
180-day forward rate of British pound	$1.50
Spot rate of British pound	$1.48

Assume that Riverside Corp. from the United States will receive £400,000 in 180 days. Would it be better off using a forward hedge or a money market hedge? Substantiate your answer with estimated revenue for each type of hedge.

18. Why would Cleveland, Inc., consider hedging net payables or net receivables with currency options rather than forward contracts? What are the disadvantages of hedging with currency options as opposed to forward contracts?

19. Relate the use of currency options to hedging net payables and receivables. That is, when should currency puts be purchased, and when should currency calls be purchased?

20. Can Brooklyn Co. determine whether currency options will be more or less expensive than a forward hedge when considering both hedging techniques to cover net payables in euros? Why or why not?

21. How can a firm hedge long-term currency positions? Elaborate on each method.

22. Under what conditions would Zona Co.'s subsidiary consider using a "leading" strategy to reduce transaction exposure?

23. Under what conditions would an Zona Co.'s subsidiary consider using a "lagging" strategy to reduce transaction exposure?

24. Explain how a firm can use cross-hedging to reduce transaction exposure.

25. Explain how how a firm can use currency diversification to reduce transaction exposure.

26. a. Assume that Carbondale Co. expects to receive S$500,000 in one year. The existing spot rate of the Singapore dollar is $.60. The one-year forward rate of the Singapore dollar is $.62. Carbondale created a probability distribution for the future spot rate in one year as follows:

Future Spot Rate	Probability
$.61	20%
.63	50
.67	30

Assume that one-year put options on Singapore dollars are available, with an exercise price of $.63 and a premium of $.04 per unit. One-year call options on Singapore dollars are available with an exercise price of $.60 and a premium of $.03 per unit. Assume the following money market rates:

	U.S.	Singapore
Deposit rate	8%	5%
Borrowing rate	9	6

Given this information, determine whether a forward hedge, money market hedge, or currency options hedge would be most appropriate. Then, compare the most appropriate hedge to an unhedged strategy, and decide whether Carbondale should hedge its receivables position.

b. Assume that Baton Rouge, Inc., expects to need S$1 million in one year. Using any relevant information in part (a) of this question, determine whether a forward hedge, money market hedge, or a currency options hedge would be most appropriate. Then, compare the most appropriate hedge to an unhedged strategy, and decide whether Baton Rouge should hedge its payables position.

27. SMU Corp. has future receivables of 4,000,000 New Zealand dollars (NZ$) in one year. It must decide whether to use options or a money market hedge to hedge this position. Use any of the following information to make the decision. Verify your answer by determining the estimate (or

probability distribution) of dollar revenue to be received in one year for each type of hedge.

Spot rate of NZ$	$.54
One-year call option	Exercise price = $.50; premium = $.07
One-year put option	Exercise price = $.52; premium = $.03

	U.S.	New Zealand
One-year deposit rate	9%	6%
One-year borrowing rate	11	8

	Rate	Probability
Forecasted spot rate of NZ$	$.50	20%
	.51	50
	.53	30

28. As treasurer of Tucson Corp. (a U.S. exporter to New Zealand), you must decide how to hedge (if at all) future receivables of 250,000 New Zealand dollars 90 days from now. Put options are available for a premium of $.03 per unit and an exercise price of $.49 per New Zealand dollar. The forecasted spot rate of the New Zealand dollar in 90 days follows:

Future Spot Rate	Probability
$.44	30%
.40	50
.38	20

Given that you hedge your position with options, create a probability distribution for dollars to be received in 90 days.

29. As treasurer of Tempe Corp., you are confronted with the following problem. Assume the one-year forward rate of the British pound is $1.59. You plan to receive £1 million in one year. A one-year put option is available. It has an exercise price of $1.61. The spot rate as of today is $1.62, and the option premium is $.04 per unit. Your forecast of the percentage change in the spot rate was determined from the following regression model:

$$e_t = a_0 + a_1 \, DINF_{t-1} + a_2 \, DINT_t + \mu$$

where

e_t = percentage change in British pound value over period t

$DINF_{t-1}$ = differential in inflation between the United States and the United Kingdom in period $t - 1$

$DINT_t$ = average differential between U.S. interest rate and British interest rate over period t

$a_0, a_1,$ and a_2 = regression coefficients

μ = error term

The regression model was applied to historical annual data, and the regression coefficients were estimated as follows:

$$a_0 = 0$$
$$a_1 = 1.1$$
$$a_2 = .6$$

Assume last year's inflation rates were 3 percent for the United States and 8 percent for the United Kingdom. Also assume that the interest rate differential ($DINT_t$) is forecasted as follows for this year:

Forecast of $DINT_t$	Probability
1%	40%
2	50
3	10

Using any of the available information, decide whether the treasurer should choose the forward hedge or a put option hedge. Show your work.

30. Would Oregon Co.'s real cost of hedging Australian dollar payables every 90 days have been positive, negative, or about zero on average over a period in which the dollar weakened consistently? What does this imply about the forward rate as an unbiased predictor of the future spot rate? Explain.

31. If interest rate parity exists, would a forward hedge be more favorable, equally favorable, or less favorable than a money market hedge on euro payables? Explain.

32. Would Montana Co.'s real cost of hedging Japanese yen receivables have been positive, negative, or about zero on average over a period in which the dollar weakened consistently? Explain.

33. If you are a U.S. importer of Mexican goods and you believe that today's forward rate of the peso is a very accurate estimate of the future spot rate, do you think Mexican peso call options would be a more appropriate hedge than the forward hedge? Explain.

34. You are an exporter of goods to the United Kingdom, and you believe that today's forward rate of the British pound substantially underestimates the future spot rate. Company policy requires you to hedge your British pound receivables in some way. Would a forward hedge or a put option hedge be more appropriate? Explain.

35. Explain how a Malaysian firm can use the forward market to hedge periodic purchases of U.S. goods denominated in U.S. dollars.

36. Explain how a French firm can use foward contracts to hedge periodic sales of goods sold to the United States that are invoiced in dollars.

37. Explain how a British firm can use the forward market to hedge periodic purchases of Japanese goods denominated in yen.

38. Cornell Co. purchases computer chips denominated in euros on a monthly basis from a Dutch supplier. To hedge its exchange rate risk, this U.S. firm negotiates a three-month forward contract three months before the next order will arrive. In other words, Cornell is always covered for the next three monthly shipments. Because Cornell consistently hedges in this manner, it is not concerned with exchange rate movements. Is Cornell insulated from exchange rate movements? Explain.

39. Malibu, Inc., is a U.S. company that imports British goods. It plans to use call options to hedge payables of £100,000 in 90 days. Three call options are available that have an expiration date 90 days from now. Fill in the number of dollars needed to pay for the payables (including the option premium paid) for each option available under each possible scenario.

Scenario	Spot Rate of Pound 90 Days from Now	Exercise Price = $1.74; Premium = $.06	Exercise Price = $1.76; Premium = $.05	Exercise Price = $1.79; Premium = $.03
1	$1.65			
2	1.70			
3	1.75			
4	1.80			
5	1.85			

If each of the five scenarios had an equal probability of occurrence, which option would you choose? Explain.

40. Wedco Technology of New Jersey exports plastics products to Europe. Wedco decided to price its exports in dollars. Telematics International, Inc. (of Florida), exports computer network systems to the United Kingdom (denominated in British pounds) and other countries. Telematics decided to use hedging techniques such as forward contracts to hedge its exposure.

a. Does Wedco's strategy of pricing its materials for European customers in dollars avoid economic exposure? Explain.

b. Explain why the earnings of Telematics International, Inc., were affected by changes in the value of the pound. Why might Telematics leave its exposure unhedged sometimes?

41. Describe how the Asian crisis could have reduced the cash flows of a U.S. firm that exported products (denominated in U.S. dollars) to Asian countries.

42. How could a U.S. firm that exported products (denominated in U.S. dollars) to Asia, and anticipated the Asian crisis before it began, have insulated itself from any currency effects while continuing to export to Asia?

Impact of 9/11/01

43. If you are a U.S. importer of products from Europe, explain whether the September 11, 2001, terrorist attact on the United States would have caused you to hedge your payables (which are denominated in euros) due a few months later.

Internet Application

44. The following website contains annual reports of many MNCs: **http://www.reportgallery.com**

   a. Review the annual report of your choice. Look for any comments in the report that describe the MNC's hedging of transaction exposure. Summarize the MNC's hedging of transaction exposure based on the comments in the annual report.

   b. The following website provides exchange rate movements against the dollar over recent months: **http://pacific.commerce.ubc.ca/xr/data.html**.

Based on the exposure of the MNC you assessed in part (a), determine whether the exchange rate movements of whatever currency (or currencies) it is exposed to moved in a favorable or unfavorable direction over the last few months.

Running Your Own MNC

 This exercise can be found on the Student CD-ROM.

Blades, Inc. Case

Management of Transaction Exposure

Blades, Inc., has recently decided to expand its international trade relationship by exporting to the United Kingdom. Jogs, Ltd., a British retailer, has committed itself to the annual purchase of 200,000 pairs of "Speedos," Blades' primary product, for a price of £80 per pair. The agreement is to last for two years, at which time it may be renewed by Blades and Jogs.

In addition to this new international trade relationship, Blades continues to export to Thailand. Its primary customer there, a retailer called Entertainment Products, is committed to the purchase of 180,000 pairs of Speedos annually for another two years at a fixed price of 4,594 Thai baht per pair. When the agreement terminates, it may be renewed by Blades and Entertainment Products.

Blades also incurs costs of goods sold denominated in Thai baht. It imports materials sufficient to manufacture 72,000 pairs of Speedos annually from Thailand. These imports are denominated in baht, and the price depends on current market prices for the rubber and plastic components imported.

Under the two export arrangements, Blades sells quarterly amounts of 50,000 and 45,000 pairs of Speedos to Jogs and Entertainment Products, respectively. Payment for these sales is made on the first of January, April, July, and October. The annual amounts are spread over quarters in order to avoid excessive inventories for the British and Thai retailers. Similarly, in order to avoid excessive inventories, Blades usually imports materials sufficient to manufacture 18,000 pairs of Speedos quarterly from Thailand. Although payment terms call for payment within 60 days of delivery, Blades generally pays for its Thai imports upon delivery on the first day of each quarter in order to maintain its trade relationships with the Thai suppliers. Blades feels that early payment is beneficial, as other customers of the Thai supplier pay for their purchases only when it is required.

Since Blades is relatively new to international trade, Ben Holt, Blades' chief financial officer (CFO), is concerned with the potential impact of exchange rate fluctuations on Blades' financial performance. Holt is vaguely familiar with various techniques available to hedge transaction exposure, but he is not certain whether one technique is superior to the others. Holt would like to know more about the forward, money market, and option hedges and has asked you, a financial analyst at Blades, to help him identify the hedging technique most appropriate for Blades. Unfortunately, no options are available for Thailand, but British call and put options are available for £31,250 per option.

Ben Holt has gathered and provided you with the following information for Thailand and the United Kingdom:

	Thailand	United Kingdom
Current spot rate	$0.0230	$1.50
90-day forward rate	$0.0215	$1.49
Put option premium	Not available	$0.020 per unit
Put option exercise price	Not available	$1.47
Call option premium	Not available	$0.015 per unit
Call option exercise price	Not available	$1.48
90-day borrowing rate (nonannualized)	4%	2%
90-day lending rate (nonannualized)	3.5%	1.8%

In addition to this information, Ben Holt has informed you that the 90-day borrowing and lending rates in the United States are 2.3 percent and 2.1 percent, respectively, on a nonannualized basis. He has also identified the following probability distributions for the exchange rates of the British pound and the Thai baht in 90 days:

Probability	Spot Rate for the British Pound in 90 Days	Spot Rate for the Thai Baht in 90 Days
5%	$1.45	$0.0200
20	1.47	0.0213
30	1.48	0.0217
25	1.49	0.0220
15	1.50	0.0230
5	1.52	0.0235

Blades' next sales to and purchases from Thailand will occur one quarter from now. If Blades decides to hedge, Holt will want to hedge the entire amount subject to exchange rate fluctuations, even if it requires overhedging (i.e., hedging more than the needed amount). Currently, Holt expects the imported components from Thailand to cost approximately 3,000 baht per pair of Speedos. Holt has asked you to answer the following questions for him:

1. Using a spreadsheet, compare the hedging alternatives for the Thai baht with a scenario under which Blades remains unhedged. Do you think Blades should hedge or remain unhedged? If Blades should hedge, which hedge is most appropriate?

2. Using a spreadsheet, compare the hedging alternatives for the British pound receivables with a scenario under which Blades remains unhedged. Do you think Blades should hedge or remain unhedged? Which hedge is the most appropriate for Blades?

3. In general, do you think it is easier for Blades to hedge its inflows or its outflows denominated in foreign currencies? Why?

4. Would any of the hedges you compared in question 2 for the British pounds to be received in 90 days require Blades to overhedge? Given Blades' exporting arrangements, do you think it is subject to overhedging with a money market hedge?

5. Could Blades modify the timing of the Thai imports in order to reduce its transaction exposure? What is the tradeoff of such a modification?

6. Could Blades modify its payment practices for the Thai imports in order to reduce its transaction exposure? What is the tradeoff of such a modification?

7. Given Blades' exporting agreements, are there any long-term hedging techniques Blades could benefit from? For this question only, assume that Blades incurs all of its costs in the United States.

Hedging Decisions by the Sports Exports Company

Jim Logan, owner of the Sports Exports Company, will be receiving about 10,000 British pounds about one month from now as payment for exports produced and sent by his firm. Jim is concerned about his exposure because he believes that there are two possible scenarios: (1) the pound will depreciate by 3 percent over the next month or (2) the pound will appreciate by 2 percent over the next month. There is a 70 percent chance that Scenario 1 will occur. There is a 30 percent chance that Scenario 2 will occur.

Jim notices that the prevailing spot rate of the pound is $1.65, and the one-month forward rate is about $1.645. Jim can purchase a put option over the counter from a securities firm that has an exercise (strike) price of $1.645, a premium of $.025, and an expiration date of one month from now.

1. Determine the amount of dollars received by the Sports Exports Company if the receivables to be received in one month are not hedged under each of the two exchange rate scenarios.

2. Determine the amount of dollars received by the Sports Exports Company if a put option is used to hedge receivables in one month under each of the two exchange rate scenarios.

3. Determine the amount of dollars received by the Sports Exports Company if a forward hedge is used to hedge receivables in one month under each of the two exchange rate scenarios.

4. Summarize the results of dollars received based on an unhedged strategy, a put option strategy, and a forward hedge strategy. Select the strategy that you prefer based on the information provided.

4

CURRENCY DERIVATIVES

This chapter is devoted entirely to currency derivatives, often used by speculators interested in trading currencies simply to achieve profits but also used by firms to cover their foreign currency positions. Since MNCs commonly use currency derivatives, their managers must understand how these derivatives can be used to achieve corporate goals.

The specific objectives of this chapter are to:
- explain how forward contracts are used to hedge based on anticipated exchange rate movements,
- describe how currency futures contracts are used to speculate or hedge based on anticipated exchange rate movements, and
- explain how currency options contracts are used to speculate or hedge based on anticipated exchange rate movements.

FORWARD MARKET

The forward market facilitates the trading of forward contracts on currencies. A **forward contract** is an agreement between a corporation and a commercial bank to exchange a specified amount of a currency at a specified exchange rate (called the **forward rate**) on a specified date in the future. When multinational corporations (MNCs) anticipate a future need for or future receipt of a foreign currency, they can set up forward contracts to lock in the rate at which they can purchase or sell a particular foreign currency. Virtually all large MNCs use forward contracts. Some MNCs, such as TRW, have forward contracts outstanding worth more than $100 million to hedge various positions.

Because forward contracts accommodate large corporations, the forward transaction will often be valued at $1 million or more. Forward contracts normally are not used by consumers or small firms. In cases when a bank does not know a corporation well or fully trust it, the bank may request that the corporation make an initial deposit to assure that it will fulfill its obligation.

The most common forward contracts are for 30, 60, 90, 180, and 360 days, although other periods (including longer periods) are available. The forward rate of a given currency will typically vary with the length (number of days) of the forward period.

How MNCs Use Forward Contracts

MNCs use forward contracts to hedge their imports. They can lock in the rate at which they obtain a currency needed to purchase imports.

Example

Turz, Inc., is an MNC based in Chicago that will need 1,000,000 Singapore dollars in 90 days to purchase Singapore imports. It can buy Singapore dollars for immediate delivery at the spot rate of $.50 per Singapore dollar (S$). At this spot rate, the firm would need $500,000 (computed as S$1,000,000 × $.50 per Singapore dollar). However, it does not have the funds right now to exchange for Singapore dollars. It could wait 90 days and then exchange dollars for Singapore dollars at the spot rate existing at that time. But, Turz does not know what the spot rate will be at that time. If the rate rises to $.60 by then, Turz will need $600,000 (computed as S$1,000,000 × $.60 per Singapore dollar), an additional outlay of $100,000 due to the appreciation of the Singapore dollar.

To avoid exposure to exchange rate risk, Turz can lock in the rate it will pay for Singapore dollars 90 days from now without having to exchange dollars for Singapore dollars immediately. Specifically, Turz can negotiate a forward contract with a bank to purchase S$1,000,000 90 days forward.

Corporations also use the forward market to lock in the rate at which they can sell foreign currencies. This strategy is used to hedge against the possibility of those currencies depreciating over time.

Example

Scanlon, Inc., based in Virginia, exports products to a French firm and will receive payment of €400,000 in four months. It can lock in the amount of dollars to be received from this transaction by selling euros forward. That is, Scanlon can negotiate a forward contract with a bank to sell the €400,000 for dollars at a specified forward rate today. Assume the prevailing four-month forward rate on euros is $.1.10. In four months, Scanlon will exchange its €400,000 for $440,000 (computed as €$400,000 × $1.10 = $440,000).

Bid/Ask Spread. Like spot rates, forward rates have a bid/ask spread. For example, a bank may set up a contract with one firm agreeing to sell the firm Singapore dollars 90 days from now at $.510 per Singapore dollar. This represents the ask rate. At the same time, the firm may agree to purchase (bid) Singapore dollars 90 days from now from some other firm at $.505 per Singapore dollar.

The spread between the bid and ask prices is wider for forward rates of currencies of developing countries, such as Chile, Mexico, South Korea, Taiwan, and Thailand. Because these markets have relatively few orders for forward contracts, banks are less able to match up willing buyers and sellers. This lack of liquidity causes banks to widen the bid/ask spread when quoting forward contracts. The contracts in these countries are generally available only for short-term horizons.

Premium or Discount on the Forward Rate. If the forward rate exceeds the existing spot rate, it contains a **premium**. If it is less than the existing spot rate, it contains a **discount**. This premium or discount is normally computed on an annual basis as shown in Exhibit 5.1. For example, assume the forward exchange rates shown in Column 2 of Exhibit 5.1 are quoted for the British pound. Based on those forward rates, the forward discount has been computed for each maturity. The forward discounts can first be computed in decimal form, which is easily converted into percentage form.

Forward rates typically differ from the spot rate for any given currency. If the forward rate were the same as the spot rate, and interest rates of the two countries differed, it would be possible for some investors (under certain assumptions) to use **arbitrage** to earn higher returns than would be possible domestically without incurring additional risk. Consequently, the forward rate usually contains a premium (or discount) that reflects the difference between the home interest rate and the foreign interest rate.

HTTP:// ONLINE APPLICATION Forward Rates Forward rates of the Canadian dollar, British pound, euro, and Japanese yen are provided for various periods at http://www.bmo.com/economic/regular/fxrates.html.

The website shows the forward rate of the Canadian dollar for many time horizons. It also shows forward rate of the British pound, the euro, and the Japanese yen against the Canadian dollar and against the U.S. dollar.

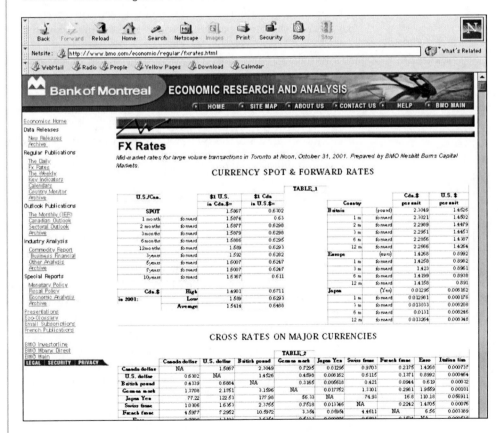

Exhibit 5.1

Computation of Forward Rate Premiums or Discounts

Type of Exchange Rate for £	Value	Maturity	Forward Rate Premium or Discount for £
Spot rate	$1.681		
30-day forward rate	$1.680	30 days	$\dfrac{\$1.680 - \$1.681}{\$1.681} \times \dfrac{360}{30} = -.71\%$
90-day forward rate	$1.677	90 days	$\dfrac{\$1.677 - \$1.681}{\$1.681} \times \dfrac{360}{90} = -.95\%$
180-day forward rate	$1.672	180 days	$\dfrac{\$1.672 - \$1.681}{\$1.681} \times \dfrac{360}{180} = -1.07\%$

Non-Deliverable Forward Contracts

A new type of forward contract called a **non-deliverable forward contract (NDF)** is frequently used for currencies in emerging markets. Like a regular forward contract, an NDF represents an agreement regarding a position in a specified amount of a specified currency, a specified exchange rate, and a specified future settlement date. However, an NDF does not result in an actual exchange of the currencies at the future date. That is, there is no delivery. Instead, one party to the agreement makes a payment to the other party based on the exchange rate at the future date.

Example   Jackson, Inc., an MNC based in Wyoming, determines as of April 1 that it will need 100 million Chilean pesos to purchase supplies on July 1. It can negotiate an NDF with a local bank as follows. The NDF will specify the currency (Chilean peso), the settlement date (90 days from now), and a so-called reference rate, which identifies the type of exchange rate that will be marked to market at the settlement. Specifically, the NDF will contain the following information:

- Buy 100 million Chilean pesos.
- Settlement date: July 1.
- Reference index: Chilean peso's closing exchange rate (in dollars) quoted by Chile's central bank in 90 days.

Assume that the Chilean peso (which is the reference index) is currently valued at $.0020, so the dollar amount of the position is $200,000 at the time of the agreement. At the time of the settlement date (July 1), the value of the reference index is determined, and a payment is made between the two parties to settle the NDF. For example, if the peso value increases to $.0023 by July 1, the value of the position specified in the NDF will be $230,000 ($.0023 × 100 million pesos). Since the value of Jackson's NDF position is $30,000 higher than when the agreement was created, Jackson will receive a payment of $30,000 from the bank.

Recall that Jackson needs 100 million pesos to buy imports. Since the peso's spot rate rose from April 1 to July 1, Jackson will need to pay $30,000 more for the imports than if it had paid for them on April 1. At the same time, however, Jackson will have received a payment of $30,000 due to its NDF. Thus, the NDF hedged the exchange rate risk.

If the Chilean peso had depreciated to $.0018 instead of rising, Jackson's position in its NDF would have been valued at $180,000 (100 million pesos × $.0018) at the settlement date, which is $20,000 less than the value when the agreement was created. Therefore, Jackson would have owed the bank $20,000 at that time. However, the decline in the spot rate of the peso means that Jackson would pay $20,000 less for the imports than if it had paid for them on April 1. Thus, an offsetting effect would also occur in this example.

As these examples show, although an NDF does not involve delivery, it can effectively hedge future foreign currency payments that are anticipated by an MNC.

Since an NDF can specify that any payments between the two parties be in dollars or some other available currency, firms can even use NDFs to hedge existing positions of foreign currencies that are not convertible. Consider an MNC that expects to receive payment in a foreign currency that cannot be converted into dollars. Though the MNC may use the currency to make purchases in the local country of concern, it still may desire to hedge against a decline in the value of the currency over the period before it receives payment. It takes a sell position in an NDF and uses the closing exchange rate of that currency as of the settlement date as the reference index. If the currency depreciates against the dollar over time, the firm will receive the difference between the dollar value of the position when the NDF contract was created and the dollar value of the position as of the settlement date. Thus, it will receive a payment in dollars from the NDF to offset any depreciation in the currency over the period of concern.

CURRENCY FUTURES MARKET

The *Futures* magazine website at www.futuresmag.com/library/contents.html covers various aspects of derivatives trading such as new products, strategies, and market analyses.

Currency futures contracts are contracts specifying a standard volume of a particular currency to be exchanged on a specific settlement date. They are commonly used by MNCs to hedge their foreign currency positions. In addition, they are traded by speculators who hope to capitalize on their expectations of exchange rate movements. A buyer of a currency futures contract locks in the exchange rate to be paid for a foreign currency at a future point in time. Alternatively, a seller of a currency futures contract locks in the exchange rate at which a foreign currency can be exchanged for the home currency. In the United States, currency futures contracts are purchased to lock in the amount of dollars needed to obtain a specified amount of a particular foreign currency; they are sold to lock in the amount of dollars to be received from selling a specified amount of a particular foreign currency.

Contract Specifications

Visit the Chicago Mercantile Exchange site at www.cme.com for a time series on financial futures and option prices. The site also allows for the generation of historic price charts.

Currency futures contracts are available for several widely traded currencies at the Chicago Mercantile Exchange (see Exhibit 5.2), and the contract for each currency specifies a standardized number of units. The trading of French franc and German mark futures has been phased out because those currencies have been replaced by the euro.

Firms or individuals can execute orders by calling brokerage firms that serve as intermediaries. The order to buy or sell a currency futures contract for a specific currency and a specific settlement date is communicated to the brokerage firm,

Exhibit 5.2

Currency Futures
Contracts Traded
on the Chicago
Mercantile
Exchange

Currency	Units per Contract
Australian dollar	100,000
Brazilian real	100,000
British pound	62,500
Canadian dollar	100,000
Euro	125,000
Japanese yen	12,500,000
Mexican peso	500,000
New Zealand dollar	100,000
Russian ruble	500,000
South African rand	500,000
Swiss franc	125,000

which in turn communicates the order to the CME. A floor broker at the CME who specializes in that type of currency futures contract stands at a specific spot at the trading pit where that type of contract is traded and attempts to find a counterparty to fulfill the order. For example, if an MNC wants to purchase a Mexican peso futures contract with a December settlement date, the floor broker assigned to execute this order will look for another floor broker who has an order to sell a Mexican peso futures contract with a December settlement date.

Currency futures contracts typically specify the third Wednesday in March, June, September, or December as the settlement date. There is also an over-the-counter currency futures market, where various financial intermediaries facilitate trading of currency futures contracts with specific settlement dates. Contracts have to be standardized, or floor trading would slow down considerably while brokers assessed contract specifications.

Trading on the floor (in the trading pits) of the CME takes place from 7:20 A.M. to 2:00 P.M. (Chicago time) Monday through Friday. After the CME's floor is closed, currency futures contracts can still be traded on the CME's automated order-entry and matching system called GLOBEX from 2:30 P.M. until 7:05 A.M. the following morning. The GLOBEX system matches buy and sell orders for each type of currency futures contract.

When participants in the currency futures market take a position, they need to establish an initial margin, which may represent as little as 10 percent of the contract value. The margin required is in the form of cash for small investors or Treasury securities for institutional investors. In addition to the initial margin, participants are subject to a variation margin, which is intended to accumulate a sufficient amount of funds to back the futures position. Full-service brokers typically charge a commission of about $50 for a round-trip trade in currency futures, while discount brokers charge a commission of about $20. Some Internet brokers also trade currency futures.

Example

Assume that as of February 10, a futures contract on 62,500 British pounds with a March settlement date is priced at $1.50 per pound. Consider the positions of two different firms on the opposite sides of this contract. The buyer of this currency futures contract will receive £62,500 on the March settlement date and will pay $93,750 for the pounds (computed as £62,500 × $1.50 per pound). The seller of this contract is obligated to sell £62,500 at a price of $1.50 per pound and therefore will receive $93,750 on the settlement date.

Comparison of Currency Futures and Forward Contracts

Currency futures contracts are similar to forward contracts in that they allow a customer to lock in the exchange rate at which a specific currency is purchased or sold for a specific date in the future. Nevertheless, there are some differences between currency futures contracts and forward contracts, which are summarized in Exhibit 5.3. Currency futures contracts are sold on an exchange, while each forward contract is negotiated between a firm and a commercial bank over a telecommunications network. Thus, forward contracts can be tailored to the needs of the firm, while the currency futures contracts are standardized.

Exhibit 5.3

Comparison of the Forward and Futures Markets

	Forward	Futures
Size of contract	Tailored to individual needs.	Standardized.
Delivery date	Tailored to individual needs.	Standardized.
Participants	Banks, brokers, and multinational companies. Public speculation not encouraged.	Banks, brokers, and multinational companies. Qualified public speculation encouraged.
Security deposit	None as such, but compensating bank balances or lines of credit required.	Small security deposit required.
Clearing operation	Handling contingent on individual banks and brokers. No separate clearinghouse function.	Handled by exchange clearinghouse. Daily settlements to the market price.
Marketplace	Over the telephone worldwide.	Central exchange floor with worldwide communications.
Regulation	Self-regulating.	Commodity Futures Trading Commission; National Futures Association.
Liquidation	Most settled by actual delivery. Some by offset, at a cost.	Most by offset, very few by delivery.
Transaction costs	Set by "spread" between bank's buy and sell prices.	Negotiated brokerage fees.

Source: Reprinted with the permission of the Chicago Mercantile Exchange.

Corporations that have established relationships with large banks tend to use forward contracts rather than futures contracts because forward contracts are tailored to the precise amount of currency to be purchased or sold in the future and the precise forward date that they prefer. Conversely, small firms and individuals who do not have established relationships with large banks or prefer to trade in smaller amounts tend to use currency futures contracts.

Pricing Currency Futures

The price of currency futures normally will be similar to the forward rate for a given currency and settlement date. This relationship is enforced by the potential arbitrage activity that would occur if there were significant discrepancies.

HTTP:// ONLINE APPLICATION **Futures Prices** Futures contract prices for major currencies are provided at http://www.cme.com/prices/daily_settlement.cfm.

Search for the currency of interest and click on <u>Futures</u>. The first column shows the settlement months. The next five columns show the open, high, low, close, and settle prices of futures contracts on the currency of concern. The seventh column shows the point change from the settle price on the previous day to the settle price today. The eighth column shows the trading volume, and the last three columns provide information over the previous trading day.

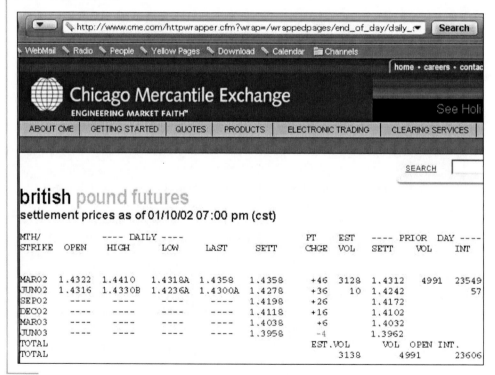

Example | Assume that the currency futures price on the pound is $1.50 and that forward contracts for a similar period are available for $1.48. Firms may attempt to purchase forward contracts and simultaneously sell currency futures contracts. If they can exactly match the settlement dates of the two contracts, they can generate guaranteed profits of $.02 per unit. These actions will place downward pressure on the currency futures price. The futures contract and forward contracts of a given currency and settlement date should have the same price, or else guaranteed profits are possible (assuming no transaction costs).

The currency futures price differs from the spot rate for the same reasons that a forward rate differs from the spot rate. If a currency's spot and futures prices were the same and the currency's interest rate were higher than the U.S. rate, U.S. speculators could lock in a higher return than they would receive on U.S. investments. They could purchase the foreign currency at the spot rate, invest the funds at the attractive interest rate, and simultaneously sell currency futures to lock in the exchange rate, at which they could reconvert the currency back to dollars. If the spot and futures rates were the same, there would be neither a gain nor a loss on the currency conversion. Thus, the higher foreign interest rate would provide a higher yield on this type of investment. The actions of investors to capitalize on this opportunity would place upward pressure on the spot rate and downward pressure on the currency futures price, causing the futures price to fall below the spot rate.

Credit Risk of Currency Futures Contracts

Each currency futures contract represents an agreement between a client and the exchange clearinghouse, even though the exchange has not taken a position. To illustrate, assume you call a broker to request the purchase of a British pound futures contract with a March settlement date. Meanwhile, another person unrelated to you calls a broker to request the sale of a similar futures contract. Neither party needs to worry about the credit risk of the counterparty. The exchange clearinghouse assures that you will receive whatever is owed to you as a result of your currency futures position.

To minimize its risk in such a guarantee, the CME imposes **margin requirements** to cover fluctuations in the value of a contract, meaning that the participants must make a deposit with their respective brokerage firms when they take a position. The initial margin requirement is typically between $1,000 and $2,000 per currency futures contract. However, if the value of the futures contract declines over time, the buyer may be asked to add to the initial margin. Margin requirements are not always required for forward contracts due to the more personal nature of the agreement; the bank knows the firm it is dealing with and may trust it to fulfill its obligation.

Speculation with Currency Futures

Currency futures contracts are sometimes purchased by speculators who are simply attempting to capitalize on their expectation of a currency's future movement.

Example   Assume that speculators expect the British pound to appreciate in the future. They can purchase a futures contract that will lock in the price at which they buy pounds at a specified settlement date. On the settlement date, they can purchase their pounds at the rate specified by the futures contract and then sell these pounds at the spot rate. If the spot rate has appreciated by this time in accordance with their expectations, they will profit from this strategy.

Currency futures are often sold by speculators who expect that the spot rate of a currency will be less than the rate at which they would be obligated to sell it.

Example   Assume that as of April 4, a futures contract specifying 500,000 Mexican pesos and a June settlement date is priced at $.09. On April 4, speculators who expect the peso will decline sell futures contracts on pesos. Assume that on June 17 (the settlement date), the spot rate of the peso is $.08. The transactions are shown in Exhibit 5.4 (the margin deposited by the speculators is not shown). The gain on the futures position is $5,000, which represents the difference between the amount received ($45,000) when selling the pesos in accordance with the futures contract versus the amount paid ($40,000) for those pesos in the spot market.

Of course, expectations are often incorrect. It is because of different expectations that some speculators decide to purchase futures contracts while other speculators decide to sell the same contracts at a given point in time.

How Firms Use Currency Futures

Corporations that have open positions in foreign currencies can consider purchasing or selling futures contracts to offset their positions.

Purchasing Futures to Hedge Payables. The purchase of futures contracts locks in the price at which a firm can purchase a currency.

Exhibit 5.4
Source of Gains from Buying Currency Futures

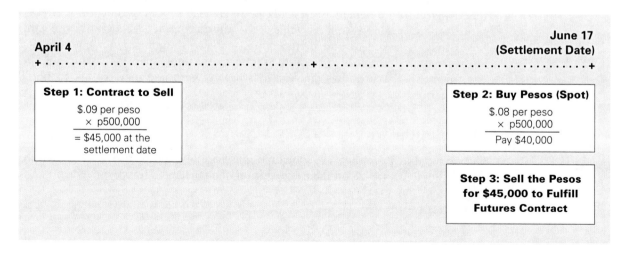

Example   Teton Co. orders Canadian goods and upon delivery will need to send C$500,000 to the Canadian exporter. Thus, Teton purchases Canadian dollar futures contracts today, thereby locking in the price to be paid for Canadian dollars at a future settlement date. By holding futures contracts, Teton does not have to worry about changes in the spot rate of the Canadian dollar over time.

Purchasing Futures to Hedge Receivables. The sale of futures contracts locks in the price at which a firm can sell a currency.

Example   Veton Co. sells futures contracts when it plans to receive a currency from exporting that it will not need (it accepts a foreign currency when the importer prefers that type of payment). By selling a futures contract, Veton locks in the price at which it will be able to sell this currency as of the settlement date. Such an action can be appropriate if Veton expects the foreign currency to depreciate against Veton's home currency.

The use of futures contracts to cover, or **hedge**, a firm's currency positions is described more thoroughly in Chapter 11.

Closing Out a Futures Position

If a firm holding a currency futures contract decides before the settlement date that it no longer wants to maintain its position, it can close out the position by selling an identical futures contract. The gain or loss to the firm from its previous futures position is dependent on the price of purchasing futures versus selling futures.

The price of a futures contract changes over time in accordance with movements in the spot rate and also with changing expectations about the spot rate's value as of the settlement date.

If the spot rate of a currency increases substantially over a one-month period, the futures price will likely increase by about the same amount. In this case, the purchase and subsequent sale of a futures contract would be profitable. Conversely, a decline in the spot rate over time will correspond with a decline in the currency futures price, meaning that the purchase and subsequent sale of a futures contract would result in a loss. While the purchasers of the futures contract could decide not to close out their position under such conditions, the losses from that position could increase over time.

Example   On January 10, Tacoma Co. anticipates that it will need Australian dollars (A$) in March when it orders supplies from an Australian supplier. Consequently, Tacoma purchases a futures contract specifying A$100,000 and a March settlement date (which is March 19 for this contract). On January 10, the futures contract is priced at $.53 per A$. On February 15, Tacoma realizes that it will not need to order supplies because it has reduced its production levels. Therefore, it has no need for A$ in March. It sells a futures contract on A$ with the March settlement date to offset the contract it purchased in January. At this time, the futures contract is priced at $.50 per A$. On March 19 (the settlement date), Tacoma has offsetting positions in futures contracts. However, the price when the futures contract was purchased was higher than the price when an identical contract was sold, so Tacoma incurs a loss from its futures positions. Tacoma's transactions are summarized in Exhibit 5.5. Move from left to right along the time line to review the transactions. The margin deposited by the firm is not shown in this exhibit.

Exhibit 5.5
Closing Out a Futures Contract

January 10	February 15	March 19 (Settlement Date)
Step 1: Contract to Buy	**Step 2: Contract to Sell**	**Step 3: Settle Contracts**
$.53 per A$	$.50 per A$	−$53,000 (Contract 1)
× A$100,000	× A$100,000	+$50,000 (Contract 2)
= $53,000 at the settlement date	= $50,000 at the settlement date	= $3,000 loss

Sellers of futures contracts can close out their positions by purchasing currency futures contracts with similar settlement dates. Most currency futures contracts are closed out before the settlement date.

Transaction Costs of Currency Futures

Brokers that fulfill orders to buy or sell futures contracts charge a transaction or brokerage fee in the form of a bid/ask spread. That is, they buy a futures contract for one price (their "bid" price) and simultaneously sell the contract to someone else for a slightly higher price (their "ask" price). The difference between a bid and an ask price on a futures contract may be as little as $7.50. Yet, even this amount is larger in percentage terms than the transaction fees for forward contracts.

CURRENCY OPTIONS MARKET

In late 1982, exchanges in Amsterdam, Montreal, and Philadelphia allowed trading in standardized foreign currency options. Since that time, options have been offered on the Chicago Mercantile Exchange and the Chicago Board Options Exchange. A currency option is an alternative type of contract that can be purchased or sold by speculators and firms. Currency options are currently available for many currencies, including the British pound, Canadian dollar, Japanese yen, euro, Swiss franc, and Australian dollar.

The options exchanges in the United States are regulated by the Securities and Exchange Commission. Options can be purchased or sold through brokers for a commission. The commission per transaction is commonly $30 to $60 for a single currency option, but it can be much lower per contract when the transaction involves multiple contracts. Brokers require that a margin be maintained during the life of the contract. The margin is increased for clients whose option positions have deteriorated. This protects against possible losses if the clients do not fulfill their obligations.

In addition to the exchanges where currency options are available, there is an over-the-counter market where currency options are offered by commercial banks and brokerage firms. Unlike the currency options traded on an exchange, currency options are tailored to the specific needs of the firm. Since these options are not standardized, all the terms must be specified in the contracts. The number of units, desired strike price, and expiration date can be tailored to the specific needs of the client. The minimum size of currency options offered by financial institutions is normally about $5 million. Since these transactions are conducted with a specific financial institution rather than an exchange, there are no credit guarantees. Thus, the agreement made is only as safe as the parties involved. For this reason, financial institutions may require some collateral from individuals or firms desiring to purchase or sell currency options. Currency options are classified as either **calls** or **puts**, as discussed in the next section.

CURRENCY CALL OPTIONS

A **currency call option** grants the right to buy a specific currency at a designated price within a specific period of time. The price at which the owner is allowed to buy that currency is known as the **exercise price** or **strike price**, and there are monthly expiration dates for each option.

Call options are desirable when one wishes to lock in a maximum price to be paid for a currency in the future. If the spot rate of the currency rises above the strike price, owners of call options can "exercise" their options by purchasing the currency at the strike price, which will be cheaper than the prevailing spot rate. This strategy is somewhat similar to that used by purchasers of futures contracts, but the futures contracts require an obligation, which the currency option does not. The owner can choose to let the option expire on the expiration date without ever exercising it. Owners of expired call options will have lost the premium they initially paid, but that is the most they can lose.

Currency options quotations are summarized each day in *The Wall Street Journal* and other business newspapers. Although currency options typically expire near the middle of the specified month, some of them expire at the end of the specific month and are designated as EOM. Some options are listed as "European Style," which means that they can be exercised only upon expiration.

A currency call option is said to be *in the money* when the present exchange rate exceeds the strike price, *at the money* when the present exchange rate equals the strike price, and *out of the money* when the present exchange rate is less than the strike price. For a given currency and expiration date, an in-the-money call option will require a higher premium than options that are at the money or out of the money.

Factors Affecting Currency Call Option Premiums

http://
Visit www.ino.com for the latest information and prices of options and financial futures as well as the corresponding historic price charts.

Premiums of call options vary due to three main factors:

- *Level of existing spot price relative to strike price.* The higher the spot rate relative to the strike price, the higher the option price will be. This is due to the higher probability of buying the currency at a substantially lower rate than what you could sell it for. This relationship can be verified by comparing premiums of options for a specified currency and expiration date that have different strike prices.
- *Length of time before the expiration date.* It is generally expected that the spot rate has a greater chance of rising high above the strike price if it has a longer period of time to do so. A settlement date in June allows two additional months

beyond April for the spot rate to move above the strike price. This explains why June option prices exceed April option prices given a specific strike price. This relationship can be verified by comparing premiums of options for a specified currency and strike price that have different expiration dates.

■ *Potential variability of currency.* The greater the variability of the currency, the higher the probability that the spot rate will be above the strike price. Thus, more volatile currencies have higher call option prices. For example, the Canadian dollar is more stable than most other currencies. If all other factors are similar, Canadian call options should be less expensive than call options on other foreign currencies.

The potential currency variability can also vary over time for a particular currency. For example, at the beginning of the Asian crisis in 1997, the Asian countries experienced financial problems, and their currency values were subject to much more uncertainty. Consequently, the premium on over-the-counter options of Asian currencies such as the Thai baht, Indonesian rupiah, and Korean won increased. The higher premium was necessary to compensate those who were willing to sell options in these currencies, as the risk to sellers had increased because the currencies had become more volatile.

How Firms Use Currency Call Options

Corporations with open positions in foreign currencies can sometimes use currency call options to cover these positions.

Using Call Options to Hedge Payables. MNCs can purchase call options on a currency to hedge future payables.

Example

When Pike Co. of Seattle orders Australian goods, it makes a payment in Australian dollars to the Australian exporter upon delivery. An Australian dollar call option locks in a maximum rate at which Pike can exchange dollars for Australian dollars. This exchange of currencies at the specified strike price on the call option contract can be executed at any time before the expiration date. In essence, the call option contract specifies the maximum price that Pike must pay to obtain these Australian dollars. If the Australian dollar's value remains below the strike price, Pike can purchase Australian dollars at the prevailing spot rate when it needs to pay for its imports and simply let its call option expire.

Options may be more appropriate than futures or forward contracts for some situations. Intel Corp. uses options to hedge its order backlog in semiconductors. If an order is canceled, it has the flexibility to let the option contract expire. With a forward contract, it would be obligated to fulfill its obligation even though the order was canceled.

Using Call Options to Hedge Project Bidding. U.S.-based MNCs that bid for foreign projects may purchase call options to lock in the dollar cost of the potential expenses.

Example

Kelly Co. is an MNC based in Fort Lauderdale that has bid on a project sponsored by the Canadian government. If the bid is accepted, Kelly will need approximately C$500,000 to purchase Canadian materials and services. However, Kelly will not know whether the bid is accepted until three months from now. In this case, it can purchase call options with a three-month expiration date. Ten call option contracts will cover the entire amount of potential exposure. If the bid is accepted, Kelly can use the options to purchase the Canadian dollars needed. If the Canadian dollar has depreciated over time, Kelly will likely let the options expire.

Assume that the exercise price on Canadian dollars is $.70 and the call option premium is $.02 per unit. Kelly will pay $1,000 per option (since there are 50,000 units per Canadian dollar option), or $10,000 for the 10 option contracts. With the options, the maximum amount necessary to purchase the C$500,000 is $350,000 (computed as $.70 per Canadian dollar × C$500,000). The amount of U.S. dollars needed would be less if the Canadian dollar's spot rate were below the exercise price at the time the Canadian dollars were purchased.

Even if Kelly's bid is rejected, it will exercise the currency call option if the Canadian dollar's spot rate exceeds the exercise price before the option expires and sell the Canadian dollars in the spot market. Any gain from exercising may partially or even fully offset the premium paid for the options.

This type of example is quite common. When Air Products and Chemicals was hired to perform some projects, it needed capital equipment from Germany. The purchase of equipment was contingent on whether the firm was hired for the projects. The company used options to hedge this possible future purchase.

Using Call Options to Hedge Target Bidding. Firms can also use call options to hedge a possible acquisition.

Example

Morrison Co. is attempting to acquire a French firm and has submitted its bid in euros. Morrison has purchased call options on the euro because it will need euros to purchase the French company's stock. The call options hedge the U.S. firm against the potential appreciation of the euro by the time the acquisition occurs. If the acquisition does not occur and the spot rate of the euro remains below the strike price, Morrison Co. can let the call options expire. If the acquisition does not occur and the spot rate of the euro exceeds the strike price, Morrison Co. can exercise the options and sell the euros in the spot market. Alternatively, Morrison Co. can sell the call options it is holding. Either of these actions may offset part or all of the premium paid for the options.

Speculating with Currency Call Options

Because this text focuses on multinational financial management, the corporate use of currency options is more important than the speculative use. The use of options for hedging is discussed in detail in Chapter 11. Speculative trading is discussed here in order to provide more of a background on the currency options market.

Individuals may speculate in the currency options market based on their expectation of the future movements in a particular currency. Speculators who expect that a foreign currency will appreciate can purchase call options on that currency. Once the spot rate of that currency appreciates, the speculators can exercise their options by purchasing that currency at the strike price and then sell the currency at the prevailing spot rate.

Just as with currency futures, for every buyer of a currency call option there must be a seller. A seller (sometimes called a **writer**) of a call option is obligated to sell a specified currency at a specified price (the strike price) up to a specified expiration date. Speculators may sometimes want to sell a currency call option on a currency that they expect will depreciate in the future. The only way a currency call option will be exercised is if the spot rate is higher than the strike price. Thus, a seller of a currency call option will receive the premium when the option is purchased and can keep the entire amount if the option is not exercised. When it appears that an option will be exercised, there will still be sellers of options. However, such options will sell for high premiums due to the high risk that the option will be exercised at some point.

The net profit to a speculator who purchases call options on a currency is based on a comparison of the selling price of the currency versus the exercise price paid for the currency and the premium paid for the call option.

Example | Jim is a speculator who buys a British pound call option with a strike price of $1.40 and a December settlement date. The current spot price as of that date is about $1.39. Jim pays a premium of $.012 per unit for the call option. Assume there are no brokerage fees. Just before the expiration date, the spot rate of the British pound reaches $1.41. At this time, Jim exercises the call option and then immediately sells the pounds at the spot rate to a bank. To determine Jim's profit or loss, first compute his revenues from selling the currency. Then, subtract from this amount the purchase price of pounds when exercising the option, and also subtract the purchase price of the option. The computations follow. Assume one option contract specifies 31,250 units.

	Per Unit	Per Contract
Selling price of £	$1.41	$44,063 ($1.41 × 31,250 units)
− Purchase price of £	−1.40	−43,750 ($1.40 × 31,250 units)
− Premium paid for option	−.012	−375 ($.012 × 31,250 units)
= Net profit	− $.002	−$62 (−$.002 × 31,250 units)

Assume that Linda was the seller of the call option purchased by Jim. Also assume that Linda would purchase British pounds only if and when the option was exercised, at which time she must provide the pounds at the exercise price of $1.40. Using the information in this example, Linda's net profit from selling the call option is derived here:

	Per Unit	Per Contract
Selling price of £	$1.40	$43,750 ($1.40 × 31,250 units)
− Purchase price of £	−1.41	−44,063 ($1.41 × 31,250 units)
+ Premium received	+.012	+375 ($.012 × 31,250 units)
= Net profit	$.002	$62 ($.002 × 31,250 units)

As a second example, assume the following information:

- Call option premium on Canadian dollars (C$) = $.01 per unit.
- Strike price = $.70.
- One option contract represents C$50,000.

A speculator who had purchased this call option decided to exercise the option shortly before the expiration date, when the spot rate reached $.74. The speculator immediately sold the Canadian dollars in the spot market. Given this information, the net profit to the speculator is computed as follows:

	Per Unit	Per Contract
Selling price of C$	$.74	$37,000 ($.74 × 50,000 units)
− Purchase price of C$	−.70	−35,000 ($.70 × 50,000 units)
− Premium paid for option	−.01	−500 ($.01 × 50,000 units)
= Net profit	$.03	$1,500 ($.03 × 50,000 units)

If the seller of the call option did not obtain Canadian dollars until the option was about to be exercised, the net profit to the seller of the call option was

	Per Unit	Per Contract
Selling price of C$	$.70	$35,000 ($.70 × 50,000 units)
− Purchase price of C$	− .74	−37,000 ($.74 × 50,000 units)
+ Premium received	+ .01	+500 ($.01 × 50,000 units)
= Net profit	− $.03	−$1,500 (−$.03 × 50,000 units)

When brokerage fees are ignored, the currency call purchaser's gain will be the seller's loss. The currency call purchaser's expenses represent the seller's revenues, and the purchaser's revenues represent the seller's expenses. Yet, because it is possible for purchasers and sellers of options to close out their positions, the relationship described here will not hold unless both parties begin and close out their positions at the same time.

An owner of a currency option may simply sell the option to someone else before the expiration date rather than exercising it. The owner can still earn profits, since the option premium changes over time, reflecting the probability that the option can be exercised and the potential profit from exercising it.

Break-Even Point from Speculation. The purchaser of a call option will break even if the revenue from selling the currency equals the payments for (1) the currency (at the strike price) and (2) the option premium. In other words, regardless of the number of units in a contract, a purchaser will break even if the spot rate at which the currency is sold is equal to the strike price plus the option premium.

Example | Based on the information in the previous example, the strike price is $.70 and the option premium is $.01. Thus, for the purchaser to break even, the spot rate existing at the time the call is exercised must be $.71 ($.70 + $.01). Of course, speculators will not purchase a call option if they think the spot rate will only reach the break-even point and not go higher before the expiration date. Nevertheless, the computation of the break-even point is useful for a speculator deciding whether to purchase a currency call option.

CURRENCY PUT OPTIONS

The owner of a **currency put option** receives the right to sell a currency at a specified price (the strike price) within a specified period of time. As with currency call options, the owner of a put option is not obligated to exercise the option. Therefore, the maximum potential loss to the owner of the put option is the price (or premium) paid for the option contract.

A currency put option is said to be *in the money* when the present exchange rate is less than the strike price, *at the money* when the present exchange rate equals the strike price, and *out of the money* when the present exchange rate exceeds the strike price. For a given currency and expiration date, an in-the-money put option will require a higher premium than options that are at the money or out of the money.

Factors Affecting Currency Put Option Premiums

The three main factors influencing call option premiums also influence put option premiums. First, the spot rate of a currency relative to the strike price is important. The lower the spot rate relative to the strike price, the more valuable the put option will be, because there is a higher probability that the option will be exercised. Recall that just the opposite relationship held for call options. A second factor influencing put option premium is the length of time until the expiration date. As with currency call options, the longer the time to expiration, the greater the put option premium will be. A longer period creates a higher probability that the currency will move into a range where it will be feasible to exercise the option (whether it is a put or a call). These relationships can be verified by assessing quotations of put option premiums for a specified currency. A third factor that influences the put option premium is the variability of a currency. As with currency call options, the greater the variability, the greater the put option premium will be, again reflecting a higher probability that the option may be exercised.

Hedging with Currency Put Options

Corporations with open positions in foreign currencies can use currency put options in some cases to cover these positions.

Example Assume Duluth Co. has exported products to Canada and invoiced the products in Canadian dollars (at the request of the Canadian importers). Duluth is concerned that the Canadian dollars it is receiving will depreciate over time. To insulate itself against possible depreciation, Duluth purchases Canadian dollar put options, which entitle it to sell Canadian dollars at the specified strike price. In essence, Duluth locks in the minimum rate at which it can exchange Canadian dollars for U.S. dollars over a specified period of time. If the Canadian dollar appreciate over this time period, Duluth can let the put options expire and sell the Canadian dollars it receives at the prevailing spot rate.

Speculating with Currency Put Options

Individuals may speculate with currency put options based on their expectations of the future movements in a particular currency. For example, speculators who expect that the British pound will depreciate can purchase British pound put options, which will entitle them to sell British pounds at a specified strike price. If the pound's spot rate depreciates as expected, the speculators can then purchase pounds at the spot rate and exercise their put options by selling these pounds at the strike price.

Speculators can also attempt to profit from selling currency put options. The seller of such options is obligated to purchase the specified currency at the strike price from the owner who exercises the put option. Speculators who believe the currency will appreciate (or at least will not depreciate) may sell a currency put option. If the currency appreciates over the entire period, the option will not be exercised.

Managing for Value: Cisco's Dilemma When Hedging with Put Options

When Cisco Systems' European subsidiaries remit funds to their U.S. parent, Cisco may consider purchasing put options to lock in the rate at which the euros will convert to dollars. The put options also offer the flexibility of letting the options expire if the prevailing exchange rate of the euro is higher than the options' exercise price. Several put options are available to Cisco and other MNCs that wish to hedge their currency positions. At a given point in time, some put options are deep out of the money, meaning that the prevailing exchange rate is high above the exercise price. These options are cheaper (have a lower premium), as they are unlikely to be exercised because their exercise price is too low. At the same time, other put options have an exercise price that is currently below the prevailing exercise price and are therefore more likely to be exercised. Consequently, these options are more expensive.

Cisco must weigh the tradeoff when using put options to hedge. It can create a hedge that is cheap, but the options can be exercised only if the currency's spot rate declines substantially. Alternatively, Cisco can create a hedge that can be exercised at a more favorable exchange rate, but it must pay a higher premium for the options. If Cisco's goal in using put options is simply to prevent a major loss if the currency weakens substantially, it may be willing to use an inexpensive put option (low exercise price, low premium). However, if its goal is to ensure that the currency can be exchanged at a more favorable exchange rate, Cisco will use a more expensive put option (high exercise price, high premium). By selecting currency options with an exercise price and premium that fits their objectives, Cisco and other MNCs can increase their value.

This is an ideal situation for put option sellers, since they keep the premiums received when selling the options and bear no cost.

The net profit to a speculator from purchasing put options on a currency is based on a comparison of the exercise price at which the currency can be sold versus the purchase price of the currency and the premium paid for the put option.

Example

A put option contract on British pounds specifies the following information:

- Put option premium on British pound (£) = $.04 per unit.
- Strike price = $1.40.
- One option contract represents £31,250.

A speculator who had purchased this put option decided to exercise the option shortly before the expiration date, when the spot rate of the pound was $1.30. The speculator purchased the pounds in the spot market at that time. Given this information, the net profit to the purchaser of the put option is calculated as follows:

	Per Unit	Per Contract
Selling price of £	$1.40	$43,750 ($1.40 × 31,250 units)
– Purchase price of £	–1.30	–40,625 ($1.30 × 31,250 units)
– Premium paid for option	–.04	–1,250 ($.04 × 31,250 units)
= Net profit	$.06	$ 1,875 ($.06 × 31,250 units)

Assuming that the seller of the put option sold the pounds received immediately after the option was exercised, the net profit to the seller of the put option is calculated as follows:

	Per Unit	Per Contract
Selling price of £	$1.30	$40,625 ($1.30 × 31,250 units)
– Purchase price of £	–1.40	–43,750 ($1.40 × 31,250 units)
+ Premium received	+.04	+1,250 ($.04 × 31,250 units)
= Net profit	–$.06	–$1,875 (–$.06 × 31,250 units)

The seller of the put options could simply refrain from selling the pounds (after being forced to buy them at $1.40 per pound) until the spot rate of the pound rose. However, there is no guarantee that the pound will reverse its direction and begin to appreciate. The seller's net loss could potentially be greater if the pound's spot rate continued to fall, unless the pounds were sold immediately.

Whatever an owner of a put option gains, the seller loses, and vice versa. This relationship would hold if brokerage costs did not exist and if the buyer and seller of options entered and closed their positions at the same time. Brokerage fees for currency options exist, however, and are very similar in magnitude to those of currency futures contracts.

Speculating with Combined Put and Call Options. For volatile currencies, one possible speculative strategy is to create a **straddle**, which uses both a put option and a call option at the same exercise price. This may seem unusual because owning a put option is appropriate for expectations that the currency will depreciate while owning a call option is appropriate for expectations that the currency will appreciate. However, it is possible that the currency will depreciate (at which time the put is exercised) and then reverse direction and appreciate (allowing for profits when exercising the call).

HTTP:// ONLINE APPLICATION **Options Prices** Options contract prices for major currencies are provided at http://www.cme.com/prices/daily_settlement.cfm.

Search for the currency of interest and click on <u>Options</u>. A heading that begins in the first column states the expiration date of the option. Below that heading in the first column are various exercise (strike) premiums that exist for a currency option with that expiration date. The next five columns show the open, high, low, close, and settle prices for options contracts on the currency of concern. The seventh column shows the point change from the settle price on the previous day to the settle price today. The eighth column shows the trading volume, while the last three columns provide information over the previous trading day.

Also, a speculator might anticipate that a currency will be substantially affected by current economic events yet be uncertain of the exact way it will be affected. By purchasing a put option and a call option, the speculator will gain if the currency moves substantially in either direction. Although two options are purchased and only one is exercised, the gains could more than offset the costs.

CONTINGENCY GRAPHS FOR CURRENCY OPTIONS

A contingency graph for currency options illustrates the potential gain or loss for various exchange rate scenarios.

Contingency Graph for a Purchaser of a Call Option

A contingency graph for a purchaser of a call option compares the price paid for the call option to potential payoffs to be received with various exchange rate scenarios.

Example

A British pound call option is available, with a strike price of $1.50 and a call premium of $.02. The speculator plans to exercise the option on the expiration date (if appropriate at that time) and to then immediately sell the pounds received in the spot market. Under these conditions, a **contingency graph** can be created to measure the profit or loss per unit (see the upper-left graph in Exhibit 5.6). Notice that if the future spot rate is $1.50 or less, the net gain per unit is –$.02 (ignoring transaction costs). This represents the loss of the premium per unit paid for the option, as the option would not be exercised. At $1.51, $.01 per unit would be earned by exercising the option, but considering the $.02 premium paid, the net gain would be –$.01.

At $1.52, $.02 per unit would be earned by exercising the option, which would offset the $.02 premium per unit. This is the break-even point. At any rate above this point, the gain from exercising the option would more than offset the premium, resulting in a positive net gain. The maximum loss to the speculator in this example is the premium paid for the option.

Contingency Graph for a Seller of a Call Option

A contingency graph compares the premium received from selling a call option to the potential payoffs made to the buyer of the call option for various exchange rate scenarios.

Example

The lower-left graph shown in Exhibit 5.6 provides a contingency graph for a speculator who sold the call option described in the previous example. It assumes that this seller would purchase the pounds in the spot market just as the option was exercised (ignoring transaction costs). At future spot rates of less than $1.50, the net gain to the seller would be the premium of $.02 per unit, as the option would not have been exercised. If the future spot rate is $1.51, the seller would lose $.01 per unit on the option transaction (paying $1.51 for pounds in the spot market and selling pounds for $1.50 to fulfill the exercise request). Yet, this loss would be more than offset by the premium of $.02 per unit received, resulting in a net gain of $.01 per unit.

The break-even point is at $1.52, and the net gain to the seller of a call option becomes negative at all future spot rates higher than that point. Notice that the contingency graphs for the buyer and seller of this call option are mirror images of one another.

Exhibit 5.6
Contingency Graphs for Currency Options

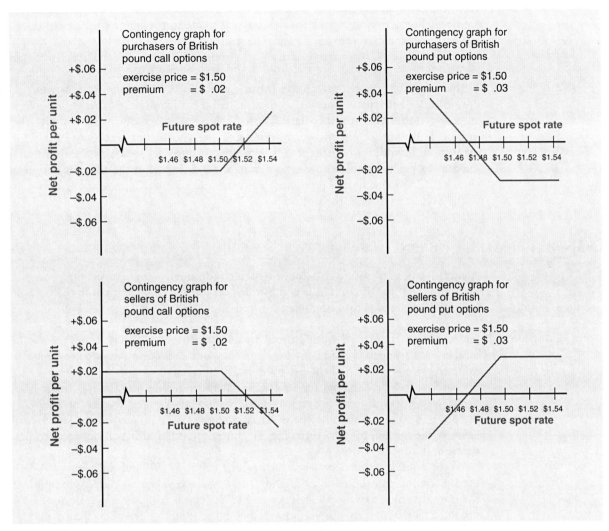

Contingency Graph for a Buyer of a Put Option

A contingency graph for a buyer of a put option compares the premium paid for the put option to potential payoffs received for various exchange rate scenarios.

Example | The upper-right graph in Exhibit 5.6 shows the net gains to a buyer of a British pound put option with an exercise price of $1.50 and a premium of $.03 per unit. If the future spot rate is above $1.50, the option will not be exercised. At a future spot rate of $1.48, the put option will be exercised. However, considering the premium of $.03 per unit, there will be a net loss of $.01 per unit. The break-even point in this example is $1.47, since this is the future spot rate that will generate $.03 per unit from exercising the option to offset the $.03 premium. At any future spot rates of less than $1.47, the buyer of the put option will earn a positive net gain.

Contingency Graph for a Seller of a Put Option

A contingency graph for the seller of this put option compares the premium received from selling the option to the possible payoffs made to the buyer of the put option for various exchange rate scenarios. The graph is shown in the lower-right graph in Exhibit 5.6. It is the mirror image of the contingency graph for the buyer of a put option.

For various reasons, an option buyer's net gain will not always represent an option seller's net loss. The buyer may be using call options to hedge a foreign currency, rather than to speculate. In this case, the buyer does not evaluate the options position taken by measuring a net gain or loss; the option is used simply for protection. In addition, sellers of call options on a currency in which they currently maintain a position will not need to purchase the currency at the time an option is exercised. They can simply liquidate their position in order to provide the currency to the person exercising the option.

CONDITIONAL CURRENCY OPTIONS

A currency option can be structured with a conditional premium, meaning that the premium paid for the option is conditioned on the actual movement in the currency's value over the period of concern.

Example | Jensen Co., a U.S.-based MNC, needs to sell British pounds that it will receive in 60 days. It can negotiate a traditional currency put option on pounds in which the exercise price is $1.70 and the premium is $.02 per unit.

Alternatively, it can negotiate a conditional currency option with a commercial bank, which has an exercise price of $1.70 and a so-called trigger of $1.74. If the pound's value falls below the exercise price by the expiration date, Jensen will exercise the option, thereby receiving $1.70 per pound, and it will not have to pay a premium for the option.

If the pound's value is between the exercise price ($1.70) and the trigger ($1.74), the option will not be exercised, and Jensen will not need to pay a premium. If the pound's value exceeds the trigger of $1.74, Jensen will pay a premium of $.04 per unit. Notice that this premium may be higher than the premium that would be paid for a basic put option. Jensen may not mind this outcome, however, because it will be receiving a high dollar amount from converting its pound receivables in the spot market.

Jensen must determine whether the potential advantage of the conditional option (avoiding the payment of a premium under some conditions) outweighs the potential disadvantage (paying a higher premium than the premium for a traditional put option on British pounds).

The potential advantage and disadvantage are illustrated in Exhibit 5.7. At exchange rates less than or equal to the trigger level ($1.74), the conditional option results in a larger payment to Jensen by the amount of the premium that would have been paid for the basic option. Conversely, at exchange rates above the trigger level, the conditional option results in a lower payment to Jensen, as its premium of $.04 exceeds the premium of $.02 per unit paid on a basic option.

Exhibit 5.7

Comparison of
Conditional and
Basic Currency
Options

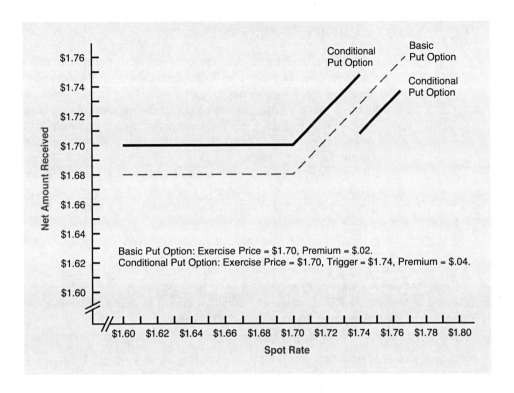

The choice of a basic option versus a conditional option is dependent on expectations of the currency's exchange rate over the period of concern. A firm that was very confident that the pound's value would not exceed $1.74 in the previous example would prefer the conditional currency option.

Conditional currency options are also available for U.S. firms that need to purchase a foreign currency in the near future.

Example

A conditional call option on pounds may specify an exercise price of $1.70 and a trigger of $1.67. If the pound's value remains above the trigger of the call option, a premium will not have to be paid for the call option. However, if the pound's value falls below the trigger, a large premium (such as $.04 per unit) will be required. Some conditional options require a premium if the trigger is reached anytime up until the expiration date; others only require a premium if the exchange rate is beyond the trigger as of the expiration date.

Firms also use various combinations of currency options. For example, a firm may purchase a currency call option to hedge payables and finance the purchase of the call option by selling a put option on the same currency.

EUROPEAN CURRENCY OPTIONS

The discussion of currency options up to this point has dealt solely with American-style options. European-style currency options are also available for speculating and hedging in the foreign exchange market. They are similar to American-style options except that they must be exercised on the expiration date if they are to be exercised at all. Consequently, they do not offer as much flexibility; however, this is not relevant to some situations. For example, firms that purchase options to hedge future foreign currency cash flows will probably not desire to exercise their options before the expiration date anyway. If European-style options are available for the same expiration date as American-style options and can be purchased for a slightly lower premium, some corporations may prefer them for hedging.

Financial Markets Perspective

Efficiency of Currency Futures and Options

Speculators may believe that speculation in the currency futures and/or currency options markets can consistently generate abnormally large profits. This would not be possible if these markets were "efficient." In an efficient foreign exchange market, any available contracts would be priced to reflect all relevant information; thus, speculators would not be able to exploit existing information to earn abnormally large profits. Any valuable information would already have caused an adjustment in "sell" or "buy" requests, thereby forcing the contract price to reflect that information.

To assess the efficiency of the currency futures market, Thomas[1] developed a trading strategy based on interest rate differentials. This strategy generated a return of about 10.3 percent above the three-month Treasury bill rate on average, suggesting that currency futures are not priced efficiently (if the excess return is assumed to more than compensate for the risk involved).

The efficiency of the currency options market has also been tested. Research by Bodurtha and Courtadon[2] and by Tucker[3] found that when accounting for transaction costs, the currency options market is efficient. This suggests that currency option prices generally reflect all available information.

A speculative strategy requires the speculator to incur risk, since the actual results from investing funds in a speculative instrument are uncertain. Although a high return (profit as a percentage of the amount invested) can sometimes be achieved by speculating in foreign exchange markets, considerable risk is involved. "Abnormal" profits from a speculative strategy would reflect above-average returns *after* accounting for the risk involved. Individuals who speculate in futures and options markets must believe that they know something the market doesn't. In contrast, corporations may use these markets even if they believe in market efficiency. Their positions in currency futures and currency options are usually intended to reduce exposure to fluctuating exchange rates rather than to earn a speculative profit.

[1]Lee R. Thomas III, "A Winning Strategy for Currency-Futures Speculation," *Journal of Portfolio Management* (Fall 1985), pp. 65–69.

[2]James Bodurtha and Georges Courtadon, "Tests of an American Option Pricing Model on the Foreign Currency Options Market," *Journal of Financial Quantitative Analysis* (June 1987), pp. 153–168.

[3]Alan L. Tucker, "Empirical Tests of the Efficiency of the Currency Option Market," *Journal of Financial Research* (Winter 1985), pp. 275–285.

Use of Currency Derivative Contracts

Nike Problem

Like many MNCs, Nike uses currency derivative contracts to hedge some future transactions that are denominated in foreign currencies. Nike's policy is to use currency derivatives for hedging and not for speculating in the foreign exchange market. In general, Nike uses forward contracts to hedge payables or receivables and purchases currency options to hedge some anticipated foreign transactions that are not confirmed commitments. Its hedged transactions are typically denominated in European currencies, the Japanese yen, or the Canadian dollar. Nike mentions in a recent annual report that the estimated fair market values of its currency derivative positions will fluctuate over time and that these values should not be assessed by themselves but in relation to the market values of the transactions that are to be hedged. For example, consider a purchase of yen future contracts by Nike that is intended to hedge future yen payments. The market value of a purchased futures position in yen could lose market value due to a decline in the yen's value. Yet, the dollar market value of the hedged position would decline by a similar amount. Thus, a reduction in the value of any currency derivative positions does not necessarily create more risk because there may be an offsetting effect when the currency derivatives are used to hedge future transactions.

Discussion: Explain why Nike may use forward contracts to hedge committed transactions and use currency options to hedge contracts that are anticipated but not committed. Why might forward contracts be advantageous for committed transactions and currency options be advantageous for anticipated transactions?

HOW THE USE OF CURRENCY FUTURES
AND OPTIONS AFFECTS AN MNC's VALUE

The use of currency futures and options can affect an MNC's value, as shown in Exhibit 5.8. Currency futures can prevent the possibility that the value of foreign currency receipts will decline because of depreciation of that currency against the dollar. In this way, the use of currency futures can increase the expected dollar cash flows to be received from converting foreign currency cash flows to dollars. Yet, by using currency futures, the MNC forgoes the possibility of a favorable effect resulting from the appreciation of foreign currencies that will be converted into dollars.

Currency options can offer the same type of protection against depreciation of currencies that will be received but allow more flexibility to capitalize on the potential appreciation of the foreign currency before conversion into dollars. However, premiums are paid for the options, reducing the MNC's cash flows.

Exhibit 5.8
Impact of Currency Derivatives on an MNC's Value

Currency Futures
Currency Options

$$V = \sum_{t=1}^{n} \left\{ \frac{\sum_{j=1}^{m} \left[E(CF_{j,t}) \times E(ER_{j,t}) \right]}{(1+k)^t} \right\}$$

V = value of the U.S.-based MNC
$E(CF_{j,t})$ = expected cash flows denominated in currency j to be received by the U.S. parent in period t
$E(ER_{j,t})$ = expected exchange rate at which currency j can be converted to dollars at the end of period t
k = weighted average cost of capital of the U.S. parent company
m = number of currencies
n = number of periods

SUMMARY

- A forward contract specifies a standard volume of a particular currency to be exchanged on a particular date. Such a contract can be purchased by a firm to hedge payables or sold by a firm to hedge receivables.

- A currency futures contract can be purchased by speculators who expect the currency to appreciate. Conversely, it can be sold by speculators who expect that currency to depreciate. If the currency depreciates, the value of the futures contract declines, allowing those speculators to benefit when they close out their positions.

- Futures contracts on a particular currency can be purchased by corporations that have payables in that currency and wish to hedge against the possible appreciation of that currency. Conversely, these contracts can be sold by corporations that have receivables in that currency and wish to hedge against the possible depreciation of that currency.

- Currency options are classified as call options or put options. Call options allow the right to purchase a specified currency at a specified exchange rate by a specified expiration date. Put options allow the right to sell a specified currency at a specified exchange rate by a specified expiration date.

- Call options on a specific currency can be purchased by speculators who expect that currency to appreciate. Put options on a specific currency can be purchased by speculators who expect that currency to depreciate.

- Currency call options are commonly purchased by corporations that have payables in a currency that is expected to appreciate. Currency put options are commonly purchased by corporations that have receivables in a currency that is expected to depreciate.

SELF TEST

(Answers are provided in Appendix A at the back of the text.)

1. A call option on Canadian dollars with a strike price of $.60 is purchased by a speculator for a premium of $.06 per unit. Assume there are 50,000 units in this option contract. If the Canadian dollar's spot rate is $.65 at the time the option is exercised, what is the net profit per unit to the speculator? What is the net profit for one contract? What would the spot rate need to be at the time the option is exercised for the speculator to break even? What is the net profit per unit to the seller of this option?

2. A put option on Australian dollars with a strike price of $.80 is purchased by a speculator for a premium of $.02. If the Australian dollar's spot rate is $.74 on the expiration date, should the speculator exercise the option on this date or let the option expire? What is the net profit per unit to the speculator? What is the net profit per unit to the seller of this put option?

3. Longer-term currency options are becoming more popular for hedging exchange rate risk. Why do you think some firms decide to hedge by using other techniques instead of purchasing long-term currency options?

QUESTIONS AND APPLICATIONS

1. Compare and contrast forward and futures contracts.

2. How can currency futures be used by corporations? How can currency futures be used by speculators?

3. What is a currency call option? What is a currency put option?

4. Compute the forward discount or premium for the Mexican peso whose 90-day forward rate is $.098 and spot rate is $.10. State whether your answer is a discount or premium.

5. How can a forward contract backfire?

6. When would a U.S. firm consider purchasing a call option in euros for hedging?

7. When would a U.S. firm consider purchasing a put option in euros for hedging?

8. When should a speculator purchase a call option on Australian dollars?

9. When should a speculator purchase a put option on Australian dollars?

10. List the factors that affect currency call option premiums, and briefly explain the relationship that exists for each. Do you think an at-the-money call option in euros has a higher or lower premium than an at-the-money call option in British pounds (assuming the expiration date and the total dollar value represented by each option are the same for both options)?

11. List the factors that affect currency put option premiums, and briefly explain the relationship that exists for each.

12. Randy Rudecki purchased a call option on British pounds for $.02 per unit. The strike price was $1.45, and the spot rate at the time the pound option was exercised was $1.46. Assume there are 31,250 units in a British pound option. What was Randy's net profit on this option?

13. Alice Duever purchased a put option on British pounds for $.04 per unit. The strike price was $1.80, and the spot rate at the time the pound option was exercised was $1.59. Assume there are 31,250 units in a British pound option. What was Alice's net profit on the option?

14. Mike Suerth sold a call option on Canadian dollars for $.01 per unit. The strike price was $.76, and the spot rate at the time the

option was exercised was $.82. Assume Mike did not obtain Canadian dollars until the option was exercised. Also assume there are 50,000 units in a Canadian dollar option. What was Mike's net profit on the call option?

15. Brian Tull sold a put option on Canadian dollars for $.03 per unit. The strike price was $.75, and the spot rate at the time the option was exercised was $.72. Assume Brian immediately sold off the Canadian dollars received when the option was exercised. Also assume there are 50,000 units in a Canadian dollar option. What was Brian's net profit on the put option?

16. What are the advantages and disadvantages to a U.S. corporation that uses currency options on euros rather than a forward contract on euros to hedge against its exposure in euros?

17. Assume that the euro's spot rate has moved in cycles over time. How might you try to use futures contracts on pounds to capitalize on this tendency? How could you determine whether such a strategy would have been profitable in previous periods?

18. Assume that the transactions listed in Column 1 of the following table are anticipated by U.S. firms that have no other foreign transactions. Place an "X" in the table wherever you see possible ways to hedge each of the transactions.

	Forward Contract		Futures Contract		Options Contract	
	Forward Purchase	Forward Sale	Buy Futures	Sell Futures	Purchase a Call	Purchase a Put
a. Georgetown Co. plans to purchase Japanese goods denominated in yen.						
b. Harvard, Inc., will sell goods to Japan, denominated in yen.						
c. Yale Corp. has a subsidiary in Australia that will be remitting funds to the U.S. parent.						
d. Brown, Inc., needs to pay off existing loans that are denominated in Canadian dollars.						
e. Princeton Co. may purchase a company in Japan in the near future (but the deal may not go through).						

19. Assume that on November 1 the spot rate of the British pound was $1.58 and the price on a December futures contract was $1.59. Assume that the pound depreciated during November so that by November 30 it was worth $1.51.

   a. What do you think happened to the futures price over the month of November? Why?

   b. If you had known that this would occur, would you have purchased or sold a December futures contract in pounds on November 1? Explain.

20. Assume that a March futures contract on Mexican pesos was available in January for $.09 per unit. Also assume that forward contracts were available for the same settlement date at a price of $.092 per peso. How could speculators capitalize on this situation, assuming zero transaction costs? How would such speculative activity affect the difference between the forward contract price and the futures price?

21. LSU Corp. purchased Canadian dollar call options for speculative purposes. If these options are exercised, LSU will immediately

sell the Canadian dollars in the spot market. Each option was purchased for a premium of $.03 per unit, with an exercise price of $.75. LSU plans to wait until the expiration date before deciding whether to exercise the options. Of course, LSU will exercise the options at that time only if it is feasible to do so. In the following table, fill in the net profit (or loss) per unit to LSU Corp. based on the listed possible spot rates of the Canadian dollar on the expiration date.

Possible Spot Rate of Canadian Dollar on Expiration Date	Net Profit (Loss) per Unit to LSU Corp.
$.76	
.78	
.80	
.82	
.85	
.87	

22. Auburn Co. has purchased Canadian dollar put options for speculative purposes. Each option was purchased for a premium of $.02 per unit, with an exercise price of $.86 per unit. Auburn Co. will purchase the Canadian dollars just before it exercises the options (if it is feasible to exercise the options). It plans to wait until the expiration date before deciding whether to exercise the options. In the following table, fill in the net profit (or loss) per unit to Auburn Co. based on the listed possible spot rates of the Canadian dollar on the expiration date.

Possible Spot Rate of Canadian Dollar on Expiration Date	Net Profit (Loss) per Unit to Auburn Co.
$.76	
.79	
.84	
.87	
.89	
.91	

23. Bama Corp. has sold British pound call options for speculative purposes. The option premium was $.06 per unit, and the exercise price was $1.58. Bama will purchase the pounds on the day the options are exercised (if the options are exercised) in order to fulfill its obligation. In the following table, fill in the net profit (or loss) to Bama Corp. if the listed spot rate exists at the time the purchaser of the call options considers exercising them.

Possible Spot Rate at the Time Purchaser of Call Options Considers Exercising Them	Net Profit (Loss) per Unit to Bama Corp.
$1.53	
1.55	
1.57	
1.60	
1.62	
1.64	
1.68	

24. Bulldog, Inc., has sold Australian dollar put options at a premium of $.01 per unit and an exercise price of $.76 per unit. It has forecasted the Australian dollar's lowest level over the period of concern as shown in the following table. Determine the net profit (or loss) per unit to Bulldog, Inc., if each level occurs and the put options are exercised at that time.

Possible Value of Australian Dollar	Net Profit (Loss) to Bulldog, Inc. If Value Occurs
$.72	
.73	
.74	
.75	
.76	

25. A U.S. professional football team plans to play an exhibition game in the United Kingdom next year. Assume that all expenses will be paid by the British government and that the team will receive a check for 1 million pounds. The team anticipates that the pound will depreciate substantially by the scheduled date of the game. In addition,

the National Football League must approve the deal, and approval (or disapproval) will not occur for three months. How can the team hedge its position? What is there to lose by waiting three months to see if the exhibition game is approved before hedging?

26. Currency futures markets are commonly used as a means of capitalizing on shifts in currency values because the value of a futures contract tends to move in line with the change in the corresponding currency value. Recently, many currencies appreciated against the dollar. Most speculators anticipated that these currencies would continue to strengthen and took large buy positions in currency futures. However, the Fed intervened in the foreign exchange market by selling foreign currencies in exchange for dollars, causing an abrupt decline in the values of foreign currencies (as the dollar strengthened). Participants that had purchased currency futures contracts incurred large losses. One floor broker responded to the effects of the Fed's intervention by immediately selling 300 futures contracts on British pounds (with a value of about $30 million). Such actions caused even more panic on the futures market.

    a. Explain why the central bank's intervention caused such panic for currency futures traders with buy positions.

    b. Explain why the floor broker's willingness to sell 300 pound futures contracts at the going market rate aroused such concern. What might this action signal to other brokers?

    c. Explain why speculators with short (sell) positions could benefit as a result of the central bank's intervention.

    d. Some traders with buy positions may have responded immediately to the central bank's intervention by selling futures contracts. Why would some speculators with buy positions leave their positions unchanged or even increase their positions by purchasing more futures contracts in response to the central bank's intervention?

Impact of 9/11/01

27. The terrorist attack on the United States on September 11, 2001, caused a decline in U.S. stock prices and caused an expectation of lower U.S. interest rates. If you were a speculator of euro futures contracts, would you buy or sell euro futures based on this information? Explain.

Internet Application

28. The website of the Chicago Mercantile Exchange provides information about currency futures and options. Its address is: **www.cme.com**

    a. Use this website to review the prevailing prices of currency futures contracts. Do today's futures prices (for contracts with the closest settlement date) generally reflect an increase or decrease from the day before? Is there any news today that might explain the change in the futures prices?

    b. Does it appear that futures prices among currencies (for the closest settlement date) are changing in the same direction? Explain.

    c. If you purchase a British pound futures contract with the closest settlement date, what is the futures price? Given that a contract is based on 62,500 pounds, what is the dollar amount you will need at the settlement date to fulfill the contract?

Running Your Own MNC

 This exercise can be found on the Student CD-ROM.

Blades, Inc. Case

Use of Currency Derivative Instruments

Blades, Inc., needs to order supplies two months ahead of the delivery date. It is considering an order from a Japanese supplier that requires a payment of 12.5 million yen payable as of the delivery date. Blades has two choices:

- Purchase two call options contracts (since each option contract represents 6,250,000 yen).
- Purchase one futures contract (which represents 12.5 million yen).

The futures price on yen has historically exhibited a slight discount from the existing spot rate. However, the firm would like to use currency options to hedge payables in Japanese yen for transactions two months in advance. Blades would prefer hedging its yen payable position because it is uncomfortable leaving the position open given the historical volatility of the yen. Nevertheless, the firm would be willing to remain unhedged if the yen becomes more stable someday.

Ben Holt, Blades' chief financial officer (CFO), prefers the flexibility that options offer over forward contracts or futures contracts because he can let the options expire if the yen depreciates. He would like to use an exercise price that is about 5 percent above the existing spot rate to ensure that Blades will have to pay no more than 5 percent above the existing spot rate for a transaction two months beyond its order date, as long as the option premium is no more than 1.6 percent of the price it would have to pay per unit when exercising the option.

In general, options on the yen have required a premium of about 1.5 percent of the total transaction amount that would be paid if the option is exercised. For example, recently the yen spot rate was $0.0072, and the firm purchased a call option with an exercise price of $0.00756, which is 5 percent above the existing spot rate. The premium for this option was $0.0001134, which is 1.5 percent of the price to be paid per yen if the option is exercised.

A recent event caused more uncertainty about the yen's future value, although it did not affect the spot rate or the forward or futures rate of the yen.

Specifically, the yen's spot rate was still $0.0072, but the option premium for a call option with an exercise price of $0.00756 was now $0.0001512. An alternative call option is available with an expiration date of two months from now; it has a premium of $0.0001134 (which is the size of the premium that would have existed for the option desired before the event), but it is for a call option with an exercise price of $.00792.

The table below summarizes the option and futures information available to Blades:

	Before Event	After Event	
Spot rate	$.0072	$.0072	$.0072
Option Information:			
Exercise price ($)	$.00756	$.00756	$.00792
Exercise price (% above spot)	5%	5%	10%
Option premium per yen ($)	$.0001134	$.0001512	$.0001134
Option premium (% of exercise price)	1.5%	2.0%	1.5%
Total premium ($)	$1,417.50	$1,890.00	$1,417.50
Amount paid for yen if option is exercised (not including premium)	$94,500	$94,500	$99,000
Futures Contract Information:			
Futures price	$.006912	$.006912	

As an analyst for Blades, you have been asked to offer insight on how to hedge. Use a spreadsheet to support your analysis of questions 4 and 6.

1. If Blades uses call options to hedge its yen payables, should it use the call option with the exercise price of $0.00756 or the call option with the exercise price of $0.00792? Describe the tradeoff.

2. Should Blades allow its yen position to be unhedged? Describe the tradeoff.

3. Assume there are speculators who attempt to capitalize on their expectation of the yen's movement over the two months between the order and delivery dates by either buying or selling yen futures now and buying or selling yen at the future spot rate. Given this information, what is the expectation on the order date of the yen spot rate by the delivery date? (Your answer should consist of one number.)

4. Assume that the firm shares the market consensus of the future yen spot rate. Given this expectation and given that the firm makes a decision (i.e., option, futures contract, remain unhedged) purely on a cost basis, what would be its optimal choice?

5. Will the choice you made as to the optimal hedging strategy in question 4 definitely turn out to be the lowest-cost alternative in terms of actual costs incurred? Why or why not?

6. Now assume that you have determined that the historical standard deviation of the yen is about $0.0005. Based on your assessment, you believe it is highly unlikely that the future spot rate will be more than two standard deviations above the expected spot rate by the delivery date. Also assume that the futures price remains at its current level of $0.006912. Based on this expectation of the future spot rate, what is the optimal hedge for the firm?

Small Business Dilemma

Use of Currency Futures and Options by the Sports Exports Company

The Sports Exports Company receives pounds each month as payment for the footballs that it exports. It anticipates that the pound will depreciate over time against the dollar.

1. How can the Sports Exports Company use currency futures contracts to hedge against exchange rate risk? Are there any limitations of using currency futures contracts that would prevent the Sports Exports Company from locking in a specific exchange rate at which it can sell all the pounds it expects to receive in each of the upcoming months?

2. How can the Sports Exports Company use currency options to hedge against exchange rate risk? Are there any limitations of using currency options contracts that would prevent the Sports Exports Company from locking in a specific exchange rate at which it can sell all the pounds it expects to receive in each of the upcoming months?

3. Jim Logan, owner of the Sports Exports Company, is concerned that the pound may depreciate substantially over the next month, but he also believes that the pound could appreciate substantially if specific situations occur. Should Jim use currency futures or currency options to hedge the exchange rate risk? Is there any disadvantage of selecting this method for hedging?

CURRENCY OPTION PRICING

The premiums paid for currency options depend on various factors that must be monitored when anticipating future movements in currency option premiums. Since participants in the currency options market typically take positions based on their expectations of how the premiums will change over time, they can benefit from understanding how options are priced.

BOUNDARY CONDITIONS

The first step in pricing currency options is to recognize boundary conditions that force the option premium to be within lower and upper bounds.

Lower Bounds

The call option premium (C) has a lower bound of at least zero or the spread between the underlying spot exchange rate (S) and the exercise price (X), whichever is greater, as shown below:

$$C = MAX(0, S - X)$$

This floor is enforced by arbitrage restrictions. For example, assume that the premium on a British pound call option is $.01, while the spot rate of the pound is $1.62 and the exercise price is $1.60. In this example, the spread ($S - X$) exceeds the call premium, which would allow for arbitrage. One could purchase the call option for $.01 per unit, immediately exercise the option at $1.60 per pound, and then sell the pounds in the spot market for $1.62 per unit. This would generate an immediate profit of $.01 per unit. Arbitrage would continue until the market forces realigned the spread ($S - X$) to be less than or equal to the call premium.

The put option premium (P) has a lower bound of zero or the spread between the exercise price (X) and the underlying spot exchange rate (S), whichever is greater, as shown below:

$$P = MAX(0, X - S)$$

This floor is also enforced by arbitrage restrictions. For example, assume that the premium on a British pound put option is $.02, while the spot rate of the pound is $1.60 and the exercise price is $1.63. One could purchase the pound put option for $.02 per unit, purchase pounds in the spot market at $1.60, and immediately exercise the option by selling the pounds at $1.63 per unit. This would generate an immediate profit of $.01 per unit. Arbitrage would continue until the market forces realigned the spread $(X - S)$ to be less than or equal to the put premium.

Upper Bounds

The upper bound for a call option premium is equal to the spot exchange rate (S), as shown below:

$$C = S$$

If the call option premium ever exceeds the spot exchange rate, one could engage in arbitrage by selling call options for a higher price per unit than the cost of purchasing the underlying currency. Even if those call options are exercised, one could provide the currency that was purchased earlier (the call option was covered). The arbitrage profit in this example is the difference between the amount received when selling the premium and the cost of purchasing the currency in the spot market. Arbitrage would occur until the call option's premium was less than or equal to the spot rate.

The upper bound for a put option is equal to the option's exercise price (X), as shown below:

$$P = X$$

If the put option premium ever exceeds the exercise price, one could engage in arbitrage by selling put options. Even if the put options are exercised, the proceeds received from selling the put options exceed the price paid (which is the exercise price) at the time of exercise.

Given these boundaries that are enforced by arbitrage, option premiums lie within these boundaries.

APPLICATION OF PRICING MODELS

Although boundary conditions can be used to determine the possible range for a currency option's premium, they do not precisely indicate the appropriate premium for the option. However, pricing models have been developed to price currency options. Based on information about an option (such as the exercise price and time to maturity) and about the currency (such as its spot rate, standard deviation, and interest rate), pricing models can derive the premium on a currency option. The currency option pricing model of Biger and Hull[1] is

$$C = e^{-r^*T} S \cdot N(d_1) - e^{-rT}X \cdot N(d_1 - \sigma\sqrt{T})$$

where

$d_1 = \{[\ln(S/X) + (r - r^* + (\sigma^2/2))T]/\sigma\sqrt{T}\}$
C = price of the currency call option
S = underlying spot exchange rate

X = exercise price

r = U.S. riskless rate of interest

r^* = foreign riskless rate of interest

σ = instantaneous standard deviation of the return on a holding of foreign currency

T = option's time maturity expressed as a fraction of a year

$N(\cdot)$ = standard normal cumulative distribution function

This equation is based on the stock option pricing model (OPM) when allowing for continuous dividends. Since the interest gained on holding a foreign security (r^*) is equivalent to a continuously paid dividend on a stock share, this version of the OPM holds completely. The key transformation in adapting the stock OPM to value currency options is the substitution of exchange rates for stock prices. Thus, the percentage change of exchange rates is assumed to follow a diffusion process with constant mean and variance.

Bodurtha and Courtadon[2] have tested the predictive ability of the currency option of the pricing model. They computed pricing errors from the model using 3,326 call options. The model's average percentage pricing error for call options was −6.90 percent, which is smaller than the corresponding error reported for the dividend-adjusted Black-Scholes stock OPM. Hence, the currency option pricing model has been more accurate than the counterpart stock OPM.

The model developed by Biger and Hull is sometimes referred to as the European model because it does not account for early exercise. European currency options do not allow for early exercise (before the expiration date), while American currency options do allow for early exercise. The extra flexibility of American currency options may justify a higher premium on American currency options than on European currency options with similar characteristics. However, there is not a closed-form model for pricing American currency options. Although various techniques are used to price American currency options, the European model is commonly applied to price American currency options because the European model can be just as accurate.

Bodurtha and Courtadon found that the application of an American currency options pricing model does not improve predictive accuracy. Their average percentage pricing error was −7.07 percent for all sample call options when using the American model.

Given all other parameters, the currency option pricing model can be used to impute the standard deviation σ. This implied parameter represents the option's market assessment of currency volatility over the life of the option.

[1]Nahum Biger and John Hull, "The Valuation of Currency Options," *Financial Management* (Spring 1983), 24–28.

[2]James Bodurtha and Georges Courtadon, "Tests of an American Option Pricing Model on the Foreign Currency Options Market," *Journal of Financial Quantitative Analysis* (June 1987): 153–168.

Pricing Currency Put Options According to Put-Call Parity

Given the premium of a European call option (called C), the premium for a European put option (called P) on the same currency and same exercise price (X) can be derived from put-call parity, as shown below:

$$P = C + Xe^{-rT} - Se^{-r^*T}$$

where

r = U.S. riskless rate of interest
r^* = foreign riskless rate of interest
T = option's time to maturity expressed as a fraction of the year

If the actual put option premium is less than what is suggested by the put-call parity equation above, arbitrage can be conducted. Specifically, one could (1) buy the put option, (2) sell the call option, and (3) buy the underlying currency. The purchases are financed with the proceeds from selling the call option and from borrowing at the rate r. Meanwhile, the foreign currency that was purchased can be deposited to earn the foreign rate r^*. Regardless of the scenario for the path of the currency's exchange rate movement over the life of the option, the arbitrage will result in a profit. First, if the exchange rate is equal to the exercise price such that each option expires worthless, the foreign currency can be converted in the spot market to dollars, and this amount will exceed the amount required to repay the loan. Second, if the foreign currency appreciates and therefore exceeds the exercise price, there will be a loss from the call option being exercised. Although the put option will expire, the foreign currency will be converted in the spot market to dollars, and this amount will exceed the amount required to repay the loan and the amount of the loss on the call option. Third, if the foreign currency depreciates and therefore is below the exercise price, the amount received from exercising the put option plus the amount received from converting the foreign currency to dollars will exceed the amount required to repay the loan. Since the arbitrage generates a profit under any exchange rate scenario, it will force an adjustment in the option premiums so that put-call parity is no longer violated.

If the actual put option premium is more than what is suggested by put-call parity, arbitrage would again be possible. The arbitrage strategy would be the reverse of that used when the actual put option premium was less than what is suggested by put-call parity (as just described). The arbitrage would force an adjustment in option premiums so that put-call parity is no longer violated. The arbitrage that can be applied when there is a violation of put-call parity on American currency options differs slightly from the arbitrage applicable to European currency options. Nevertheless, the concept still holds that the premium of a currency put option can be determined according to the premium of a call option on the same currency and the same exercise price.

The International Financial Environment

Mesa Co. specializes in the production of small fancy picture frames, which are exported from the United States to the United Kingdom. Mesa invoices the exports in pounds and converts the pounds to dollars when they are received. The British demand for these frames is positively related to economic conditions in the United Kingdom. Assume that British inflation and interest rates are similar to the rates in the United States. Mesa believes that the U.S. balance of trade deficit from trade between the United States and the United Kingdom will adjust to changing prices between the two countries, while capital flows will adjust to interest rate differentials. Mesa believes that the value of the pound is very sensitive to changing international flows and is moderately sensitive to changing international trade flows. Mesa is considering the following information:

- The U.K. inflation rate is expected to decline, while the U.S. inflation rate is expected to rise.
- British interest rates are expected to decline, while U.S. interest rates are expected to increase.

Questions

1. Explain how the international trade flows should initially adjust in response to the changes in inflation (holding exchange rates constant). Explain how the international capital flows should adjust in response to the changes in interest rates (holding exchange rates constant).
2. Using the information provided, will Mesa expect the pound to appreciate or depreciate in the future? Explain.
3. Mesa believes international capital flows shift in response to changing interest rate differentials. Is there any reason why the changing interest rate differentials in this example will not necessarily cause international capital flows to change significantly? Explain.
4. Based on your answer to question 2, how would Mesa's cash flows be affected by the expected exchange rate movements? Explain.
5. Based on your answer to question 4, should Mesa consider hedging its exchange rate risk? If so, explain how it could hedge using forward contracts, futures contracts, and currency options.

5

MANAGING ECONOMIC EXPOSURE AND TRANSLATION EXPOSURE

As the previous chapter described, MNCs can manage the exposure of their international transactions to exchange rate movements (referred to as transaction exposure) in various ways. Nevertheless, cash flows of MNCs may still be sensitive to exchange rate movements (economic exposure) even if anticipated international transactions are hedged. Furthermore, the consolidated financial statements of MNCs may still be exposed to exchange rate movements (translation exposure). By managing economic exposure and translation exposure, financial managers may increase the value of their MNCs.

The specific objectives of this chapter are to
- Explain how an MNC's economic exposure can be hedged.
- Explain how an MNC's translation exposure can be hedged.

In general, it is more difficult to effectively hedge economic or translation exposure than to hedge transaction exposure, for reasons explained in this chapter.

ECONOMIC EXPOSURE

From a U.S. firm's perspective, transaction exposure represents only the exchange rate risk when converting net foreign cash inflows to U.S. dollars or when purchasing foreign currencies to send payments. Economic exposure represents any impact of exchange rate fluctuations on a firm's future cash flows. Corporate cash flows can be affected by exchange rate movements in ways not directly associated with foreign transactions. Thus, firms cannot focus just on hedging their foreign currency payables or receivables but must also attempt to determine how all their cash flows will be affected by possible exchange rate movements.

Financial Markets Perspective

How Financial Markets Affected Laker Airlines

A firm's economic exposure is determined by its use of the debt markets, as well as by foreign exchange market conditions. Consider the case of Laker Airways, a British airline that generated much of its revenue in British pounds. A large proportion of its expenses (such as fuel, oil, and debt payments), however, were denominated in dollars. As the dollar strengthened in the foreign exchange market in 1981, Laker needed larger amounts in pounds to cover its dollar-denominated expenses.

In January 1981, Laker borrowed $131 million in the financial markets from a group of U.S. and European banks. The debt was denominated in U.S. dollars and therefore had to be repaid in U.S. dollars. Laker's decision to obtain dollar-denominated debt in the financial markets further increased its economic exposure. As the dollar continued to strengthen, the firm's revenues could not adequately cover its dollar-denominated expenses. Consequently, Laker Airways went bankrupt. It might have avoided bankruptcy if it had reduced its economic exposure, either by reducing its dollar-denominated expenses or by increasing its dollar-denominated revenue. Overall, Laker's performance was affected by conditions in the foreign exchange market along with its decision to borrow dollars in the debt markets.

Many MNCs are subject to a high degree of economic exposure and can experience financial problems if they do not manage it properly. The 1997–1998 Asian crisis illustrates the importance of managing economic exposure. MNCs from the United States and other countries that exported to Asia and invoiced the products in their own currencies were not subject to transaction exposure from this business. However, when the Asian currencies declined by as much as 80 percent over this period, Asian importers simply could not afford to purchase products denominated in other currencies. Thus, they discontinued orders for foreign imports unless the exporters were willing to accept the Asian currencies as payment. If those MNCs had denominated some of their expenses in the Asian currencies, they could have reduced their economic exposure.

MNCs typically recognize the importance of managing economic exposure. For example, in a recent annual report IBM identified "the continued adverse effects of a strong dollar on our non-U.S. results" as one of its primary challenges. The following comments reflect the situation for many MNCs.

The economic impact of currency exchange rates on us is complex because such changes are often linked to variability in real growth, inflation, interest rates, governmental actions, and other factors. These changes, if material, can cause us to adjust our financing and operating strategies.

PepsiCo

http://

See www.ibm.com as an example of an MNC's website. The websites of various MNCs make available financial statements such as annual reports that describe the use of financial derivatives to hedge interest rate risk and foreign exchange rate risk.

How to Assess Economic Exposure

An MNC must determine its economic exposure before it can manage its exposure. It can determine its exposure to each currency in terms of its cash inflows and cash outflows. The income statements for each subsidiary can be used to derive estimates.

Example	Recall from Chapter 10 that Madison, Inc., is subject to economic exposure. Madison can assess its economic exposure to exchange rate movements by determining the sensitivity of its expenses and revenue to various possible exchange rate scenarios. Exhibit 12.1. reproduces Madison's revenue and expense information from Exhibit 10.9 of Chapter 10. The U.S. revenues are assumed to be sensitive to different exchange rate scenarios because of the foreign competition. Regardless of the exchange rate scenario, Canadian sales are expected to be C$4 million, but the dollar amount received from these sales will depend on the scenario. The cost of goods sold attributable to U.S. orders is assumed to be $50 million and insensitive to exchange rate movements. The cost of goods sold attributable to Canadian orders is assumed to be C$200 million. The U.S. dollar amount of this cost varies with the exchange rate scenario. The gross profit shown in Exhibit 12.1 is determined by subtracting the total dollar value of cost of goods sold from the total dollar value of sales.

Operating expenses are separated into fixed and variable categories. The fixed expenses are $30 million per year, while the projected variable expenses are dictated by projected sales. The earnings before interest and taxes are determined by the total U.S. dollar amount of gross profit minus the total U.S. dollar amount of operating expenses. The interest owed to U.S. banks is insensitive to the exchange rate scenario, but the projected amount of dollars needed to pay interest on existing Canadian loans varies with the exchange rate scenario. Earnings before taxes are estimated by subtracting total interest expense from earnings before interest and taxes.

Exhibit 12.1

Original Impact of Exchange Rate Movements on Earnings: Madison, Inc. (in Millions)

	Exchange Rate Scenario					
	C$ = $.75		**C$ = $.80**		**C$ = $.85**	
Sales:						
(1) U.S.		$300.0		$304.00		$307.00
(2) Canadian	C$4 =	3.0	C$4 =	3.20	C$4 =	3.40
(3) Total		$303.0		$307.20		$310.40
Cost of goods sold:						
(4) U.S.		$ 50.0		$ 50.00		$ 50.00
(5) Canadian	C$200 =	150.0	C$200 =	160.00	C$200 =	170.00
(6) Total		$200.0		$210.00		$220.00
(7) Gross profit		$103.0		$ 97.20		$ 90.40
Operating expenses:						
(8) U.S.: Fixed		$ 30.0		$ 30.00		$ 30.00
(9) U.S.: Variable (10% of total sales)		30.3		30.72		31.04
(10) Total		$ 60.3		$ 60.72		$ 61.04
(11) EBIT		$ 42.7		$ 36.48		$ 29.36
Interest expense:						
(12) U.S.		$ 3.0		$ 3.00		$ 3.00
(13) Canadian	C$10 =	7.5	C$10 =	8.00	C$10 =	8.50
(14) Total		$ 10.5		$ 11.00		$ 11.50
(15) EBT		$ 32.2		$ 25.48		$ 17.86

Exhibit 12.1 enables Madison to assess how its income statement items will be affected by different exchange rate movements. A stronger Canadian dollar increases Madison's U.S. sales and the dollar revenue earned from Canadian sales. However, it also increases Madison's cost of materials purchased from Canada and the dollar amount needed to pay interest on loans from Canadian banks. The higher expenses more than offset the higher revenue in this scenario. Thus, the amount of Madison's earnings before taxes is inversely related to the strength of the Canadian dollar.

If the Canadian dollar strengthens consistently over the long run, Madison's cost of goods sold and interest expense likely will rise at a higher rate than its U.S. dollar revenue. Consequently, it may wish to institute some policies to ensure that movements of the Canadian dollar will have a more balanced impact on its revenue and expenses. At the current time, Madison's high exposure to exchange rate movements occurs because its expenses are more susceptible than its revenue to the changing value of the Canadian dollar.

Now that Madison has assessed its exposure, it recognizes that it can reduce this exposure by either increasing Canadian sales or reducing orders of Canadian materials. These actions would allow some offsetting of cash flows and therefore reduce its economic exposure.

How Restructuring Can Reduce Economic Exposure

MNCs may restructure their operations to reduce their economic exposure. The restructuring involves shifting the sources of costs or revenue to other locations in order to match cash inflows and outflows in foreign currencies.

Example   Reconsider the previous example of Madison, Inc., which has more cash outflows than cash inflows in Canadian dollars. Madison could create more balance by increasing Canadian sales. It believes that it can achieve Canadian sales of C$20 million if it spends $2 million more on advertising (which is part of its fixed operating expenses). The increased sales will also require an additional expenditure of $10 million on materials from U.S. suppliers. In addition, it plans to reduce its reliance on Canadian suppliers and increase its reliance on U.S. suppliers. Madison anticipates that this strategy will reduce the cost of goods sold attributable to Canadian suppliers by C$100 million and increase the cost of goods sold attributable to U.S. suppliers by $80 million (not including the $10 million increase resulting from increased sales to the Canadian market). Furthermore, it plans to borrow additional funds in the United States and retire some existing loans from Canadian banks. The result will be an additional interest expense of $4 million to U.S. banks and a reduction of C$5 million owed to Canadian banks. Exhibit 12.2 shows the anticipated impact of these strategies on Madison's income statement. For each of the three exchange rate scenarios, the initial projections are in the left column, and the revised projections (as a result of the proposed strategy) are in the right column.

Note first that the projected total sales increase in response to Madison's plan to penetrate the Canadian market. Second, the U.S. cost of goods sold is now $90 million higher as a result of the $10 million increase to accommodate increased Canadian sales and the $80 million increase due to the shift from Canadian suppliers to U.S. suppliers. The Canadian cost of goods sold decreases from C$200 million to C$100 million as a result of this shift. The revised fixed operating

Exhibit 12.2

Impact of Possible Exchange Rate Movements on Earnings under Two Alternative Operational Structures (in Millions)

	Exchange Rate Scenario C$ = $.75		Exchange Rate Scenario C$ = $.80		Exchange Rate Scenario C$ = $.85	
	Original Operational Structure	Proposed Operational Structure	Original Operational Structure	Proposed Operational Structure	Original Operational Structure	Proposed Operational Structure
Sales:						
U.S.	$300.0	$300.00	$304.00	$304	$307.00	$307.00
Canadian	C$4 = 3.0	C$20 = 15.00	C$4 = 3.20	C$20 = 16	C$4 = 3.40	C$20 = 17.00
Total	$303.0	$315.00	$307.20	$320	$310.40	$324.00
Cost of goods sold:						
U.S.	$ 50.0	$140.00	$ 50.00	$140	$ 50.00	$140.00
Canadian	C$200 = 150.0	C$100 = 75.00	C$200 = 160.00	C$100 = 80	C$200 = 170.00	C$100 = 85.00
Total	$200.0	$215.00	$210.00	$220	$220.00	$225.00
Gross profit	$103.0	$100.00	$ 97.20	$100	$ 90.40	$ 99.00
Operating expenses:						
U.S.: Fixed	$ 30.0	$ 32.00	$ 30.00	$ 32	$ 30.00	$ 32.00
U.S.: Variable (10% of total sales)	30.3	31.50	30.72	32	31.04	32.40
Total	$ 60.3	$ 63.50	$ 60.72	$ 64	$ 61.04	$ 64.40
Earnings before interest and taxes	$ 42.7	$ 36.50	$ 36.48	$ 36	$ 29.36	$ 34.60
Interest expense:						
U.S.	$ 3.0	$ 7.00	$ 3.00	$ 7	$ 3.00	$ 7.00
Canadian	C$10 = 7.5	C$5 = 3.75	C$10 = 8.00	C$5 = 4	C$10 = 8.50	C$5 = 4.25
Total	$ 10.5	$ 10.75	$ 11.00	$ 11	$ 11.50	$ 11.25
Earnings before taxes	$ 32.2	$ 25.75	$ 25.48	$ 25	$ 17.86	$ 23.35

expenses of $32 million include the increase in advertising expenses necessary to penetrate the Canadian market. The variable operating expenses are revised because of revised estimates for total sales. The interest expenses are revised because of the increased loans from the U.S. banks and reduced loans from Canadian banks.

If Madison increases its Canadian dollar inflows and reduces its Canadian dollar outflows as proposed, its revenue and expenses will be affected by movements of the Canadian dollar in a somewhat similar manner. Thus, its performance will be less susceptible to movements in the Canadian dollar. Exhibit 12.3 illustrates the sensitivity of Madison's earnings before taxes to the three exchange rate scenarios (derived from Exhibit 12.2). The reduced sensitivity of Madison's proposed restructured operations to exchange rate movements is obvious.

The way a firm restructures its operations to reduce economic exposure to exchange rate risk depends on the form of exposure. For Madison, Inc., future expenses are more sensitive than future revenue to the possible values of a foreign currency. Therefore, it can reduce its economic exposure by increasing the sensitivity of revenue and reducing the sensitivity of expenses to exchange rate movements. Firms that have a greater level of exchange-rate-sensitive revenue than expenses, however, would reduce their economic exposure by decreasing the level of exchange-rate-sensitive revenue or by increasing the level of exchange-rate-sensitive expenses.

It should be mentioned that some revenue or expenses may be more sensitive to exchange rates than others. Therefore, simply matching the level of exchange-rate-sensitive revenue to the level of exchange-rate-sensitive expenses may not completely insulate a firm from exchange rate risk. The firm can best evaluate a proposed restructuring of operations by forecasting various income statement items for various possible exchange rate scenarios (as shown in Exhibit 12.2) and then assessing the sensitivity of earnings to these different scenarios.

Expediting the Analysis with Computer Spreadsheets. Determining the sensitivity of earnings before taxes to alternative exchange rate scenarios can be expedited by using a computer to create a spreadsheet similar to Exhibit 12.2. The analyst then

Exhibit 12.3

Economic Exposure Based on the Original and Proposed Operating Structures

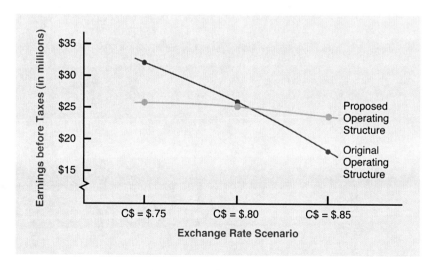

inputs forecasts for items such as sales, cost of goods sold, and fixed operating expenses. A formula is used to define the remaining items so that the computer can provide estimates after the forecasts are input. For example, the exchange rate forecast influences projections of (1) dollars received from Canadian sales, (2) cost of goods sold attributable to purchases of Canadian materials, and (3) amount in dollars needed to cover the Canadian interest payments. By revising the input to reflect various possible restructurings, the analyst can determine how each operational structure would affect the firm's economic exposure.

Example

Recall that Madison, Inc., assessed one alternative operational structure in which it increased Canadian sales by C$16 million, reduced its purchases of Canadian materials by C$100 million, and reduced its interest owed to Canadian banks by C$5 million. By using a computerized spreadsheet, Madison can easily assess the impact of alternative strategies, such as increasing Canadian sales by other amounts and/or reducing the Canadian expenses by other amounts. This provides Madison with more information about its economic exposure under various operational structures and enables it to devise the operational structure that will reduce its economic exposure to the degree desired.

Issues Involved in the Restructuring Decision

Restructuring operations to reduce economic exposure is a more complex task than hedging any single foreign currency transaction, which is why managing economic exposure is normally perceived to be more difficult than managing transaction exposure. By managing economic exposure, however, the firm is developing a long-term solution because once the restructuring is complete, it should reduce economic exposure over the long run. In contrast, the hedging of transaction exposure deals with each upcoming foreign currency transaction separately. Note, however, that it can be very costly to reverse or eliminate restructuring that was undertaken to reduce economic exposure. Therefore, MNCs must be very confident about the potential benefits before they decide to restructure their operations.

When deciding how to restructure operations to reduce economic exposure, one must address the following questions:

- Should the firm attempt to increase or reduce sales in new or existing foreign markets?
- Should the firm increase or reduce its dependency on foreign suppliers?
- Should the firm establish or eliminate production facilities in foreign markets?
- Should the firm increase or reduce its level of debt denominated in foreign currencies?

Each of these questions reflects a different part of the firm's income statement. The first relates to foreign cash inflows and the remaining ones to foreign cash outflows. Some of the more common solutions to balancing a foreign currency's inflows and outflows are summarized in Exhibit 12.4. Any restructuring of operations that can reduce the periodic difference between a foreign currency's inflows and outflows can reduce the firm's economic exposure to that currency's movements.

MNCs that have production and marketing facilities in various countries may be able reduce any adverse impact of economic exposure by shifting the allocation of their operations.

Exhibit 12.4
How to Restructure Operations to Balance the Impact of Currency Movements on Cash Inflows and Outflows

Type of Operation	Recommended Action When a Foreign Currency Has a Greater Impact on Cash Inflows	Recommended Action When a Foreign Currency Has a Greater Impact on Cash Outflows
Sales in foreign currency units	Reduce foreign sales	Increase foreign sales
Reliance on foreign supplies	Increase foreign supply orders	Reduce foreign supply orders
Proportion of debt structure representing foreign debt	Restructure debt to increase debt payments in foreign currency	Restructure debt to reduce debt payments in foreign currency

Example

Deland Co. produces products in the United States, Japan, and Mexico and sells these products (denominated in the currency where they are produced) to several countries. If the Japanese yen strengthens against many currencies, Deland may boost production in Mexico, expecting a decline in demand for the Japanese subsidiary's products. Deland may even transfer some machinery from Japan to Mexico and allocate more marketing funds to the Mexican subsidiary at the expense of the Japanese subsidiary. By following this strategy, however, Deland may have to forgo economies of scale that could be achieved if it concentrated production at one subsidiary while other subsidiaries focused on warehousing and distribution.

Nike Problem

Management of Economic Exposure

Nike's economic exposure comes in various forms. First, it is subject to transaction exposure because of its numerous purchase and sale transactions in foreign currencies, and this transaction exposure is a subset of economic exposure. Second, any remitted earnings from foreign subsidiaries to the U.S. parent also reflect transaction exposure and therefore reflect economic exposure. Third, a change in exchange rates that affects the demand for shoes at other athletic shoe companies (such as Adidas) can indirectly affect the demand for Nike's athletic shoes. Nike attempts to hedge some of its transaction exposure, but it cannot eliminate transaction exposure because it cannot predict all future transactions ahead of time. Moreover, even if it could eliminate its transaction exposure, it cannot perfectly hedge its remaining economic exposure; it is difficult to determine exactly how a specific exchange rate movement will affect the demand for a competitor's athletic shoes, and therefore how it will indirectly affect the demand for Nike's shoes.

Discussion: Given that Nike conducts much business in Japan, what are the expected results from a regression analysis of percentage changes in Nike's stock price against percentage changes in the value of the yen over several months (after controlling for U.S. stock market movements)? That is, should Nike's stock return be positively or inversely related to movements in the yen's value (measured in dollars)? Explain.

Managing for Value: How Auto Manufacturers Restructure to Reduce Exposure

To illustrate how the shifting of production can reduce economic exposure, consider the actual case of Honda, the Japanese automobile producer. By developing plants in the United States to produce automobiles for sale there, Honda not only circumvents possible trade restrictions but also reduces its economic exposure to exchange rate risk. When Honda exported automobiles to the United States, the U.S. demand for Hondas would decline if the yen appreciated because the dollar cost of the autos would increase. Thus, Honda's cash flows were adversely affected when a strong yen reduced demand for its exports. By producing automobiles in the United States and invoicing them in dollars, Honda has reduced the sensitivity of U.S. demand for its automobiles to the value of the Japanese yen. Nevertheless, Honda is not completely insulated from exchange rate risk for two reasons. First, the Honda plants in the United States purchase various components from Japan (invoiced in yen), so the dollar costs of these components rises when the yen appreciates. Second, earnings remitted from Honda's plants in the United States to its parent in Japan convert to a smaller number of yen when the yen appreciates. Nevertheless, by transferring production to the location where the product is sold, Honda has reduced its economic exposure.

In 2000, Honda's British subsidiary was adversely affected by its economic exposure. As a result of the decline of the euro against the British pound, consumers throughout Europe reduced their demand for vehicles produced at Honda's subsidiary in the United Kingdom and denominated in pounds. Consequently, Honda shifted some of its supply sources from the United Kingdom to European countries that have adopted the euro. This strategy is intended to reduce the impact of the euro on the performance of Honda's British subsidiary. When the euro declines, the decline in revenue (because of a reduced demand for Hondas produced in the United Kingdom) will be partially offset by a decline in the costs of obtaining supplies denominated in euros. If the euro's value increases, Honda's cost of euro-denominated supplies will rise, but the demand for its pound-denominated vehicles (and therefore its revenue) should also increase (see Exhibit 12.5). By shifting its operations, Honda hopes to reduce its exposure to exchange rate risk, thereby increasing its value.

As a result of Honda's decision to use suppliers in the euro-zone countries to hedge its exposure, it is buying less from suppliers in the United Kingdom. Thus, the U.K. auto suppliers have lost local business because of Honda's desire to offset its exposure. Ironically, these auto suppliers are subject to increased economic exposure as a result of Honda's decision to reduce its exposure.

Exhibit 12.5

Honda's Decision to Obtain Supplies outside the United Kingdom

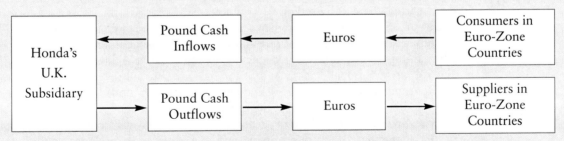

- Weak euro: Weak European demand for Honda's pound-denominated vehicles offset by reduced cost of euro-denominated supplies
- Strong euro: High cost of euro-denominated supplies offset by strong European demand for Honda's pound-denominated vehicles

MANAGING TRANSLATION EXPOSURE

Translation exposure occurs when an MNC translates each subsidiary's financial data to its home currency for consolidated financial statements. Because cash flow is not affected, some people argue that it is not necessary to hedge or even reduce translation exposure. Still, some firms are concerned with translation exposure because of its potential impact on reported consolidated earnings. A recent survey of firms by *Institutional Investor* magazine found that more than one-third of firms consider hedging translation exposure to be a major concern.

Some MNCs attempt to avoid translation exposure by matching foreign liabilities with foreign assets. For example, Philip Morris uses foreign financing to match its level of foreign assets.

http://

See www.futures.com/library/contents/html, the website of *Futures* magazine, for coverage of various aspects of derivatives trading such as new products, strategies, and market analyses.

Use of Forward Contracts to Hedge Translation Exposure

MNCs can use forward contracts or futures contracts to hedge translation exposure. Specifically, they can sell the currency forward that their foreign subsidiaries receive as earnings. In this way, they create a cash outflow in the currency to offset the earnings received in that currency.

Example

Columbus, Inc., is a U.S.-based MNC with just one subsidiary. As of the beginning of its fiscal year, the subsidiary, which is located in the the United Kingdom, forecasts that its annual earnings will be £20 million. The subsidiary plans to reinvest the entire amount of earnings within the United Kingdom and does not plan to remit any earnings back to the parent in the United States. While there is no foreseeable transaction exposure in the near future from the future earnings (since the pounds will remain in the United Kingdom), Columbus, Inc., is exposed to translation exposure.

The British earnings will be translated at the weighted average value of the pound over the course of the year. If the British pound is currently worth $1.50 and its value remains constant during the year, the forecasted translation of British earnings into U.S. dollars would be $30 million (computed as £20 million × $1.50 per pound).

The parent of Columbus, Inc., may be concerned that the translated value of the British earnings will be reduced if the pound's average value declines during the year. To hedge this translation exposure, it can implement a forward hedge on the expected earnings by selling £20 million one year forward. Assume the forward rate at that time is $1.50, the same as the spot rate. At the end of the year, the MNC can buy £20 million at the spot rate and fulfill its forward contract obligation to sell £20 million. If the pound depreciates during the fiscal year, then the MNC will be able to purchase pounds at the end of the fiscal year to fulfill the forward contract at a cheaper rate than it can sell them ($1.50 per pound). Thus, it will have generated income that can offset the translation loss.

The precise level of income generated by the forward contract will depend on the spot rate of the pound at the end of the fiscal year. Under conditions in which the pound depreciates, the translation loss will be somewhat offset by the gain generated from the forward contract position.

Managing for Value: Compaq's Decision to Hedge Translation Exposure

During 1999, Compaq Computer experienced weak sales and weak profit performance in Europe, which caused its stock price to decline substantially. Its sales in Europe increased in 2000, but Compaq was concerned about the possible decline of the euro against the dollar. A weak euro would cause Compaq's European profits to be translated at a relatively low exchange rate. From January through June 2000, the euro declined against the dollar, so Compaq's strong European sales were offset by the weak exchange rate at which the European sales and profits were translated. In the third quarter, its European sales surged, but the reported European sales and profits on financial statements did not appear as strong because of the euro's continued decline against the dollar. Compaq expected strong European sales in the fourth quarter, but was concerned that the decline in the euro could reduce its pretax profits by as much as $100 million. As Exhibit 12.6 shows, Compaq's share price was affected by the translation effect because some investors derive forecasts of a firm's future cash flows

from its recent earnings.

Compaq decided to hedge its translation exposure to the euro in the fourth quarter. Its hedging strategy was successful because the gains from taking short positions in the euro partially offset the adverse effects of the weak euro. Though Compaq realized that hedging could result in a loss if the euro strengthened, such effects would have been partially offset by the higher exchange rate at which its European profits would be translated on the consolidated financial statements.

While Compaq hedged its translation exposure, Hewlett-Packard (HP) did not. In November 2000, HP announced that its earnings were going to be worse than anticipated because of adverse currency effects and other reasons. Its stock price immediately declined by 11 percent in response to this announcement. If HP had hedged its translation exposure, it might have been able to prevent its earnings from declining and therefore might have insulated its value from exchange rate fluctuations.

Exhibit 12.6

How Translation Exposure Affects Compaq's Share Price

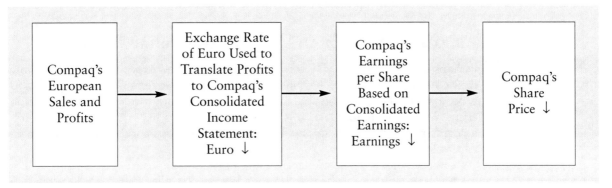

Limitations of Hedging Translation Exposure

There are four limitations in hedging translation exposure:

- *Inaccurate earnings forecasts.* A subsidiary's forecasted earnings for the end of the year are not guaranteed. In the previous example involving Columbus, Inc., British earnings were projected to be £20 million. If the actual earnings turned out to be much higher, the translation loss would likely exceed the gain generated from the forward contract strategy.
- *Inadequate forward contracts for some currencies.* A second limitation is that forward contracts are not available for all currencies. Thus, an MNC with subsidiaries in some smaller countries may not be able to obtain forward contracts for the currencies of concern.
- *Accounting distortions.* A third limitation is that the forward rate gain or loss reflects the difference between the forward rate and the future spot rate, whereas the translation gain or loss reflects the difference between the average exchange rate over the period of concern and the future spot rate. In addition, the translation losses are not tax deductible, whereas gains on forward contracts used to hedge translation exposure are taxed.
- *Increased transaction exposure.* The fourth and most critical limitation with a hedging strategy (forward or money market hedge) on translation exposure is that the MNC may be increasing its transaction exposure. For example, consider a situation in which the subsidiary's currency appreciates during the fiscal year, resulting in a translation gain. If the MNC enacts a hedge strategy at the start of the fiscal year, this strategy will generate a transaction loss that will somewhat offset the translation gain.

  Some MNCs may not be comfortable with this offsetting effect. The translation gain is simply a paper gain; that is, the reported dollar value of earnings is higher due to the subsidiary currency's appreciation. If the subsidiary reinvests the earnings, however, the parent does not receive any more income due to this appreciation. The MNC parent's net cash flow is not affected. Conversely, the loss resulting from a hedge strategy is a *real* loss; that is, the net cash flow to the parent will be reduced due to this loss. Thus, in this situation, the MNC reduces its translation exposure at the expense of increasing its transaction exposure.

Alternative Solution to Hedging Translation Exposure

Perhaps the best way for MNCs to deal with translation exposure is to clarify how their consolidated earnings have been affected by exchange rate movements. In this way, shareholders and potential investors will be more aware of the translation effect. An unusually low level of consolidated earnings may not discourage shareholders and potential investors if it is attributed to translation of subsidiary earnings at low exchange rates.

Some MNCs do not consider hedging translation exposure because they do not perceive this exposure to be relevant. For example, Phillips Petroleum has stated in its annual report that it does not hedge its translation exposure because translation effects do not influence its cash flows. Many other MNCs follow similar policies. PepsiCo's view on the hedging of translation exposure, as summarized in a recent annual report, is consistent with these comments:

We do not generally hedge translation risks because cash flows from international operations are generally reinvested locally. We do not enter into hedges to minimize volatility of reported earnings because we do not believe it is justified by the exposure or the cost.

How Managing Exposure Affects an MNC's Value

An MNC's management of economic exposure can affect its value, as shown in Exhibit 12.7. First, since transaction exposure is a subset of economic exposure, foreign subsidiaries that exchange their local currencies for others as part of their normal business must manage their transaction exposure, which affects their expected foreign currency cash flows. Second, the dollar cash flows that the U.S. parent expects to receive from the foreign subsidiaries are dependent on the expected exchange rates at which foreign currency cash flows are remitted from the foreign subsidiaries to the U.S. parent, which are determined by management of transaction exposure (whether to hedge those transactions).

An MNC's value is also affected by the way it manages other forms of economic exposure that are unrelated to transaction exposure. For example, foreign subsidiaries may attempt to restructure their operations such that their levels of foreign currency cash flows generated each period are less sensitive to exchange rate movements and therefore are more predictable. They may attempt to sell most of their products locally so that the demand for their products denominated in their local currency is less sensitive to exchange rate movements. However, managing economic exposure in this way may result in the loss of some additional business for the foreign subsidiaries, which will affect the expected foreign currency cash flows of the MNC.

Exhibit 12.7

Impact of Hedging Economic Exposure on an MNC's Value

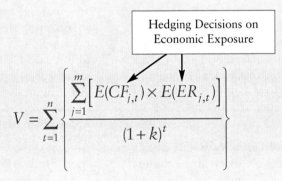

$$V = \sum_{t=1}^{n} \left\{ \frac{\sum_{j=1}^{m} \left[E(CF_{j,t}) \times E(ER_{j,t}) \right]}{(1+k)^t} \right\}$$

Hedging Decisions on Economic Exposure

V = value of the U.S.-based MNC
$E(CF_{j,t})$ = expected cash flows denominated in currency j to be received by the U.S. parent in period t
$E(ER_{j,t})$ = expected exchange rate at which currency j can be converted to dollars at the end of period t
k = weighted average cost of capital of the U.S. parent
m = number of currencies
n = number of periods

SUMMARY

- Economic exposure can be managed by balancing the sensitivity of revenue and expenses to exchange rate fluctuations. To accomplish this, however, the firm must first recognize how its revenue and expenses are affected by exchange rate fluctuations. For some firms, revenue is more susceptible. These firms are most concerned that their home currency will appreciate against foreign currencies, since the unfavorable effects on revenue will more than offset the favorable effects on expenses. Conversely, firms whose expenses are more sensitive to exchange rates than their revenue are most concerned that their home currency will depreciate against foreign currencies. When firms reduce their economic exposure, they reduce not only these unfavorable effects but also the favorable effects if the home currency value moves in the opposite direction.

- Translation exposure can be reduced by selling forward the foreign currency used to measure a subsidiary's income. If the foreign currency depreciates against the home currency, the adverse impact on the consolidated income statement can be offset by the gain on the forward sale in that currency. If the foreign currency appreciates over the time period of concern, there will be a loss on the forward sale that is offset by a favorable effect on the reported consolidated earnings. However, many MNCs would not be satisfied with a "paper gain" that offsets a "cash loss."

SELF TEST

Answers are provided in Appendix A at the back of the text.

1. Salem Exporting Co. purchases chemicals from U.S. sources and uses them to make pharmaceutical products that are exported to Canadian hospitals. Salem prices its products in Canadian dollars and is concerned about the possibility of the long-term depreciation of the Canadian dollar against the U.S. dollar. It periodically hedges its exposure with short-term forward contracts, but this does not insulate against the possible trend of continuing Canadian dollar depreciation. How could Salem offset some of its exposure resulting from its export business?

2. Using the information in question 1, give a possible disadvantage of offsetting exchange rate exposure from the export business.

3. Coastal Corp. is a U.S. firm with a subsidiary in the United Kingdom. It expects that the pound will depreciate this year. Explain Coastal's translation exposure. How could Coastal hedge its translation exposure?

4. Arlington Co. has substantial translation exposure in European subsidiaries. The treasurer of Arlington Co. suggests that the translation effects are not relevant because the earnings generated by the European subsidiaries are not being remitted to the U.S. parent, but are simply being reinvested in Europe. Nevertheless, the vice president of finance of Arlington Co. is concerned about translation exposure because the stock price is highly dependent on the consolidated earnings, which are dependent on the exchange rates at which the earnings are translated. Who is correct?

5. Lincolnshire Co. exports 80 percent of its total production of goods in New Mexico to Latin American countries. Kalafa Co. sells all the goods it produces in the United States, but it has a subsidiary in Spain that usually generates about 20 percent of its total earnings. Compare the translation exposure of these two U.S. firms.

QUESTIONS AND APPLICATIONS

1. St. Paul Co. does business in the United States and New Zealand. In attempting to assess its economic exposure, it compiled the following information.

   a. St. Paul's U.S. sales are somewhat affected by the value of the New Zealand dollar (NZ$) because it faces competition from New Zealand exporters. It forecasts the U.S. sales based on the following three exchange rate scenarios:

Exchange Rate of NZ$	Revenue from U.S. Business (in millions)
NZ$ = $.48	$100
NZ$ = .50	105
NZ$ = .54	110

   b. Its New Zealand dollar revenue on sales to New Zealand invoiced in New Zealand dollars is expected to be NZ$600 million.

   c. Its anticipated cost of goods sold is estimated at $200 million from the purchase of U.S. materials and NZ$100 million from the purchase of New Zealand materials.

   d. Fixed operating expenses are estimated at $30 million.

   e. Variable operating expenses are estimated at 20 percent of total sales (after including New Zealand sales, translated to a U.S. dollar amount).

   f. Interest expense is estimated at $20 million on existing U.S. loans, and the company has no existing New Zealand loans.

   Create a forecasted income statement for St. Paul Co. under each of the three exchange rate scenarios. Explain how St. Paul's projected earnings before taxes are affected by possible exchange rate movements. Explain how it can restructure its operations to reduce the sensitivity of its earnings to exchange rate movements without reducing its volume of business in New Zealand.

2. Baltimore, Inc., is a U.S.-based MNC that obtains 10 percent of its supplies from European manufacturers. Sixty percent of its revenues are due to exports to Europe, where its product is exported and invoiced in euros. Explain how Baltimore can attempt to reduce its economic exposure to exchange rate fluctuations in the euro.

3. UVA Co. is a U.S.-based MNC that obtains 40 percent of its foreign supplies from Thailand. It also borrows Thailand's currency (the baht) from Thai banks and converts the baht to dollars to support U.S. operations. It currently receives about 10 percent of its revenue from Thai customers. Its sales to Thai customers are denominated in baht. Explain how UVA Co. can reduce its economic exposure to exchange rate fluctuations.

4. Albany Corp. is a U.S.-based MNC that has a large government contract with Australia. The contract will continue for several years and generate more than half of Albany's total sales volume. The Australian government pays Albany in Australian dollars. About 10 percent of Albany's operating expenses are in Australian dollars; all other expenses are in U.S. dollars. Explain how Albany Co. can reduce its economic exposure to exchange rate fluctuations.

5. When an MNC restructures its operations to reduce its economic exposure, it may sometimes forgo economies of scale. Explain.

6. Explain how a U.S.-based MNC's consolidated earnings are affected during a period such as the Asian crisis.

7. Explain how a firm can hedge its translation exposure.

8. Bartunek Co. is a U.S.-based MNC that has European subsidiaries and wants to hedge its translation exposure to fluctuations in the

euro's value. Explain some limitations when it hedges translation exposure.

9. Would a more established MNC or a less established MNC be better able to effectively hedge its given level of translation exposure? Why?

10. Denver, Inc., is concerned with how shareholders react to changes in consolidated earnings but prefers not to hedge its translation exposure. How can it attempt to reduce shareholder reaction to a decline in consolidated earnings that results from a strengthened dollar?

11. Carlton Co. and Palmer, Inc., are U.S.-based MNCs with subsidiaries in Mexico that distribute medical supplies (produced in the United States) to customers throughout Latin America. Both subsidiaries purchase the products at cost and sell the products at 90 percent markup. The other operating costs of the subsidiaries are very low. Carlton Co. has a research and development center in the United States that focuses on improving its medical technology. Palmer, Inc., has a similar center based in Mexico. The parent of each firm subsidizes its respective research and development center on an annual basis. Which firm is subject to a higher degree of economic exposure? Explain.

12. Nelson Co. is a U.S. firm with annual export sales to Singapore worth about $800 million in Singapore dollars (S$). Its main competitor is Mez Co., also based in the United States, with a subsidiary in Singapore that generates about S$800 million in annual sales. Any earnings generated by the subsidiary are reinvested to support its operations. Based on the information provided, which firm is subject to a higher degree of translation exposure? Explain.

Impact of 9/11/01

13. Minnesota, Inc., has subsidiaries in Canada that produce most of the products it sells in the United States. Its revenue is in U.S. dollars, and most of its expenses are in Canadian dollars. After the September 11, 2001, terrorist attack on the United States, do you think Minnesota, Inc., was more exposed to exchange rate risk? If Minnesota, Inc., wanted to reduce its risk to economic exposure, how might it restructure its operations?

Internet Application

14. The following website provides annual reports of numerous MNCs: **http://report-gallery.com**

a. Review an annual report of an MNC of your choice. Look for any comments that relate to the MNC's economic or translation exposure. Does it appear that the MNC hedges its economic exposure or translation exposure? If so, what methods does it uses to hedge its exposure?

b. The following website provides exchange rate movements against the dollar over recent months: **http://dominostat-usa.gov/econtest.nsf**

Based on the translation exposure of the MNC you assessed in exercise (a), determine whether the exchange rate movements of whatever currency (or currencies) it is exposed to moved in a favorable or unfavorable direction over the last few months.

Running Your Own MNC

 This exercise can be found on the Student CD-ROM.

Blades, Inc. Case

Assessment of Economic Exposure

Blades, Inc., has been exporting to Thailand since its decision to supplement its declining U.S. sales by exporting there. Furthermore, Blades has recently begun exporting to a retailer in the United Kingdom. The suppliers of the components needed by Blades for roller blade production (such as rubber and plastic) are located in the United States and Thailand. Blades decided to use Thai suppliers for rubber and plastic components needed to manufacture roller blades because of cost and quality considerations. All of Blades' exports and imports are denominated in the respective foreign currency; for example, Blades pays for the Thai imports in baht.

The decision to export to Thailand was supported by the fact that Thailand had been one of the world's fastest growing economies in recent years. Furthermore, Blades found an importer in Thailand that was willing to commit itself to the annual purchase of 180,000 pairs of Blades' "Speedos," which are among the highest quality roller blades in the world. The commitment began last year and will last another two years, at which time it may be renewed by the two parties. Due to this commitment, Blades is selling its roller blades for 4,594 baht per pair (approximately $100 at current exchange rates) instead of the usual $120 per pair. Although this price represents a substantial discount from the regular price for a pair of Speedo blades, it still constitutes a considerable markup above cost. Because importers in other Asian countries were not willing to make this type of commitment, this was a decisive factor in the choice of Thailand for exporting purposes. Although Ben Holt, Blades' chief financial officer (CFO), believes the sports product market in Asia has very high future growth potential, Blades has recently begun exporting to Jogs, Ltd., a British retailer. Jogs has committed itself to purchase 200,000 pair of Speedos annually for a fixed price of £80 per pair.

For the coming year, Blades expects to import rubber and plastic components from Thailand sufficient to manufacture 80,000 pairs of Speedos, at a cost of approximately 3,000 baht per pair of Speedos.

You, as Blades' financial analyst, have pointed out to Ben Holt that recent events in Asia have fundamentally affected the economic condition of Asian countries, including Thailand. For example, you have pointed out that the high level of consumer spending on leisure products such as roller blades has declined considerably. Thus, the Thai retailer may not renew its commitment with Blades in two years. Furthermore, you are worried that the current economic conditions in Thailand may lead to a substantial depreciation of the Thai baht, which would affect Blades negatively.

Despite recent developments, however, Ben Holt remains optimistic; he is convinced that Southeast Asia will exhibit high potential for growth when the impact of recent events in Asia subsides. Consequently, Holt has no doubt that the Thai customer will renew its commitment for another three years when the current agreement terminates. In your opinion, Holt is not considering all of the factors that might directly or indirectly affect Blades. Moreover, you are worried that he is ignoring Blades' future in Thailand even if the Thai importer renews its commitment for another three years. In fact, you believe that a renewal of the existing agreement with the Thai customer may affect Blades negatively due to the high level of inflation in Thailand.

Since Holt is interested in your opinion and wants to assess Blades' economic exposure in Thailand, he has asked you to conduct an analysis of the impact of the value of the baht on next year's earnings to assess Blades' economic exposure. You have gathered the following information:

- Blades has forecasted sales in the United States of 520,000 pairs of Speedos at regular prices; exports to Thailand of 180,000 pairs of Speedos for 4,594 baht a pair; and exports to the United Kingdom of 200,000 pairs of Speedos for £80 per pair.

- Cost of goods sold for 80,000 pairs of Speedos are incurred in Thailand; the remainder is incurred in the United States, where the cost of goods sold per pair of Speedos runs approximately $70.

- Fixed costs are $2 million, and variable operating expenses other than costs of goods sold represent approximately 11 percent of U.S. sales. All fixed and variable operating expenses other than cost of goods sold are incurred in the United States.

- Recent events in Asia have increased the uncertainty regarding certain Asian currencies considerably, making it extremely difficult to forecast the value of the baht at which the Thai revenues will be converted. The current spot rate of the baht is $.022, and the current spot rate of the pound is $1.50. You have created three scenarios and derived an expected value on average for the upcoming year based on each scenario:

Scenario	Effect on the Average Value of Baht	Average Value of Baht	Average Value of Pound
1	No change	$.0220	$1.530
2	Depreciate by 5%	.0209	1.485
3	Depreciate by 10%	.0198	1.500

- Blades currently has no debt in its capital structure. However, it may borrow funds in Thailand if it establishes a subsidiary in the country.

Ben Holt has asked you to answer the following questions:

1. How will Blades be negatively affected by the high level of inflation in Thailand if the Thai customer renews its commitment for another three years?

2. Holt believes that the Thai importer will renew its commitment in two years. Do you think his assessment is correct? Why or why not? Also, assume that the Thai economy returns to the high growth level that existed prior to the recent unfavorable economic events. Under this assumption, how likely is it that the Thai importer will renew its commitment in two years?

3. For each of the three possible values of the Thai baht and the British pound, use a spreadsheet to construct a pro forma income statement for the next year. Briefly comment on the level of Blades' economic exposure.

4. Now repeat your analysis in question 3 but assume that the British pound and the Thai baht are perfectly correlated. For example, if the baht depreciates by 5 percent, the pound will also depreciate by 5 percent. Under this assumption, is Blades subject to a greater degree of economic exposure? Why or why not?

5. Based on your answers to the previous three questions, what actions could Blades take to reduce its level of economic exposure to Thailand?

Small Business Dilemma

Hedging the Sports Exports Company's Economic Exposure to Exchange Rate Risk

Jim Logan, owner of the Sports Exports Company, remains concerned about his exposure to exchange rate risk. Even if Jim hedges his transactions from one month to another, he recognizes that a long-term trend of depreciation in the British pound could have a severe impact on his firm. He believes that he must continue to focus on the British market for selling his footballs. However, he plans to consider various ways in which he can reduce his economic exposure. At the current time, he obtains material from a local manufacturer and uses a machine to produce the footballs, which are then exported. He still uses his garage as a place of production and would like to continue using his garage to maintain low operating expenses.

1. How could Jim adjust his operations to reduce his economic exposure? What is a possible disadvantage of such an adjustment?

2. Offer another solution to hedging the economic exposure in the long run, as Jim's business grows. What are the disadvantages of this solution?

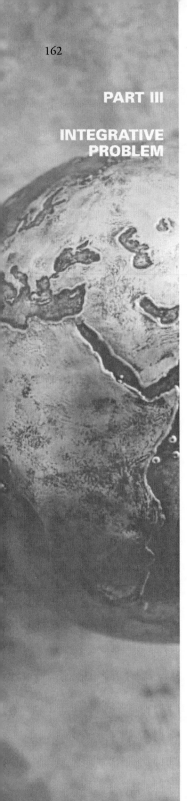

Exchange Rate Risk Management

Vogl Co. is a U.S. firm conducting a financial plan for the next year. It has no foreign subsidiaries, but more than half of its sales are from exports. Its foreign cash inflows to be received from exporting and cash outflows to be paid for imported supplies over the next year are shown in the following table:

Currency	Total Inflow	Total Outflow
Canadian dollar (C$)	C$32,000,000	C$2,000,000
New Zealand dollar (NZ$)	NZ$5,000,000	NZ$1,000,000
Mexican peso (MXP)	MXP11,000,000	MXP10,000,000
Singapore dollar (S$)	S$4,000,000	S$8,000,000

The spot rates and one-year forward rates as of today are shown below:

Currency	Spot Rate	One-Year Forward Rate
C$	$.90	$.93
NZ$	.60	.59
MXP	.18	.15
S$	.65	.64

Questions

1. Based on the information provided, determine Vogl's net exposure to each foreign currency in dollars.
2. Assume that today's spot rate is used as a forecast of the future spot rate one year from now. The New Zealand dollar, Mexican peso, and Singapore dollar are expected to move in tandem against the U.S. dollar over the next year. The Canadian dollar's movements are expected to be unrelated to movements of the other currencies. Since exchange rates are difficult to predict, the forecasted net dollar cash flows per currency may be inaccurate. Do you anticipate any offsetting exchange rate effects from whatever exchange movements do occur? Explain.
3. Given the forecast of the Canadian dollar along with the forward rate of the Canadian dollar, what is the expected increase or decrease in dollar cash flows that would result from hedging the net cash flows in Canadian dollars? Would you hedge the Canadian dollar position?
4. Assume that the Canadian dollar net inflows may range from C$20,000,000 to C$40,000,000 over the next year. Explain the risk of hedging C$30,000,000 in net inflows. How can Vogl Co. avoid such a risk? Is there any tradeoff resulting from your strategy to avoid that risk?
5. Vogl Co. recognizes that its year-to-year hedging strategy hedges the risk only over a given year but does not insulate it from long-term trends in the Canadian dollar's value. It has considered establishing a subsidiary in Canada. The goods

would be sent from the United States to the Canadian subsidiary and distributed by the subsidiary. The proceeds received would be reinvested by the Canadian subsidiary in Canada. In this way, Vogl Co. would not have to convert Canadian dollars to U.S. dollars each year. Has Vogl eliminated its exposure to exchange rate risk by using this strategy? Explain.

6

Direct Foreign Investment

MNCs commonly capitalize on foreign business opportunities by engaging in **direct foreign investment (DFI)**, which is investment in real assets (such as land, buildings, or even existing plants) in foreign countries. They engage in joint ventures with foreign firms, acquire foreign firms, and form new foreign subsidiaries. Any of these types of DFI can generate high returns when managed properly. However, DFI requires a substantial investment and can therefore put much capital at risk. Moreover, if the investment does not perform as well as expected, the MNC may have difficulty selling the foreign project it created. Given these return and risk characteristics of DFI, MNCs tend to carefully analyze the potential benefits and costs before implementing any type of DFI. Financial managers must understand the potential return and risk associated with DFI so that they can make investment decisions that maximize the MNC's value.

The specific objectives of this chapter are to
- Describe common motives for initiating direct foreign investment.
- Illustrate the benefits of international diversification.

Motives for Direct Foreign Investment

MNCs commonly consider direct foreign investment because it can improve their profitability and enhance shareholder wealth. In most cases, MNCs engage in DFI because they are interested in boosting revenues, reducing costs, or both.

Revenue-Related Motives

The following are typical motives of MNCs that are attempting to boost revenues:

- *Attract new sources of demand.* A corporation often reaches a stage when growth is limited in its home country, possibly because of intense competition. Even if it faces little competition, its market share in its home country may already be near its potential peak. Thus, the firm may consider foreign markets where there is potential demand. Many developing countries, such as Argentina, Chile, Mexico, Hungary, and China, have been perceived as attractive sources of new demand. Many MNCs have penetrated these countries since barriers have been removed. Because the consumers in these countries have historically been restricted from purchasing goods produced by firms outside their countries, the markets for some goods are not well established and offer much potential for penetration by MNCs.

Example Blockbuster Entertainment Corp. has recently established video stores in Australia, Chile, Japan, and several European countries where the video-rental concept is relatively new. With over 2,000 stores in the United States, Blockbuster's growth potential in the United States was limited.

China has also attracted MNCs. Motorola recently invested more than $1 billion in joint ventures in China. The Coca-Cola Co. has invested about $500 million in bottling facilities in China, and PepsiCo has invested about $200 million in bottling facilities. Tricon Global Restaurants has KFC franchises and Pizza Hut franchises in China. Other MNCs, such as Ford Motor Co., United Technologies, General Electric, Hewlett-Packard, and IBM, have also invested more than $100 million in China to attract demand by consumers there.

- *Enter profitable markets.* If other corporations in the industry have proved that excessive earnings can be realized in other markets, an MNC may also decide to sell in those markets. It may plan to undercut the prevailing, excessively high prices. A common problem with this strategy is that previously established sellers in a new market may prevent a new competitor from taking away their business by lowering their prices just when the new competitor attempts to break into this market.
- *Exploit monopolistic advantages.* Industrial organization theory states that firms may become internationalized if they possess resources or skills not available to competing firms. If a firm possesses advanced technology and has exploited this advantage successfully in local markets, the firm may attempt to exploit it internationally as well. In fact, the firm may have a more distinct advantage in markets that have less advanced technology.
- *React to trade restrictions.* In some cases, MNCs use DFI as a defensive rather than an aggressive strategy. Specifically, MNCs may pursue DFI to circumvent trade barriers.

Example Japanese automobile manufacturers established plants in the United States in anticipation that their exports to the United States would be subject to more stringent trade restrictions. Japanese companies recognized that trade barriers could be established that would limit or prohibit their exports. Since 1980, the United States has imposed numerous trade restrictions on automobile imports.

■ *Diversify internationally.* Since economies of countries do not move perfectly in tandem over time, net cash flow from sales of products across countries should be more stable than comparable sales if the products were sold in a single country. By diversifying sales (and possibly even production) internationally, a firm can make its net cash flows less volatile. Thus, the possibility of a liquidity deficiency is less likely. In addition, the firm may enjoy a lower cost of capital as shareholders and creditors perceive the MNC's risk to be lower as a result of more stable cash flows. Potential benefits to MNCs that diversify internationally are examined more thoroughly later in the chapter.

Example

In 2001, several technology firms experienced weak sales because of reduced U.S. demand for their products. They responded by increasing their expansion in foreign markets. AT&T, Lucent Technologies, and Nortel Networks pursued new business in China. U.S. Technology planned substantial expansion in Europe and Asia. IBM increased its expansion in China, India, South Korea, and Taiwan. Cisco Systems expanded substantially in China, Japan, and South Korea. Foreign expansion diversifies an MNC's sources of revenue and thus reduces its reliance on the U.S. economy.

Cost-Related Motives

MNCs also engage in DFI in an effort to reduce costs. The following are typical motives of MNCs that are trying to cut costs:

■ *Fully benefit from economies of scale.* A corporation that attempts to sell its primary product in new markets may increase its earnings and shareholder wealth due to **economies of scale** (lower average cost per unit resulting from increased production). Firms that utilize much machinery are most likely to benefit from economics of scale.

Example

The removal of trade barriers by the Single European Act allowed MNCs to achieve greater economies of scale. Some U.S.-based MNCs consolidated their European plants because the removal of tariffs between countries in the European Union (EU) enabled firms to achieve economies of scale at a single European plant without incurring excessive exporting costs. The act also enhanced economies of scale by making regulations on television ads, automobile standards, and other products and services uniform across the EU. As a result, Colgate-Palmolive Co. and other MNCs are manufacturing more homogeneous products that can be sold in all EU countries. The adoption of the euro also encouraged consolidation by eliminating exchange rate risk within these countries.

■ *Use foreign factors of production.* Labor and land costs can vary dramatically among countries. MNCs often attempt to set up production in locations where land and labor are cheap. Due to market imperfections (as discussed in Chapter 1) such as imperfect information, relocation transaction costs, and barriers to industry entry, specific labor costs do not necessarily become equal among markets. Thus, it is worthwhile for MNCs to survey markets to determine whether they can benefit from cheaper costs by producing in those markets.

Example

Many U.S.-based MNCs, including Black & Decker, Eastman Kodak, Ford Motor Co., and General Electric, have established subsidiaries in Mexico to achieve lower labor costs.

Mexico has attracted almost $8 billion in direct foreign investment from firms in the automobile industry, primarily because of the low-cost labor. Mexican workers at General Motors' subsidiaries who manufacture sedans and trucks earn daily wages that are less than the average hourly rate for similar workers in the United States. Ford is also producing trucks at subsidiaries based in Mexico.

Non-U.S. automobile manufacturers are also capitalizing on the low-cost labor in Mexico. Volkswagen of Germany produces its Beetle in Mexico. DaimlerChrysler of Germany manufactures its 12-wheeler trucks in Mexico, and Nissan Motor Co. of Japan produces some of its wagons in Mexico.

Other Japanese companies are also increasingly using Mexico and other low-wage countries for production. For example, Sony Corp. recently established a plant in Tijuana. Matsushita Electrical Industrial Co. has a large plant in Tijuana.

Baxter International has established manufacturing plants in Mexico and Malaysia to capitalize on lower costs of production (primarily wage rates). Honeywell has joint ventures in countries such as Korea and India where production costs are low. It has also established subsidiaries in countries where production costs are low, such as Mexico, Malaysia, Hong Kong, and Taiwan.

- *Use foreign raw materials.* Due to transportation costs, a corporation may attempt to avoid importing raw materials from a given country, especially when it plans to sell the finished product back to consumers in that country. Under such circumstances, a more feasible solution may be to develop the product in the country where the raw materials are located.
- *Use foreign technology.* Corporations are increasingly establishing overseas plants or acquiring existing overseas plants to learn the technology of foreign countries. This technology is then used to improve their own production processes and increase production efficiency at all subsidiary plants around the world.
- *React to exchange rate movements.* When a firm perceives that a foreign currency is undervalued, the firm may consider direct foreign investment in that country, as the initial outlay should be relatively low.

Example

Suppose that Canisius, Inc., can build a manufacturing plant in the United Kingdom for £40 million at a time when the dollar cost of this project would be $77.2 million. Over the next six months, the value of the British pound declines by 15.5 percent. Thus, just six months later the dollar cost of the project has fallen to $65.2 million (or $12 million less) because of the decline in the pound's value. Since the decision of whether to engage in direct foreign investment is partially dependent on the cost, exchange rate movements may influence this decision.

A related reason for such DFI is to offset the changing demand for a company's exports due to exchange rate fluctuations. For example, when Japanese automobile manufacturers build plants in the United States, they can reduce exposure to exchange rate fluctuations by incurring dollar costs that offset dollar revenues. Although MNCs do not engage in large projects simply as an indirect means of speculating on currencies, the feasibility of proposed projects may be dependent on existing and expected exchange rate movements.

The conversion of many European currencies to the euro in 1999 reduced the influence of exchange rates on the selection of a European country for DFI because the future exchange rate effects will be the same across all countries that use the euro as their currency. For example, a U.S.-based MNC considering building a manufacturing plant in Germany versus Italy or Spain does not have to take exchange rate effects into account because those countries have adopted the euro as their currency. Exchange rates must still be considered, however, if the MNC is considering European countries that have not adopted the euro along with those that have.

Comparing Benefits of DFI among Countries

http://
Visit Morgan Stanley's Economic Forum at www.ms.com/GEF for analyses, discussions, statistics, and forecasts related to non-U.S. economies.

The optimal way for a firm to penetrate a foreign market is partially dependent on the characteristics of the market. For example, direct foreign investment by U.S. firms is common in Europe but not so common in Asia, where the people are accustomed to purchasing products from Asians. Thus, licensing arrangements or joint ventures may be more appropriate when firms are expanding into Asia.

Exhibit 13.1 summarizes the possible benefits of DFI and explains how MNCs can use DFI to achieve those benefits. Most MNCs pursue DFI based on their expectations of capitalizing on one or more of the potential benefits summarized in Exhibit 13.1. Although most attempts to increase international business are motivated by one or more of the benefits listed here, some disadvantages are also associated with DFI.

HTTP:// USING THE WEB

DFI Indicators Information about economic growth and other macroeconomic indicators used when considering direct foreign investment is provided for each country at http://biz.yahoo.com/ifc/.

Click on any country listed, and then click on Country Fact Sheet. Estimates of the country's population, gross domestic product (GDP), GDP growth rate, and GDP per person are shown. In addition, information about the country's political structure and policy issues is provided.

Example

Iowa Co., a large clothing manufacturer, wants to pursue DFI in the Philippines or Mexico because the cost of producing its clothing will be much lower in either country. Iowa Co. determines that the direct costs of production would be lower in the Philippines. However, there are some other indirect costs of DFI that should also be considered. Iowa Co. determines that economic conditions in the Philippines are uncertain, that government restrictions might be imposed on a subsidiary there, and that inflation and exchange rate movements might be unfavorable. Most importantly, the safety of employees who would be sent there to manage the subsidiary might be threatened by terrorist groups. After considering all the costs, Iowa Co. decides to pursue DFI in Mexico.

Exhibit 13.1

Summary of Motives for Direct Foreign Investment

Possible Benefit	Means of Using DFI to Achieve This Benefit
1. Attract new sources of demand.	Establish a subsidiary or acquire a competitor in a new market.
2. Enter markets where superior profits are possible.	Acquire a competitor that has controlled its local market.
3. Fully benefit from economies of scale.	Establish a subsidiary in a new market that can sell products produced elsewhere; this allows for increased production and possibly greater production efficiency.
4. Use foreign factors of production.	Establish a subsidiary in a market that has relatively low costs of labor or land; sell the finished product to countries where the cost of production is higher.
5. Use foreign raw materials.	Establish a subsidiary in a market where raw materials are cheap and accessible; sell the finished product to countries where the raw materials are more expensive.
6. Use foreign technology.	Participate in a joint venture in order to learn about a production process or other operations.
7. Exploit monopolistic advantages.	Establish a subsidiary in a market where competitors are unable to produce the identical product; sell products in that country.
8. React to exchange rate movements.	Establish a subsidiary in a new market where the local currency is weak but is expected to strengthen over time.
9. React to trade restrictions.	Establish a subsidiary in a market where tougher trade restrictions will adversely affect the firm's export volume.
10. Diversify internationally.	Establish subsidiaries in markets whose business cycles differ from those where existing subsidiaries are based.

Financial Markets Perspective

How Financial Markets Can Motivate DFI

It should be clear from the list of key motives for DFI that the product markets play a major role in MNCs' decisions regarding where to expand their business. Nevertheless, the impact of the financial markets should not be ignored. As already mentioned, the foreign exchange markets have a major impact, but the financial markets can also affect DFI in other ways. The interest rates in any country can influence the cost of obtaining debt to finance local operations. An MNC might be able to save millions of dollars in debt payments simply by pursuing DFI in a country where the prevailing interest rate is relatively low. Consequently, a new project may be feasible in that country even though it would not be feasible in other countries. Countries with relatively low nominal interest rates tend to have lower expected rates of inflation, which could possibly result in lower cash flows to the subsidiary. A counterargument, however, is that a low inflation rate should allow the foreign currency to appreciate against the dollar in the future, which would enhance the dollar value of remitted earnings. Although it is impossible to offer a clear-cut conclusion here, the point is that financial market conditions should be considered along with product markets when making DFI decisions.

HTTP:// **USING THE WEB**

Direct Foreign Investment The direct foreign investment in each country for a recent year is provided at http://www.worldbank.org/data/wdi2000/pdfs/tab6_7.pdf.

Comparing Benefits of DFI over Time

As conditions change over time, so do possible benefits from pursuing direct foreign investment in various countries. Thus, some countries may become more attractive targets while other countries become less attractive. The choice of target countries for DFI has changed over time, as illustrated in Exhibit 13.2. Canada now receives a smaller proportion of total DFI than it received in the past, while Europe, Latin America, and Asia receive a larger proportion than in the past. More than one-half of all DFI by U.S. firms is in European countries. The opening of the Eastern European countries accounts for some of the increased DFI in Europe. The increased focus on Latin America is partially attributed to its high economic growth, which has encouraged MNCs to capitalize on new sources of demand for their products. In addition, MNCs have targeted Latin America and Asia to use factors of production that are less expensive in foreign countries than in the United States.

Nike Problem

Motives for Direct Foreign Investment

Nike is a classic example of a firm that has pursued international business in Asia and Europe because of some of the motives described in this chapter. In 1990, about 22 percent of Nike's revenue of $2.2 billion was from foreign countries. In 2000, Nike's revenue had grown to $8.9 billion, about 44 percent of which was from foreign countries. Specifically, revenue from Europe increased from $334 million to $2.4 billion over this 10-year period, reflecting growth of about 688 percent. Revenue from Asia increased from $29 million to $955 million, reflecting growth of about 3,293 percent.

Exhibit 13.2

Change in Distribution of Direct Foreign Investment (DFI) by U.S. Firms Over Time

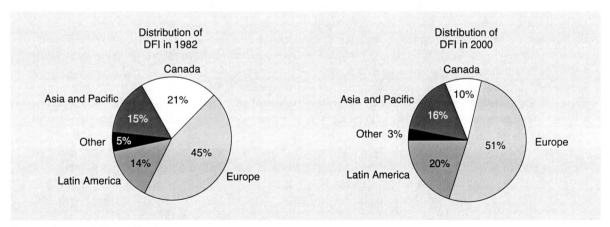

Source: *Survey of Current Business.*

Much of Nike's growth occurred because it attracted new sources of demand by consumers in foreign countries, where many consumers viewed Nike athletic shoes as unique (global name, image). In some cases, Nike may have increased its economies of scale by increasing production capacity and exporting part of the production. Nike benefits from relatively low labor costs by producing some of its athletic footwear in Indonesia, China, and Vietnam. It has also diversified so that it does not rely solely on the demand within any one country or region of the world. Therefore, Nike's overall cash flows are less sensitive to economic conditions in any given region.

Discussion: Nike has plans to expand its athletic footwear sales in Latin America. What motives do you think have encouraged Nike to expand in Latin America?

Example

In 1997, Georgia, Inc., contemplated DFI in Thailand, where it would produce and sell cell phones. It decided that costs were too high. In 1999, it reconsidered DFI in Thailand because costs had declined as a result of the Asian crisis. In 1999, Georgia could lease office space at a much lower rate than in 1997. It could also purchase a manufacturing plant at a lower cost because factories that had failed during the crisis were standing empty. In addition, the Thai baht had depreciated substantially against the dollar during the crisis, so Georgia Co. could invest in Thailand at a time when the dollar could be exchanged at a favorable exchange rate.

Georgia Co. also dicovered, however, that while the cost-related characteristics had improved, the revenue-related characteristics were now less desirable. In 1999, a new subsidiary in Thailand might not attract new sources of demand due to the country's weak economy. In addition, Georgia Co. might be unable to earn excessive profits there because the crisis had caused existing firms to keep their prices very low in order to survive. Georgia Co. would have to compare the favorable aspects of DFI in Thailand with the unfavorable aspects by using multinational capital budgeting, which is explained in the following chapter.

Managing for Value: Yahoo!'s Decision to Expand in Taiwan

Since Yahoo! successfully created a portal in the United States, it has engaged in direct foreign investment so that it can capitalize on its technology in foreign markets. By 2000, it had successfully established portals in Europe and Asia. However, it believed that it could improve its presence in Asia by focusing on the Greater China area. China has much potential because of its population base, but it also imposes restrictions that discourage DFI by firms. Meanwhile, Kimo, a privately held company and the leading portal in Taiwan, was planning to grow throughout Asia. It had 4 million registered users in Taiwan and had considered an initial public offering in the United States to support its growth, but gave up that idea when Internet valuations declined substantially, preventing Kimo from offering shares at a high price. In November 2000, Yahoo! agreed to acquire Kimo for about $150 million. Since the acquisition occurred at a time when Internet stock valuations were reduced, Yahoo! was able to purchase Kimo at a relatively low price. With this DFI, Yahoo! not only established a presence in Taiwan, but also established a link to mainland China. By timing its international expansion to a period when the cost (initial outlay) was low, Yahoo! was able to maximize its value.

BENEFITS OF INTERNATIONAL DIVERSIFICATION

An international project can reduce a firm's overall risk as a result of international diversification benefits. The key to international diversification is selecting foreign projects whose performance levels are not highly correlated over time. In this way, the various international projects should not experience poor performance simultaneously.

Example

Merrimack Co., a U.S. firm, plans to invest in a new project in either the United States or the United Kingdom. Once the project is completed, it will constitute 30 percent of the firm's total funds invested in itself. The remaining 70 percent of its investment in its business is exclusively in the United States. Characteristics of the proposed project are forecasted for a five-year period for both a U.S. and a British location, as shown in Exhibit 13.3.

Merrimack Co. plans to assess the feasibility of each proposed project based on expected risk and return, using a five-year time horizon. Its expected annual after-tax return on investment on its prevailing business is 20 percent, and its variability of returns (as measured by the standard deviation) is expected to be .10. The firm can assess its expected overall performance based on developing the project in the United States and in the United Kingdom. In doing so, it is essentially comparing two portfolios. In the first portfolio, 70 percent of its total funds are invested in its prevailing U.S. business, with the remaining 30 percent invested in a new project located in the United States. In the second portfolio, again 70 percent of the firm's total funds are invested in its prevailing business, but the remaining 30 percent are invested in a new project located in the United Kingdom. Therefore, 70 percent of the portfolios' investments are identical. The difference is in the remaining 30 percent of funds invested.

If the new project is located in the United States, the overall firm's expected after-tax return (r_p) is

$r_p =$	[(70%)	$\times$	(20%)]	+	[(30%)	$\times$	(25%)]	=	21.5%
	% of funds invested in prevailing business		Expected return on prevailing business		% of funds invested in new U.S. project		Expected return on new U.S. project		Firm's overall expected return

Exhibit 13.3

Evaluation of Proposed Projects in Alternative Locations

	Characteristics of Proposed Project	
	If Located in the United States	If Located in the United Kingdom
Mean expected annual return on investment (after taxes)	25%	25%
Standard deviation of expected annual after-tax returns on investment	.09	.11
Correlation of expected annual after-tax returns on investment with after-tax returns of prevailing U.S. business	.80	.02

This computation is based on weighting the returns according to the percentage of total funds invested in each investment.

If the firm calculates its overall expected return with the new project located in the United Kingdom instead of the United States, the results are unchanged. This is because the new project's expected return is the same regardless of the country of location. Therefore, in terms of return, neither new project has an advantage.

With regard to risk, the new project is expected to exhibit slightly less variability in returns during the five-year period if it is located in the United States (see Exhibit 13.3). Since firms typically prefer more stable returns on their investments, this is an advantage. However, estimating the risk of the individual project without considering the overall firm would be a mistake. The expected correlation of the new project's returns with those of the prevailing business must also be considered. Recall that portfolio variance is determined by the individual variability of each component as well as their pairwise correlations. The variance of a portfolio (σ_p^2) composed of only two investments (A and B) is computed as

$$\sigma_p^2 = w_A^2 \sigma_A^2 + w_B^2 \sigma_B^2 + 2 w_A w_B \sigma_A \sigma_B (CORR_{AB})$$

where w_A and w_B represent the percentage of total funds allocated to Investments A and B, respectively; σ_A and σ_B are the standard deviations of returns on Investments A and B, respectively, and $CORR_{AB}$ is the correlation coefficient of returns between Investments A and B. This equation for portfolio variance can be applied to the problem at hand. The portfolio reflects the overall firm. First, compute the overall firm's variance in returns assuming it locates the new project in the United States (based on the information provided in Exhibit 13.3). This variance (σ_p^2) is

$$\begin{aligned}
\sigma_p^2 &= (.70)^2 (.10)^2 + (.30)^2 (.09)^2 + 2 (.70)(.30)(.10)(.09)(.80) \\
&= (.49)(.01) + (.09)(.0081) + .003024 \\
&= .0049 + .000729 + .003024 \\
&= .008653
\end{aligned}$$

If Merrimack Co. decides to locate the new project in the United Kingdom instead of the United States, its overall variability in returns will be different, because that project differs from the new U.S. project in terms of individual variability in returns and correlation with the prevailing business. The overall variability of the firm's returns based on locating the new project in the United Kingdom is estimated by variance in the portfolio returns (σ_p^2):

$$\begin{aligned}
\sigma_p^2 &= (.70)^2 (.10)^2 + (.30)^2 (.11)^2 + 2(.70)(.30)(.10)(.11)(.02) \\
&= (.49)(.01) + (.09)(.0121) + .0000924 \\
&= .0049 + .001089 + .0000924 \\
&= .0060814
\end{aligned}$$

Thus, Merrimack will generate more stable returns if the new project is located in the United Kingdom. The firm's overall variability in returns is almost 29.7 percent less if the new project is located in the United Kingdom rather than in the United States.

The variability is reduced when locating in the foreign country because of the correlation of the new project's expected returns with the expected returns of the prevailing business. If the new project is located in Merrimack's home country (the United States), its returns are expected to be more highly correlated with those of the prevailing business than they would be if the project was located in the United Kingdom. When economic conditions of two countries (such as the United States and the United Kingdom) are not highly correlated, then a firm may reduce its risk by diversifying its business in both countries instead of concentrating in just one.

Diversification Benefits during a Global Crisis

When a global crisis occurs, many countries are adversely affected, so an MNC is not insulated from the crisis. For example, during the Asian crisis, an MNC with business diversified among several Asian countries would likely have experienced a major decline in performance. Asian countries experienced a substantial decline in GDP during the crisis. Nevertheless, an MNC that was diversified among several Asian countries would have suffered less than an MNC whose business was heavily focused in Indonesia, which experienced the largest percentage decline in GDP.

Diversification Benefits of Multiple Projects

International diversification across countries may also be more effective for MNCs that diversify their product line. Consider a set of 40 possible U.S. projects, each of which has expected returns to a firm over the next five years. Assume that the variance of each project's expected returns has been estimated and that the average variance of these 40 projects also has been determined. Now consider all possible sets of two projects combined (and equally weighted). If the returns on these projects are not all perfectly positively correlated, the average variance of a typical two-project portfolio will be less than the average variance of individual projects. Similarly, the variance of all possible three-project portfolios (equally weighted) should be even lower. As more projects are added, the portfolio variance should decrease on average. Initially, the average reduction in variance of returns (a measure of risk) associated with the addition of one more project is substantial. After some point, however, the average reduction in variance becomes negligible, meaning that the remaining risk cannot be diversified away by adding more U.S. projects. This is illustrated as the U.S. curve in Exhibit 13.4.

Now consider another set of 40 projects, some of which are in the United States and the rest are in various foreign countries. If the procedure just described is applied to this set, the outcome will be similar to the global curve in Exhibit 13.4. Notice that the degree of risk reduction resulting from adding an additional project is greater for the global set than for the U.S. set. For any given number of projects, the global portfolio has less risk. The advantage to the global set is attributed to the lower correlations between returns of projects implemented in different economies.

Diversification Analysis of International Projects

Like any investor, an MNC with projects positioned around the world is concerned with the risk and return characteristics of the projects. The portfolio of all projects reflects the MNC in aggregate.

Exhibit 13.4
Domestic versus
International
Diversification

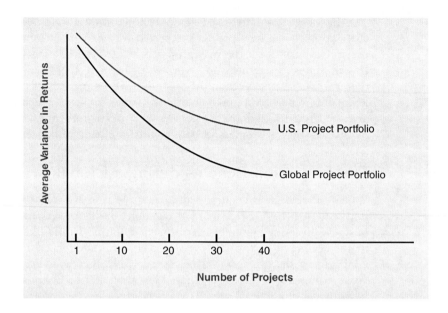

Example

http://
The CIA's homepage at
www.odci.gov/cia/
ciahome.html provides
access to various national
and international surveys,
analyses, maps, and
publications such as
the *World Factbook*.

Virginia, Inc., considers a global strategy of developing projects as shown in Exhibit 13.5. Each point on the graph reflects a specific project that either has been implemented or is being considered. The return axis may be measured by potential return on assets or return on equity. The risk may be measured by potential fluctuation in the returns generated by each project.

Exhibit 13.5 shows that Project A has the highest expected return of all the projects. While Virginia, Inc., could devote most of its resources toward this project to attempt to achieve such a high return, its risk is possibly too high by itself. In addition, such a project may not be able to absorb all available capital anyway if its potential market for customers is limited. Thus, Virginia, Inc., develops a portfolio of projects. By combining Project A with several other projects, Virginia, Inc., may decrease its expected return. On the other hand, it may also reduce its risk substantially.

Exhibit 13.5
Risk-Return Analysis
of International
Projects

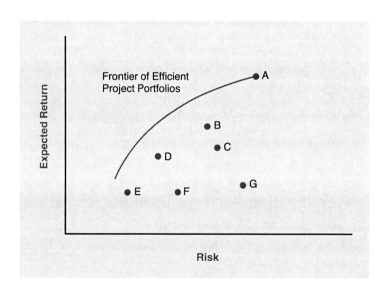

If Virginia, Inc., appropriately combines projects, its project portfolio may be able to achieve a risk-return tradeoff exhibited by any of the points on the curve in Exhibit 13.5. This curve represents a frontier of efficient project portfolios that exhibit desirable risk-return characteristics, in that no single project could outperform any of these portfolios. The term *efficient* refers to a minimum risk for a given expected return. Project portfolios outperform the individual projects considered by Virginia, Inc., because of the diversification attributes discussed earlier. The lower, or more negative, the correlation in project returns over time, the lower will be the project portfolio risk. As new projects are proposed, the frontier of efficient project portfolios available to Virginia, Inc., may shift.

HTTP:// USING THE WEB

Conditions for Direct Foreign Investment The environment for direct foreign investment in each country is provided at http://www.usatrade.gov/website/ccg.nsf.
Click on a specific country, and then click on Investment Climate.

Comparing Portfolios along the Frontier. Along the frontier of efficient project portfolios, no portfolio can be singled out as "optimal" for all MNCs. This is because MNCs vary in their willingness to accept risk. If the MNC is very conservative and has the choice of any portfolios represented by the frontier in Exhibit 13.5, it will probably prefer one that exhibits low risk (near the bottom of the frontier). Conversely, a more aggressive strategy would be to implement a portfolio of projects that exhibits risk-return characteristics such as those near the top of the frontier.

Comparing Frontiers among MNCs. The actual location of the frontier of efficient project portfolios depends on the business in which the firm is involved. Some MNCs have frontiers of possible project portfolios that are more desirable than the frontiers of other MNCs.

Example

Eurosteel, Inc., sells steel solely to European nations and is considering other related projects. Its frontier of efficient project portfolios exhibits considerable risk (because it sells just one product to countries whose economies move in tandem). In contrast, Global Products, Inc., which sells a wide range of products to countries all over the world, has a lower degree of project portfolio risk. Therefore, its frontier of efficient project portfolios is closer to the vertical axis. This comparison is illustrated in Exhibit 13.6. Of course, this comparison assumes that Global Products, Inc., is knowledgeable about all of its products and the markets where it sells.

Our discussion suggests that MNCs can achieve more desirable risk-return characteristics from their project portfolios if they sufficiently diversify among products and geographic markets. This also relates to the advantage an MNC has over a purely domestic firm with only a local market. The MNC may be able to develop a more efficient portfolio of projects than its domestic counterpart.

The international diversification of sales for three U.S.-based MNCs is shown in Exhibit 13.7. Notice that each of these MNCs has diversified its sales across

Exhibit 13.6
Risk-Return
Advantage of a
Diversified MNC

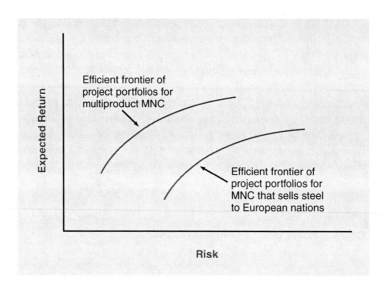

several regions. By diversifying their business across regions, these firms have reduced their exposure to economic conditions in the United States. However, they have become more exposed to conditions in foreign countries.

DECISIONS SUBSEQUENT TO DFI

Once direct foreign investment takes place, periodic decisions are necessary to determine whether further expansion should take place in a given location. In addition, as the project generates earnings, the MNC must decide whether to have the funds remitted to the parent or used by the subsidiary. If the subsidiary has a use for the funds that would be of more value than the parent's use, the subsidiary should retain the funds. Of course, a certain percentage of the funds will be needed to maintain operations, but the remaining funds can be sent to the parent, sent to another subsidiary, or reinvested for expansion purposes.

Exhibit 13.7
International Diversification of Sales (2001)

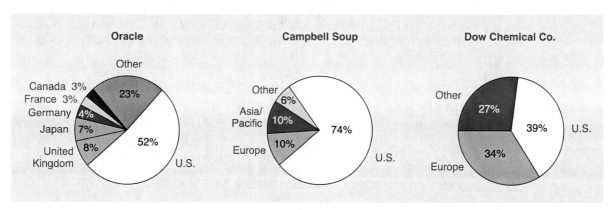

Exhibit 13.8

Earnings from Direct Foreign Investment Abroad by U.S.-Based MNCs Reported in 1998 (in Millions of Dollars)

Location	Earnings			Reinvestment Ratio
	Total	Distributed	Reinvested	
All areas	95,067	37,182	57,885	0.61
Canada	8,642	1,767	6,875	0.80
Europe	46,183	2,713	43,470	0.94
Latin America	17,404	3,105	14,299	0.82
Asia and Pacific	18,937	4,185	14,752	0.78

Source: *Survey of Current Business*, U.S. Department of Commerce.

Facts relevant to the decision of whether the subsidiary should reinvest the earnings should be analyzed on a case-by-case basis. There is no simple guideline to follow. The appropriate decision depends on the economic conditions in the subsidiary's country and the parent's country, as well as restrictions imposed by the host country government. Exhibit 13.8 provides a breakdown of reported earnings from U.S. DFI in regions as of 1998. The total earnings for each region are divided into "distributed" (sent to parent or elsewhere) and "reinvested" earnings. Notice how the reinvestment ratio (computed as reinvested earnings divided by total earnings) varies among regions.

HTTP:// USING THE WEB

DFI Information for a Particular Country Direct foreign investment in specific countries can be assessed by reviewing websites focused on those countries. For example, conditions in China are described at http://www.chinaonline.com.

HOST GOVERNMENT VIEWS OF DFI

Each government must weigh the advantages and disadvantages of direct foreign investment in its country. It may provide incentives to encourage some forms of DFI, barriers to prevent other forms of DFI, and impose conditions on some other forms of DFI.

Incentives to Encourage DFI

The ideal DFI solves problems such as unemployment and lack of technology without taking business away from local firms.

Example   Consider an MNC that is willing to build a production plant in a foreign country that will use local labor and produce goods that are not direct substitutes of other locally produced goods. In this case, the plant will not cause a reduction in sales by local firms. The host government would normally be receptive toward this type of DFI. Another desirable form of DFI from the perspective of the host government is a manufacturing plant that uses local labor and then exports the products (assuming no other local firm exports such products to the same areas).

In some cases, a government will offer incentives to MNCs that consider DFI in its country. Governments are particularly willing to offer incentives for DFI that will result in the employment of local citizens or an increase in technology. Common incentives offered by the host government include tax breaks on the income earned there, rent-free land and buildings, low-interest loans, subsidized energy, and reduced environmental regulations. The degree to which a government will offer such incentives depends on the extent to which the MNC's DFI will benefit that country.

Example

The decision by Allied Research Associates, Inc., (a U.S.-based MNC), to build a production facility and office in Belgium was highly motivated by Belgian government subsidies. The Belgian government subsidized a large portion of the expenses incurred by Allied Research Associates and offered tax concessions and favorable interest rates on loans to Allied.

While many governments encourage DFI, they use different types of incentives. France has periodically sold government land at a discount, while Finland and Ireland attracted MNCs in the late 1990s by imposing a very low corporate tax rate on specific businesses.

Barriers to DFI

Governments are less anxious to encourage DFI that adversely affects locally owned companies, unless they believe that the increased competition is needed to serve consumers. Therefore, they tend to closely regulate any DFI that may affect local firms, consumers, and economic conditions.

Barriers That Protect Local Firms or Consumers. When MNCs consider engaging in DFI by acquiring a foreign company, they may face various barriers imposed by host government agencies. All countries have one or more government agencies that monitor mergers and acquisitions. The acquisition activity in any given country is influenced by the regulations enforced by these agencies.

Example

In France, the Treasury can reject any deal if the acquirer is based outside the European Union. The French government may also reject a deal if the target is in some closely monitored industry, such as defense or health care. The Monopolies Commission of France also reviews acquisitions to prevent any combined firms from controlling more than 25 percent of an industry or from severely reducing competition.

The European Union (EU) Commisionn assesses mergers that may affect competition in Europe. The EU Commission rejected the merger between General Electric and Honeywell, because it believed that the merger would have resulted in a monopoly.

Acquisitions in Japan are reviewed by the Fair Trade Commission. Japan has historically imposed barriers to discourage international acquisitions. Recently, however, these barriers have been reduced (as long as the Japanese target is agreeable), enabling U.S.-based MNCs such as Corning Glass Works, Data General, Eastman Kodak, and Motorola to acquire Japanese firms.

Acquisitions in the United States are also reviewed by several agencies, including the Securities and Exchange Commission, which regulates the conduct of acquisitions, and the Justice Department and Federal Trade Commission, which analyzes the potential impact on competition.

Barriers That Restrict Ownership. Some governments restrict foreign ownership of local firms. Such restrictons may limit or prevent international acquisitions.

Example Many governments in Asia and Latin America have traditionally restricted foreign majority ownership. In recent years, however, these restrictions have been reduced. Governments of Asian countries removed restrictions on international acquisitions during the Asian crisis to encourage MNCs to develop new business there. Mexico also recently announced that it would allow foreign companies to own 100 percent of their subsidiaries established in Mexico.

"Red Tape" Barriers. An implicit barrier to DFI in some countries is the "red tape" involved, such as procedural and documentation requirements. An MNC pursuing DFI is subject to a different set of requirements in each country. Therefore, it is difficult for an MNC to become proficient at the process unless it concentrates on DFI within a single foreign country. The current efforts to make regulations uniform across Europe have simplified the paperwork required to acquire European firms.

Government-Imposed Conditions to Engage in DFI

Some governments allow international acquisitions but impose special requirements on MNCs that desire to acquire a local firm. For example, the MNC may be required to ensure pollution control for its manufacturing or to structure the business to export the products it produces so that it does not threaten the market share of other local firms. The MNC may even be required to retain all the employees of the target firm so that unemployment and general economic conditions in the country are not adversely affected.

Example Mexico requires that the parts used to produce automobiles there make up a specified minimum proportion of an automobile. The proportion is lower for automobiles that are to be exported.

Spain's government allowed Ford Motor Co. to set up production facilities in Spain only if it would abide by certain provisions. These included limiting Ford's local sales volume to 10 percent of the previous year's local automobile sales. In addition, two-thirds of the total volume of automobiles produced by Ford in Spain must be exported. The idea behind these provisions was to create jobs for workers in Spain without seriously affecting local competitors. Allowing a subsidiary that primarily exports its product achieved this objective.

Government-imposed conditions do not necessarily prevent an MNC from pursuing DFI in a specific foreign country, but they can be costly. Thus, MNCs should be willing to consider DFI that requires costly conditions only if the potential benefits outweigh the costs.

Exhibit 13.9

Impact of Direct Foreign Investment Decisions on an MNC's Value

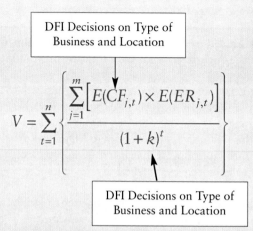

V = value of the U.S.-based MNC

$E(CF_{j,t})$ = expected cash flows denominated in currency j to be received by the U.S. parent in period t

$E(ER_{j,t})$ = expected exchange rate at which currency j can be converted to dollars at the end of period t

k = weighted average cost of capital of the U.S. parent

m = number of currencies

n = number of periods

IMPACT OF THE DFI DECISION ON AN MNC'S VALUE

An MNC's direct foreign investment decision affects its value, as shown in Exhibit 13.9. Decisions on which countries to target for expansion affect the revenue generated by the foreign subsidiaries and the operating expenses of the foreign subsidiaries. Thus, the DFI decisions determine the expected foreign currency cash flows that will be earned by each foreign subsidiary and therefore affect the expected dollar cash flows ultimately received by the U.S. parent.

Since the DFI decisions by the U.S. parent determine the types of new operations and the locations of foreign operations, they can affect the perceived risk of these operations that are supported by the parent's DFI. Therefore, DFI can affect the MNC's cost of capital, which also affects the MNC's value.

SUMMARY

- MNCs may be motivated to initiate direct foreign investment in order to attract new sources of demand or to enter markets where superior profits are possible. These two motives are normally based on opportunities to generate more revenue in foreign markets. Other motives for using DFI are typically related to cost efficiency, such as using foreign factors of production, raw materials, or technology. In addition MNCs may engage in DFI to protect their foreign market share, to react to exchange rate movements, or to avoid trade restrictions.

■ International diversification is a common motive for direct foreign investment. It allows an MNC to reduce its exposure to domestic economic conditions. In this way, the MNC may be able to stabilize its cash flows and reduce its risk. Such a goal is desirable because it may reduce the firm's cost of financing. International projects may allow MNCs to achieve lower risk than is possible from only domestic projects without reducing their expected returns. International diversification tends to be better able to reduce risk when the DFI is targeted to countries whose economies are somewhat unrelated to an MNC's home country economy.

SELF TEST

Answers are provided in Appendix A at the back of the text.

1. Offer some reasons why U.S. firms might prefer to direct their direct foreign investment (DFI) to Canada rather than Mexico.

2. Offer some reasons why U.S. firms might prefer to direct their DFI to Mexico rather than Canada.

3. One U.S. executive said that Europe was not considered as a location for DFI because of the euro's value. Interpret this statement.

4. Why do you think U.S. firms commonly use joint ventures as a strategy to enter China?

5. Why would the United States offer a foreign automobile manufacturer large incentives for establishing a production subsidiary in the United States? Isn't this strategy indirectly subsidizing the foreign competitors of U.S. firms?

QUESTIONS AND APPLICATIONS

1. Describe some potential benefits to an MNC as a result of direct foreign investment (DFI). Elaborate on each type of benefit.

2. Packer, Inc., a U.S. producer of computer disks, plans to establish a subsidiary in Mexico in order to penetrate the Mexican market. Packer's executives believe that the Mexican peso's value is relatively strong and will weaken against the dollar over time. If their expectations about the peso value are correct, how will this affect the feasibility of the project? Explain.

3. Bear Co. and Viking, Inc., are automobile manufacturers that desire to benefit from economies of scale. Bear Co. has decided to establish distributorship subsidiaries in various countries, while Viking, Inc., has decided to establish manufacturing subsidiaries in various countries. Which firm is more likely to benefit from economies of scale?

4. Raider Chemical Co. and Ram, Inc., had similar intentions to reduce the volatility of their cash flows. Raider implemented a long-range plan to establish 40 percent of its business in Canada. Ram, Inc., implemented a long-range plan to establish 30 percent of its business in Europe and Asia, scattered among 12 different countries. Which company will more effectively reduce cash flow volatility once the plans are achieved?

5. If the United States imposed long-term restrictions on imports, would the amount of DFI by non-U.S. MNCs in the United States increase, decrease, or be unchanged? Explain.

6. Some MNCs establish manufacturing facilities where there is a relatively low cost of labor. However, they sometimes close their facilities later, because the cost advantage dissipates. Why do you think the relative

cost advantage of operating facilities in these countries is reduced over time? (Ignore possible exchange rate effects.)

7. Offer your opinion on why economies of some less developed countries with strict restrictions on international trade and DFI are somewhat independent from economies of other countries. Why would MNCs desire to enter such countries? If these countries relaxed their restrictions, would their economies continue to be independent of other economies? Explain.

8. Dolphin, Inc., a U.S.-based MNC with a European subsidiary, expects that the euro will appreciate for several years. How might Dolphin adjust its policy on remitted earnings from the European subsidiary?

9. Bronco Corp. has decided to establish a subsidiary in Taiwan that will produce stereos and sell them there. It expects that its cost of producing these stereos will be one-third the cost of producing them in the United States. Assuming that its production cost estimates are accurate, is Bronco's strategy sensible? Explain.

10. What does this chapter reveal about the relationship between an MNC's degree of international business and its risk? What does this imply about the feasibility of increasing international business?

11. Starter Corp. of New Haven, Connecticut, produces sportswear that is licensed by professional sports teams. It recently decided to expand in Europe. What are the potential benefits for this firm from using DFI?

12. What potential benefits do you think were most important in the decision of the Walt Disney Co. to build a theme park in France?

13. Once an MNC establishes a subsidiary, DFI remains an ongoing decision. What does this statement mean?

14. Why would foreign governments provide MNCs with incentives to undertake DFI there?

15. This chapter concentrates on possible benefits to a firm that increases its international business. What are some risks of international business that may not exist for local business?

16. J.C. Penney has recognized numerous opportunities to expand in foreign countries and has assessed many foreign markets, including Brazil, Greece, Mexico, Portugal, Singapore, and Thailand. It has opened new stores in Europe, Asia, and Latin America. In each case, the firm was aware that it did not have sufficient understanding of the culture of each country that it had targeted; consequently, it engaged in joint ventures with local partners who knew the preferences of the local customers.

    a. What comparative advantage does J.C. Penney have when establishing a store in a foreign country, relative to an independent variety store?

    b. Why might the overall risk of J.C. Penney decrease or increase as a result of its recent global expansion?

    c. J.C. Penney has been more cautious about entering China. Explain the potential obstacles associated with entering China.

17. Consider the typical motives for a U.S. firm to engage in DFI. Which of these motives might have encouraged a U.S. firm to invest in Asia since the Asian crisis? (Assume the firm previously had no business in Asia.)

18. From the perspective of a U.S. firm that has DFI throughout Asia, did the Asian crisis increase or decrease the international diversification benefits achievable in the Asian countries?

Impact of 9/11/01

19. In August 2001, Ohio, Inc., considered establishing a manufacturing plant in central Asia, which would be used to cover its exports to Japan and Hong Kong. The cost of labor was very low in central Asia. On September 11, 2001, the terrorist attack on the United States caused Ohio, Inc., to reassess the potential cost savings. Why would the estimated expenses of the plant increase after the terrorist attack?

Internet Application

20. Information related to DFI can be retrieved from the following website of the Michigan State University Center for International Business Education and Research: **http://ciber.bus.msu.edu.**

    a. Use this site to identify emerging markets that appear to have favorable characteristics for DFI.

    b. The following website provides information about conditions that could affect an MNC's decision to invest in a specific country: **http://lcweb2.loc.gov/ gov/frd/cs/cshome.html.**

    Use this site to review the related information about a country of your choice. Describe the current economic environment and political environment of that country.

Running Your Own MNC

This exercise can be found on the Student CD-ROM.

Blades, Inc. Case

Consideration of Direct Foreign Investment

For the last year, Blades, Inc., has been exporting to Thailand in order to supplement its declining U.S. sales. Under the existing arrangement, Blades sells 180,000 pairs of roller blades annually to Entertainment Products, a Thai retailer, for a fixed price denominated in Thai baht. The agreement will last for another two years. Furthermore, to diversify internationally and to take advantage of an attractive offer by Jogs, Ltd., a British retailer, Blades has recently begun exporting to the United Kingdom. Under the resulting agreement, Jogs will purchase 200,000 pairs of "Speedos," Blades' primary product, annually at a fixed price of £80 per pair.

Blades' suppliers of the needed components for its roller blade production are located primarily in the United States, where Blades incurs the majority of its cost of goods sold. Although prices for inputs needed to manufacture roller blades vary, recent costs have run approximately $70 per pair. Blades also imports components from Thailand because of the relatively low price of rubber and plastic components and because of their high quality. These imports are denominated in Thai baht, and the exact price (in baht) depends on prevailing market prices for these components in Thailand. Currently, inputs sufficient to manufacture a pair of roller blades cost approximately 3,000 Thai baht per pair of roller blades.

Although Thailand had been among the world's fastest growing economies, recent events in Thailand have increased the level of economic uncertainty. Specifically, the Thai baht, which had been pegged to the dollar, is now a freely floating currency and has depreciated substantially in recent months. Furthermore, recent levels of inflation in Thailand have been very high. Hence, future economic conditions in Thailand are highly uncertain.

Ben Holt, Blades' chief financial officer (CFO), is seriously considering DFI in Thailand. He believes that this is a perfect time to either establish a subsidiary or acquire an existing business in Thailand because the uncertain economic conditions and the depreciation of the baht have substantially lowered the initial costs required for DFI. Holt believes the growth potential in Asia will be extremely high once the Thai economy stabilizes.

Although Holt has also considered DFI in the United Kingdom, he would prefer that Blades invest in Thailand as opposed to the United Kingdom. Forecasts indicate that the demand for roller blades in the United Kingdom is similar to that in the United States; since Blades' U.S. sales have recently declined because of the high prices it charges, Holt expects that DFI in the United Kingdom will yield similar results, especially since the components required to manufacture roller blades are more expensive in the United Kingdom than in the United States. Furthermore, both domestic and foreign roller blade manufacturers are relatively well established in the United Kingdom, so the growth potential there is limited. Holt believes the Thai roller blade market offers more growth potential.

Blades can sell its products at a lower price but generate higher profit margins in Thailand than it can in the United States. This is because the Thai customer has committed itself to purchase a fixed number of Blades' products annually only if it can purchase Speedos at a substantial discount from the U.S. price. Nevertheless, since the cost of goods sold incurred in Thailand is substantially below that incurred in the United States, Blades has managed to generate higher profit margins from its Thai exports and imports than in the United States.

As a financial analyst for Blades, Inc., you generally agree with Ben Holt's assessment of the situation. However, you are concerned that Thai consumers have not been affected yet by the unfavorable economic conditions. You believe that they may reduce their spending on leisure products within the next year. Therefore, you think it would be beneficial to wait until next year, when the unfavorable economic conditions in Thailand may subside, to make a decision regarding DFI in Thailand. However, if economic conditions in Thailand improve over the next year, DFI may become more expensive both because existing firms will be more expensive and because the baht may appreciate. You are also aware that several of Blades' U.S. competitors are considering expanding into Thailand in the next year.

If Blades acquires an existing business in Thailand or establishes a subsidiary there by the end of next year, it would fulfill its agreement with Entertainment Products for the subsequent year. The Thai retailer has expressed an interest in renewing the contractual agreement with Blades at that time if Blades establishes operations in Thailand. However, Holt believes that Blades could charge a higher price for its products if it establishes its own distribution channels.

Holt has asked you to answer the following questions:

1. Identify and discuss some of the benefits that Blades, Inc., could obtain from DFI.

2. Do you think Blades should wait until next year to undertake DFI in Thailand? What is the tradeoff if Blades undertakes the DFI now?

3. Do you think Blades should renew its agreement with the Thai supplier for another three years? What is the tradeoff if Blades renews the agreement?

4. Assume a high level of unemployment in Thailand and a unique production process employed by Blades, Inc. How do you think the Thai government would view the establishment of a subsidiary in Thailand by firms such as Blades? Do you think the Thai government would be more or less supportive if firms such as Blades acquired existing businesses in Thailand? Why?

Small Business Dilemma

Direct Foreign Investment Decision by the Sports Exports Company

Jim Logan's business, the Sports Exports Company, continues to grow. His primary product is the footballs he produces and exports to a distributor in the United Kingdom. However, his recent joint venture with a British firm has also been successful. Under this arrangement, a British firm produces other sporting goods for Jim's firm; these goods are then delivered to that distributor. Jim intentionally started his international business by exporting because it was easier and cheaper to export than to establish a place of business in the United Kingdom. However, he is considering establishing a firm in the United Kingdom to produce the footballs there instead of in his garage (in the United States). This firm would also produce the other sporting goods that he now sells, so he would no longer have to rely on another British firm (through the joint venture) to produce those goods.

1. Given the information provided here, what are the advantages to Jim of establishing the firm in the United Kingdom?

2. Given the information provided here, what are the disadvantages to Jim of establishing the firm in the United Kingdom?

7

MULTINATIONAL RESTRUCTURING

Multinational Corporations (MNCs) commonly engage in [**multinational restructuring**, which involves restructuring the composition of their multinational assets or liabilities.] Thus, multinational restructuring decisions not only determine the types of assets, but also the countries where those assets are located. Financial managers must understand how to assess restructuring alternatives so that they can make restructuring decisions that maximize the value of the MNC.

The specific objectives of this chapter are to:
- Provide a background on how MNCs use international acquisitions as a form of multinational restructuring.
- Explain how MNCs conduct valuations of foreign target firms.
- Explain why valuations of a target firm vary among MNCs that plan to restructure by acquiring a target.
- Identify other types of multinational restructuring, besides international acquisitions.

BACKGROUND ON MULTINATIONAL RESTRUCTURING

Decisions by an MNC to build a new subsidiary in the Netherlands, to acquire a company in Italy, to sell its Singapore subsidiary, to downsize its operations in New Zealand, or to shift some production from its British subsidiary to its Mexican subsidiary all represent forms of multinational restructuring. Even the most successful MNCs continuously assess possible forms of multinational restructuring so that they can capitalize on changing economic, political, or industry conditions across countries.

MNCs reevaluate their existing businesses and other proposed projects when determining the ideal composition of assets to employ and the locations where the assets are employed. Even if an existing business adds value to the MNC, it may be worthwhile to assess whether the business would generate more value to the MNC if it was restructured.

Trends in International Acquisitions

The volume of foreign acquisitions of U.S. firms has increased consistently since 1993. In particular, European firms have been attractive targets for U.S. firms attempting to establish a presence in Europe due to the more uniform regulations across countries in the European Union, the momentum for free enterprise in Eastern Europe, and the inception of the euro. U.S. firms acquire more targets in the United Kingdom than in any other country. British and Canadian firms are the most common non-U.S. acquirers of U.S. targets.

Model for Valuing a Foreign Target

An MNC's decision to invest in a foreign company is similar to its decision to invest in other projects, in that it is based on a comparison of benefits and costs as measured by net present value. From an MNC's parent's perspective, the foreign target's value can be estimated as the present value of cash flows that it would receive from the target, as the target would become a foreign subsidiary owned by the parent.

The MNC's parent would consider investing in the target only if the estimated present value of the cash flows it would ultimately receive from the target over time exceeds the initial outlay necessary to purchase the target. Thus, capital budgeting

http://
Visit the homepage of the CIA at www.odci.gov/cia/ciahome.html for access to various national and international surveys, analyses, maps, and publications such as the *World Factbook*. This information can be useful when valuing a foreign target.

Managing for Value: International Acquisitions

An international acquisition of a firm is similar to other international projects in that it requires an initial outlay and is expected to generate cash flows whose present value will exceed the initial outlay. Many international acquisitions are motivated by the desire to increase global market share or to capitalize on economies of scale through global consolidation. Many U.S.-based MNCs including Rockwell International, Ford Motor Co., Scott Paper Co., Borden, Inc., and Dow Chemical Co. have recently engaged in international acquisitions.

MNCs may view international acquisitions as a better form of direct foreign investment (DFI) than establishing a new subsidiary. However, there are distinct differences between these two forms of DFI. Through an international acquisition, the firm can immediately expand its international business since the target is already in place. Establishing a new subsidiary requires time. Second, an international acquisition can benefit from the customer relationships that have already been established. These advantages of an international acquisition over the establishment of a foreign subsidiary must be weighed against the higher costs of the acquisition. When viewed as a project, the international acquisition usually generates quicker and larger cash flows than the establishment of a new subsidiary, but it also requires a larger initial outlay. International acquisitions also necessitate the integration of the parent's management style with that of the foreign target.

analysis can be used to determine whether a firm should be acquired. The net present value of a company from the acquiring firm's perspective (NPV_a) is

$$NPV_a = -IO_a + \sum_{t=1}^{n} \frac{CF_{a,t}}{(1+k)^t} + \frac{SV_a}{(1+k)^n}$$

where

IO_a = initial outlay needed by the acquiring firm to acquire the target
$CF_{a,t}$ = cash flow to be generated by the target for the acquiring firm
k = required rate of return on the acquisition of the target
SV_a = salvage value of the target (expected selling price of the target at a point in the future)
n = time when the target will be sold by the acquiring firm

The capital budgeting analysis of a foreign target must account for the exchange rate of concern. For example, consider a U.S.-based MNC that assesses the acquisition of a foreign company. The dollar initial outlay ($IO_{U.S.}$) needed by the U.S. firm is determined by the acquisition price in foreign currency units (IO_f) and the spot rate of the foreign currency (S):

$$IO_{U.S.} = IO_f(S)$$

The dollar amount of cash flows to the U.S. firm is determined by the foreign currency cash flows ($CF_{f,t}$) per period remitted to the United States and the spot rate at that time (S_t):

$$CF_{a,t} = (CF_{f,t})S_t$$

This ignores any withholding taxes or blocked-funds restrictions imposed by the host government and any income taxes imposed by the U.S. government. The dollar amount of salvage value to the U.S. firm is determined by the salvage value in foreign currency units (SV_f) and the spot rate at the time (period n) when it is converted to dollars (S_n):

$$SV_a = (SV_f)S_n$$

The net present value of a foreign target can be derived by substituting the equalities just described in the capital budgeting equation:

$$NPV_a = -IO_a + \sum_{t=1}^{n} \frac{CF_{a,t}}{(1+k)^t} + \frac{SV_a}{(1+k)^n}$$

$$= -(IO_f)S + \sum_{t=1}^{n} \frac{(CF_{f,t})S_t}{(1+k)^t} + \frac{(SV_f)S_n}{(1+k)^n}$$

Assessing Potential Acquisitions in Asia

Although the Asian crisis had devastating effects, it created an opportunity for some MNCs to pursue new business in Asia. The initial outlay for acquiring a firm in Asia was lower as a result of the crisis. First, property values in Asia had declined. Second, the parent's currency (for parents in the United States or Europe) had more purchasing power due to the weakening of the Asian currencies. Third, many firms in Asia were near bankruptcy and were unable to obtain necessary funding. Fourth, the governments in these countries were more willing to allow foreign acquisitions of local firms (especially those that were failing) as a means of resolving the crisis. Consequently, some U.S. and European firms pursued direct foreign investment in Asia during the Asian crisis.

Example

In the first six months of 1998, U.S. firms invested more than $8 billion in Asia—more than double the amount they had invested there in all of 1997. Procter & Gamble agreed to acquire Sanyong Paper (a large conglomerate in South Korea) during the crisis. Citicorp obtained a large stake of First City Bank in Thailand.

Firms that made aquistions had to consider the obvious adverse effects of the crisis in their capital budgeting analysis. The lower economic growth meant that most Asian projects would generate lower cash flows, and the weak currencies reduced the amount of cash flows (in the parent's currency) that would ultimately be received as a return on the parent's investment.

To the extent that the firms believed that the Asian currency values had hit bottom and would rebound, they could assume that any new acquisitions of Asian firms would benefit from future exchange rate movements. Firms could initiate their investment in Asia by investing their home currency in exchange for the weak Asian currency. Then, if the Asian currency appreciated over time, the earnings generated there would be worth more (in terms of the parent's currency) when remitted to the parent.

Assessing Potential Acquisitions in Europe

Before the adoption of the euro, a U.S.-based MNC had to separately consider the exchange rate effects from acquiring firms in different European countries. For example, Italy's currency (the lira) was considered more likely to weaken against the dollar than some of the other European currencies, and this could affect the decision of whether to acquire an Italian firm versus a firm in Germany or France. The adoption of the euro as the local currency by several European countries simplifies the analysis for an MNC that is comparing possible target firms in those countries. The U.S.-based MNC can be affected by future movements in the euro's value against the dollar, but those effects should occur regardless of whether the MNC purchases a firm in Italy or in any other euro-zone country. Thus, the MNC can make its decision on which firm to acquire within these countries without being concerned about differential exchange rate effects. If the MNC is also considering firms in European countries that have not adopted the euro as their currency, however, it will still have to compare the potential exchange rate effects that could result from the acquisition.

FACTORS THAT AFFECT THE EXPECTED CASH FLOWS OF THE FOREIGN TARGET

When an MNC estimates the future cash flows that it will ultimately receive after acquiring a foreign target, it considers several factors that reflect either conditions in the country of concern or conditions of the target itself.

Target-Specific Factors

The following characteristics of the foreign target are typically considered when estimating the cash flows that the target will provide to the parent.

Target's Previous Cash Flows. Since the foreign target has been conducting business, it has a history of cash flows that it has generated. The recent cash flows per period may serve as an initial base from which future cash flows per period can be estimated after accounting for other factors. Since the target firm has already been conducting business, it may be easier to estimate the cash flows it will generate than to estimate the cash flows to be generated from a new foreign subsidiary.

A company's previous cash flows are not necessarily an accurate indicator of future cash flows, however, especially when the target's future cash flows would have to be converted into the acquirer's home currency as they are remitted to the parent. Therefore, the MNC needs to carefully consider all the factors that could influence the cash flows that will be generated from a foreign target.

Managerial Talent of the Target. An acquiring firm must assess the target's existing management so that it can determine how the target firm will be managed after the acquisition. The way the acquirer plans to deal with the managerial talent will affect the estimated cash flows to be generated by the target.

If the MNC acquires the target, it may allow the target firm to be managed as it was before the acquisition. Under these conditions, however, the acquiring firm may have less potential for enhancing the target's cash flows.

A second alternative for the MNC is to downsize the target firm after acquiring it. For example, if the acquiring firm introduces new technology that reduces the need for some of the target's employees, it can attempt to downsize the target. Downsizing reduces expenses but may also reduce productivity and revenue, so the effect on cash flows can vary with the situation. In addition, an MNC may encounter significant barriers to increasing efficiency by downsizing in several countries. Governments of some countries are likely to intervene and prevent the acquisition if downsizing is anticipated.

A third alternative for the MNC is to maintain the existing employees of the target but restructure the operations so that labor is used more efficiently. For example, the MNC may infuse its own technology into the target firm and then restructure operations so that many of the employees receive new job assignments. This strategy may cause the acquirer to incur some additional expenses, but there is potential for improved cash flows over time.

Country-Specific Factors

http://
Visit the Web page of the International Institute for Management (IMD) at www.imd.ch/wcy/wcyonline.html for the results of a comprehensive World Competitiveness Analysis that ranks about 50 countries by factors such as infrastructure, financial environment, science and technological capabilities, international business environment, and political freedom.

An MNC typically considers the following country-specific factors when estimating the cash flows that will be provided by the foreign target to the parent.

Target's Local Economic Conditions. Potential targets in countries where economic conditions are strong are more likely to experience strong demand for their products in the future and may generate higher cash flows. However, some firms are more sensitive to economic conditions than others. Also, some acquisitions of firms are intended to focus on exporting from the target's home country, so the economic conditions in the target's country may not be as important. Economic conditions are difficult to predict over a long-term period, especially for emerging countries.

Target's Local Political Conditions. Potential targets in countries where political conditions are favorable are less likely to experience adverse shocks to their cash flows. The sensitivity of cash flows to political conditions is dependent on the firm's type of business. Political conditions are also difficult to predict over a long-term period, especially for emerging countries.

Target's Industry Conditions. Industry conditions within a country can cause some targets to be more desirable than others. Some industries in a particular country may be extremely competitive while others are not. In addition, some industries exhibit much stronger potential for growth in a particular country, while others exhibit very little potential for growth. When an MNC assesses targets among countries, it would prefer a country where the growth potential for its industry is high and the competition within the industry is not excessive.

http://
Visit Fred, the Federal Reserve's data bank, at www.stls.frb.org/fred for numerous economic and financial time series, e.g., on balance-of-payments statistics, interest rates, and foreign exchange rates.

Target's Currency Conditions. If a U.S.-based MNC plans to acquire a foreign target, it must consider how future exchange rate movements may affect the target's local currency cash flows. It must also consider how exchange rates will affect the conversion of the target's remitted earnings to the U.S. parent. In the typical case, ideally the foreign currency would be weak at the time of the acquisition (so that the MNC's initial outlay is low) but strengthen over time as funds are periodically remitted to the U.S. parent. There can be exceptions to this general statement, but the point is that the MNC forecasts future exchange rates and then applies those forecasts to determine the impact on cash flows.

Target's Local Stock Market Conditions. Potential target firms that are publicly held are continuously valued in the market, so their stock prices can change rapidly. As the target firm's stock price changes, the acceptable bid price necessary to buy that firm will likely change as well. Thus, there are substantial swings in the purchase price that would be acceptable to a target. This is especially true for publicly traded firms in emerging markets in Asia, Eastern Europe, and Latin America where stock prices commonly change by 5 percent or more in a week. Therefore, an MNC that plans to acquire a target would prefer to make its bid at a time when the local stock market prices are generally low.

Taxes Applicable to the Target. When an MNC assesses a foreign target, it must estimate the expected after-tax cash flows that it will ultimately receive in the form of remitted funds to the parent. Thus, the tax laws applicable to the foreign target are used to derive the after-tax cash flows. First, the applicable corporate tax rates are applied to the estimated future earnings of the target to determine the after-tax earnings. Second, the after-tax proceeds are determined by applying any withholding tax rates to the funds that are expected to be remitted to the parent in each period. Third, if the acquiring firm's government imposes an additional tax on remitted earnings or allows a tax credit, that tax or credit must be applied.

EXAMPLE OF THE VALUATION PROCESS

Lincoln Co. desires to expand in Latin America or Canada. The methods Lincoln uses to initially screen targets in various countries and then to estimate a target's value are discussed next.

International Screening Process

Lincoln Co. considers the factors just described when it conducts an initial screening of prospective targets. It has identified prospective targets in Mexico, Brazil, Colombia, and Canada, as shown in Exhibit 15.1. The target in Mexico has no plans to sell its business and is unwilling to even consider an offer from Lincoln Co. Therefore, this firm is no longer considered. Lincoln anticipates potential political problems that could create barriers to an acquisition in Colombia, even though the Colombian target is willing to be acquired. Stock market conditions are not favorable in Brazil, as the stock prices of most Brazilian companies have recently risen substantially. Lincoln does not want to pay as much as the Brazilian target is now worth based on its prevailing market value.

Based on this screening process, the only foreign target that deserves a closer assessment is the target in Canada. According to Lincoln's assessment, Canadian currency conditions are slightly unfavorable, but this is not a reason to eliminate the target from further consideration. Thus, the next step would be for Lincoln to obtain as much information as possible about the target and conditions in Canada. Then Lincoln can use this information to derive the target's expected cash flows and to determine whether the target's value exceeds the initial outlay that would be required to purchase it, as explained next.

Exhibit 15.1

Example of Process Used to Screen Foreign Targets

Target Based in:	Is the Target Receptive to an Acquisition?	Local Economic and Industry Conditions	Local Political Conditions	Local Currency Conditions	Prevailing Stock Market Prices	Tax Laws
Mexico	No	Favorable	OK	OK	OK	May change
Brazil	Maybe	OK	OK	OK	Too high	May change
Colombia	Yes	Favorable	Volatile	Favorable	OK	Reasonable
Canada	Yes	OK	Favorable	Slightly unfavorable	OK	Reasonable

Estimating the Target's Value

Once Lincoln Co. has completed its initial screening of targets, it conducts a valuation of all targets that passed the screening process. Continuing with our simplified example, Lincoln's screening process resulted in only one eligible target, a Canadian firm. Assume the Canadian firm has conducted all of its business locally. Assume also that Lincoln expects that it can obtain materials at a lower cost than the target can because of its relationships with some Canadian suppliers and that it also expects to implement a more efficient production process. Lincoln also plans to use its existing managerial talent to manage the target and therefore reduce the administrative and marketing expenses incurred by the target. It also expects that the target's revenue will increase when its products are sold under Lincoln's name. Lincoln expects to maintain prices of the products as they are.

   The target's expected cash flows can be measured by first determining the revenue and expense levels in recent years and then adjusting those levels to reflect the changes that would occur after the acquisition.

Revenue. The target's annual revenue has ranged between $80 million and $90 million in Canadian dollars (C$) over the last four years. Lincoln Co. expects that it can improve sales, and forecasts revenue to be C$ 100 million next year, C$93.3 million in the following year, and $121 million in the year after. The cost of goods sold has been about 50 percent of the revenue in the past, but Lincoln expects it will fall to 40 percent of revenue because of improvements in efficiency. The estimates are shown in Exhibit 15.2.

Expenses. Selling and administrative expenses have been about C$20 million annually, but Lincoln believes that through restructuring it can reduce these expenses to C$15 million in each of the next three years. Depreciation expenses have been about C$10 million in the past and are expected to remain at that level

Exhibit 15.2
Valuation of Canadian Target Based on the Assumptions Provided (in Millions of Dollars)

	Last Year	Year 1	Year 2	Year 3
Revenue	C$90	C$100	C$93.3	C$121
Cost of goods sold	C$45	C$40	C$37.3	C$ 48.4
Gross profit	C$45	C$60	C$56	C$ 72.6
Selling & administrative expenses	C$20	C$15	C$15	C$15
Depreciation	C$10	C$10	C$10	C$10
Earnings before taxes	C$15	C$35	C$31	C$47.6
Tax (30%)	C$ 4.5	C$10.5	C$ 9.3	C$14.28
Earnings after taxes	C$10.5	C$24.5	C$21.7	C$33.32
+Depreciation		C$10	C$10	C$10
−Funds to reinvest		C$5	C$ 5	C$ 5
Sale of firm		___	___	C$230
Cash flows in C$		C$29.5	C$26.7	C$268.32
Exchange rate of C$		$ .80	$ .80	$ .80
Cash flows in $		$23.6	$21.36	$214.66
PV (20% discount rate)		$19.67	$14.83	$124.22
Cumulative PV		$19.67	$34.50	$158.72

for the next three years. The Canadian tax rate on the target's earnings is expected to be 30 percent.

Earnings and Cash Flows. Given the information assumed here, the after-tax earnings that the target would generate under Lincoln's ownership are estimated in Exhibit 15.2. The cash flows generated by the target are determined by adding the depreciation expenses back to the after-tax earnings. Assume that the target will need C$5 million in cash each year to support existing operations (including the repair of existing machinery) and that the remaining cash flow can be remitted to the U.S. parent. Assume that the target firm is financially supported only by its equity. It currently has 10 million shares of stock outstanding that are priced at C$17 per share.

Cash Flows to Parent. Since Lincoln's parent wishes to assess the target from its own perspective, it focuses on the dollar cash flows that it expects to receive. Assuming no additional taxes, the expected cash flows generated in Canada that are to be remitted to Lincoln's parent are converted into U.S. dollars at the expected exchange rate at the end of each year. Lincoln uses the prevailing exchange rate of the Canadian dollar (which is $.80) as the expected exchange rate for the Canadian dollar in future years.

Estimating the Target's Future Sales Price. If Lincoln purchases the target, it will sell the target in three years, after improving the target's performance. Lincoln expects to receive C$230 million (after capital gains taxes) from the sale. The price at which the target can actually be sold will depend on its expected future cash flows from that point forward, but those expected cash flows are partially dependent on its performance prior to that time. Thus, Lincoln can enhance the sales price by improving the target's performance over the three years it plans to own the target.

Valuing the Target Based on Estimated Cash Flows. The expected U.S. dollar cash flows to Lincoln's parent over the next three years are shown in Exhibit 15.2. The high cash flow in Year 3 is due to Lincoln's plans to sell the target at that time. Assuming that Lincoln has a required rate of return of 20 percent on this project, the cash flows are discounted at that rate to derive the net present value of acquiring this target. From Lincoln's perspective, the net present value of the target is about $158.72 million.

Given that the target's shares are currently valued at C$17 per share, the 10 million shares are worth C$170 million. At the prevailing exchange rate of $.80 per dollar, the target is currently valued at $136 million by the market (computed as C$170 million × $.80). Lincoln's valuation of the target of about $159 million is about 17 percent above the market valuation. However, Lincoln will have to pay a premium on the shares to entice the target's board of directors to approve the acquisition. Premiums commonly range from 10 percent to 40 percent of the market price. If Lincoln allows for a premium of 10 percent above the prevailing stock price of C$17 per share, it would pay C$18.7 per share for the target. At this price per share, the price paid for the Canadian firm would be C$187 million, or $149.6 million at the existing exchange rate. This price is less than the perceived net present value of the target, so Lincoln may be willing to pay this amount.

Lincoln recognizes that the target may reject its offer of a 10 percent premium and ask for a higher premium, but it will not pay more than its estimate of the target's net present value. Since Lincoln values the target at about $159 million, it will not pay more than about C$199 million at the prevailing exchange rate (computed as $159 million divided by $.80 per Canadian dollar), or a share price of C$19.90 (computed as C$199 million divided by 10 million shares).

Sources of Uncertainty. This example shows how the acquisition of a publicly traded foreign firm differs from the creation of a new foreign subsidiary. Although the valuation of a publicly traded foreign firm can utilize information about an existing business, the cash flows resulting from the acquisition are still subject to uncertainty for several reasons, which can be identified by reviewing the assumptions made in the valuation process. First, the growth rate of revenue is subject to uncertainty. If this rate is overestimated (perhaps because Canadian economic growth is overestimated), the earnings generated in Canada will be lower, and cash flows remitted to the U.S. parent will be lower as well.

Second, the cost of goods sold could exceed the assumed level of 40 percent of revenue, which would reduce cash flows remitted to the parent. Third, the selling and administrative expenses could exceed the assumed amount of C$15 million, especially when considering that the annual expenses were C$20 million prior to the acquisition. Fourth, Canada's corporate tax rate could increase, which would reduce the cash flows remitted to the parent. Fifth, the exchange rate of the Canadian dollar may be weaker than assumed, which would reduce the cash flows received by the parent. Sixth, the estimated selling price of the target three years from now could be incorrect for any of these five reasons, and this estimate is very influential on the valuation of the target today.

Since one or more of these conditions could occur, the estimated net present value of the target could be overestimated. Consequently, it is possible for Lincoln to acquire the target at a purchase price exceeding its actual value. In particular, the future cash flows are very sensitive to exchange rate movements. This can be illustrated by using sensitivity analysis and reestimating the value of the target based on different scenarios for the exchange rate over time.

Changes in Valuation over Time. If Lincoln Co. decides not to bid for the target at this time, it will need to redo its analysis if it later reconsiders acquiring the target. As the factors that affect the expected cash flows or the required rate of return from investing in the target change, so will the value of the target. For example, changes in the expected economic conditions in Canada will affect the cash flows generated by the target. Changes in exchange rates will affect the purchase price paid by Lincoln's parent and the expected cash flows to be received by the parent. Changes in the parent's cost of financing or political risk in Canada could cause a change in the required rate of return on the Canadian target.

Changes in the Market Valuation. Just as Lincoln's valuation of the target changes over time, so does the market value of the target. The target's stock price may change in response to conditions that affect its expected cash flows. The price may increase if investors anticipate that the target will be acquired, since they are aware that stock prices of targets rise abruptly after a bid by the acquiring firm. Thus, it is important that Lincoln keep its intentions about acquiring the target confidential.

Financial Markets Perspective

How Financial Market Conditions Affect Market Valuations

The price that a U.S. acquirer must pay for a foreign target's stock price could change simply because of general stock market conditions or because of foreign exchange market conditions.

- *Impact of stock market conditions.* A change in stock market conditions affects the price per share of each stock in that market. Thus, the value of publicly traded firms in that market will change. Remember that an acquirer needs to pay a premium above the market valuation to acquire a foreign firm.

Continuing with our example involving Lincoln Co.'s pursuit of a Canadian target, assume that the target firm has a market price of C$17 per share, representing a valuation of C$170 million, but that before Lincoln makes its decision to acquire the target, the Canadian stock market level rises by 20 percent. If the target's stock price rises by this same percentage, the firm is now valued at

New stock price = C$170 million × 1.2
= C$204 million

Using the 10 percent premium assumed in the earlier example, Lincoln must now pay C$224.4 million (computed as C$204 million × 1.1) if it wants to acquire the target. This example illustrates how the price paid for the target can change abruptly simply because of a change in the general level of the stock market.

- *Impact of stock market conditions on the value of private firms.* Even if a target is privately held, general stock market conditions will affect the amount that an acquirer has to pay for the target because a privately held company's value is influenced by the market price multiples of related firms in the same country. A simple method of valuing a private company is to apply the price-earnings (PE) ratios of publicly traded firms in the same industry to the private company's earnings.

For example, if the earnings of a private Canadian company are C$8 million and the average PE ratio of publicly traded Canadian firms in the same industry is 15, the company's market valuation can be estimated as:

Market valuation = earnings × average PE ratio
= C$8 million × 15
= C$120 milion

If the stock market level rises by 20 percent, the average PE ratio of the firms in the same industry will likely rise by about 20 percent, which represents an increase in the PE ratio from 15 to 18. The new market valuation of the Canadian firm will be:

New market valuation = C$8 million × 18
= C$144 million

As this example illustrates, private companies also become more expensive targets when local stock market conditions improve.

- *Impact of exchange rates.* Whether a foreign target is publicly traded or private, a U.S. acquirer must convert dollars to the local currency to purchase the target. If the foreign currency appreciates by the time the acquirer makes payment, the acquisition will be more costly. The cost of the acquisition changes in the same proportion as the change in the exchange rate.

- *Combined stock market and exchange rate effects.* In reality, stock market levels and exchange rates change simultaneously. The effects on the cost of acquiring a foreign target are especially pronounced in emerging markets where stock and currency values are volatile.

For example, assume that Mizner, Inc., a U.S. firm, wanted to acquire a firm in the Czech Republic so that it could expand its business in Eastern Europe. Also assume that the Czech target's valuation moved in tandem with general Czech stock market conditions. Exhibit 15.3 shows how the cost to Mizner of acquiring the Czech target changed over time based on actual stock market and foreign exchange market conditions (assuming no change in the performance of the firm itself). Notice that the the cost of the acquisition increased by 20 percent in a single month (December 2000) as a result of a very strong stock market in that month and also appreciation of the Czech currency (koruna). At the other extreme, the cost of the acquisition declined by 20 percent in March 2001 as a result of a weakening stock market and koruna over that month. This exhibit illustrates how sensitive the cost of an acquisition of a foreign target is to foreign market conditions.

Example 15.3

Influence of Czech Stock Market and Currency Conditions on the Cost of Acquiring a Czech Target

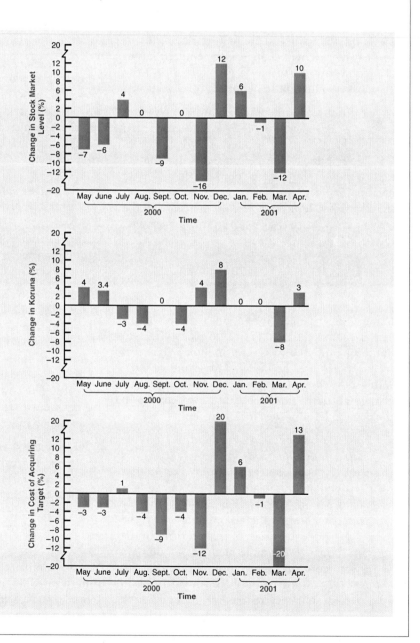

WHY VALUATIONS OF A TARGET MAY VARY AMONG MNCs

Most MNCs that consider acquiring a specific target will use a somewhat similar process for valuing the target. Nevertheless, their valuations will differ because of differences in the way the MNC's estimate the key determinants of a given target's valuation: (1) cash flows to be generated by the target, (2) exchange rate effects on funds remitted to the MNC's parent, and (3) required rate of return when investing in the target.

Estimated Cash Flows of the Foreign Target

The target's expected future cash flows will vary among MNCs because the cash flows will be dependent on the MNC's management or oversight of the target's operations. If an MNC can improve the production efficiency of the target without reducing the target's production volume, it can improve the target's cash flows.

Each MNC may have a different plan as to how the target will fit within its structure and how the target will conduct future operations. The target's expected cash flows will be influenced by the way it is utilized. An MNC with production plants in Asia that purchases another Asian production plant may simply be attempting to increase its market share and production capacity. This MNC's cash flows change because of a higher production and sales level. Conversely, an MNC with all of its production plants in the United States may purchase an Asian production plant to shift its production where costs are lower. This MNC's cash flows change because of lower expenses.

Tax laws can create competitive advantages for acquirers based in some countries. Acquirers based in low-tax countries may be able to generate higher cash flows from acquiring a foreign target than acquirers in high-tax countries simply because they are subject to lower taxes on the future earnings remitted by the target (after it is acquired).

Exchange Rate Effects on the Funds Remitted

The valuation of a target among MNCs can vary simply because of differences in the exchange rate effects on funds remitted by the foreign target to the MNC's parent. If the target remits funds frequently in the near future, its value will be partially dependent on the expected exchange rate of the target's local currency in the near future. If the target does not remit funds in the near future, its value is more dependent on its local growth strategy and on exchange rates in the distant future.

Required Return of Acquirer

The valuation of the target could also vary among MNCs because of differences in their required rate of return from investing funds to acquire the target. If an MNC targets a successful foreign company with plans to continue the target's local business in a more efficient manner, the risk of the business will be relatively low, and therefore the MNC's required return from acquiring the target will be relatively low. Conversely, if an MNC targets the company because it plans to turn the company into a major exporter, the risk is much higher. The target has not established itself in foreign markets, so the cash flows that would result from the exporting business are very uncertain. Thus, the required return to acquire the target company will be relatively high as well.

If potential acquirers are based in different countries, their required rates of return from a specific target will vary even if they plan to use the target in similar ways. Recall that an MNC's required rate of return on any project is dependent on the local risk-free interest rate (since that influences the cost of funds for that MNC). Therefore, the required rate of return for MNCs based in countries with relatively high interest rates such as Brazil and Venezuela may differ from MNCs based in low-interest-rate countries such as the United States or Japan. The higher required rate of return for MNCs based in Latin American countries will not necessarily lead to a lower valuation. The target's currency might be expected to appreciate substantially against Latin American currencies (since some Latin American currencies have consistently weakened over time), which would enhance the amount of cash flows received as a result of remitted funds and could possibly offset the effects of the higher required rate of return.

OTHER TYPES OF MULTINATIONAL RESTRUCTURING

Besides acquiring foreign firms, MNCs can engage in multinational restructuring through international partial acquisitions, acquisitions of privatized businesses, international alliances, and international divestitures. Each type is described in turn.

International Partial Acquisitions

In many cases, an MNC may consider a partial international acquisition of a firm, in which it purchases part of the existing stock of a foreign firm. A partial international acquisition requires less funds because only a portion of the foreign target's shares are purchased. With this type of investment, the foreign target normally continues operating and may not experience the employee turnover that commonly occurs after a target's ownership changes. Nevertheless, by acquiring a substantial fraction of the shares, the MNC may have some influence on the target's management and be in a position to complete the acquisition in the future. Some MNCs buy substantial stakes in foreign companies to have some control over their operations. For example, Coca-Cola has purchased stakes in many foreign bottling companies that bottle its syrup. In this way, it can ensure that the bottling operations meet its standards.

Valuation of a Foreign Firm That May Be Partially Acquired. When an MNC considers a partial acquisition in which it will purchase sufficient shares so that it can control the firm, the MNC can conduct its valuation of the target in much the same way as when it purchases the entire firm. If the MNC buys only a small proportion of the firm's shares, however, the MNC cannot restructure the firm's operations to make it more efficient. Therefore, its estimates of the firm's cash flows must be made from the perspective of a passive investor rather than as a decision maker for the firm.

International Acquisitions of Privatized Businesses

In recent years, government-owned businesses of many developing countries in Eastern Europe and South America have been sold to individuals or corporations. Many MNCs have capitalized on this wave of so-called privatization by acquiring the businesses being sold by governments. These businesses may be attractive because of the potential for MNCs to increase their efficiency.

Valuation of a Privatized Business. An MNC can conduct a valuation of a foreign business that was owned by the government in a developing country by using capital budgeting analysis, as illustrated earlier. However, the valuation of such businesses is difficult for the following reasons:

- The future cash flows are very uncertain because the businesses were previously operating in environments of little or no competition. Thus, previous sales volume figures may not be useful indicators of future sales.
- Data concerning what businesses are worth are very limited in some countries because there are not many publicly traded firms in their markets, and there is limited disclosure of prices paid for targets in other acquisitions. Consequently, there may not be any benchmarks to use when valuing a business.
- Economic conditions in these countries are very uncertain during the transition to a market-oriented economy.
- Political conditions tend to be volatile during the transition, as government policies for businesses are sometimes unclear or subject to abrupt changes.

Even with the difficulties of measuring the value of privatized businesses, MNCs such as Gerber Products and PepsiCo have acquired these businesses as a means of entering new markets. Hungary serves as a model country for privatizations. More than 25,000 MNCs have a foreign stake in Hungary's businesses. Hungary's government has been quick and efficient at selling off its assets to MNCs.

International Alliances

MNCs commonly engage in international alliances such as joint ventures and licensing agreements with foreign firms. International alliances are quite different from international acquisitions. The initial outlay is typically smaller because the MNC is not acquiring a foreign firm, and the cash flows to be received are typically smaller as well.

Example | Laredo, Inc., plans to provide a Mexican firm with technology. In return, the Mexican firm will pay royalties amounting to 10 percent of its future sales of products resulting from use of this technology over the next five years. Laredo's initial outlay for this international alliance is the initial expense incurred as a result of providing the technology. Laredo can estimate the cash flows to be received from the Mexican firm by first forecasting the Mexican firm's annual sales (in pesos) of products based on the technology. Laredo will receive 10 percent of this amount. Then, it must forecast the value of the peso over each of the next five years so that it can determine the dollar cash flows resulting from these royalties. It must also consider any tax effects.

International Divestitures

An MNC should periodically reassess its direct foreign investments to determine whether they should be retained or sold (divested). Some foreign projects may no longer be feasible as a result of the MNC's increased cost of capital, increased host government taxes, increased political risk in the host country, or revised projections of exchange rates. Many divestitures occur as a result of a revised assessment of industry or economic conditions. For example, Warner-Lambert Co., Johnson & Johnson, and several other U.S.-based MNCs recently divested some of their Latin American subsidiaries when economic conditions deteriorated there.

Assessing Whether to Divest Existing Operations in Asia. During the Asian crisis in the 1997–1998 period, some MNCs with direct foreign investment in Asia reassessed the feasibility of their existing operations. The expected cash flows that these operations would generate for the parent had declined in many cases for two obvious reasons. First, the rate of economic growth in Asia declined, which led to a decline in expected local sales by the foreign subsidiaries and therefore a decline in the expected level of foreign currency cash flow. Second, the weak currencies of Asian countries led to a decline in the expected amount of the parent's currency to be received when foreign subsidiaries in Asian countries remitted funds. At the same time, however, market valuations had declined so much that any operations could be divested only if the parent was willing to sell them at a low price. The low prices deterred some divestitures.

Valuation of an International Project That May Be Divested. The valuation of a proposed international divestiture can be determined by comparing the present value of the cash flows if the project is continued to the proceeds that would be received (after taxes) if the project is divested.

Example

Reconsider the example from the previous chapter in which Spartan, Inc., considered establishing a Singapore subsidiary. Assume that the Singapore subsidiary was created and, after two years, the spot rate of the Singapore dollar (S$) is $.46. In addition, forecasts have been revised for the remaining two years of the project, indicating that the Singapore dollar should be worth $.44 in Year 3 and $.40 in the project's final year. Because these forecasted exchange rates have an adverse effect on the project, Spartan, Inc., considers divesting the subsidiary. For simplicity, assume that the original forecasts of the other variables remain unchanged and that a potential acquirer has offered S$13 million (after adjusting for any capital gains taxes) for the subsidiary if the acquirer can retain the existing working capital.

Spartan can conduct a divestiture analysis by comparing the after-tax proceeds from the possible sale of the project (in U.S. dollars) to the present value of the expected U.S. dollar inflows that the project will generate if it is not sold. This comparison will determine the net present value of the divestiture (NPV_d), as illustrated in Exhibit 15.4. Since the present value of the subsidiary's cash flows from Spartan's perspective exceeds the price at which it can sell the subsidiary, the divestiture is not feasible. Thus, Spartan should not divest the subsidiary at the price offered. Spartan may still search for another firm that is willing to acquire the subsidiary for a price that exceeds its present value.

Example 15.4

Divestiture Analysis: Spartan, Inc.

	End of Year 2 (Today)	End of Year 3 (One Year from Today)	End of Year 4 (Two Years from Today)
S$ remitted after withholding taxes		S$6,840,000	S$19,560,000
Selling price	S$13,000,000		
Exchange rate	$.46	$.44	$.40
Cash flow received from divestiture	$5,980,000		
Cash flows forgone due to divestiture		$3,009,600	$7,824,000
PV of forgone cash flows (15% discount rate)		$2,617,044	$5,916,068

NPV_d = $5,980,000 − ($2,617,044 + $5,916,068)
         = $5,980,000 − $8,533,112
         = −$2,553,112

RESTRUCTURING DECISIONS AS REAL OPTIONS

Some restructuring issues faced by MNCs involve **real options**, or implicit options on real assets (such as buildings, machinery, and other assets used by MNCs to facilitate their production). A real option can be classified as a call option on real assets or a put option on real assets, as explained next.

Managing for Value: Mazda's Decision to Restructure

Mazda's main production facilities are based in Japan, but it relies heavily on exports to the United States and Europe. In 1996, Ford Motor Co. purchased about one-third of Mazda's shares. In the late 1990s, Mazda's performance was weak despite Ford's efforts to improve its operations. It had an excessive amount of debt. It was also highly susceptible to the weakness of the euro in the 1999–2000 period. When the euro weakened against the yen, the European demand for exports made in Japan (and priced in Japanese yen) was reduced. Mazda's costs of producing its vehicles in Japan were not reduced, however, because those costs were denominated in yen. In the first six months of 2000, Mazda experienced losses of more than $9 billion yen (about $90 million), and much of the loss was attributed to the euro's weakness.

In November 2000, Mazda decided to engage in major multinational restructuring to resolve its financial problems. It shifted some of its production from Japan to Europe so that its expenses and revenue from its sales in Europe would be denominated in the same currency. This strategy reduced Mazda's exposure to exchange rate risk because it could sell the cars in Europe at a markup above the cost (in euros) necessary to produce them. The euro's movements against other currencies would not have a direct effect on the European demand for Mazdas. This multinational restructuring was politically tense because it required the closing of some facilities in Japan, which resulted in layoffs. However, it was expected to increase the value of the firm and therefore to benefit shareholders.

Call Option on Real Assets

A **call option on real assets** represents a proposed project that contains an option of pursuing an additional venture. Some possible forms of restructuring by MNCs contain a call option on real assets. Multinational capital budgeting can be conducted in a manner to account for the option.

Example   Coral, Inc., an Internet firm in the United States, is considering the acquisition of an Internet business in Mexico. Coral estimates and discounts the expected dollar cash flows that would result from acquiring this business and compares them to the initial outlay. At this time, the present value of the future cash flows that are directly attributable to the Mexican business is slightly lower than the initial outlay that would be required to purchase that business, so the business appears to be an unfeasible investment.

A Brazilian Internet firm is also for sale, but its owners will only sell the business to a firm that they know and trust, and Coral, Inc., has no relationship with this business. A possible advantage of the Mexican firm that is not measured by the traditional multinational capital budgeting analysis is that it frequently does business with the Brazilian Internet firm and could use its relationship to help Coral acquire the Brazilian firm. Thus, if Coral purchases the Mexican business, it will have an option to also acquire the Internet firm in Brazil. In essence, Coral will have a call option on real assets (of the Brazilian firm), because it will have the option (not the obligation) to purchase the Brazilian firm. The expected purchase price of the Brazilian firm over the next few months serves as the exercise price in the call option on real assets. If Coral acquires the Brazilian firm, it now has a second initial outlay and will generate a second stream of cash flows.

When the call option on real assets is considered, the acquisition of the Mexican Internet firm may now be feasible, even though it was not feasible when considering only the cash flows directly attributable to that firm. The project can be analyzed by segmenting it into two scenarios. In the first scenario, Coral, Inc., acquires the Mexican firm but, after taking a closer look at the Brazilian firm, decides not to exercise its call option (decides not to purchase the Brazilian firm). The net present value in this scenario is simply a measure of the present value of expected dollar cash flows directly attributable to the Mexican firm minus the initial outlay necessary to purchase the Mexican firm. In the second scenario, Coral, Inc., acquires the Mexican firm and then exercises its option by also purchasing the Brazilian firm. In this case, the present value of combined (Mexican firm plus Brazilian firm) cash flow streams (in dollars) would be compared to the combined initial outlays.

If the outlay necessary to acquire the Brazilian firm was made after the initial outlay of the Mexican firm, the outlay for the Brazilian firm should be discounted. If Coral, Inc., knows the probability of these two scenarios, it can determine the probability of each scenario and then determine the expected value of the net present value of the proposed project by summing the products of the probability of each scenario times the respective net present value for that scenario.

Put Option on Real Assets

A **put option on real assets** represents a proposed project that contains an option of divesting part or all of the project. As with a call option on real assets, a put option on real assets can be accounted for by multinational capital budgeting.

Example

Jade, Inc., an office supply firm in the United States, is considering the acquisition of a similar business in Italy. Jade, Inc., believes that if future economic conditions in Italy are favorable, the net present value of this project is positive. However, given that weak economic conditions in Italy are more likely, the proposed project appears to be unfeasible.

Assume now that Jade, Inc., knows that it can sell the Italian firm at a specified price to another firm over the next four years. In this case, Jade has an implied put option attached to the project.

The feasibility of this project can be assessed by determining the net present value under both the scenario of strong economic conditions and the scenario of weak economic conditions. The expected value of the net present value of this project can be estimated as the sum of the products of the probability of each scenario times its respective net present value. If economic conditions are favorable, the net present value is positive. If economic conditions are weak, Jade, Inc., may sell the Italian firm at the locked-in sales price (which resembles the exercise price of a put option) and therefore may still achieve a positive net present value over the short time that it owned the Italian firm. Thus, the put option on real assets may turn an unfeasible project into a feasible project.

IMPACT OF MULTINATIONAL RESTRUCTURING ON AN MNC'S VALUE

An MNC's multinational restructuring can affect its value, as shown in Exhibit 15.5. A strategy of foreign expansion creates additional expected cash flows to be generated by the MNC's foreign subsidiaries and therefore increases the expected cash flows that will ultimately be received by the parent. The expansion also typically requires a large initial outlay by the parent. Conversely, a MNC's strategy of divesting creates an initial inflow of funds to the parent when a foreign subsidiary is sold, at the expense of a reduction in the future expected cash flows because the business will no longer be part of the MNC.

Nike Problem

Multinational Restructuring at Nike

An obvious starting point for Nike when considering whether to restructure its international operations is to determine where it currently generates most of its revenues and income. In 2000, Nike generated about 45 percent of its revenue from foreign countries. About 27 percent of its revenue was derived from Europe, and 11 percent was derived from Asia. Yet, about 44 percent of its total assets were in Asia. This imbalance reflected Nike's manufacturing in Asia, so that it could keep expenses low and increase value.

Discussion: Explain the risk to Nike resulting from relying so heavily on Asia for production, while revenue generated in Asian countries is limited.

Exhibit 15.5

Impact of Multinational Restructuring on an MNC's Value

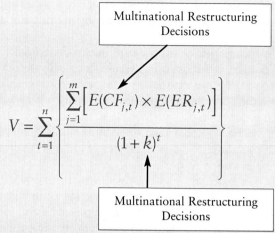

V = value of the U.S.-based MNC

$E(CF_{j,t})$ = expected cash flows denominated in currency j to be received by the U.S. parent in period t

$E(ER_{j,t})$ = expected exchange rate at which currency j can be converted to dollars at the end of period t

k = weighted average cost of capital of the U.S. parent

m = number of currencies

n = number of periods

SUMMARY

- International acquisitions are one of the most common types of multinational restructuring. MNCs can use capital budgeting to determine whether a foreign target is worth acquiring. The expected cash flows of a foreign target are affected by target-specific factors (such as the target's previous cash flows and its managerial talent) and country-specific factors (such as economic conditions, political conditions, currency conditions, and stock market conditions).

- In the typical valuation process, an MNC initially screens prospective targets based on willingness to be acquired and country barriers. Then, each prospective target is valued by estimating its cash flows, based on target-specific characteristics and the target's country characteristics, and by discounting the expected cash flows. Then the perceived value is compared to the target's market value to determine whether the target can be purchased at a price

that is below the perceived value from the MNC's perspective.

- Valuations of a foreign target may vary among potential acquirers because of differences in estimates of the target's cash flows or exchange rate movements or differences in the required rate of return among acquirers. These differences may be especially pronounced when the acquirers are from different countries.

- Besides international acquisitions of firms, the more common types of multinational restructuring include international partial acquisitions, international acquisitions of privatized businesses, international alliances (such as international licensing or joint ventures), and international divestitures. Each of these types of multinational restructuring can be assessed by applying multinational capital budgeting.

SELF TEST

Answers are provided in Appendix A at the back of the text.

1. Explain why more acquisitions have taken place in Europe in recent years.

2. What are some of the barriers to international acquisitions?

3. Why might a U.S.-based MNC prefer to establish a foreign subsidiary rather than acquire an existing firm in a foreign country?

4. Provo, Inc. (based in Utah), has been considering the divestiture of a Swedish subsidiary that produces ski equipment and sells it locally. A Swedish firm has already offered to acquire this Swedish subsidiary. Assume that the U.S. parent has just revised its projections of the Swedish krona's value downward. Will the proposed divestiture now seem more or less feasible than it did before? Explain.

QUESTIONS AND APPLICATIONS

1. Why do you think MNCs continuously assess possible forms of multinational restructuring, such as foreign acquisitions or downsizing of a foreign subsidiary?

2. Maude, Inc., a U.S.-based MNC, has recently acquired a firm in Singapore. To eliminate inefficiencies, Maude downsized the target substantially, eliminating two-thirds of the workforce. Why might this action affect the regulations imposed on the subsidiary's business by the Singapore government?

3. Poki, Inc., a U.S.-based MNC, considers expanding into Thailand because of decreasing profit margins in the United States. The demand for Poki's product in Thailand is very strong. However, forecasts indicate that the baht is expected to depreciate substantially over the next three years. Should Poki expand into Thailand? What factors may affect its decision?

4. Rastell, Inc., a U.S.-based MNC, is considering the acquisition of a Russian target to produce personal computers (PCs) and market them throughout Russia, where demand for PCs has increased substantially in recent years. Assume that stock market conditions are not favorable in Russia, as the stock prices of most Russian companies rose substantially just prior to Rastell's assessment of the target. What are some alternatives available to Rastell?

5. Savannah, Inc., a manufacturer of clothing, wants to increase its market share by acquiring a target producing a popular clothing line in Europe. This clothing line is well established. Forecasts indicate a relatively stable euro over the life of the project. Marquette, Inc., wants to increase its market share in the personal computer market by acquiring a target in Thailand that currently produces radios and converting the operations. Forecasts indicate a depreciation of the baht over the life of the project. Funds resulting from both projects will be remitted to the respective U.S. parent on a regular basis. Which target do you think will result in a higher net present value? Why?

6. Why are valuations of privatized businesses previously owned by the governments of developing countries more difficult than valuations of existing firms in developed countries?

7. Blore, Inc., a U.S.-based MNC, has screened several targets. Based on economic and political considerations, only one eligible target remains in Malaysia. Blore would like you to value this target and has provided you with the following information:

   ■ Blore expects to keep the target for three

years, at which time it expects to sell the firm for 300 million Malaysian ringgit (MYR) after any taxes.

- Blore expects a strong Malaysian economy. Consequently, the estimates for revenues for the next year are MYR200 million. Revenues are expected to increase by 8 percent over the following two years.

- Cost of goods sold are expected to be 50 percent of revenues.

- Selling and administrative expenses are expected to be MYR30 million in each of the next three years.

- The Malaysian tax rate on the target's earnings is expected to be 35 percent.

- Depreciation expenses are expected to be MYR20 million per year for each of the next three years.

- The target will need MYR7 million in cash each year to support existing operations.

- The target's stock price is currently MYR30 per share. The target has 9 million shares outstanding.

- Any remaining cash flows will be remitted by the target to Blore, Inc. Blore uses the prevailing exchange rate of the Malaysian ringgit as the expected exchange rate for the next three years. This exchange rate is currently $.25.

- Blore's required rate of return on projects is 20 percent.

a. Prepare a worksheet to estimate the value of the Malaysian target based on the information provided.

b. Will Blore, Inc., be able to acquire the Malaysian target for a price lower than its valuation of the target?

8. Refer to question 7. What are some of the key sources of uncertainty in Blore's valuation of the target? Identify two reasons why the expected cash flows from an Asian subsidiary of a U.S.-based MNC would have been lower as a result of the Asian crisis.

9. The reduction in expected cash flows of Asian subsidiaries as a result of the Asian crisis likely resulted in a reduced valuation of these subsidiaries from the parent's perspective. Explain why a U.S.-based MNC might not have sold its Asian subsidiaries.

10. Identify two reasons why the expected cash flows from the Asian subsidiary of a U.S.-based MNC might have been lower during the Asian crisis than in other periods.

Impact of 9/11/01

11. Ethridge Co. of Atlanta, Georgia, has a subsidiary in India that produces products and sells them throughout Asia. In response to the September 11, 2001, terrorist attack on the United States, Ethridge Co. decided to conduct a capital budgeting analysis to determine whether it should divest the subsidiary. Why might this decision be different after the attack as opposed to before the attack? Describe the general method for determining whether the divestiture is financially feasible.

Internet Application

12. The following website provides information about recent economic events around the world: **http://biz.yahoo.com/reports/world.html**

Use this site to review international events over the last week. Select three economic events that could affect economic or political conditions in foreign countries and explain how an MNC might restructure its business in response to these events. Would the MNC increase or reduce its business in that country due to that event?

Running Your Own MNC

 This exercise can be found on the Student CD-ROM.

Blades, Inc. Case

Assessment of an Acquisition in Thailand

Recall that Ben Holt, Blades' chief financial officer (CFO), has suggested to the board of directors that Blades proceed with the establishment of a subsidiary in Thailand. Due to the high growth potential of the roller blade market in Thailand, his analysis suggests that the venture will be profitable. Specifically, his view is that Blades should establish a subsidiary in Thailand to manufacture roller blades, whether an existing agreement with Entertainment Products (a Thai retailer) is renewed or not. Under this agreement, Entertainment Products is committed to the purchase of 180,000 pairs of "Speedos," Blades' primary product, annually. The agreement was initially for three years and will expire two years from now. At this time, the agreement may be renewed. Due to delivery delays, Entertainment Products has indicated that it will renew the agreement only if Blades establishes a subsidiary in Thailand. In this case, the price per pair of roller blades would be fixed at 4,594 Thai baht per pair. If Blades decides not to renew the agreement, Entertainment Products has indicated that it would purchase only 5,000 pairs of Speedos annually at prevailing market prices.

According to Ben Holt's analysis, renewing the agreement with Entertainment Products and establishing a subsidiary in Thailand will result in a net present value (*NPV*) of $2,638,735. Conversely, if the agreement is not renewed and a subsidiary is established, the resulting *NPV* is $8,746,688. Consequently, Holt has suggested to the board of directors that Blades establish a subsidiary without renewing the existing agreement with Entertainment Products.

Recently, a Thai roller blade manufacturer called Skates'n'Stuff contacted Holt regarding the potential sale of the company to Blades. Skates'n'Stuff entered the Thai roller blade market a decade ago and has generated a profit in every year of operation. Furthermore, Skates'n'Stuff has established distribution channels in Thailand. Consequently, if Blades acquires the company, it could begin sales immediately and would not require an additional year to build the plant in Thailand. Initial forecasts indicate that Blades would be able to sell 280,000 pairs of roller blades annually. These sales are incremental to the acquisition of Skates'n'Stuff. Furthermore, all sales resulting from the acquisition would be made to retailers in Thailand. Blades' fixed expenses would be 20 million baht annually. Although Holt has not previously considered the acquisition of an existing business, he is now wondering whether aquiring Skates'n'Stuff may be a better course of action than building a subsidiary in Thailand.

Holt is also aware of some disadvantages associated with such an acquisition. Skates'n'Stuff's CFO has indicated that he would be willing to accept a price of 1 billion baht in payment for the company, which is clearly more expensive than the 550 million baht outlay that would be required to establish a subsidiary in Thailand. However, Skates'n'Stuff's CFO has indicated that it is willing to negotiate. Furthermore, Blades' employs a high-quality production process, which enables it to charge relatively high prices for roller blades produced in its plants. If Blades acquires Skates'n'Stuff, which uses an inferior production process (resulting in lower quality roller blades), it would have to charge a lower price for the roller blades it produces there. Initial forecasts indicate that Blades will be able to charge a price of 4,500 Thai baht per pair of roller blades without affecting demand. However, because Skates'n'Stuff uses a production process that results in lower quality roller blades than Blades' Speedos, operating costs incurred would be similar to the amount incurred if Blades establishes a subsidiary in Thailand. Thus, Blades estimates that it would incur operating costs of about 3,500 baht per pair of roller blades.

Ben Holt has asked you, a financial analyst for Blades, Inc., to determine whether the acquisition of Skates'n'Stuff is a better course of action for Blades than the establishment of a subsidiary in Thailand. Acquiring Skates'n'Stuff will be more favorable than establishing a subsidiary if the present value of the cash flows generated by the company exceeds the purchase price by more than $8,746,688, the *NPV* of establishing a new subsidiary. Thus, Holt has asked you to construct a spreadsheet that determines the *NPV* of the acquisition.

To aid you in your analysis, Holt has provided the following additional information, which he gathered from various sources, including unaudited financial statements of Skates'n'Stuff for the last three years:

- Blades, Inc., requires a return on the Thai acquisition of 25 percent, the same rate of return it would require if it established a subsidiary in Thailand.

- If Skates'n'Stuff is acquired, Blades, Inc., will operate the company for 10 years, at which time Skates'n'Stuff will be sold for an estimated 1.1 million baht.

- Of the 1 billion baht purchase price, 600 million baht constitutes the cost of the plant and equipment. These items are depreciated using straight-line depreciation. Thus, 60 million baht will be depreciated annually for 10 years.

- Sales of 280,000 pairs of roller blades annually will begin immediately at a price of 4,500 baht per pair.

- Variable costs per pair of roller blades will be 3,500 per pair.

- Fixed operating costs, including salaries and administrative expenses, will be 20 million baht annually.

- The current spot rate of the Thai baht is $0.023. Blades expects the baht to depreciate by an average of 2 percent per year for the next 10 years.

- The Thai government will impose a 25 percent tax on income and a 10 percent withholding tax on any funds remitted by Skates'n'Stuff to Blades, Inc. Any earnings remitted to the United States will not be taxed again in the United States All earnings generated by Skates'n'Stuff will be remitted to Blades, Inc.

- The average inflation rate in Thailand is expected to be 12 percent annually. Revenues, variable costs, and fixed costs are subject to inflation and are expected to change by the same annual rate as the inflation rate.

In addition to the information outlined above, Ben Holt has informed you that Blades, Inc., will need to manufacture all of the 180,000 pairs to be delivered to Entertainment Products this year and next year in Thailand. Since Blades previously only used components from Thailand (which are of a lower quality but cheaper than U.S. components) sufficient to manufacture 72,000 pairs annually, it will incur cost savings of 32.4 million baht this year and next year. However, since Blades will sell 180,000 pairs of Speedos annually to Entertainment Products this year and next year whether it acquires Skates'n'Stuff or not, Holt has urged you not to include these sales in your analysis. The agreement with Entertainment Product will not be renewed at the end of next year.

Ben Holt would like you to answer the following questions:

1. Using a spreadsheet, determine the *NPV* of the acquisition of Skates'n'Stuff. Based on your numerical analysis, should Blades establish a subsidiary in Thailand or acquire Skates'n'Stuff?

2. If Blades negotiates with Skates'n'Stuff, what is the maximum amount (in Thai baht) Blades should be willing to pay?

3. Are there any other factors Blades should consider in making its decision? In your answer, you should consider the price Skates'n'Stuff is asking relative to your analysis in question (1), other potential businesses for sale in Thailand, the source of the information your analysis is based on, the production process that will be employed by the target in the future, and the future management of Skates'n'Stuff.

Small Business Dilemma

Multinational Restructuring by the Sports Exports Company

The Sports Exports Company has been successful in producing footballs in the United States and exporting them to the United Kingdom. Recently, Jim Logan (owner of the Sports Exports Company) has considered restructuring his company by expanding throughout Europe. He plans to export footballs and other sporting goods that were not already popular in Europe to one large sporting goods distributor in Germany; the goods will then be distributed to any retail sporting goods stores throughout Europe that are willing to purchase these goods. This distributor will make payments in euros to the Sports Exports Company.

1. Are there any reasons why the business that has been so successful in the United Kingdom will not necessarily be successful in other European countries?

2. If the business is diversified throughout Europe, will this substantially reduce the exposure of the Sports Exports Company to exchange rate risk?

3. Now that several countries in Europe participate a single currency system, will this affect the performance of new expansion throughout Europe?

8

COUNTRY RISK ANALYSIS

An MNC conducts country risk analysis when assessing whether to continue conducting business in a particular country. The analysis can also be used when determining whether to implement new projects in foreign countries. Country risk can be partitioned into the country's political risk and its financial risk. Financial managers must understand how to measure country risk so that they can make investment decisions that maximize their MNC's value.

The specific objectives of this chapter are to
- Identify the common factors used by MNCs to measure a country's political risk.
- Identify the common factors used by MNCs to measure a country's financial risk.
- Explain the techniques used to measure country risk.
- Explain how MNCs use the assessment of country risk when making financial decisions.

WHY COUNTRY RISK ANALYSIS IS IMPORTANT

Country risk is the potentially adverse impact of a country's environment on an MNC's cash flows. Country risk analysis can be used to monitor countries where the MNC is currently doing business. If the country risk level of a particular country begins to increase, the MNC may consider divesting its subsidiaries located there. Country risk analysis can also be used by MNCs as a screening device to avoid conducting business in countries with excessive risk. Events that heighten country risk tend to discourage U.S. direct foreign investment in that particular country.

Country risk analysis is not restricted to predicting major crises. It is also used by an MNC to revise its investment or financing decisions in light of recent events. Consider the following events that occurred in just a single week, the last week of June 2001:

- President Milosevic of Yugoslavia is tried for war crimes; this event carries implications for firms that conduct business in Yugoslavia.
- The Belgian government pushed for reform within the European Union, which could affect policies implemented in several European countries.
- Several technology firms in Europe announced layoffs and profit warnings, which triggered concerns about a recession in Europe.
- The European Commission blocked a proposed merger between General Electric and Honeywell; this action may have implications for other mergers that could create more competition in Europe.
- The International Monetary Fund postponed its approval of funding for Turkey citing that the Turkish government had not satisfied various conditions. This caused concerns about the future of Turkey's economy.
- Negotiations between the union and management of Volkswagen (Europe's largest car manufacturer) broke down, which raised concerns about strikes throughout the European car industry.
- President Koizumi of Japan announced that he would pursue a radical agenda on bank reform and fiscal policy. While the intent was to improve economic conditions in Japan, there were concerns that the efforts would push Japan into severe depression.
- Speculation about a change in trade sanctions imposed on Iraq by the United States continued, which created concerns about oil prices, and therefore, inflation in several oil-importing countries.
- Pilots for Iberia Airlines of Spain refused management's wage proposal, which caused concerns about a possible strike that could result in travel complications to Spain and lead to other airline strikes in Europe.
- Counterfeiting in China escalated, as many stores used false branding to create the appearance of name brand products. Firms were discouraged from pursuing expansion in China, because they could not compete with the counterfeit products.
- The Belgian government threatened a lawsuit against Swissair, minority owner of Belgian-owned Sabena Airlines, if Swissair did not provide funding that Sabena needed to survive. This event had implications for European alliances and inter-country relations.
- Berlin considered radical changes in its policy on immigration, which could result in 50,000 workers outside of the European Union entering Germany every year.
- The European Union moved to accept new members, but there was much disagreement among the existing members about whether the potential members are meeting conditions for entry related to issues such as freedom of movement for labor, the environment, and free rights to purchase land.

This list is typical for a single week. Even if an MNC reduces its exposure to all events in a given week, a new set of events will occur in the following week. For each of these events, an MNC must consider whether its cash flows will be affected and whether there is a change in policy to which it should enact in response. Since these events occurred in just a single week, it should be obvious that country risk analysis is an ongoing process throughout each year. Most MNCs will not be affected by every event, but they will pay close attention to those events that may have an impact on the industries or countries in which they do business. They also recognize that they cannot eliminate their exposure to all events but may at least attempt to limit their exposure to any single country-specific event.

POLITICAL RISK FACTORS

An MNC must assess country risk not only in countries where it currently does business but also in those where it expects to export or establish subsidiaries. Several risk characteristics of a country may significantly affect performance, and the MNC should be concerned about the likely degree of impact for each. The September 11, 2001, terrorist attack on the United States heightened the awareness of political risk.

As one might expect, many country characteristics related to the political environment can influence an MNC. An extreme form of political risk is the possibility that the host country will take over a subsidiary. In some cases of expropriation, some compensation (the amount decided by the host country government) is awarded. In other cases, the assets are confiscated and no compensation is provided. Expropriation can take place peacefully or by force. The folllowing are some of the more common forms of political risk:

- Attitude of consumers in the host country
- Actions of host government
- Blockage of fund transfers
- Currency inconvertibility
- War
- Bureaucracy
- Corruption

Each of these characteristics will be examined.

Attitude of Consumers in the Host Country

A mild form of political risk (to an exporter) is a tendency of residents to purchase only locally produced goods. Even if the exporter decides to set up a subsidiary in the foreign country, this philosophy could prevent its success. All countries tend to exert some pressure on consumers to purchase from locally owned manufacturers. (In the United States, consumers are encouraged to look for the "Made in the U.S.A." label.) MNCs that consider entering a foreign market (or have already entered that market) must monitor the general loyalty of consumers toward locally produced products. If consumers are very loyal to local products, a joint venture with a local company may be more feasible than an exporting strategy. The September 11, 2001, terrorist attack caused some consumers to pay more attention to the country where products are produced.

Actions of Host Government

Various actions of a host government can affect the cash flow of an MNC. For example, a host government might impose pollution control standards (which affect costs) and additional corporate taxes (which affect after-tax earnings) as well as withholding taxes and fund transfer restrictions (which affect after-tax cash flows sent to the parent).

HTTP:// **ONLINE APPLICATION** **Political Conditions**   A description of the political environment including factors that affect political risk) for each country is provided at http://www. usatrade.gov/website/ccg.nsf.

Click on a specific country, and then click on Political Environment.

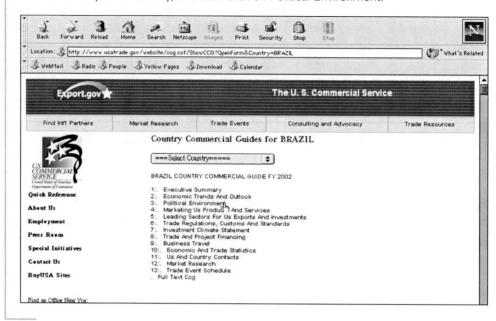

Some analysts use turnover in government members or philosophy as a proxy for a country's political risk. While this can significantly influence the MNC's future cash flows, it alone does not serve as a suitable representation of political risk. A subsidiary will not necessarily be affected by changing governments. Furthermore, a subsidiary can be affected by new policies of the host government or by a changed attitude toward the subsidiary's home country (and therefore the subsidiary), even when the host government has no risk of being overthrown.

A host government can use various means to make an MNC's operations coincide with its own goals. It may, for example, require the use of local employees for managerial positions at a subsidiary. In addition, it may require social facilities (such as an exercise room or nonsmoking areas) or special environmental controls (such as air pollution controls). Furthermore, it is not uncommon for a host government to require special permits, impose extra taxes, or subsidize competitors. All of these actions represent political risk, in that they reflect a country's political characteristics and could influence an MNC's cash flows.

One of the most troubling issues for MNCs is the failure by host governments to enforce copyright laws against local firms that illegally copy the MNC's product. For example, local firms in Asia commonly copy software produced by MNCs and sell it to customers at a lower price. Software producers lose an estimated $3 billion in sales annually in Asia for this reason.

Blockage of Fund Transfers

Subsidiaries of MNCs often send funds back to the headquarters for loan repayments, purchases of supplies, administrative fees, remitted earnings, or other purposes. In some cases, a host government may block fund transfers, which could force subsidiaries to undertake projects that are not optimal (just to make use of the funds). Alternatively, the MNC could invest the funds in local securities that would provide some return while funds were blocked. But this return might be inferior to what could have been earned on funds remitted to the parent.

Currency Inconvertibility

Some governments do not allow the home currency to be exchanged into other currencies. Thus, the earnings generated by a subsidiary in these countries cannot be remitted to the parent through currency conversion. When the currency is inconvertible, an MNC's parent may need to exchange it for goods to extract benefits from projects in that country.

War

Some countries tend to engage in constant battles with neighboring countries or experience internal battles. This can affect the safety of employees hired by an MNC's subsidiary or by salespeople who attempt to establish export markets for the MNC. In addition, countries plagued by the threat of war typically have volatile business cycles, which make the MNC's cash flows generated from such countries more uncertain. The terrorist attack on the United States on September 11, 2001, caused the expectation that the United States would be involved in a war. MNCs were adversely affected by their potential exposure to terrorist attacks, especially if their subsidiaries were located in countries where there may be anti-U.S. sentiment. Even if an MNC is not directly damaged due to a war, it may incur costs from ensuring the safety of its employees.

Bureaucracy

Another country risk factor is government bureaucracy, which can complicate the MNC's business. Although this factor may seem irrelevant, it was a major deterrent for MNCs that considered projects in Eastern Europe in the early 1990s. Many of the Eastern European governments were not experienced at facilitating the entrance of MNCs into their markets.

HTTP:// USING THE WEB

Political Risk Ratings If an MNC wants to review an assessment of various political risk characteristics by outside evaluators, it can obtain this information at http://biz.yahoo.com/ifc/.

Click on any country listed, and then click on Country Outlook. Click on Politics to review the political situation in that country. Click on International Relations to review how this country interacts with other countries.

Exhibit 16.1
Corruption Ratings
among Countries

Country	Corruption Perception Index
Denmark	9.94
New Zealand	9.23
Canada	9.10
Australia	8.85
Germany	8.23
Hong Kong	7.28
Japan	6.57
Chile	6.05
Hungary	5.18
Taiwan	5.02
Malaysia	5.01
South Korea	4.29
Brazil	3.56
Thailand	3.06
China	2.88
Argentina	2.81
Indonesia	2.72
Mexico	2.66
Russia	2.72

Corruption

Corruption can adversely affect an MNC's international business because it can increase the cost of conducting business or reduce revenue. Various forms of corruption can occur between firms or between a firm and the government. For example, an MNC may lose revenue because a government contract is awarded to a local firm that paid off a government official. A sampling of corruption perception index ratings (drawn from *Euromoney* magazine) is provided in Exhibit 16.1. The highest possible rating is 10.0. Many countries in Western Europe were assigned ratings of 8.0 or above, while countries in Asia and South America were assigned lower ratings.

FINANCIAL RISK FACTORS

Along with political factors, financial factors should be considered when assessing country risk. One of the most obvious financial factors is the current and potential state of the country's economy. An MNC that exports to a country or develops a subsidiary in a country is highly concerned about that country's demand for its products. This demand is, of course, strongly influenced by the country's economy. A recession in the country could severely reduce demand for the MNC's exports or products sold by the MNC's local subsidiary. In the early 1990s and again in the early 2000s, the European business performance of Ford Motor Co., Nike, Walt Disney Co., and many other U.S.-based MNCs was adversely affected by a weak European economy.

Indicators of Economic Growth

http://
The Department of Statistics, Singapore, site at www.singstat.gov.sg/BES provides access to the department's current business expectation surveys and country analyses.

A country's economic growth is dependent on several financial factors, which are identified here:

- *Interest rates.* Higher interest rates tend to slow the growth of an economy and reduce demand for the MNC's products. Lower interest rates often stimulate the economy and increase demand for the MNC's products.

- *Exchange rates.* Exchange rates can influence the demand for the country's exports, which in turn affects the country's production and income level. A strong currency may reduce demand for the country's exports, increase the volume of products imported by the country, and therefore reduce the country's production and national income. A very weak currency can cause speculative outflows and reduce the amount of funds available to finance growth by businesses.

- *Inflation.* Inflation can affect consumers' purchasing power and therefore their demand for an MNC's goods. It also indirectly affects a country's financial condition by influencing the counrty's interest rates and currency value. A high level of inflation may also lead to a decline in economic growth.

Most financial factors that affect a country's economic conditions are difficult to forecast. Thus, even if an MNC considers them in its country risk assessment, it may still make poor decisions because of an improper forecast of the country's financial factors.

Some financial conditions may be caused by political risk. For example, the September 11, 2001, terrorist attack on the United States affected U.S.-based MNCs because of political risk and financial risk. Political uncertainty caused uncertainty about economic conditions, which resulted in a reduction in spending by consumers, and therefore, a reduction in cash flows of MNCs.

Nike Problem

Potential Exposure to Country Risk

Since Nike conducts a large amount of international business, it must monitor country risk in many countries. Nike could be affected by country risk in several ways. First, a conflict between the United States and a specific foreign country could cause either the foreign country's government or its people to vent their anger toward a Nike subsidiary in that country. Thus, Nike could be a target simply because it is viewed as a U.S. company, even if all the employees at that subsidiary are locals. Second, a change in a foreign government could result in new tax laws and other restrictions imposed on subsidiaries of U.S. firms or firms from any other country that are based there. Third, other local shoe manufacturers could possibly use government ties to impose more restrictions against Nike so that they could have a competitive advantage in the country of concern. Fourth, Nike's subsidiary could be adversely affected by other political problems that cause a deterioration in economic conditions in that country. Any of these events could cause an increase in the subsidiary's expenses or a decline in its revenue.

Discussion: When Nike decides to conduct a multinational capital budgeting analysis to assess the establishment of a new shoe factory in Latin America, how can it capture the potential effects of country risk in its analysis?

TYPES OF COUNTRY RISK ASSESSMENT

Although there is no consensus as to how country risk can best be assessed, some guidelines have been developed. The first step is to recognize the difference between (1) an overall risk assessment of a country without consideration of the MNC's business and (2) the risk assessment of a country as it relates to the MNC's type of business. The first type can be referred to as **macroassessment** of country risk and the latter type as a **microassessment**. Each type is discussed in turn.

Macroassessment of Country Risk

http://
Visit lcweb2.loc.gov/frd/cs/ cshome.html for detailed studies of 85 countries provided by the Library of Congress.

A macroassessment involves consideration of all variables that affect country risk except those unique to a particular firm or industry. This type of risk is convenient in that it remains the same for a given country, regardless of the firm or industry of concern; however, it excludes relevant information that could improve the accuracy of the assessment. While a macroassessment of country risk is not ideal for any individual MNC, it serves as a foundation that can then be modified to reflect the particular business of the MNC.

HTTP:// USING THE WEB

Information Used To Measure Country Risk Information about a country's government is provided at http://www.odci.gov/cia/publications/factbook/indexgeo.html.

Click on Government to obtain this information, which can be used to assess the country risk surrounding a foreign project.

Any macroassessment model should consider both political and financial characteristics of the country being assessed:

- *Political factors.* Political factors include the relationship of the host government with the MNC's home country government, the attitude of people in the host country toward the MNC's government, the historical stability of the host government, the vulnerability of the host government to political takeovers, and the probability of war between the host country and neighboring countries. Consideration of such political factors will indicate the probability of political events that may affect an MNC and the magnitude of the impact. The September 11, 2001, terrorist attack on the United States caused more concern about political risk for U.S.-based MNCs because of all the factors cited here.
- *Financial factors.* The financial factors of a macroassessment model should include GDP growth, inflation trends, government budget levels (and the government deficit), interest rates, unemployment, the country's reliance on export income, the balance of trade, and foreign exchange controls. The list of financial factors could easily be extended several pages. The factors listed here represent just a subset of the financial factors considered when evaluating the financial strength of a country.

Country Characteristics That Affect Profits. A survey by Petry and Sprow[1] was conducted to determine what country characteristics have the greatest potential impact on the profitability of large MNCs. Each characteristic was assigned a weight from 1 to 5, with 5 reflecting the most negative impact. An average weight across all MNCs was then computed; those characteristics with a higher average weight are perceived to have a larger negative impact on the MNC's profitability. The average weights for the seven most critical characteristics are shown here.

The authors also found that the weights assigned by MNCs in the consumer/retail sector were lower than those assigned by MNCs in the industrial sector. MNCs with a relatively large proportion of international business assigned higher weights, or greater importance, to restrictive practices and unstable currencies.

Country Characteristic	Average Weight
Restrictive practices	3.44
Tariffs or regulations	3.16
Unstable currencies	3.07
Foreign government subsidies	3.07
Shaky governments in less developed countries	2.84
Debt problems in less developed countries	2.67
Varying standards between countries	2.58

There is clearly a degree of subjectivity in identifying the relevant political and financial factors for a macroassessment of country risk. There is also some subjectivity in determining the importance of each factor for the overall macroassessment for a particular country. For instance, one assessor may assign a much higher weight (degree of importance) to real GDP growth than another assessor. Finally, there is some subjectivity in predicting these financial factors. Because of the types of subjectivity mentioned here, it is not surprising that risk assessors often arrive at different opinions after completing a macroassessment of country risk.

Microassessment of Country Risk

While a macroassessment of country risk provides an indication of the country's overall status, it does not assess country risk from the perspective of the particular business of concern. A microassessment of country risk is needed to determine how the country risk relates to the specific MNC.

Example

Country Z has been assigned a relatively low macroassessment by most experts due to its poor financial condition. Two MNCs are deciding whether to set up subsidiaries in Country Z. Carco, Inc., is considering developing a subsidiary that would produce automobiles and sell them locally, while Milco, Inc., plans to build a subsidiary that would produce military supplies. Carco's plan to build an

---

[1]Glenn H. Petry and James Sprow, "International Trends and Events in Corporate Finance and Management: A Survey," *Financial Practice and Education*, Spring/Summer 1993, pp. 21–28.

automobile subsidiary does not appear to be feasible, unless Country Z does not have a sufficient number of automobile producers already.

Country Z's government may be committed to purchasing a given amount of military supplies, regardless of how weak the economy is. Thus, Milco's plan to build a military supply subsidiary may still be feasible, even though Country Z's financial condition is poor.

It is possible, however, that Country Z's government will order its military supplies from a locally owned firm because it wants its supply needs to remain confidential. This possibility is an element of country risk because it is a country characteristic (or attitude) that can affect the feasibility of a project. Yet, this specific characteristic is relevant only to Milco, Inc., and not to Carco, Inc.

This example illustrates how an appropriate country risk assessment varies with the firm, industry, and project of concern and therefore why a macro-assessment of country risk has its limitations. A microassessment is also necessary when evaluating the country risk related to a particular project proposed by a particular firm.

In addition to political variables, financial variables are also necessary for microassessment of country risk. Microfactors include the sensitivity of the firm's business to real GDP growth, inflation trends, interest rates, and other factors. Due to differences in business characteristics, some firms are more susceptible to the host country's economy than others.

In summary, the overall assessment of country risk consists of four parts:

1. Macropolitical risk
2. Macrofinancial risk
3. Micropolitical risk
4. Microfinancial risk

Although these parts can be consolidated to generate a single country risk rating, it may be useful to keep them separate so that an MNC can identify the various ways its direct foreign investment or exporting operations are exposed to country risk.

TECHNIQUES TO ASSESS COUNTRY RISK

Once a firm identifies all the macro- and microfactors that deserve consideration in the country risk assessment, it may wish to implement a system for evaluating these factors and determining a country risk rating. Various techniques are available to achieve this objective. The following are some of the more popular techniques:

- Checklist approach
- Delphi technique
- Quantitative analysis
- Inspection visits
- Combination of techniques

Each technique is briefly discussed in turn.

Checklist Approach

A checklist approach involves making a judgment on all the political and financial factors (both macro and micro) that contribute to a firm's assessment of country risk. Ratings are assigned to a list of various financial and political factors, and these ratings are then consolidated to derive an overall assessment of country risk. Some factors (such as real GDP growth) can be measured from available data, while others (such as probability of entering a war) must be subjectively measured.

A substantial amount of information about countries is available on the Internet. This information can be used to develop ratings of various factors used to assess country risk. The factors are then converted to some numerical rating in order to assess a particular country. Those factors thought to have a greater influence on country risk should be assigned greater weights. Both the measurement of some factors and the weighting scheme implemented are subjective.

Delphi Technique

The **Delphi technique** involves the collection of independent opinions on country risk without group discussion by the assessors (such as employees or outside consultants) who provide these opinions. Though the Delphi technique can be useful, it is based on subjective opinions, which may vary among assessors. The MNC can average these opinions in some manner and even assess the degree of disagreement by measuring the dispersion of opinions.

Quantitative Analysis

Once the financial and political variables have been measured for a period of time, models for quantitative analysis can attempt to identify the characteristics that influence the level of country risk. For example, regression analysis may be used to assess risk, since it can measure the sensitivity of one variable to other variables. A firm could regress a measure of its business activity (such as its percentage increase in sales) against country characteristics (such as real growth in GDP) over a series of previous months or quarters. Results from such an analysis will indicate the susceptibility of a particular business to a country's economy. This is valuable information to incorporate into the overall evaluation of country risk.

Although quantitative models can quantify the impact of variables on each other, they do not necessarily indicate a country's problems before they actually occur (preferably before the firm's decision to pursue a project in that country). Nor can they evaluate subjective data that cannot be quantified. In addition, historical trends of various country characteristics are not always useful for anticipating an upcoming crisis.

Inspection Visits

Inspection visits involve traveling to a country and meeting with government officials, business executives, and/or consumers. Such meetings can help clarify any uncertain opinions the firm has about a country. Indeed, some variables, such as intercountry relationships, may be difficult to assess without a trip to the host country.

Combination of Techniques

A survey of 193 corporations heavily involved in foreign business found that about half of them have no formal means for making country risk assessments. This does not mean that they neglect to assess country risk, but rather that there is no proven method to use. Consequently, many MNCs use a variety of techniques, possibly using a checklist approach to develop an overall country risk rating and then using the Delphi technique, quantitative analysis, and inspection visits to assign ratings to the various factors.

Example   Missouri, Inc., recognizes that it must consider several financial and political factors in its country risk analysis of Mexico, where it plans to establish a subsidiary. Missouri creates a checklist of several factors and will assign a rating to each factor. It uses the Delphi technique to rate various political factors. It uses quantitaitve analysis to predict future economic conditions in Mexico so that it can rate various financial factors. It conducts an inspection visit to complement its assessment of the financial and political factors.

MEASURING COUNTRY RISK

Deriving an overall country risk rating using a checklist approach requires separate ratings for political and financial risk. First, the political factors are assigned values within some arbitrarily chosen range (such as values from 1 to 5, where 5 is the best value/lowest risk). Next, these political factors are assigned weights (representing degree of importance), which should add up to 100 percent. The assigned values of the factors times their respective weights can then be summed to derive a political risk rating.

The process is then repeated to derive the financial risk rating. All financial factors are assigned values (from 1 to 5, where 5 is the best value/lowest risk). Then the assigned values of the factors times their respective weights can be summed to derive a financial risk rating.

Once the political and financial ratings have been derived, a country's overall country risk rating as it relates to a specific project can be determined by assigning weights to the political and financial ratings according to their perceived importance. The importance of political risk versus financial risk varies with the intent of the MNC. An MNC considering direct foreign investment to attract demand in that country must be highly concerned about financial risk. An MNC establishing a foreign manufacturing plant and planning to export the goods from there should be more concerned with political risk.

If the political risk is thought to be much more influential on a particular project than the financial risk, it will receive a higher weight than the financial risk rating (together both weights must total 100 percent). The political and financial ratings multiplied by their respective weights will determine the overall country risk rating for a country as it relates to a particular project.

Example   Assume that Cougar Co. plans to build a steel plant in the Mexico. It has used the Delphi technique and quantitative analysis to derive ratings for various political and financial factors. The discussion here focuses on how to consolidate the ratings to derive an overall country risk rating.

Exhibit 16.2 illustrates Cougar's country risk assessment of Mexico. Notice in Exhibit 16.2 that three political factors and five financial factors contribute to the overall country risk rating in this example. Cougar Co. will consider projects only in countries that have a country risk rating of 3.5 or higher, based on its country risk rating.

Cougar Co. has assigned the values and weights to the factors as shown in Exhibit 16.3. In this example, the company generally assigns the financial factors higher ratings than the political factors. The financial condition of Mexico has therefore been assessed more favorably than the political condition. Industry growth is the most important financial factor in Mexico, based on its 40 percent weighting. The bureaucracy is thought to be the most important political factor, based on a weighting of 70 percent; regulation of international fund transfers receives the remaining 30 percent weighting. The political risk rating is estimated at 3.3 by adding the products of the assigned ratings (Column 2) and weights (Column 3) of the political risk factors.

The financial risk is computed to be 3.9, based on adding the products of the assigned ratings and the weights of the financial risk factors. Once the political and financial ratings are determined, the overall country risk rating can be derived (as shown at the bottom of Exhibit 16.3), given the weights assigned to political and financial risk. Column 3 at the bottom of Exhibit 16.3 indicates that Cougar perceives political risk (receiving an 80 percent weight) to be much more important than financial risk (receiving a 20 percent weight) in Mexico for the proposed project. The overall country risk rating of 3.42 may appear low given the individual category ratings. This is due to the heavy weighting given to political risk, which in this example is critical from the firm's perspective. In particular,

Exhibit 16.2

Determining the Overall Country Risk Rating

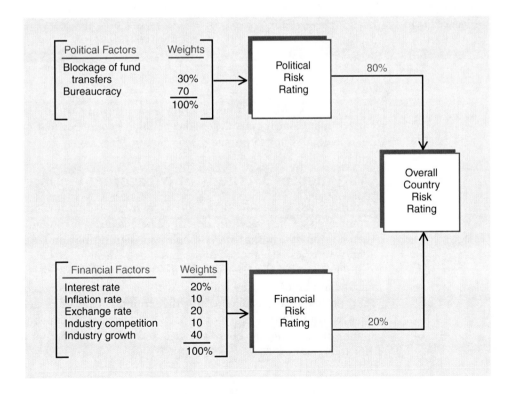

Exhibit 16.3

Derivation of the Overall Country Risk Rating Based on Assumed Information

(1)	(2)	(3)	(4) = (2) × (3)
Political Risk Factors	Rating Assigned by Company to Factor (within a Range of 1–5)	Weight Assigned by Company to Factor According to Importance	Weighted Value of Factor
Blockage of fund transfers	4	30%	1.2
Bureaucracy	3	70	2.1
		100%	3.3 = Political risk rating
Financial Risk Factors			
Interest rate	5	20%	1.0
Inflation rate	4	10	.4
Exchange rate	4	20	.8
Industry competition	5	10	.5
Industry growth	3	40	1.2
		100%	3.9 = Financial risk rating

(1)	(2)	(3)	(4) = (2) × (3)
Category	Rating as Determined Above	Weight Assigned by Company to Each Risk Category	Weighted Rating
Political risk	3.3	80%	2.64
Financial risk	3.9	20	.78
		100%	3.42 = Overall country risk rating

Cougar views Mexico's bureaucracy as a critical factor and assigns it a low rating. Given that Cougar considers projects only in countries that have a rating of at least 3.5, it decides not to pursue the project in Mexico.

Variation in Methods of Measuring Country Risk

Country risk assessors have their own individual procedures for quantifying country risk. The procedure described here is just one of many. Most procedures are similar, though, in that they somehow assign ratings and weights to all individual characteristics relevant to country risk assessment.

The number of relevant factors comprising both the political risk and the financial risk categories will vary with the country being assessed and the type of corporate operations planned for that country. The assignment of values to the factors, along with the degree of importance (weights) assigned to the factors, will also vary with the country being assessed and the type of corporate operations planned for that country.

Using the Country Risk Rating for Decision Making

If the country risk is too high, then the firm does not need to analyze the feasibility of the proposed project any further. Some firms may contend that no risk is too high when considering a project. Their reasoning is that if the potential return is high enough, the project is worth undertaking. When employee safety is a concern, the project may be rejected regardless of its potential return.

Even after a project is accepted and implemented, the MNC must continue to monitor country risk. With a labor-intensive MNC, the host country may feel it is benefiting from a subsidiary's existence (due to the subsidiary's employment of local people), and the chance of expropriation may be low. Nevertheless, several other forms of country risk could suddenly make the MNC consider divesting the project. Furthermore, decisions regarding subsidiary expansion, fund transfers to the parent, and sources of financing can all be affected by any changes in country risk. Since country risk can change dramatically over time, periodic reassessment is required, especially for less stable countries.

Regardless of how country risk analysis is conducted, MNCs are often unable to predict crises in various countries. MNCs should recognize their limitations when assessing country risk and consider ways they might limit their exposure to a possible increase in that risk.

COMPARING RISK RATINGS AMONG COUNTRIES

An MNC may evaluate country risk for several countries, perhaps to determine where to establish a subsidiary. One approach to comparing political and financial ratings among countries, advocated by some foreign risk managers, is a **foreign investment risk matrix (FIRM)**, which displays the financial (or economic) and political risk by intervals ranging across the matrix from "poor" to "good." Each

Financial Markets Perspective

Financial Market Indicators of Country Risk

By observing the financial markets, MNCs can obtain insight about country risk. First, the risk-free rate that is determined by the country's debt market offers some information about the minimum funding for a project in the country. The volatility of that rate over time indicates how the minimum funding costs may change over time. The risk premium on risky debt issued by firms based in that country indicates the perceived level of risk of those firms. The volatility of the risk premium over time indicates the degree to which the perception of risk changes in this country. The volatility of the foreign exchange market indicates how the local currency's value may change over time. If the MNC's subsidiary plans to issue stock locally, the volatility of the local stock market indicates how the firm's stock value may change over time.

Though financial market indicators of country risk are useful, they do not capture all aspects of country risk. For example, they may not be useful in detecting conflict between two countries. Therefore, the financial market indicators should be used to complement rather than replace other methods of assessing country risk.

country can be positioned in its appropriate location on the matrix based on its political rating and financial rating.

HTTP:// **ONLINE APPLICATION** **Country Risk Ratings** If an MNC wants to consider a country risk assessment by outside evaluators, it can obtain a country risk rating for any country at http://biz.yahoo.com/ifc/.

Click on any country listed, then click on Country Risk, and then click on Risk Rating. A country risk rating is provided for the near future, as well as for a longer time period. An overall country risk rating is provided in the second column, with an overall score in the third column. Various components used to derive the overall country risk rating are rated in Columns 4 to 7, including the country's political risk and economic risk.

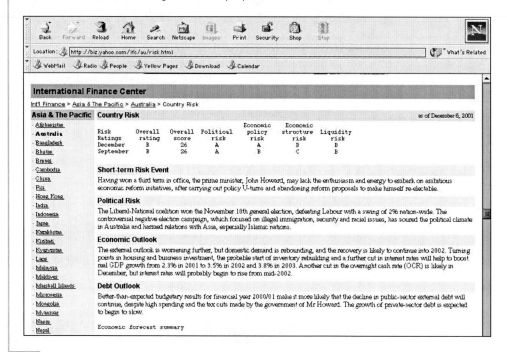

ACTUAL COUNTRY RISK RATINGS ACROSS COUNTRIES

Country risk ratings are shown in Exhibit 16.4. This exhibit is not necessarily applicable to a particular MNC that wants to pursue international business because the risk assessment here may not focus on the factors that are relevant to that MNC. Nevertheless, the exhibit illustrates how the risk rating can vary substantially among countries. Many industrialized countries such as Germany and Switzerland are rated highly. Emerging countries tend to have lower risk ratings. Country risk ratings change over time in response to the factors that influence a country's rating.

Exhibit 16.4
Country Risk Ratings among Countries (Maximum Rating Is 100)

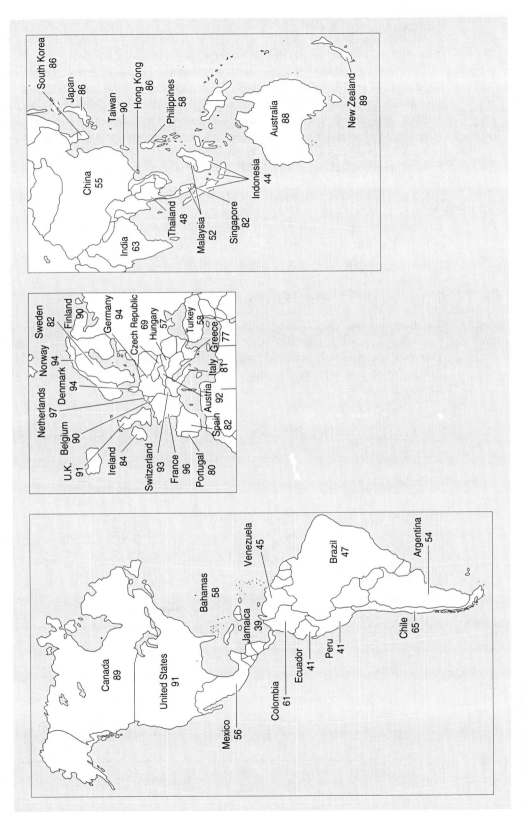

South Korea 86
Japan 86
Taiwan 90
Hong Kong 86
Philippines 58
China 55
India 63
Thailand 48
Malaysia 52
Singapore 82
Indonesia 44
Australia 88
New Zealand 89

Netherlands 97
Norway 94
Denmark 94
Sweden 82
Finland 90
Germany 94
Czech Republic 69
Hungary 57
Turkey 58
Greece 77
Italy 81
Austria 92
Spain 82
Portugal 80
France 96
Switzerland 93
Ireland 84
Belgium 90
U.K. 91

Canada 89
United States 91
Mexico 56
Bahamas 58
Jamaica 39
Colombia 61
Ecuador 41
Peru 41
Venezuela 45
Brazil 47
Chile 65
Argentina 54

Source: World Bank, 2000.

Economic and Political Ratings of Countries

Exhibit 16.5 shows the economic performance (which is a subset of the financial risk rating) and political risk for various countries. These two factors were assigned a maximum of 50 points (25 points each), out of a total of 100 points. Other financial factors to be discussed shortly made up the other 50 points. Notice from Exhibit 16.5 that industrialized countries such as Germany and Japan are assigned a higher political risk rating than economic performance rating. Conversely, emerging markets such as China and Hungary receive a higher economic performance rating than political risk rating.

HTTP:// **USING THE WEB**

Country Debt Ratings Ratings of a country's creditworthiness and its debt are provided at http://www.worldbank.org/data/wdi2000/pdfs/tab5_3.pdf.

Ratings of Eastern European Countries

To illustrate the characteristics that are given much attention when assessing country risk, consider the assessment of Eastern European countries in recent years. Hungary has generally received relatively high ratings because of its capable labor force, the ease in remitting profits from the country, and its government's efforts to promote direct foreign investment. Poland, Romania, and the countries that

Exhibit 16.5

Comparison of Economic Performance and Political Risk across Countries

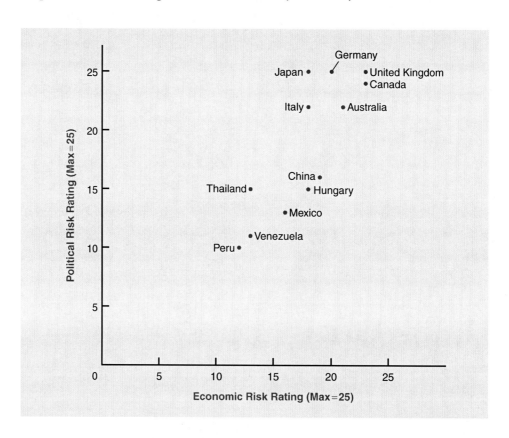

formerly made up Yugoslavia have received low ratings because of internal political battles, large budget deficits, poor economic conditions, large government bureaucracies, and little effort to encourage direct foreign investment. Some other important characteristics assessed when measuring country risk in these countries are availability of hotels, office space, phone lines, and public transportation.

INCORPORATING COUNTRY RISK IN CAPITAL BUDGETING

If the risk rating of a country is in the tolerable range, any project related to that country deserves further consideration. Country risk can be incorporated in the capital budgeting analysis of a proposed project by adjusting the discount rate or by adjusting the estimated cash flows. Each method is discussed here.

Adjustment of the Discount Rate

The discount rate of a proposed project is supposed to reflect the required rate of return on that project. Thus, the discount rate can be adjusted to account for the country risk. The lower the country risk rating, the higher the perceived risk and the higher the discount rate applied to the project's cash flows. This approach is convenient in that one adjustment to the capital budgeting analysis can capture country risk. However, there is no precise formula for adjusting the discount rate to incorporate country risk. The adjustment is somewhat arbitrary and may therefore cause feasible projects to be rejected or unfeasible projects to be accepted.

Adjustment of the Estimated Cash Flows

Perhaps the most appropriate method for incorporating forms of country risk in a capital budgeting analysis is to estimate how the cash flows would be affected

---

Managing for Value: TheStreet.com's Decision to Close Its British Subsidiary

TheStreet.com is a U.S.-based Internet firm that provides financial information on its website. In February 2000, it decided to expand its operations into the United Kingdom where it created a website specific to British investors. One country characteristic in its favor was that many individual investors in Europe are based in the United Kingdom. However, a key characteristic of any country is the preferences of its consumers, which affect the demand for a firm's products.

It appears that TheStreet.com's assessment of the United Kingdom's environment was overly optimistic. The Internet and online brokerage accounts are not used as much in the United Kingdom as in some other European countries.

Therefore, TheStreet.com attracted fewer customers than it had expected. In November 2000, TheStreet.com decided to close its operations in the United Kingdom because the website was costly to maintain and was not generating sufficient advertising revenue.

This example illustrates the danger of generalizing about Europe rather than recognizing the specific characteristics of each European country. Although there are more individual investors in the United Kingdom, individuals in Germany and the Scandinavian countries use the Internet more. TheStreet.com's decision to close its operations in the United Kingdom enhanced its value because it discontinued a value-decreasing project.

by each form of risk. For example, if there is a 20 percent probability that the host government will temporarily block funds from the subsidiary to the parent, the MNC should estimate the project's net present value (*NPV*) under these circumstances, realizing that there is a 20 percent chance that this *NPV* will occur.

If there is a chance that the host government takeover will occur, the foreign project's *NPV* under these conditions should be estimated. Each possible form of risk has an estimated impact on the foreign project's cash flows and therefore on the project's *NPV*. By analyzing each possible impact, the MNC can determine the probability distribution of *NPV*s for the project. Its accept/reject decision on the project will be based on its assessment of the probability that the project will generate a positive *NPV*, as well as the size of possible *NPV* outcomes. Though this procedure may seem somewhat tedious, it directly incorporates forms of country risk into the cash flow estimates and explicitly illustrates the possible results from implementing the project. The more convenient method of adjusting the discount rate in accordance with the country risk rating does not indicate the probability distribution of possible outcomes.

Example

Reconsider the example of Spartan, Inc., that was discussed in Chapter 14. Assume for the moment that all the initial assumptions regarding Spartan's initial investment, project life, pricing policy, exchange rate projections, and so on still apply. Now, however, we will incorporate two country risk characteristics that were not included in the initial analysis. First, assume that there is a 30 percent chance that the withholding tax imposed by the Singapore government will be at a 20 percent rate rather than a 10 percent rate. Second, assume that there is a 40 percent chance that the Singapore government will provide Spartan a payment (salvage value) of S$7 million rather than S$12 million. These two possibilities represent a form of country risk.

Assume that these two possible situations are unrelated. To determine how the *NPV* is affected by each of these scenarios, a capital budgeting analysis similar to that shown in Exhibit 14.2 in Chapter 14 can be used. If this analysis is already on a spreadsheet, the *NPV* can easily be estimated by adjusting line items no. 15 (withholding tax on remitted funds) and no. 17 (salvage value). The capital budgeting analysis measures the effect of a 20 percent withholding tax rate in Exhibit 16.6. Since none of the items before line no. 14 are affected, these items are not shown here. If the 20 percent withholding tax rate is imposed, the *NPV* of the four-year project is $1,252,160.

Now consider the possibility of the lower salvage value, while using the initial assumption of a 10 percent withholding tax rate. The capital budgeting analysis accounts for the lower salvage value in Exhibit 16.7. The estimated *NPV* is $800,484, based on this scenario.

Finally, consider the possibility that both the higher withholding tax and the lower salvage value occur. The capital budgeting analysis in Exhibit 16.8 accounts for both of these situations. The *NPV* is estimated to be –$177,223.

Once estimates for the *NPV* are derived for each scenario, Spartan, Inc., can attempt to determine whether the project is feasible. There are two country risk variables that are uncertain, and there are four possible *NPV* outcomes, as illustrated in Exhibit 16.9. Given the probability of each possible situation and the assumption that the withholding tax outcome is independent from the salvage value outcome, joint probabilities can be determined for each pair of outcomes by multiplying the probabilities of the two outcomes of concern. Since the probability

Exhibit 16.6

Analysis of Project Based on a 20 Percent Withholding Tax: Spartan, Inc.

	Year 0	Year 1	Year 2	Year 3	Year 4
14. S$ remitted by subsidiary		S$6,000,000	S$6,000,000	S$7,600,000	S$8,400,000
15. Withholding tax imposed on remitted funds (20%)		S$1,200,000	S$1,200,000	S$1,520,000	S$1,680,000
16. S$ remitted after withholding taxes		S$4,800,000	S$4,800,000	S$6,080,000	S$6,720,000
17. Salvage value					S$12,000,000
18. Exchange rate of S$		$.50	$.50	$.50	$.50
19. Cash flows to parent		$2,400,000	$2,400,000	$3,040,000	$9,360,000
20. *PV* of parent cash flows (15% discount rate)		$2,086,956	$1,814,745	$1,998,849	$5,351,610
21. Initial investment by parent	$10,000,000				
22. Cumulative *NPV*		−$7,913,044	−$6,098,299	−$4,099,450	$1,252,160

of a 20 percent withholding tax is 30 percent, the probability of a 10 percent withholding tax is 70 percent. Given that the probability of a lower salvage value is 40 percent, the probability of the initial estimate for the salvage value is 60 percent. Thus, scenario no. 1 (10 percent withholding tax and S$12 million salvage value) created in Chapter 14 has a joint probability (probability that both outcomes will occur) of 70% × 60% = 42%.

Exhibit 16.7

Analysis of Project Based on a Reduced Salvage Value: Spartan, Inc.

	Year 0	Year 1	Year 2	Year 3	Year 4
14. S$ remitted by subsidiary		S$6,000,000	S$6,000,000	S$7,600,000	S$8,400,000
15. Withholding tax imposed on remitted funds (10%)		S$ 600,000	S$ 600,000	S$ 760,000	S$ 840,000
16. S$ remitted after withholding taxes		S$5,400,000	S$5,400,000	S$6,840,000	S$7,560,000
17. Salvage value					S$7,000,000
18. Exchange rate of S$		$.50	$.50	$.50	$.50
19. Cash flows to parent		$2,700,000	$2,700,000	$3,420,000	$7,280,000
20. *PV* of parent cash flows (15% discount rate)		$2,347,826	$2,041,588	$2,248,706	$4,162,364
21. Initial investment by parent	$10,000,000				
22. Cumulative *NPV*		−$7,652,174	−$5,610,586	−$3,361,880	$800,484

Exhibit 16.8

Analysis of Project Based on a 20 Percent Withholding Tax and a Reduced Salvage Value: Spartan, Inc.

	Year 0	Year 1	Year 2	Year 3	Year 4
14. S$ remitted by subsidiary		S$6,000,000	S$6,000,000	S$7,600,000	S$8,400,000
15. Withholding tax imposed on remitted funds (20%)		S$1,200,000	S$1,200,000	S$1,520,000	S$1,680,000
16. S$ remitted after withholding taxes		S$4,800,000	S$4,800,000	S$6,080,000	S$6,720,000
17. Salvage value					S$7,000,000
18. Exchange rate of S$		$.50	$.50	$.50	$.50
19. Cash flows to parent		$2,400,000	$2,400,000	$3,040,000	$6,860,000
20. PV of parent cash flows (15% discount rate)		$2,086,956	$1,814,745	$1,998,849	$3,922,227
21. Initial investment by parent	$10,000,000				
22. Cumulative NPV		−$7,913,044	−$6,098,299	−$4,099,450	−$177,223

In Exhibit 16.9, scenario no. 4 is the only scenario in which there is a negative *NPV*. Since this scenario has a 12 percent chance of occurring, there is a 12 percent chance that the project will adversely affect the value of the firm. Put another way, there is an 88 percent chance that the project will enhance the firm's value. The expected value of the project's *NPV* can be measured as the sum of each scenario's estimated *NPV* multiplied by its respective probability across all four scenarios, as shown at the bottom of Exhibit 16.9. Most MNCs would accept the proposed project, given the likelihood that the project will have a positive *NPV* and the limited loss that would occur even under the worst case scenario.

Exhibit 16.9

Summary of Estimated *NPV*s across the Possible Scenarios: Spartan, Inc.

Scenario	Withholding Tax Imposed by Singapore Government	Salvage Value of Project	NPV	Probability
1	10%	S$12,000,000	$2,229,867	(70%)(60%) = 42%
2	20%	S$12,000,000	$1,252,160	(30%)(60%) = 18%
3	10%	S$7,000,000	$800,484	(70%)(40%) = 28%
4	20%	S$7,000,000	−$177,223	(30%)(40%) = 12%

$$E(NPV) = \$2,229,867(42\%)$$
$$+ \$1,252,160(18\%)$$
$$+ \$800,484(28\%)$$
$$- \$177,223(12\%)$$
$$= \$1,364,801$$

Using an Electronic Spreadsheet to Account for Uncertainty. In the previous example, the initial assumptions for most input variables were used as if they were known with certainty. However, Spartan, Inc. could account for the uncertainty of country risk characteristics (as in our current example) while also allowing for uncertainty in the other variables as well. This process can be facilitated if the analysis is on a computer spreadsheet.

Example If Spartan, Inc., wishes to allow for three possible exchange rate trends, it can adjust the exchange rate projections for each of the four scenarios assessed in the current example. Each scenario will reflect a specific withholding tax outcome, a specific salvage value outcome, and a specific exchange rate trend. There will be a total of 12 scenarios, with each scenario having an estimated *NPV* and a probability of occurrence. Based on the estimated *NPV* and the probability of each scenario, Spartan, Inc., can then measure the expected value of the *NPV* and the probability that the *NPV* will be positive, which leads to a decision regarding whether the project is feasible.

Applications of Country Risk Analysis

In some cases, country risk assessment has enabled MNCs to avoid further involvement and even reduce current involvement in politically tense countries.

Gulf War. As a result of the crisis that culminated in the Gulf War in 1991, many MNCs attempted to reassess country risk. Terrorism became a major concern. MNCs used various methods to protect against terrorism. Cross-country travel by executives was reduced, as MNCs used teleconference calls instead. Some MNCs with subsidiaries in Saudi Arabia temporarily closed some of their operations, allowing employees from other countries to return home. Some projects that were being considered for countries that could be subject to terrorist attacks were postponed. Even projects that appeared to be feasible from a financial perspective were postponed because of the potential danger to employees.

In addition to the threat of terrorism, the crisis influenced cash flows of MNCs in many other ways. The effects varied with the characteristics of each MNC. The more obvious effects of the crisis were reduced travel and higher oil prices. The reduction in travel adversely affected airlines, hotels, restaurants, luggage manufacturers, tourist attractions, rental car agencies, and cruise lines.

Asian Crisis. As a result of the 1997–1998 Asian crisis, MNCs realized that they had underestimated the potential financial problems that could occur in the high-growth Asian countries. The high degree of economic growth was overemphasized and comforted country risk analysts, even though the Asian countries had high debt levels, and commercial banks had massive loan problems. The loan problems were not obvious because commercial banks were typically not required to disclose much information about their loans. Some MNCs recognized the potential problems in Asia, and limited their exports to those Asian businesses that were not willing to pay in advance.

Terrorist Attack on United States. Following the September 11, 2001, attack on the United States, some MNCs reduced their exposure to various forms of country risk by discontinuing business in countries where U.S. firms might be subject to more terrorist attacks. Some MNCs also reduced employee travel to protect employees from attacks. MNCs recognize that some unpredictable events will unfold that will affect their exposure to country risk. Yet, they can at least be prepared to revise their operations in order to reduce their exposure.

REDUCING EXPOSURE TO HOST GOVERNMENT TAKEOVERS

Although direct foreign investment offers several possible benefits, country risk can offset such benefits. The most severe country risk is a host government takeover. This type of takeover may result in major losses, especially when the MNC does not have any power to negotiate with the host government.

The following are the most common strategies used to reduce exposure to a host government takeover:

- Use a short-term horizon.
- Rely on unique supplies or technology.
- Hire local labor.
- Borrow local funds.
- Purchase insurance.

Use a Short-Term Horizon

An MNC may concentrate on recovering cash flow quickly so that in the event of expropriation, losses are minimized. An MNC would also exert only a minimum effort to replace worn-out equipment and machinery at the subsidiary. It may even phase out its overseas investment by selling off its assets to local investors or the government in stages over time.

Rely on Unique Supplies or Technology

If the subsidiary can bring in supplies from its headquarters (or a sister subsidiary) that cannot be duplicated locally, the host government will not be able to take over and operate the subsidiary without those supplies. Also the MNC can cut off the supplies if the subsidiary is treated unfairly.

If the subsidiary can hide the technology in its production process, a government takeover will be less likely. A takeover would be successful in this case only if the MNC would provide the necessary technology, and the MNC would do so only under conditions of a friendly takeover that would ensure that it received adequate compensation.

Hire Local Labor

If local employees of the subsidiary would be affected by the host government's takeover, they can pressure their government to avoid such action. However, the government could still keep those employees after taking over the subsidiary. Thus, this strategy has only limited effectiveness in avoiding or limiting a government takeover.

Borrow Local Funds

If the subsidiary borrows funds locally, local banks will be concerned about its future performance. If for any reason a government takeover would reduce the probability that the banks would receive their loan repayments promptly, they might attempt to prevent a takeover by the host government. However, the host government may guarantee repayment to the banks, so this strategy has only limited effectiveness. Nevertheless, it could still be preferable to a situation in which the MNC not only loses the subsidiary but also still owes home country creditors.

Purchase Insurance

Insurance can be purchased to cover the risk of expropriation. For example, the U.S. government provides insurance through the Overseas Private Investment Corporation (OPIC). The insurance premiums paid by a firm depend on the degree of insurance coverage and the risk associated with the firm. Yet, any insurance policy will typically cover only a portion of the company's total exposure to country risk.

Many home countries of MNCs have investment guarantee programs that insure to some extent the risks of expropriation, wars, or currency blockage. Some guarantee programs have a one-year waiting period or longer before compensation is paid on losses due to expropriation. Also, some insurance policies do not cover all forms of expropriation. Furthermore, to be eligible for such insurance, the subsidiary might be required by the country to concentrate on exporting rather than on local sales. Even if a subsidiary qualifies for insurance, there is a cost. Any insurance will typically cover only a portion of the assets and may specify a maximum duration of coverage, such as 15 or 20 years. A subsidiary must weigh the benefits of this insurance against the cost of the policy's premiums and potential losses in excess of coverage. The insurance can be helpful, but it does not by itself prevent losses due to expropriation.

In 1993, Russia established an insurance fund to protect MNCs against various forms of country risk. The Russian government took this action to encourage more direct foreign investment in Russia.

The World Bank has established an affiliate called the Multilateral Investment Guarantee Agency (MIGA) to provide political insurance for MNCs with direct foreign investment in less developed countries. MIGA offers insurance against expropriation, breach of contract, currency inconvertibility, war, and civil disturbances.

IMPACT OF AN MNC's COUNTRY RISK ANALYSIS ON ITS VALUE

An MNC's country risk analysis can affect its value, as shown in Exhibit 16.10. The country risk analysis determines the expected cash flows derived from each foreign subsidiary in the future. A country risk analysis may also lead to a decision to divest a subsidiary, which means that the expected foreign currency cash flows generated by that subsidiary will terminate after that point. Thus, the expected foreign currency cash flows that will ultimately be remitted to the U.S. parent are influenced by the country risk analysis.

The parent's required rate of return on the funds it provides to support operations in foreign countries is also affected by its country risk analysis. During

Exhibit 16.10
Impact of Country Risk on an MNC's Value

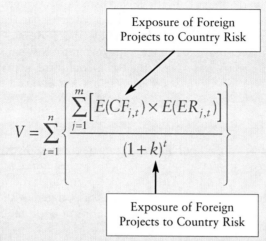

V = value of the U.S.-based MNC
$E(CF_{j,t})$ = expected cash flows denominated in currency j to be received by the U.S. parent in period t
$E(ER_{j,t})$ = expected exchange rate at which currency j can be converted to dollars at the end of period t
k = weighted average cost of capital of the U.S. parent company
m = number of currencies
n = number of periods

the Asian crisis, many MNCs revised their country risk assessment upward for Asian countries. Thus, the required rate of return for investment in Asian operations would have been revised upward even if no other factors changed, which reduced the value of the MNC.

SUMMARY

- The factors used by MNCs to measure a country's political risk include attitude of consumers toward purchasing locally produced goods, the host government's actions toward the MNC, the blockage of fund transfers, currency inconvertibility, war, bureaucracy, and corruption. These factors can increase the costs of international business.

- The factors used by MNCs to measure a country's financial risk are the country's interest rates, exchange rates, and inflation rates.

- The techniques typically used by MNCs to measure the country risk are the checklist

approach, the Delphi technique, quantitative analysis, and inspection visits. Since no one technique covers all aspects of country risk, a combination of these techniques is commonly used. The measurement of country risk is essentially a weighted average of the political or financial factors that are perceived to comprise country risk. Each MNC has its own view as to the weights that should be assigned to each factor. Thus, the overall rating for a country may vary among MNCs.

- Once country risk is measured, it can be incorporated into a capital budgeting analysis by adjustment of the discount rate. The adjustment is somewhat arbitrary, however, and may lead to improper decision making. An alternative method of incorporating country risk analysis into capital budgeting is to explicitly account for each factor that affects country risk. For each possible form of risk, the MNC can recalculate the foreign project's net present value under the condition that the event (such as blocked funds, increased taxes, etc.) occurs.

SELF TEST

Answers are provided in Appendix A at the back of the text.

1. Key West Co. exports highly advanced phone system components to its subsidiary shops on islands in the Caribbean. The components are purchased by consumers to improve their phone systems. These components are not produced in other countries. Explain how political risk factors could adversely affect the profitability of Key West Co.

2. Using the information in question 1, explain how financial risk factors could adversely affect the profitability of Key West Co.

3. Given the information in question 1, do you expect that Key West Co. is more concerned about the adverse effects of political risk or of financial risk?

4. Explain what types of firms would be most concerned about an increase in country risk as a result of the terrorist attack on the World Trade Center on September 11, 2001.

5. Rockford Co. plans to expand its successful business by establishing a subsidiary in Canada. However, it is concerned that after two years the Canadian government will either impose a special tax on any income sent back to the U.S. parent or order the subsidiary to be sold at that time. The executives have estimated that either of these scenarios has a 15 percent chance of occurring. They have decided to add four percentage points to the project's required rate of return to incorporate the country risk that they are concerned about in the capital budgeting analysis. Is there a better way to more precisely incorporate the country risk of concern here?

QUESTIONS AND APPLICATIONS

1. List some forms of country risk other than a takeover of a subsidiary by the host government.

2. Identify common political factors for an MNC to consider when assessing country risk. Briefly elaborate on how each factor can affect the risk to the MNC.

3. Identify common financial factors for an MNC to consider when assessing country risk. Briefly elaborate on how each factor can affect the risk to the MNC.

4. Discuss the use of the foreign investment risk matrix (FIRM) to compare country risk among countries. Why do firms have different acceptable zones when using this matrix?

5. Describe the steps involved in assessing country risk once all relevant information has been gathered.

6. Describe the possible errors involved in assessing country risk. In other words, explain why country risk analysis is not always accurate.

7. Explain an MNC's strategy of diversifying projects internationally in order to maintain a low level of overall country risk.

8. Once a project is accepted, country risk

analysis for the foreign country involved is no longer necessary, assuming that no other proposed projects are being evaluated for that country. Do you agree with this statement? Why or why not?

9. If the potential return is high enough, any degree of country risk can be tolerated. Do you agree with this statement? Why or why not?

10. Niagra, Inc., has decided to call a well-known country risk consultant to conduct a country risk analysis on a small country where it plans to develop a large subsidiary. Niagra prefers to hire the consultant, since it plans to use its employees for other important corporate functions. The consultant uses a computer program that has assigned weights of importance linked to the various factors. The consultant will evaluate the factors for this small country and insert a rating for each factor into the computer. The weights assigned to the factors are not adjusted by the computer, but the factor ratings are adjusted for each country the consultant assesses. Do you think Niagra, Inc., should use this consultant? Why or why not?

11. Explain the microassessment of country risk.

12. How could a country risk assessment be used to adjust a project's required rate of return? How could such an assessment be used instead to adjust a project's estimated cash flows?

13. Explain some methods of reducing exposure to existing country risk while maintaining the same amount of business within a particular country.

14. Why do some subsidiaries maintain a low profile as to where their parents are located?

15. Do you think that a proper country risk analysis can replace a capital budgeting analysis of a project considered for a foreign country? Explain.

16. When NYU Corp. considered establishing a subsidiary in Zenland, it performed a country risk analysis to help make the decision. It first retrieved a country risk analysis performed about one year earlier, when it had planned to begin a major exporting business to Zenland firms. Then it updated the analysis by incorporating all current information on the key variables that were used in that analysis, such as Zenland's willingness to accept exports, its existing quotas, and existing tariff laws. Is this country risk analysis adequate? Explain.

17. MNCs such as Alcoa, DuPont, Heinz, and IBM donated products and technology to foreign countries where they had subsidiaries. How could these actions have reduced some forms of country risk?

18. Hoosier, Inc., is planning a project in the United Kingdom. It would lease space for one year in a shopping mall to sell expensive clothes manufactured in the United States. The project would end in one year, when all earnings would be remitted to Hoosier, Inc. Assume that no additional corporate taxes would be incurred beyond those imposed by the British government. Since Hoosier, Inc., would rent space, it would not have any long-term assets in the United Kingdom, and it expects that the salvage (terminal) value of the project will be about zero.

Assume that the project's required rate of return is 18 percent. Also assume that the initial outlay required by the parent to fill the store with clothes is $200,000. The pretax earnings are expected to be £300,000 at the end of one year. The British pound is expected to be worth $1.60 at the end of one year, when the after-tax earnings will be converted to dollars and remitted to the United States. The following forms of country risk must be considered:

■ The British economy may weaken (probability = 30%), which would cause the expected pretax earnings to be £200,000.

■ The British corporate tax rate on income earned by U.S. firms may increase from 40 percent to 50 percent (probability = 20 percent).

These two forms of country risk are independent. Calculate the expected value of the project's net present value (*NPV*) and determine the probability that the project will have a negative *NPV*.

19. Explain how capital budgeting analysis would need to be adjusted for question 18 if there were three possible outcomes for the British pound, in addition to the possible outcomes for the British economic growth and the corporate tax rate.

20. Recently, J.C. Penney decided to consider expanding into various foreign countries; it applied a comprehensive country risk analysis before making its expansion decisions. Initial screenings of 30 foreign countries were based on political and economic factors that contribute to country risk. For the remaining 20 countries where country risk was considered to be tolerable, specific country risk characteristics of each country were considered. One of J.C. Penney's biggest targets is Mexico, where it planned to build and operate seven large stores.

    a. Identify the political factors that you think may possibly affect the performance of the J.C. Penney stores in Mexico.

    b. Explain why the J.C. Penney stores in Mexico and in other foreign markets are subject to financial risk (a subset of country risk).

    c. Assume that J.C. Penney anticipated that there was a 10 percent chance that the Mexican government would temporarily prevent conversion of peso profits into dollars because of political conditions. This event would prevent J.C. Penney from remitting earnings generated in Mexico and could adversely affect the performance of these stores (from the U.S. perspective). Offer a way in which this type of political risk could be explicitly incorporated into a capital budgeting analysis when assessing the feasibility of these projects.

    d. Assume that J.C. Penney decides to use dollars to finance the expansion of stores in Mexico. Second, assume that J.C. Penney decides to use one set of dollar cash flow estimates for any project that it assesses. Third, assume that the stores in Mexico are not subject to political risk. Do you think that the required rate of return on these projects would differ from the required rate of return on stores built in the United States at the same time? Explain.

    e. Based on your answer to the previous question, does this mean that proposals for any new stores in the United States have a higher probability of being accepted than proposals for any new stores in Mexico?

Impact of 9/11/01

21. Arkansas, Inc., exports to various less-developed countries, and its receivables are denominated in the foreign currencies of the importers. It considers reducing its exchange rate risk by establishing small subsidiaries to produce products in the countries where it sells products. By incurring some expenses in the countries where it generates revenue, it reduces its exposure to exchange rate risk. Since September 11, 2001, when terrorists attacked the United States, it questioned whether it should restructure its operations. Its CEO believed that its cash flows may be less exposed to exchange rate risk but more exposed to other types of risk as a result of restructuring. What is your opinion?

Internet Application

22. The following website offers information on countries that are more transparent than others, meaning that one can recognize that they are having political or economic problems: **asiarisk.com/library2/html**.

    Use this website to identify the Asian countries that have recently been rated very transparent. What Asian countries are not perceived to be transparent?

Running Your Own MNC

This exercise can be found on the Student CD-ROM.

Blades, Inc. Case

Country Risk Assessment

Recently, Ben Holt, Blades' chief financial officer (CFO), has assessed whether it would be more beneficial for Blades to establish a subsidiary in Thailand to manufacture roller blades or to acquire an existing manufacturer, Skates'n'Stuff, which has offered to sell the business to Blades for 1 billion Thai baht. In Holt's view, establishing a subsidiary in Thailand yields a higher net present value (*NPV*) than acquiring the existing business. Furthermore, the Thai manufacturer has rejected an offer by Blades, Inc., for 900 million baht. A purchase price of 900 million baht for Skates'n'Stuff would make the acquisition as attractive as the establishment of a subsidiary in Thailand in terms of *NPV*. Skates'n'Stuff has indicated that it is not willing to accept less than 950 million baht.

Although Holt is confident that the *NPV* analysis was conducted correctly, he is troubled by the fact that the same discount rate, 25 percent, was used in each analysis. In his view, establishing a subsidiary in Thailand may be associated with a higher level of country risk than acquiring Skates'n'Stuff. Although either approach would result in approximately the same level of financial risk, the political risk associated with establishing a subsidiary in Thailand may be higher then the political risk of operating Skates'n'Stuff. If the establishment of a subsidiary in Thailand is associated with a higher level of country risk overall, then a higher discount rate should have been used in the analysis. Based on these considerations, Holt wants to measure the country risk associated with Thailand on both a macro and a micro level and then to reexamine the feasibility of both approaches.

First, Holt has gathered some more detailed political information for Thailand. For example, he believes that consumers in Asian countries prefer to purchase goods produced by Asians, which might

prevent a subsidiary in Thailand from being successful. This cultural characteristic might not prevent an acquisition of Skates'n'Stuff from succeeding, however, especially if Blades retains the company's management and employees. Furthermore, the subsidiary would have to apply for various licenses and permits to be allowed to operate in Thailand, while Skates'n'Stuff obtained these licenses and permits long ago. However, the number of licenses required for Blades' industry is relatively low compared to other industries. Moreover, there is a high possibility that the Thai government will implement capital controls in the near future, which would prevent funds from leaving Thailand. Since Blades, Inc., has planned to remit all earnings generated by its subsidiary or by Skates'n'Stuff back to the United States, regardless of which approach to direct foreign investment it takes, capital controls may force Blades to reinvest funds in Thailand.

Ben Holt has also gathered some information regarding the financial risk of operating in Thailand. Thailand's economy has been weak lately, and recent forecasts indicate that a recovery may be slow. A weak economy may affect the demand for Blades' products, roller blades. The state of the economy is of particular concern to Blades since it produces a leisure product. In the case of an economic turndown, consumers will first eliminate these types of purchases. Holt is also worried about the high interest rates in Thailand, which may further slow economic growth if Thai citizens begin saving more. Furthermore, Holt is also aware that inflation levels in Thailand are expected to remain high. These high inflation levels can affect the purchasing power of Thai consumers, who may adjust their spending habits to purchase more essential products than roller blades. However, high levels of inflation also indicate that consumers in Thailand are still spending a relatively high proportion of their earnings.

Another financial factor that may affect Blades' operations in Thailand is the baht-dollar exchange rate. Current forecasts indicate that the Thai baht may depreciate in the future. However, recall that Blades will sell all roller blades produced in Thailand to Thai consumers. Therefore, Blades is not subject to a lower level of U.S. demand resulting from a weak baht. Blades will remit the earnings generated in Thailand back to the United States, however, and a weak baht would reduce the dollar amount of these translated earnings.

Based on these initial considerations, Holt feels that the level of political risk of operating may be higher if Blades decides to establish a subsidiary to manufacture roller blades (as opposed to acquiring Skates'n'Stuff). Conversely, the financial risk of operating in Thailand will be roughly the same whether Blades establishes a subsidiary or acquires Skates'n'Stuff. Holt is not satisfied with this initial assessment, however, and would like to have numbers at hand when he meets with the board of directors next week. Thus, he would like to conduct a quantitative analysis of the country risk associated with operating in Thailand. He has asked you, a financial analyst at Blades, to develop a country risk analysis for Thailand and to adjust the discount rate for the riskier venture (i.e., establishing a subsidiary or acquiring Skates'n'Stuff). Holt has provided the following information for your analysis:

- Since Blades produces leisure products, it is more susceptible to financial risk factors than political risk factors. You should use weights of 60 percent for financial risk factors and 40 percent for political risk factors in your analysis.

- You should use the attitude of Thai consumers, capital controls, and bureaucracy as political risk factors in your analysis. Holt perceives capital controls as the most important political risk factor. In his view, the consumer attitude and bureaucracy factors are of equal importance.

- You should use interest rates, inflation levels, and exchange rates as the financial risk factors in your analysis. In Holt's view, exchange rates

and interest rates in Thailand are of equal importance, while inflation levels are slightly less important.

- Each factor used in your analysis should be assigned a rating in a range of 1 to 5, where 5 indicates the most unfavorable rating.

Ben Holt has asked you to provide answers to the following questions for him, which he will use in his meeting with the board of directors:

1. Based on the information provided in the case, do you think the political risk associated with Thailand is higher or lower for a manufacturer of leisure products such as Blades as opposed to, say, a food producer? That is, conduct a microassessment of political risk for Blades, Inc.

2. Do you think the financial risk associated with Thailand is higher or lower for a manufacturer of leisure products such as Blades as opposed to, say, a food producer? That is, conduct a microassessment of financial risk for Blades, Inc. Do you think a leisure product manufacturer such as Blades will be more affected by political or financial risk factors?

3. Without using a numerical analysis, do you think establishing a subsidiary in Thailand or acquiring Skates'n'Stuff will result in a higher assessment of political risk? Of financial risk? Substantiate your answer.

4. Using a spreadsheet, conduct a quantitative country risk analysis for Blades, Inc., using the information Ben Holt has provided for you. Use your judgment to assign weights and ratings to each political and financial risk factor and determine an overall country risk rating for Thailand. Conduct two separate analyses for (a) the establishment of a subsidiary in Thailand and (b) the acquisition of Skates'n'Stuff.

5. Which method of direct foreign investment should utilize a higher discount rate in the capital budgeting analysis? Would this strengthen or weaken the tentative decision of establishing a subsidiary in Thailand?

Small Business Dilemma

Country Risk Analysis at the Sports Exports Company

The Sports Exports Company produces footballs in the United States and exports them to the United Kingdom. It also has an ongoing joint venture with a British firm that produces some sporting goods for a fee. The Sports Exports Company is considering the establishment of a small subsidiary in the United Kingdom.

1. Under the current conditions, is the Sports Exports Company subject to country risk?

2. If the firm does decide to develop a small subsidiary in the United Kingdom, will its exposure to country risk change? If so, how?

9

MULTINATIONAL COST OF CAPITAL AND CAPITAL STRUCTURE

An MNC finances its operations by using a capital structure (proportion of debt versus equity financing) that can minimize its cost of capital. By minimizing the cost of capital used to finance a given level of operations, financial managers minimize the required rate of return necessary to make the foreign operations feasible and therefore maximize the value of those operations.

The specific objectives of this chapter are to:
- Explain how corporate and country characteristics influence an MNC's cost of capital.
- Explain why there are differences in the costs of capital among countries.
- Explain how corporate and country characteristics are considered by an MNC when it establishes its capital structure.

BACKGROUND ON COST OF CAPITAL

A firm's capital consists of equity (retained earnings and funds obtained by issuing stock) and debt (borrowed funds). The firm's cost of retained earnings reflects an opportunity cost: what the existing shareholders could have earned if they had received the earnings as dividends and invested the funds themselves. The firm's cost of new common equity (issuing new stock) also reflects an opportunity cost: what the new shareholders could have earned if they had invested their funds elsewhere instead of in the stock. This cost exceeds that of retained earnings because it also includes the expenses associated with selling the new stock (flotation costs).

The firm's cost of debt is easier to measure because the firm incurs interest expenses as a result of borrowing funds. Firms attempt to use a specific capital structure, or mix of capital components, that will minimize their cost of capital. The lower a firm's cost of capital, the lower is its required rate of return on a given proposed project. Firms estimate their cost of capital before they conduct capital budgeting, because the net present value of any project is partially dependent on the cost of capital.

Comparing the Costs of Equity and Debt

A firm's weighted average cost of capital (referred to as k_c) can be measured as

$$k_c = \left(\frac{D}{D+E}\right)k_d(1-t) + \left(\frac{E}{D+E}\right)k_e$$

where D is the amount of the firm's debt, k_d is the before-tax cost of its debt, t is the corporate tax rate, E is the firm's equity, and k_e is the cost of financing with equity. These ratios reflect the percentage of capital represented by debt and equity, respectively.

There is an advantage to using debt rather than equity as capital because the interest payments on debt are tax deductible. The greater the use of debt, however, the greater the interest expense is and the higher the probability that the firm will be unable to meet its expenses. Consequently, the rate of return required by potential new shareholders or creditors will increase to reflect the higher probability of bankruptcy.

The tradeoff between debt's advantage (tax deductibility of interest payments) and its disadvantage (increased probability of bankruptcy) is illustrated in Exhibit 17.1. As the exhibit shows, the firm's cost of capital initially decreases as the ratio of debt to total capital increases. However, after some point (labeled X in Exhibit 17.1), the cost of capital rises as the ratio of debt to total capital increases. This suggests that the firm should increase its use of debt financing until the point at which the bankruptcy probability becomes large enough to offset the tax advantage of using debt. To go beyond that point would increase the firm's overall cost of capital.

Exhibit 17.1

Searching for the
Appropriate Capital
Structure

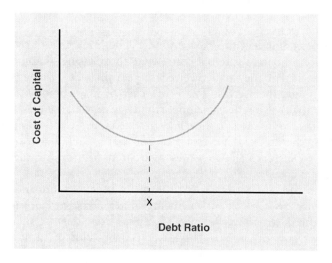

COST OF CAPITAL FOR MNCs

The cost of capital for MNCs may differ from that for domestic firms because of the following characteristics that differentiate MNCs from domestic firms:

- *Size of firm.* An MNC that often borrows substantial amounts may receive preferential treatment from creditors, thereby reducing its cost of capital. Furthermore, its relatively large issues of stocks or bonds allow for reduced flotation costs (as a percentage of the amount of financing). Note, however, that these advantages are due to the MNC's size and not to its internationalized business. A domestic corporation may receive the same treatment if it is large enough. Nevertheless, a firm's growth is more restricted if it is not willing to operate internationally. Because MNCs may more easily achieve growth, they may be more able than purely domestic firms to reach the necessary size to receive preferential treatment from creditors.

- *Access to international capital markets.* MNCs are normally able to obtain funds through the international capital markets. Since the cost of funds can vary among markets, the MNC's access to the international capital markets may allow it to obtain funds at a lower cost than that paid by domestic firms. In addition, subsidiaries may be able to obtain funds locally at a lower cost than that available to the parent if the prevailing interest rates in the host country are relatively low.

Example
The Coca-Cola Co.'s recent annual report stated: "Our global presence and strong capital position afford us easy access to key financial markets around the world, enabling us to raise funds with a low effective cost. This posture, coupled with the aggressive management of our mix of short-term and long-term debt, results in a lower overall cost of borrowing."

The use of foreign funds will not necessarily increase the MNC's exposure to exchange rate risk since the revenues generated by the subsidiary will most likely be denominated in the same currency. In this case, the subsidiary is not relying on the parent for financing, although some centralized managerial support from the parent will most likely still exist.

- *International diversification.* As explained earlier, a firm's cost of capital is affected by the probability that it will go bankrupt. If a firm's cash inflows come from sources all over the world, those cash inflows may be more stable because the firm's total sales will not be highly influenced by a single economy. To the extent that individual economies are independent of each other, net cash flows from a portfolio of subsidiaries should exhibit less variability, which may reduce the probability of bankruptcy and therefore reduce the cost of capital.

- *Exposure to exchange rate risk.* An MNC's cash flows could be more volatile than those of a domestic firm in the same industry if it is highly exposed to exchange rate risk. If foreign earnings are remitted to the U.S. parent of an MNC, they will not be worth as much when the U.S. dollar is strong against major currencies. Thus, the capability of making interest payments on outstanding debt is reduced, and the probability of bankruptcy is higher. This could force creditors and shareholders to require a higher return, which increases the MNC's cost of capital.

Overall, a firm more exposed to exchange rate fluctuations will usually have a wider (more dispersed) distribution of possible cash flows in future periods. Since the cost of capital should reflect that possibility, and since the possibility of bankruptcy will be higher if the cash flow expectations are more uncertain, exposure to exchange rate fluctuations could lead to a higher cost of capital.

- *Exposure to country risk.* An MNC that establishes foreign subsidiaries is subject to the possibility that a host country government may seize a subsidiary's assets. The probability of such an occurrence is influenced by many factors, including the attitude of the host country government and the industry of concern. If assets are seized and fair compensation is not provided, the probability of the MNC's going bankrupt increases. The higher the percentage of an MNC's assets invested in foreign countries and the higher the overall country risk of operating in these countries, the higher will be the MNC's probability of bankruptcy (and therefore its cost of capital), other things being equal.

  Other forms of country risk, such as changes in a host government's tax laws, could also affect an MNC's subsidiary's cash flows. These risks are not necessarily incorporated into the cash flow projections because there is no reason to believe that they will arise. Nevertheless, there is a possibility that these events will occur, so the capital budgeting process should incorporate such risk.

Example

ExxonMobil has much experience in assessing the feasibility of potential projects in foreign countries. If it detects a radical change in government or tax policy, it adds a premium to the required return of related projects. The adjustment also reflects a possible increase in its cost of capital.

The five factors that distinguish the cost of capital for an MNC and the cost for a domestic firm in a particular industry are summarized in Exhibit 17.2. In general, the first three factors listed (size, access to international capital markets, and international diversification) have a favorable effect on an MNC's cost of capital, while exchange rate risk and country risk have an unfavorable effect. It is impossible to generalize as to whether MNCs have an overall cost–of-capital advantage over domestic firms. Each MNC should be assessed separately to determine whether the net effects of its international operations on the cost of capital are favorable.

Cost-of-Capital Comparison Using the CAPM

To assess how required rates of return of MNCs differ from those of purely domestic firms, the capital asset pricing model (CAPM) can be applied. It defines the required return (k_e) on a stock as

$$k_e = R_f + B(R_m - R_f)$$

where

R_f = risk-free rate of return
R_m = market return
B = beta of stock

Exhibit 17.2

Summary of Factors
That Cause the Cost
of Capital of MNCs
to Differ from That of
Domestic Firms

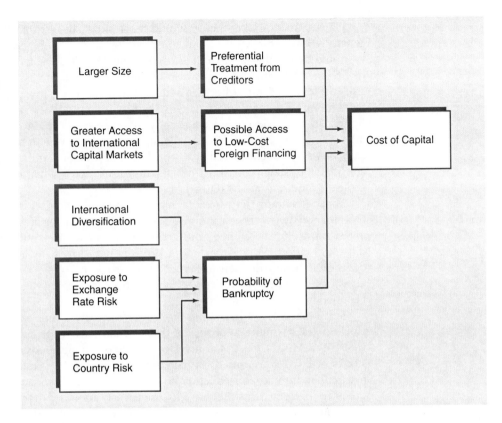

The CAPM suggests that the required return on a firm's stock is a positive function of (1) the risk-free rate of interest, (2) the market rate of return, and (3) the stock's beta. The beta represents the sensitivity of the stock's returns to market returns (a stock index is normally used as a proxy for the market). Advocates of the CAPM may suggest that a project's beta can be used to determine the required rate of return for that project. A project's beta represents the sensitivity of the project's cash flow to market conditions. A project whose cash flow is insulated from market conditions will exhibit a low beta.

For a well-diversified firm with cash flows generated by several projects, each project contains two types of risk: (1) unsystematic variability in cash flows unique to the firm and (2) systematic risk. Capital asset pricing theory suggests that the unsystematic risk of projects can be ignored because it will be diversified away. However, systematic risk is not diversified away because all projects are similarly affected. The lower a project's beta, the lower is the project's systematic risk and the lower its required rate of return.

Implications of the CAPM for an MNC's Risk

An MNC that increases the amount of its foreign sales may be able to reduce its stock's beta and therefore reduce the return required by investors. In this way, it will reduce its cost of capital. If projects of MNCs exhibit lower betas than projects of purely domestic firms, then the required rates of return on MNC projects should be lower. This translates into a lower overall cost of capital.

Capital asset pricing theory would most likely suggest that the cost of capital is generally lower for MNCs than for domestic firms for the reasons just presented. It should be emphasized, though, that some MNCs consider unsystematic project risk to be relevant. And if it is also considered within the assessment of a project's risk, the required rate of return will not necessarily be lower for MNCs' projects than for projects of domestic firms. In fact, many MNCs would perceive a large project in a less developed country with very volatile economic conditions and a high degree of country risk as being very risky, even if the project's expected cash flows are uncorrelated with the U.S. market. This indicates that MNCs may consider unsystematic risk to be an important factor when determining a foreign project's required rate of return.

When assuming that financial markets are segmented, it is acceptable to use the U.S. market when measuring a U.S.-based MNC's project beta. If U.S. investors invest mostly in the United States, their investments are systematically affected by the U.S. market. MNCs that adopt projects with low betas may be able to reduce their own betas (the sensitivity of their stock returns to market returns). U.S. investors consider such firms desirable because they offer more diversification benefits due to their low betas.

Since markets are becoming more integrated over time, one could argue that a world market is more appropriate than a U.S. market for determining the betas of U.S.-based MNCs. That is, if investors purchase stocks across many countries, their stocks will be substantially affected by world market conditions, not just U.S. market conditions. Consequently, to achieve more diversification benefits, they will prefer to invest in firms that have low sensitivity to world market conditions. MNCs that adopt projects that are somewhat isolated from world market conditions may be able to reduce their overall sensitivity to these conditions and therefore could be viewed as desirable investments by investors.

Though markets are becoming more integrated, U.S. investors still tend to focus on U.S. stocks and to capitalize on lower transaction and information costs. Thus, their investments are systematically affected by U.S. market conditions; this causes them to be most concerned about the sensitivity of investments to the U.S. market.

In summary, we cannot say with certainty whether an MNC will have a lower cost of capital than a purely domestic firm in the same industry. However, we can use this discussion to understand how an MNC may attempt to take full advantage of the favorable aspects that reduce its cost of capital, while minimizing exposure to the unfavorable aspects that increase its cost of capital.

Costs of Capital across Countries

An understanding of why the cost of capital can vary among countries is relevant for three reasons. First, it can explain why MNCs based in some countries may have a competitive advantage over others. Just as technology and resources differ across countries, so does the cost of capital. Therefore, MNCs based in some countries will have a larger set of feasible (positive net present value) projects because their cost of capital is lower; thus, these MNCs can more easily increase their world market share. MNCs operating in countries with a high cost of capital will be forced to decline projects that might be feasible for MNCs operating in countries with a low cost of capital.

Second, MNCs may be able to adjust their international operations and sources of funds to capitalize on differences in the cost of capital among countries. Third, differences in the costs of each capital component (debt and equity) can help explain why MNCs based in some countries tend to use a more debt-intensive capital structure than MNCs based elsewhere. Country differences in the cost of debt are discussed next, followed by country differences in the cost of equity.

Country Differences in the Cost of Debt

The cost of debt to a firm is primarily determined by the prevailing risk-free interest rate in the currency borrowed and the risk premium required by creditors. The cost of debt for firms is higher in some countries than in others because the corresponding risk-free rate is higher at a specific point in time or because the risk premium is higher. Explanations for country differences in the risk-free rate and in the risk premium follow.

Differences in the Risk-Free Rate. The risk-free rate is determined by the interaction of the supply and demand for funds. Any factors that influence the supply and/or demand will affect the risk-free rate. These factors include tax laws, demographics, monetary policies, and economic conditions, all of which differ among countries.

Tax laws in some countries offer more incentives to save than those in others, which can influence the supply of savings and, therefore, interest rates. A country's corporate tax laws related to depreciation and investment tax credits can also affect interest rates through their influence on the corporate demand for funds.

A country's demographics influence the supply of savings available and the amount of loanable funds demanded. Since demographics differ among countries, so will supply and demand conditions and, therefore, nominal interest rates. Countries with younger populations are likely to experience higher interest rates because younger households tend to save less and borrow more.

The monetary policy implemented by a country's central bank influences the supply of loanable funds and therefore influences interest rates. Each central bank implements its own monetary policy, and this can cause interest rates to differ among countries. One exception is the set of European countries that rely on the European Central Bank to control the supply of euros. All of these countries now have the same risk-free rate because they use the same currrency.

Since economic conditions influence interest rates, they can cause interest rates to vary across countries. The cost of debt is much higher in many less developed countries than in industrialized countries, primarily because of economic conditions. Some less developed countries have a high expected rate of inflation, which causes creditors to require a high risk-free interest rate.

Differences in the Risk Premium. The risk premium on debt must be large enough to compensate creditors for the risk that the borrower may be unable to meet its payment obligations. This risk can vary among countries because of differences in economic conditions, relationships between corporations and creditors, government intervention, and degree of financial leverage.

http://

Morgan Stanley's Economic Forum at www.ms.com/GEF provides analysis, discussions, statistics, and forecasts related to non-U.S. economies.

When economic conditions tend to be stable, the risk of a recession in that country is relatively low. Thus, the probability that a firm might not meet its obligations is lower, allowing for a lower risk premium.

Corporations and creditors have closer relationships in some countries than in others. In Japan, creditors stand ready to extend credit in the event of a corporation's financial distress, which reduces the risk of illiquidity. The cost of a Japanese firm's financial problems may be shared in various ways by the firm's management, business customers, and consumers. Since the financial problems are not borne entirely by creditors, all parties involved have more incentive to see that the problems are resolved. Thus, there is less likelihood (for a given level of debt) that Japanese firms will go bankrupt, allowing for a lower risk premium on the debt of Japanese firms.

Governments in some countries are more willing to intervene and rescue failing firms. For example, in the United Kingdom many firms are partially owned by the government. It may be in the government's best interest to rescue firms that it partially owns. Even if the government is not a partial owner, it may provide direct subsidies or extend loans to failing firms. In the United States, government rescues are less likely because taxpayers prefer not to bear the cost of corporate misman-agement. While there has been some government intervention in the United States to protect particular industries, the probability that a failing firm will be rescued by the government is lower there than in other countries. Therefore, the risk premium on a given level of debt may be higher for U.S. firms than for firms of other countries.

Firms in some countries have greater borrowing capacity because their creditors are willing to tolerate a higher degree of financial leverage. For example, firms in Japan and Germany have a higher degree of financial leverage than firms in the United States. If all other factors were equal, these high-leverage firms would have to pay a higher risk premium. However, all other factors are not equal. In fact, these firms are allowed to use a higher degree of financial leverage because of their unique relationships with the creditors and governments.

Comparative Costs of Debt across Countries. The before-tax cost of debt (as measured by corporate bond yields) for various countries is displayed in Exhibit 17.3. There is some positive correlation between country cost-of-debt levels over time. The nominal cost of debt for firms in many countries declined in the early 1990s during a global recession and then increased in the mid-1990s before declin-ing again in the late 1990s and early 2000s. The disparity in the cost of debt among the countries is due primarily to the disparity in their risk-free interest rates.

Country Differences in the Cost of Equity

A firm's cost of equity represents an opportunity cost: what shareholders could earn on investments with similar risk if the equity funds were distributed to them. This return on equity can be measured as a risk-free interest rate that could have been earned by shareholders, plus a premium to reflect the risk of the firm. As risk-free interest rates vary among countries, so does the cost of equity.

The cost of equity is also based on investment opportunities in the country of concern. In a country with many investment opportunities, potential returns may be relatively high, resulting in a high opportunity cost of funds and, therefore, a high

Exhibit 17.3

Costs of Debt across Countries

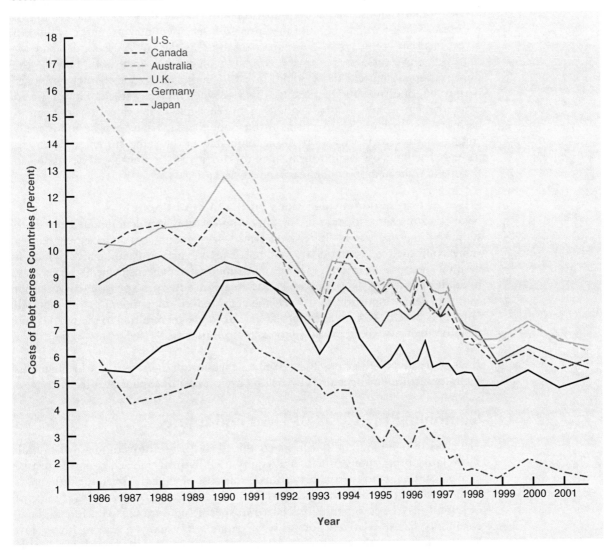

cost of capital. According to McCauley and Zimmer, a firm's cost of equity in a particular country can be estimated by first applying the price-earnings multiple to a given stream of earnings.[1]

The price-earnings multiple is related to the cost of capital because it reflects the share price of the firm in proportion to the firm's performance (as measured by earnings). A high price-earnings multiple implies that the firm receives a high price when selling new stock for a given level of earnings, which means that the cost of equity financing is low. The price-earnings multiple must be adjusted for the effects of a country's inflation, earnings growth, and other factors, however.

---

[1]Robert N. McCauley and Steven A. Zimmer, "Explaining International Differences in the Cost of Capital," *FRBNY Quarterly Review* (Summer 1989): 7–28.

Impact of the Euro. It can be argued that the adoption of the euro has reduced the cost of equity capital in the European countries that use this currency by reducing market imperfections. The adoption of the euro has facilitated the integration of European stock markets because investors from each country are more willing to invest in other countries where the euro is used as the currency. As demand for shares by investors has increased, trading volume has increased, making the European stock markets more liquid. Investors in one euro-zone country no longer need to be concerned about exchange rate risk when they buy stock of a firm based in another euro-zone country. In addition, the euro allows the valuations of firms to be more transparent because firms throughout the euro-zone can be more easily compared since their values are all denominated in the same currency. Given the increased willingness of European investors to invest in stocks, MNCs based in Europe have been more willing to issue stock.

Nike Problem

Effect of International Operations on the Cost of Capital

Nike has substantial operations in Japan, and it uses yen-denominated bonds to support these operations. It recently issued yen-denominated bonds that have a value equivalent to about $100 million. The use of yen-denominated bonds is desirable because the interest rate on yen-denominated debt instruments is very low. In addition, the yen-denominated bonds create an interest expense each year that can be offset by a portion of the revenue. This reduces the amount of yen that will ultimately have to be converted into dollars as funds are remitted to the parent, and therefore reduces Nike's exposure to exchange rate risk.

Discussion: If Nike decides to expand further in South America, why might its capital structure be affected? Why will its overall cost of capital be affected?

Combining the Costs of Debt and Equity

The costs of debt and equity can be combined to derive an overall cost of capital. The relative proportions of debt and equity used by firms in each country must be applied as weights to reasonably estimate this cost of capital. Given the differences in the costs of debt and equity across countries, it is understandable that the cost of capital may be lower for firms based in specific countries. Japan, for example, commonly has a relatively low cost of capital. It usually has a relatively low risk-free interest rate, which not only affects the cost of debt but also indirectly affects the cost of equity. In addition, the price-earnings multiples of Japanese firms are usually high, allowing these firms to obtain equity funding at a relatively low cost. MNCs can attempt to access capital from countries where capital costs are low, but when the capital is used to support operations in other countries, the MNCs are usually exposed to exchange rate risk. Thus, the cost of capital may ultimately turn out to be higher than expected.

USING THE COST OF CAPITAL FOR ASSESSING FOREIGN PROJECTS

When an MNC's parent proposes an investment in a foreign project that has the same risk as the MNC itself, it can use its weighted average cost of capital as the required rate of return for the project. However, many foreign projects exhibit different risk levels than the risk of the MNC. There are various ways for an MNC to account for the risk differential in its capital budgeting process.

Derive Net Present Values Based on the Weighted Average Cost of Capital

First, an MNC can account for the risk within its cash flow estimates. Many possible values for each input variable (such as demand, price, labor cost, etc.) can be incorporated to estimate net present values *NPVs* under alternative scenarios and then derive a probability distribution of the *NPVs*. When the weighted average cost of capital (WACC) is used as the required rate of return, the probability distribution of *NPVs* can be assessed to determine the probability that the foreign project will generate a return that is at least equal to the firm's weighted average cost of capital. If the project exhibits much risk, an area of the probability distribution will reflect negative *NPVs*, suggesting that the project could backfire.

This method is useful in accounting for risk because it explicitly incorporates the various possible scenarios in the *NPV* estimation and therefore can measure the probability that a project may backfire. Computer software programs that perform sensitivity analysis and simulation can be used to facilitate the process.

Adjust the Weighted Average Cost of Capital for the Risk Differential

An alternative method of accounting for a foreign project's risk is to adjust the firm's weighted average cost of capital for the risk differential. For example, if the foreign project is thought to exhibit more risk than the MNC exhibits, a premium can be added to the weighted average cost of capital to derive the required rate of return on the project. Then, the capital budgeting process will incorporate this required rate of return as the discount rate. If the foreign project exhibits lower risk, the MNC will use a required rate of return on the project that is less than its weighted average cost of capital.

This method is easy to use, but there is no perfect formula to adjust for the project's unique risk. The MNC's parent could estimate its cost of equity and the after-tax cost of debt on the funds to be obtained to finance the foreign project. The after-tax cost of debt can be estimated with reasonable accuracy using public information on the present costs of debt (bond yields) incurred by other firms whose risk level is similar to the foreign project. The cost of equity is an opportunity cost: what investors could earn on alternative equity investments with similar risk. The MNC could attempt to measure the expected return on a set of stocks that exhibit the same risk as its foreign project. This expected return could serve as the cost of equity. The required rate of return on the project would be the project's weighted cost of capital, based on the estimates explained here.

THE MNC'S CAPITAL STRUCTURE DECISION

An MNC's capital structure decision involves the choice of debt versus equity financing within all of its subsidiaries. Thus, its overall capital structure is essentially a combination of all of its subsidiaries' capital structures. MNCs recognize the tradeoff between using debt and using equity for financing their operations. The advantages of using debt as opposed to equity vary with corporate characteristics specific to each MNC and specific to the countries where the MNC has established subsidiaries. Some of the more relevant corporate characteristics specific to the MNC that can affect its capital structure are identified first, followed by country characteristics.

Influence of Corporate Characteristics

http://

Visit www.worldbank.org for country profiles, analyses, and sectoral surveys.

Characteristics unique to each MNC can influence its capital structure. Some of the more common firm-specific characteristics that affect the MNC's capital structure are identified here.

Stability of MNC's Cash Flows. MNCs with more stable cash flows can handle more debt because there is a constant stream of cash inflows to cover periodic interest payments. Conversely, MNCs with erratic cash flows may prefer less debt because they are not assured of generating enough cash in each period to make larger interest payments on debt. MNCs that are diversified across several countries may have more stable cash flows since the conditions in any single country should not have a major impact on their cash flows. Consequently, these MNCs may be able to handle a more debt-intensive capital structure.

MNC's Credit Risk. MNCs that have lower credit risk (risk of default on loans provided by creditors) have more access to credit. Any factors that influence credit risk can affect an MNC's choice of using debt versus equity. For example, if an MNC's management is thought to be strong and competent, the MNC's credit risk may be low, allowing for easier access to debt. MNCs with assets that serve as acceptable collateral (such as buildings, trucks, and adaptable machinery) are more able to obtain loans and may prefer to emphasize debt financing. Conversely, MNCs with assets that are not marketable have less acceptable collateral and may need to use a higher proportion of equity financing.

MNC's Access to Retained Earnings. Highly profitable MNCs may be able to finance most of their investment with retained earnings and therefore use an equity-intensive capital structure. Conversely, MNCs that have small levels of retained earnings may rely on debt financing. Growth-oriented MNCs are less able to finance their expansion with retained earnings and tend to rely on debt financing. MNCs with less growth need less new financing and may rely on retained earnings (equity) rather than debt.

MNC's Guarantees on Debt. If the parent backs the debt of its subsidiary, the subsidiary's borrowing capacity might be increased. Therefore, the subsidiary might need less equity financing. At the same time, however, the parent's borrowing capacity might be reduced, as creditors will be less willing to provide funds to the parent if those funds might be needed to rescue the subsidiary.

MNC's Agency Problems. If a subsidiary in a foreign country cannot easily be monitored by investors from the parent's country, agency costs are higher. To maximize the firm's stock price, the parent may induce the subsidiary to issue stock rather than debt in the local market so that its managers there will be monitored. In this case, the foreign subsidiary is referred to as "partially owned" rather than "wholly owned" by the MNC's parent. This strategy can affect the MNC's capital structure. It may be feasible when the MNC's parent can enhance the subsidiary's image and presence in the host country or can motivate the subsidiary's managers by allowing them partial ownership.

One concern about a partially owned foreign subsidiary is a potential conflict of interest, especially when its managers are minority shareholders. These managers may make decisions that can benefit the subsidiary at the expense of the MNC overall. For example, they may use funds for projects that are feasible from their perspective but not from the parent's perspective.

Influence of Country Characteristics

In addition to characteristics unique to each MNC, the characteristics unique to each host country can influence the MNC's choice of debt versus equity financing and therefore influence the MNC's capital structure. Specific country characteristics that can influence an MNC's choice of equity versus debt financing are described here.

Stock Restrictions in Host Countries. In some countries, governments allow investors to invest only in local stocks. Even when investors are allowed to invest in other countries, they may not have complete information about stocks of companies outside their home countries. This represents an implicit barrier to cross-border investing. Furthermore, potential adverse exchange rate effects and tax effects can discourage investors from investing outside their home countries. Such impediments to worldwide investing can cause some investors to have fewer stock investment opportunities than others. Consequently, an MNC operating in countries where investors have fewer investment opportunities may be able to raise equity in those countries at a relatively low cost. This could entice the MNC to use more equity by issuing stock in these countries to finance its operations.

HTTP:// USING THE WEB

Stock Market Conditions If an MNC's subsidiary is considering issuing its own stock to local investors as a means of obtaining equity, it should assess the general stock market conditions of the country. Information about stock market conditions for each country is provided at http://biz.yahoo.com/ifc/.

Click on any country listed. Then click on Equity Consensus.

Interest Rates in Host Countries. Because of government-imposed barriers on capital flows along with potential adverse exchange rate, tax, and country risk effects, loanable funds do not always flow to where they are needed most. Thus, the price of loanable funds (the interest rate) can vary across countries. MNCs may be able to obtain loanable funds (debt) at a relatively low cost in specific countries, while the cost of debt in other countries may be very high. Consequently, an MNC's preference for debt may depend on the costs of debt in the countries where it operates. If markets are somewhat segmented and the cost of funds in the subsidiary's country appears excessive, the parent may use its own equity to support projects implemented by the subsidiary.

Strength of Host Country Currencies. If an MNC is concerned about the potential weakness of the currencies in its subsidiaries' host countries, it may attempt to finance a large proportion of its foreign operations by borrowing those currencies instead of relying on parent funds. In this way, the subsidiaries will remit a smaller amount in earnings because they will be making interest payments on local debt. This strategy reduces the MNC's exposure to exchange rate risk.

If the parent believes that a subsidiary's local currency will appreciate against the parent's currency, it may have the subsidiary retain and reinvest more of its earnings. The parent may also provide an immediate cash infusion to finance growth in the subsidiary. As a result, there will be a transfer of internal funds from the parent to the subsidiary, possibly resulting in more external financing by the parent and less debt financing by the subsidiary.

Country Risk in Host Countries. A relatively mild form of country risk is the possibility that the host government will temporarily block funds to be remitted by the subsidiary to the parent. Subsidiaries that are prevented from remitting earnings over a period may prefer to use local debt financing. This strategy reduces the amount of funds that can be blocked because the subsidiary must pay interest on local debt.

If an MNC's subsidiary is exposed to risk that a host government might confiscate its assets, the subsidiary may use much debt financing in that host country. Then local creditors that have lent funds will have a genuine interest in ensuring that the subsidiary is treated fairly by the host government. In addition, if the MNC's operations in a foreign country are terminated by the host government, it will not lose as much if its operations are financed by local creditors. Under these circumstances, the local creditors will have to negotiate with the host government to obtain all or part of the funds they have lent after the host government liquidates the assets it confiscates from the MNC.

A less likely way to reduce exposure to a high degree of country risk is for the subsidiary to issue stock in the host country. Minority shareholders benefit directly from a profitable subsidiary. Therefore, they could pressure their government to refrain from imposing excessive taxes, environmental constraints, or any other provisions that would reduce the profits of the subsidiary. Having local investors own a minority interest in a subsidiary may also offer some protection against threats of adverse actions by the host government. Another advantage of a partially owned subsidiary is that it may open up additional opportunities in the host country. The subsidiary's name will become better known when its shares are acquired by minority shareholders in that country.

Tax Laws in Host Countries. Foreign subsidiaries of an MNC may be subject to a withholding tax when they remit earnings. By using local debt financing instead of relying on parent financing, they will have to make interest payments on the local debt and thus may be able to reduce the amount to be remitted periodically. Thus, they may reduce the withholding taxes by using more local debt financing. Foreign subsidiaries may also consider using local debt if the host governments impose high corporate tax rates on foreign earnings; in this way, the subsidiaries can benefit from the tax advantage of using debt where taxes are high (unless the higher taxes paid would be fully offset by tax credits received by the parent).

In recent years, MNCs have restructured their capital structures to reduce their withholding taxes on remitted earnings by subsidiaries.

Example

Clayton, Inc., is a U.S.-based MNC whose parent plans to raise $50 million of capital in the United States by issuing stock in the United States. The parent plans to convert the $50 million into 70 million Australian dollars (A$) and use the funds to build a subsidiary in Australia. Since the parent may need some return on this capital to pay its shareholders' dividends, it will require that its Australian subsidiary remit A$2 million per year. Assume that the Australian government will impose a withholding tax of 10 percent on the remitted earnings, which will amount to A$200,000 per year. Clayton, Inc., can revise its capital structure in several different ways to reduce or avoid this tax. Most solutions involve reducing the reliance of the subsidiary on the parent's capital.

First, Clayton's Australian subsidiary could borrow funds in Australia as its main source of capital instead of relying on the U.S. parent. Thus, it would use some of its earnings to pay its local creditors interest instead of remitting a large amount of earnings to the U.S parent. This financing strategy minimizes the amount of funds that would be remitted and can therefore minimize the withholding taxes that would be paid to the Australian government . In addition, the subsidiary would not need as much equity investment from the parent. One limitation of this strategy is that the subsidiary may increase its debt to an excessive level.

If Clayton prefers not to increase the subsidiary's debt, the subsidiary could raise funds by issuing stock in the host country. In this case, the subsidiary would use a portion of its funds to pay dividends to local shareholders rather than remit those funds to the parent. Once again, withholding taxes are minimized because the

Managing for Value: Capital Structure of European Subsidiaries

In 2000, Europe experienced some inflationary pressure as a result of high oil prices. The European Central Bank attempted to reduce the inflationary pressure by raising the euro's interest rate. Subsidiaries of U.S.-based MNCs that were located in euro-zone countries were directly affected by the increase in the interest rate because it raised their cost of local borrowing. Under these conditions, the subsidiaries faced a dilemma in managing their capital structures. If a subsidiary replaced local borrowing with the use of more retained earnings, it would remit less earnings to the parent. Whether the parent would approve of this strategy would depend, in part, on how much it needed the funds. The euro's exchange rate also played a role in this decision. The euro weakened throughout much of 2000, reaching its lowest level in that year. To the extent that the parent expected the euro to rebound in the future, it might prefer that the subsidiary defer its remittances anyway. In general, the parent and its subsidiaries can maximize the value of the MNC by pinpointing the capital structure that will achieve the lowest cost of capital to support a given set of projects. However, the optimal capital structure is a moving target that is affected by shifts in interest rates and exchange rates.

Exhibit 17.4

Adjusting the
Multinational Capital
Structure to Reduce
Withholding Taxes

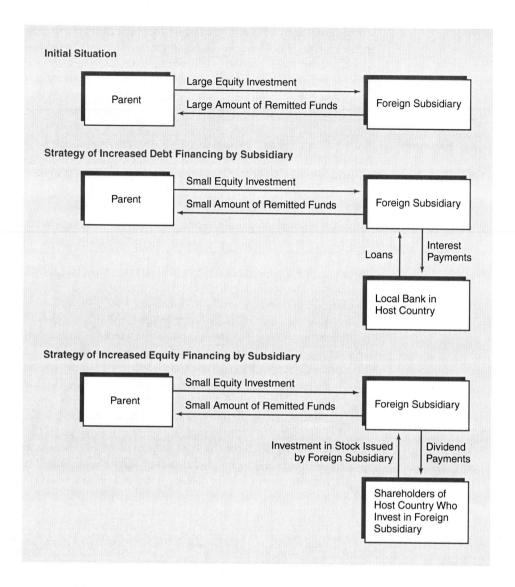

subsidiary would not remit much money to the parent. The issuance of stock would create a minority ownership in Australia, which reduces the parent's control over the subsidiary. The parent could retain control, however, by instructing the subsidiary to issue nonvoting stock.

Both strategies minimize Clayton's withholding tax, but the first strategy reflects a more debt-intensive capital structure while the second strategy reflects a more equity-intensive capital structure. The two strategies are illustrated in Exhibit 17.4. These strategies could also have been used to reduce Clayton's exposure to exchange rate risk because they minimize the amount of Australian dollars that will be converted into U.S. dollars.

INTERACTION BETWEEN SUBSIDIARY AND PARENT FINANCING DECISIONS

The decision by a subsidiary to use internal equity financing (retaining and reinvesting its earnings) or obtain debt financing can affect its degree of reliance on parent financing and the amount of funds that it can remit to the parent. Thus, its financing decisions should be made in consultation with the parent. The potential impact of two common subsidiary financing situations on the parent's capital structure are explained next.

HTTP:// **USING THE WEB**

Capital Structure Regulations When an MNC revises its capital structure by ordering a subsidiary to remit some of the capital back to the parent, it needs to review the country's regulations. The capital repatriation regulations imposed by each country are provided at http://biz.yahoo.com/ifc/.

Impact of Increased Debt Financing by the Subsidiary

When global conditions increase a subsidiary's debt financing, the amount of internal equity financing needed by the subsidiary is reduced. As these extra internal funds are remitted to the parent, the parent will have a larger amount of internal funds to use for financing before resorting to external financing. Assuming that the parent's operations absorb all internal funds and require some debt financing, there are offsetting effects on the capital structures of the subsidiary and the parent. The increased use of debt financing by the subsidiary is offset by the reduced debt financing of the parent. Nevertheless, the cost of capital for the MNC overall could have changed for two reasons. First, the revised composition of debt financing (more by the subsidiary, less by the parent) could affect the interest charged on the debt. Second, it could affect the MNC's overall exposure to exchange rate risk and therefore influence the risk premium on capital.

In some situations, the subsidiary's increased use of debt financing will not be offset by the parent's reduced debt financing. For example, if there are any restrictions or excessive taxes on remitted funds, the parent may not be able to rely on the subsidiary and may need some debt financing as well. In this case, international conditions that encourage increased use of debt financing by the subsidiary will result in a more debt-intensive capital structure for the MNC. Again, for reasons already mentioned, the cost of capital to the MNC could be affected by the subsidiary's increased debt financing. In addition, the use of a higher proportion of debt financing for the MNC overall would also affect the cost of capital.

Impact of Reduced Debt Financing by the Subsidiary

When global conditions encourage the subsidiary to use less debt financing, the subsidiary will need to use more internal financing. Consequently, it will remit fewer funds to the parent, reducing the amount of internal funds available to the parent. If the parent's operations absorb all internal funds and require some debt financing, there are offsetting effects on the capital structures of the subsidiary and parent. The subsidiary's reduced use of debt financing is offset by the parent's increased use. For reasons expressed earlier, the cost of capital may change even if the MNC's overall capital structure does not.

If the parent's operations can be fully financed with internal funds, the parent will not use debt financing. Thus, the subsidiary's reduced debt financing is not offset by the parent's increased debt financing, and the MNC's overall capital structure becomes more equity-intensive.

Summary of Interaction between Subsidiary and Parent Financing Decisions

Exhibit 17.5 provides a summary of some of the more relevant characteristics of the host country that can affect a subsidiary's preference for debt or equity financing. The decision by a subsidiary to finance with local debt affects the amount of funds remitted to the parent and therefore affects the amount of internal financing available to the parent. Since the subsidiary's local debt financing decisions are influenced by country-specific characteristics like those shown in Exhibit 17.5, the MNC's overall capital structure is partially influenced by the locations of the foreign subsidiaries.

LOCAL VERSUS GLOBAL TARGET CAPITAL STRUCTURE

An MNC may deviate from its "local" target capital structure in each country where financing is obtained, yet still achieve its "global" target capital structure (based on consolidating the capital structures of all its subsidiaries). The following examples of particular foreign country conditions illustrate the motive behind deviating from a local target capital structure while still satisfying a global target capital structure.

Exhibit 17.5

Effect of Global Conditions on Financing

Host Country Conditions	Amount of Local Debt Financing by Subsidiary	Amount of Internal Funds Available to Parent	Amount of Debt Financing Provided by Parent
Higher country risk	Higher	Higher	Lower
Higher interest rates	Lower	Lower	Higher
Lower interest rates	Higher	Higher	Lower
Expected weakness of local currency	Higher	Higher	Lower
Expected strength of local currency	Lower	Lower	Higher
Blocked funds	Higher	Higher	Lower
High withholding taxes	Higher	Higher	Lower
Higher corporate taxes	Higher	Higher	Lower

Offsetting a Subsidiary's High Degree of Financial Leverage

First, consider that Country A does not allow MNCs with headquarters elsewhere to list their stocks on its local stock exchange. Under these conditions, an MNC's subsidiary that desires to expand its operations will likely decide to borrow funds by issuing bonds or obtaining bank loans rather than by issuing stock in this country. By being forced to use debt financing here, the MNC may deviate from its target capital structure, which could raise its overall cost of capital. The parent might offset this concentration in debt by using more equity financing for its own operations.

Alternatively, consider an MNC that desires financing in Country B, which is experiencing political turmoil. The use of local bank loans would be most appropriate since local banks may be able to prevent the subsidiary's operations from being affected by political conditions in that country. If the local banks serve as creditors to the MNC's subsidiary, it is in their interest to ensure that the subsidiary's operations are sufficiently profitable to repay its loans. Since the subsidiary may have more financial leverage than is desired for the MNC overall, the parent may use less financial leverage to finance its own operations in order to achieve its overall ("global") target capital structure.

Offsetting a Subsidiary's Low Degree of Financial Leverage

Suppose that Country C allows the MNC's subsidiary to issue stock there and list its stock on its local exchange. Also assume that the project to be implemented in that country will not generate net cash flows for five years, thereby limiting the subsidiary's ability to generate internal financing. In this case, equity financing by the subsidiary may be more appropriate. The subsidiary could issue stock, and, by paying low or zero dividends, it could avoid any major cash outflows for the next five years. The parent might offset the subsidiary's concentration in equity by instructing one of its other foreign subsidiaries in some other host country to use mostly debt financing. Alternatively, the parent could use more debt financing to support its own operations.

Limitations in Offsetting a Subsidiary's Abnormal Degree of Financial Leverage

The examples provided up to this point suggest that the parent can offset the imbalance created by a foreign subsidiary by adjusting the way it finances its own operations. However, the revision of the parent's capital structure may result in a higher cost of capital for the parent. Given that the subsidiary's financing decision could affect the parent's capital structure and therefore affect the parent's cost of capital, the subsidiary must consider the impact of its decision on the parent. The subsidiary's decision to use an unusually high or low degree of financial leverage should be made only if the benefits outweigh any costs for the MNC overall.

The strategy of ignoring a "local" target capital structure in favor of a "global" target capital structure is rational as long as it is acceptable to foreign creditors and investors. However, if foreign creditors and investors monitor each subsidiary's local capital structure, they may require a higher rate of return on funds provided to the

Financial Markets Perspective

Differences in Financing Tendencies among Countries

The volume of debt and equity issued in financial markets varies among countries, which can affect the degree of financial leverage used by a subsidiary in a particular country. Firms in Japan and Germany have traditionally used a much higher degree of financial leverage (on average) than firms in the United States or the United Kingdom. Nevertheless, the probability of bankruptcy may generally be lower for Japanese and German firms because their respective governments may rescue them. Furthermore, banks in Japan and Germany commonly serve as creditors and large shareholders of firms and have a vested interest in rescuing these firms.

The use of equity is changing in Germany, however, as a result of a greater emphasis by financial managers on maximizing shareholder wealth. With the shift in managerial focus, German investors are more willing to purchase stock, so the German market now has more potential to absorb stock offerings by firms. Other countries in Europe are also shifting toward more equity investments for the same reason. Firms still use some debt, but have shifted toward the use of debt security markets, while reducing their reliance on local bank loans. In many cases, they are able to secure lower financing costs with a debt offering than by obtaining bank loans.

MNC. For example, the "local" target capital structures for the subsidiaries based in Country A (from the earlier example) and in Country B are debt-intensive. Creditors in these two countries may penalize the subsidiary for its highly leveraged local capital structure, even though the MNC's global capital structure is more balanced, because they believe that the subsidiary may be unable to meet its high debt repayments. If the parent plans to back the subsidiaries, however, it could guarantee debt repayment to the creditors in the foreign countries, which might reduce their risk perception and lower the cost of the debt. Many MNC parents stand ready to financially back their subsidiaries because, if they did not, their subsidiaries would be unable to obtain adequate financing.

IMPACT OF AN MNC'S CAPITAL STRUCTURE DECISIONS ON ITS VALUE

An MNC's capital structure decisions affect its value, as shown in Exhibit 17.6. In general, the capital structure decisions of an MNC involve the mix of debt and equity to use for financing its businesses. Its choice of equity instead of debt reduces the perceived risk of the MNC, but also dilutes the ownership of the MNC.

When an MNC's parent uses equity to provide most of the financing for foreign subsidiaries, this financing is initiated with a large cash outflow from the parent to the foreign subsidiaries. Equity financing by the parent typically increases the expected amount of foreign currency cash flows that can be remitted by foreign subsidiaries to the parent because it reduces the need for the foreign subsidiaries to borrow funds.

Alternatively, when a foreign subsidiary uses local debt to finance most of its operations, the cash flows remitted on a periodic basis to the parent will be smaller because the subsidiary makes interest payments on the debt before remitting

Exhibit 17.6
Impact of Multinational Capital Structure Decisions on an MNC's Value

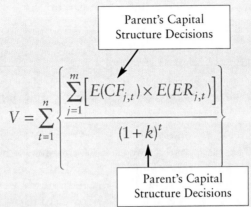

V = value of the U.S.-based MNC

$E(CF_{j,t})$ = expected cash flows denominated in currency j to be received by the U.S. parent in period t

$E(ER_{j,t})$ = expected exchange rate at which currency j can be converted to dollars at the end of period t

k = weighted average cost of capital of the U.S. parent company

m = number of currencies

n = number of periods

cash flows to the parent. Although this reduces the amount of foreign cash flows received by the parent, it also reduces the amount of foreign cash flows that have to be converted to dollars and therefore reduces the exposure to exchange rate risk. In addition, the local financing means that the subsidiaries require less financial support from the parent. The parent must consider the tradeoff described here when determining whether its provision of equity financing for its foreign subsidiaries will enhance the MNC's overall value.

SUMMARY

- The cost of capital may be lower for an MNC than for a domestic firm because of characteristics peculiar to the MNC, including its size, its access to international capital markets, and its degree of international diversification. Yet, some characteristics peculiar to an MNC can increase the MNC's cost of capital, such as exposure to exchange rate risk and to country risk.

- Costs of capital vary across countries because of country differences in the components that comprise the cost of capital. Specifically, there are differences in the risk-free rate, the risk pre-

mium on debt, and the cost of equity among countries. Countries with a higher risk-free rate tend to exhibit a higher cost of capital.

- An MNC's capital structure decision is influenced by corporate characteristics such as the stability of the MNC's cash flows, its credit risk, and its access to earnings. The capital structure is also influenced by characteristics of the countries where the MNC conducts business, such as stock restrictions, interest rates, strength of local currencies, country risk, and tax laws. Some characteristics favor an equity-intensive capital structure because they discourage the use of debt. Other characteristics favor a debt-intensive structure because of the desire to protect against risks by creating foreign debt. Given that the relative costs of capital components vary among countries, the MNC's capital structure may be dependent on the specific mix of countries in which it conducts operations.

SELF TEST

Answers are provided in Appendix A at the back of the text.

1. When Goshen, Inc., focused only on domestic business in the United States, it had a low debt level. As it expanded into other countries, it increased its degree of financial leverage (on a consolidated basis). What factors would have caused Goshen to increase its financial leverage (assuming that country risk was not a concern)?

2. Lynde Co. is a U.S.-based MNC with a large subsidiary in the Philippines financed with equity from the parent. In response to news about a possible change in the Philippine government, the subsidiary revised its capital structure by borrowing from local banks and transferring the equity investment back to the U.S. parent. Explain the likely motive behind these actions.

3. Duever Co. (a U.S. firm) noticed that its financial leverage was substantially lower than that of most successful firms in Germany and Japan in the same industry. Is Duever's capital structure less than optimal?

4. Atlanta, Inc., has a large subsidiary in Venezuela, where interest rates are very high and the currency is expected to weaken. Assume that Atlanta perceives the country risk to be high. Explain the tradeoff involved in financing the subsidiary with local debt versus an equity investment from the parent.

5. Reno, Inc., is considering a project to establish a plant for producing and selling consumer goods in an undeveloped country. Assume that the host country's economy is very dependent on oil prices, the local currency of the country is very volatile, and the country risk is very high. Also assume that the country's economic conditions are unrelated to U.S. conditions. Should the required rate of return (and therefore the risk premium) on the project be higher or lower than that of other alternative projects in the United States?

QUESTIONS AND APPLICATIONS

1. Present an argument in support of an MNC's favoring a debt-intensive capital structure.

2. Present an argument in support of an MNC's favoring an equity-intensive capital structure.

3. Wizard, Inc., has substantial operations in a country where the government allows only a small amount of earnings to be remitted to the United States each year. Should Wizard use debt financing by the parent, equity financing by the parent, or financing by local banks in the foreign country?

4. Describe general differences between the capital structures of firms based in the United States and those of firms based in Japan. Offer an explanation for these differences.

5. Why might a firm use a "local" capital structure at a particular subsidiary that differs substantially from its "global" capital structure?

6. Explain how characteristics of MNCs can affect the cost of capital.

7. Explain why managers of a wholly owned subsidiary may be more likely to satisfy the shareholders of the MNC.

8. LaSalle Corp. is a U.S.-based MNC with subsidiaries in various less developed countries where stock markets are not well established. How can LaSalle still achieve its "global" target capital structure of 50 percent debt and 50 percent equity, if it plans to use only debt financing for the subsidiaries in these countries?

9. Drexel Co. is a U.S.-based company that is establishing a project in a politically unstable country. It is considering two possible sources of financing. Either the parent could provide most of the financing, or the subsidiary could be supported by local loans from banks in that country. Which financing alternative is more appropriate to protect the subsidiary?

10. Charleston Corp. is considering establishing a subsidiary in either Germany or the United Kingdom. The subsidiary will be mostly financed with loans from the local banks in the host country chosen. Charleston has determined that the revenue generated from the British subsidiary will be slightly more favorable than the revenue generated by the German subsidiary, even after considering tax and exchange rate effects. The initial outlay will be the same, and both countries appear to be politically stable. Charleston decides to establish the subsidiary in the United Kingdom because of the revenue advantage. Do you agree with its decision? Explain.

11. Fairfield Corp., a U.S. firm, recently established a subsidiary in a less developed country that consistently experiences an annual inflation rate of 80 percent or more. The country does not have an established stock market, but loans by local banks are available with a 90 percent interest rate. Fairfield has decided to use a strategy in which the subsidiary is financed entirely with funds from the parent. It believes that in this way it can avoid the excessive interest rate in the host country. What is a key disadvantage of using this strategy that may cause Fairfield to be no better off than if it paid the 90 percent interest rate?

12. Veer Co. is a U.S.-based MNC that has most of its operations in Japan. Noticing that the Japanese companies with which it competes use more financial leverage, it has decided to adjust its financial leverage to be in line with theirs. With this heavy emphasis on debt, Veer should reap more tax advantages. It believes that the market's perception of its risk will remain unchanged since its financial leverage will still be no higher than that of its Japanese competitors. Comment on this strategy.

13. Pullman, Inc., a U.S. firm, has been highly profitable but prefers not to pay out higher dividends because its shareholders want the funds to be reinvested. It plans for large growth in several less developed countries. Pullman would like to finance the growth with local debt in the host countries of concern to reduce its exposure to country risk. Explain the dilemma faced by Pullman and offer possible solutions.

14. Forest Co. produces goods in the United States, Germany, and Australia and sells the goods in the areas where they are produced. Foreign earnings are periodically remitted to the U.S. parent. As the euro's interest rates have declined to a very low level, Forest Co. has decided to finance its German operations with borrowed funds in place of the parent's equity investment. Forest will transfer the U.S. parent's equity investment in the German subsidiary over to its Australian subsidiary. These funds will be used to pay off a floating rate loan, as Australian interest rates have been high and are rising. Explain the expected effects of these actions on the consolidated capital structure and cost of capital of Forest Co.

15. Using the information in question 14, explain how the exposure of Forest Co. to exchange rate risk may have changed.

16. Explain why the cost of capital for a U.S.-

based MNC with a large subsidiary in Brazil is higher than for a U.S.-based MNC in the same industry with a large subsidiary in Japan. Assume that the subsidiary operations for each MNC are financed with local debt in the host country.

17. In recent years, several U.S. firms have penetrated Mexico's market. One of the biggest challenges is the cost of capital to finance businesses in Mexico. Mexican interest rates tend to be much higher than U.S. interest rates. In some periods, the Mexican government does not attempt to lower the interest rates because higher rates may attract foreign investment in Mexican securities.

     a. How might U.S.-based MNCs expand in Mexico without incurring the high Mexican interest expenses when financing the expansion? Are any disadvantages associated with this strategy?

     b. Are there any additional alternatives for a Mexican subsidiary to finance its business itself after it has been well established? How might this strategy affect the subsidiary's capital structure?

Impact of 9/11/01

18. Rose, Inc., of Dallas, Texas, needed to infuse capital into its foreign subsidiaries to support their expansion. As of August 2001, it planned to issue stock in the United States. However, after the September 11, 2001, terrorist attack on the United States, it decided that long-term debt was a cheaper source of capital. Explain how the terrorist attack could have altered the two forms of capital.

Internet Application

19. The Bloomberg website provides interest rate data for many countries and various maturities. Its address is **www.bloomberg.com**

     Go to the "Markets" section and then to "International Yield Curves." Assume that an MNC would pay 1 percent more on borrowed funds than the risk-free (government) rates shown at the Bloomberg website. Determine the cost of debt (use a 10-year maturity) for the U.S. parent that borrows dollars. Then determine the cost of funds for a foreign subsidiary in Japan that borrows funds locally. Then determine the cost of debt for a subsidiary in Thailand that borrows funds locally. Offer some explanations as to why the cost of debt may vary among the three countries.

Running Your Own MNC

 This exercise can be found on the Student CD-ROM.

Blades, Inc. Case

Assessment of Cost of Capital

Recall that Blades has tentatively decided to establish a subsidiary in Thailand to manufacture roller blades. The new plant will be utilized to produce "Speedos," Blades' primary product. Once the subsidiary has been established in Thailand, it will be operated for 10 years, at which time it is expected to be sold. Ben Holt, Blades' chief financial officer (CFO), believes the growth potential in Thailand will be extremely high over the next few years. However, his optimism is not shared by most economic fore-

casters, who predict a slow recovery of the Thai economy, which has been very negatively affected by recent events in that country. Furthermore, forecasts for the future value of the baht indicate that the currency may continue to depreciate over the next few years.

Despite the pessimistic forecasts, Ben Holt believes Thailand is a good international target for Blades' products because of the high growth potential and lack of competitors in Thailand. At a recent meeting of the board of directors,

Holt presented his capital budgeting analysis and pointed out that the establishment of a subsidiary in Thailand had a net present value (*NPV*) of over $8 million even when a 25 percent required rate of return is used to discount the cash flows resulting from the project. Blades' board of directors, while favorable to the idea of international expansion, remained skeptical. Specifically, the directors wondered where Holt obtained the 25 percent discount rate to conduct his capital budgeting analysis and whether this discount rate was high enough. Consequently, the decision to establish a subsidiary in Thailand has been delayed until the directors' meeting next month.

The directors also asked Holt to determine how operating a subsidiary in Thailand would affect Blades' required rate of return and its cost of capital. The directors would like to know how Blades' characteristics would affect its cost of capital relative to roller blade manufacturers operating solely in the United States. Furthermore, the capital asset pricing model (CAPM) was mentioned by two directors, who would like to know how Blades' systematic risk would be affected by expanding into Thailand. Another issue that was raised is how the cost of debt and equity in Thailand differ from the corresponding costs in the United States, and whether these differences would affect Blades' cost of capital. The last issue that was raised during the meeting was whether Blades' capital structure would be affected by expanding into Thailand. The directors have asked Holt to conduct a thorough analysis of these issues and report back to them at their next meeting.

Ben Holt's knowledge of cost of capital and capital structure decisions is somewhat limited, and he requires your help. You are a financial analyst for Blades, Inc. Holt has gathered some information regarding Blades' characteristics that distinguish it from roller blade manufacturers operating solely in the United States, its systematic risk, and the costs of debt and equity in Thailand, and he wants to know whether and how this information will affect Blades' cost of capital and its capital structure decision.

Regarding Blades' characteristics, Holt has gathered information regarding Blades' size, its access to the Thai capital markets, its diversification benefits from a Thai expansion, its exposure to exchange rate risk, and its exposure to country risk. Although Blades' expansion into Thailand classifies the company as an MNC, Blades is still relatively small compared to U.S. roller blade manufacturers. Also, Blades' expansion into Thailand will give it access to the capital and money markets there. However, negotiations with various commercial banks in Thailand indicate that Blades will be able to borrow at interest rates of approximately 15 percent, versus 8 percent in the United States.

Expanding into Thailand will diversify Blades' operations. As a result of this expansion, Blades would be subject to economic conditions in Thailand as well as the United States. Ben Holt sees this as a major advantage since Blades' cash flows would no longer be solely dependent on the U.S. economy. Consequently, he believes that Blades' probability of bankruptcy would be reduced. Nevertheless, if Blades establishes a subsidiary in Thailand, all of the subsidiary's earnings will be remitted back to the U.S. parent, which would create a high level of exchange rate risk. This is of particular concern because current economic forecasts for Thailand indicate that the baht will depreciate further over the next few years. Furthermore, Holt has already conducted a country risk analysis for Thailand, which resulted in an unfavorable country risk rating.

Regarding Blades' level of systematic risk, Holt has determined how Blades' beta, which measures systematic risk, would be affected by the establishment of a subsidiary in Thailand. Holt believes that Blades' beta would drop from its current level of 2.0 to 1.8 because the firm's exposure to U.S. market conditions would be reduced by the expansion into Thailand. Moreover, Holt estimates that the risk-free interest rate is 5 percent and the required return on the market is 12 percent.

Holt has also determined that the costs of both debt and equity are higher in Thailand than in the United States. Lenders such as commercial banks in Thailand require interest rates higher than U.S. rates. This is partially attributed to a higher risk premium, which reflects the larger degree of economic uncertainty in Thailand. The cost of equity is also higher in Thailand than in the United States. Thailand is not as developed as the United States in many ways, and various investment opportunities are available to Thai investors, which increases their opportunity cost. However, Holt is not sure that this higher cost of equity in Thailand would affect Blades, as all of Blades' shareholders are located in the United States.

Ben Holt has asked you to analyze this information and to determine how it may affect Blades' cost of capital and its capital structure. To help you in your analysis, Holt would like you to provide answers to the following questions:

1. If Blades expands into Thailand, do you think its cost of capital will be higher or lower than the cost of capital of roller blade manufacturers operating solely in the United States? Substantiate your answer by outlining how Blades' characteristics distinguish it

from domestic roller blade manufacturers.

2. According to the CAPM, how would Blades' required rate of return be affected by an expansion into Thailand? How do you reconcile this result with your answer to question 1? Do you think Blades should use the required rate of return resulting from the CAPM to discount the cash flows of the Thai subsidiary to determine its *NPV*?

3. If Blades borrows funds in Thailand to support its Thai subsidiary, how would this affect its cost of capital? Why?

4. Given the high level of interest rates in Thailand, the high level of exchange rate risk, and the high (perceived) level of country risk, do you think Blades will be more or less likely to use debt in its capital structure as a result of its expansion into Thailand? Why?

Small Business Dilemma

Multinational Capital Structure Decision at the Sports Exports Company

The Sports Exports Company has considered a variety of projects, but all of its business is still in the United Kingdom. Since most of its business comes from exporting of footballs (denominated in pounds), it remains exposed to exchange rate risk. On the favorable side, the British demand for its footballs has risen consistently every month. Jim Logan, the owner of the Sports Exports Company, has retained more than $100,000 (after the pounds were converted into dollars) in earnings since he began his business. At this point in time, his capital structure is mostly his own equity, with very little debt. Jim has periodically considered establishing a very small subsidiary in the United Kingdom to produce the footballs there (so that he would not have to export them from the United States). If he does establish this subsidiary, he has several

options for the capital structure that would be used to support it: (1) use all of his equity to invest in the firm, (2) use pound-denominated long-term debt, or (3) use dollar-denominated long-term debt. The interest rate on British long-term debt is slightly higher than the interest rate on U.S. long-term debt.

1. What is an advantage of using equity to support the subsidiary? What is a disadvantage?

2. If Jim decides to use long-term debt as the primary form of capital to support this subsidiary, should he use dollar-denominated debt or pound-denominated debt?

3. How can the equity proportion of this firm's capital structure increase over time after it is established?

ANSWERS TO SELF-TEST QUESTIONS

ANSWERS TO SELF-TEST QUESTIONS FOR CHAPTER 1

1. MNCs can capitalize on comparative advantages (such as a technology or cost of labor) that they have relative to firms in other countries, which allows them to penetrate those other countries' markets. Given a world of imperfect markets, comparative advantages across countries are not freely transferable. Therefore, MNCs may be able to capitalize on comparative advantages. Many MNCs initially penetrate markets by exporting but ultimately establish a subsidiary in foreign markets and attempt to differentiate their products as other firms enter those markets (product cycle theory).

2. In the late 1980s and early 1990s, West European countries removed many barriers, which allowed more potential for efficient expansion throughout Europe. Consequently, U.S. firms may be able to expand across European countries at a lower cost than before.

   During the same period, Eastern European countries opened their markets to foreign firms and privatized many of the state-owned firms. This allowed U.S. firms to penetrate these countries to offer products that previously had been unavailable.

3. First, there is the risk of poor economic conditions in the foreign country. Second, there is country risk, which reflects the risk of changing government or public attitudes toward the MNC. Third, there is exchange rate risk, which can affect the performance of the MNC in the foreign country.

ANSWERS TO SELF-TEST QUESTIONS FOR CHAPTER 2

1. Each of the economic factors is described, holding other factors constant.

   a. *Inflation.* A relatively high U.S. inflation rate relative to other countries can make U.S. goods less attractive to U.S. and non-U.S. consumers, which results in fewer U.S. exports, more U.S. imports, and a lower (or more negative) current account balance. A relatively low U.S. inflation rate would have the opposite effect.

   b. *National Income.* A relatively high increase in the U.S. national income (compared to other countries) tends to cause a large increase in demand for imports and can cause a lower (or more negative) current account balance. A relatively low increase in the U.S. national income would have the opposite effect.

   c. *Exchange Rates.* A weaker dollar tends to make U.S. products cheaper to non-U.S. firms and makes non-U.S. products expensive to U.S. firms. Thus, U.S. exports are expected to increase, while U.S. imports are expected to decrease. However, some conditions can prevent these effects from occurring, as explained in the chapter. Normally, a stronger dollar causes U.S. exports to decrease and U.S. imports to increase because it makes U.S. goods more expensive to non-U.S. firms and makes non-U.S. goods less expensive to U.S. firms.

d. *Government Restrictions.* When the U.S. government imposes new barriers on imports, the U.S. imports decline, causing the U.S. balance of trade to increase (or be less negative). When non-U.S. governments impose new barriers on imports from the United States, the U.S. balance of trade may decrease (or be more negative). When governments remove trade barriers, the opposite effects are expected.

2. When the U.S. imposes tariffs on imported goods, foreign countries may retaliate by imposing tariffs on goods exported by the United States. Thus, there is a decline in U.S. exports that may offset any decline in U.S. imports.

3. The Asian crisis caused a decline in Asian income levels and therefore resulted in a reduced demand for U.S. exports. In addition, Asian exporters experienced problems, and some U.S. importers discontinued their relationships with the Asian exporters.

ANSWERS TO SELF-TEST QUESTIONS FOR CHAPTER 3

1. Bid/ask spread = (Ask rate − Bid rate)/Ask rate
    = ($.80 − $.784)/$.80
    = .02, or 2%

2. The bid-ask percentage spread of the Peruvian sol is 1.05 percent based on the quotations provided.

3. MNCs use the spot foreign exchange market to exchange currencies for immediate delivery. They use the forward foreign exchange market and the currency futures market to lock in the exchange rate at which currencies will be exchanged at a future point in time. They use the currency options market when they wish to lock in the maximum (minimum) amount to be paid (received) in a future currency transaction but maintain flexibility in the event of favorable exchange rate movements.

    MNCs use the Eurocurrency market to engage in short-term investing or financing or the Eurocredit market to engage in medium-term financing. They can obtain long-term financing by issuing bonds in the Eurobond market or by issuing stock in the international markets.

ANSWERS TO SELF-TEST QUESTIONS FOR CHAPTER 4

1. Economic factors affect the yen's value as follows:

    a. If U.S. inflation is higher than Japanese inflation, the U.S. demand for Japanese goods may increase (to avoid the higher U.S. prices), and the Japanese demand for U.S. goods may decrease (to avoid the higher U.S. prices). Consequently, there is upward pressure on the value of the yen.

    b. If U.S. interest rates increase and exceed Japanese interest rates, the U.S. demand for Japanese interest-bearing securities may decline (since U.S. interest-bearing securities are more attractive), while the Japanese demand for U.S. interest-bearing securities may rise. Both forces place downward pressure on the yen's value.

 c. If U.S. national income increases more than Japanese national income, the U.S. demand for Japanese goods may increase more than the Japanese demand for U.S. goods. Assuming that the change in national income levels does not affect exchange rates indirectly through effects on relative interest rates, the forces should place upward pressure on the yen's value.

 d. If government controls reduce the U.S. demand for Japanese goods, they place downward pressure on the yen's value. If the controls reduce the Japanese demand for U.S. goods, they place upward pressure on the yen's value.

The opposite scenarios of those described here would cause the expected pressure to be in the opposite direction.

2.   U.S. capital flows with Country A may be larger than U.S. capital flows with Country B. Therefore, the change in the interest rate differential has a larger effect on the capital flows with Country A, causing the exchange rate to change. If the capital flows with Country B are nonexistent, interest rate changes do not change the capital flows and therefore do not change the demand and supply conditions in the foreign exchange market.

3.   Smart Banking Corp. should not pursue the strategy because a loss would result, as shown here.

 a. Borrow $5 million.

 b. Convert $5 million to C$5,263,158 (based on the spot exchange rate of $.95 per C$).

 c. Invest the C$ at 9% annualized, which represents a return of .15% over six days, so the C$ received after six days = C$5,271,053 (computed as C$5,263,158 × [1+.0015]).

 d. Convert the C$ received back to U.S. dollars after six days: C$5,271,053 = $4,954,789 (based on anticipated exchange rate of $.94 per C$ after six days).

 e. The interest rate owed on the U.S.-dollar loan is .10% over the six-day period. Thus, the amount owed as a result of the loan is $5,005,000 (computed as $5,000,000 × [1+.001]).

 f. The strategy is expected to cause a gain of ($4,954,789 − $5,005,000) = −$50,211.

ANSWERS TO SELF-TEST QUESTIONS FOR CHAPTER 5

1.   The net profit to the speculator is −$.01 per unit.
 The net profit to the speculator for one contract is −$500 (computed as −$.01 × 50,000 units).
 The spot rate would need to be $.66 for the speculator to break even.
 The net profit to the seller of the call option is $.01 per unit.

2.   The speculator should exercise the option.
 The net profit to the speculator is $.03 per unit.
 The net profit to the seller of the put option is −$.03 per unit.

3.   The premium paid is higher for options with longer expiration dates (other things being equal). Firms may prefer not to pay such high premiums.

Answers to Self-Test Questions for Chapter 6

1. Market forces cause the demand and supply of yen in the foreign exchange market to change, which causes a change in the equilibrium exchange rate. The central banks could intervene to affect the demand or supply conditions in the foreign exchange market, but they would not always be able to offset the changing market forces. For example, if there were a large increase in the U.S. demand for yen and no increase in the supply of yen for sale, the central banks would have to increase the supply of yen in the foreign exchange market to offset the increased demand.

2. The Fed could use direct intervention by selling some of its dollar reserves in exchange for pesos in the foreign exchange market. It could also use indirect intervention by attempting to reduce U.S. interest rates through monetary policy. Specifically, it could increase the U.S. money supply, which places downward pressure on U.S. interest rates (assuming that inflationary expectations do not change). The lower U.S. interest rates should discourage foreign investment in the U.S. and encourage increased investment by U.S. investors in foreign securities. Both forces tend to weaken the dollar's value.

3. A weaker dollar tends to increase the demand for U.S. goods because the price paid for a specified amount in dollars by non-U.S. firms is reduced. In addition, the U.S. demand for foreign goods is reduced because it takes more dollars to obtain a specified amount in foreign currency once the dollar weakens. Both forces tend to stimulate the U.S. economy and therefore improve productivity and reduce unemployment in the United States.

Answers to Self-Test Questions for Chapter 7

1. No. The cross exchange rate between the pound and the C$ is appropriate, based on the other exchange rates. There is no discrepancy to capitalize on.

2. No. Covered interest arbitrage involves the exchange of dollars for pounds. Assuming that the investors begin with $1 million (the starting amount will not affect the final conclusion), the dollars would be converted to pounds as shown here:

$$\text{\$1 million/\$1.60 per £} = £625,000$$

The British investment would accumulate interest over the 180-day period, resulting in

$$£625,000 \times 1.04 = £650,000$$

After 180 days, the pounds would be converted to dollars:

$$£650,000 \times \text{\$1.56 per pound} = \$1,014,000$$

This amount reflects a return of 1.4 percent above the amount U.S. investors initially started with. The investors could simply invest the funds in the United States at 3 percent. Thus, U.S. investors would earn less using the covered interest arbitrage strategy than investing in the United States.

3. No. The forward rate discount on the pound does not perfectly offset the interest rate differential. In fact, the discount is 2.5 percent, which is larger than the interest rate differential. U.S. investors do worse when attempting covered interest arbitrage than when investing their funds in the United States because the interest rate advantage on the British investment is more than offset by the forward discount.

   Further clarification may be helpful here. While the U.S. investors could not benefit from covered interest arbitrage, British investors could capitalize on covered interest arbitrage. While British investors would earn 1-percent interest less on the U.S. investment, they would be purchasing pounds forward at a discount of 2.5 percent at the end of the investment period. When interest rate parity does not exist, investors from only one of the two countries of concern could benefit from using covered interest arbitrage.

4. If there is a discrepancy in the pricing of a currency, one may capitalize on it by using the various forms of arbitrage described in the chapter. As arbitrage occurs, the exchange rates will be pushed toward their appropriate levels because arbitrageurs will buy an underpriced currency in the foreign exchange market (increase in demand for currency places upward pressure on its value) and will sell an overpriced currency in the foreign exchange market (increase in the supply of currency for sale places downward pressure on its value).

5. The one-year forward discount on pounds would become more pronounced (by about one percentage point more than before) because the spread between the British interest rates and U.S. interest rates would increase.

ANSWERS TO SELF-TEST QUESTIONS FOR CHAPTER 8

1. If the Japanese prices rise because of Japanese inflation, the value of the yen should decline. Thus, even though the importer might need to pay more yen, it would benefit from a weaker yen value (it would pay fewer dollars for a given amount in yen). Thus, there could be an offsetting effect if PPP holds.

2. Purchasing power parity does not necessarily hold. In our example, Japanese inflation could rise (causing the importer to pay more yen), and yet the Japanese yen would not necessarily depreciate by an offsetting amount, or at all. Therefore, the dollar amount to be paid for Japanese supplies could increase over time.

3. High inflation will cause a balance of trade adjustment, whereby the United States will reduce its purchases of goods in these countries, while the demand for U.S. goods by these countries should increase (according to PPP). Consequently, there will be downward pressure on the values of these currencies.

4. $$e_f = I_h - I_f$$
   $$= 3\% - 4\%$$
   $$= -.01 \text{ or } -1\%$$
   $$S_{t+1} = S(1 + e_f)$$
   $$= \$.85[1 + (-.01)]$$
   $$= \$.8415$$

5.

$$e_f = \frac{(1+i_b)}{(1+i_f)} - 1$$

$$= \frac{(1+.06)}{(1+.11)} - 1$$

$$\cong -.045, \text{ or } -4.5\%$$

$$S_{t+1} = S(1+e_f)$$

$$= \$.90[1+(-.045)]$$

$$= \$.8595$$

6. According to the IFE, the increase in interest rates by 5 percentage points reflects an increase in expected inflation by 5 percentage points.

   If the inflation adjustment occurs, the balance of trade should be affected, as Australian demand for U.S. goods rises while the U.S. demand for Australian goods declines. Thus, the Australian dollar should weaken.

   If U.S. investors believed in the IFE, they would not attempt to capitalize on higher Australian interest rates because they would expect the Australian dollar to depreciate over time.

ANSWERS TO SELF-TEST QUESTIONS FOR CHAPTER 9

1. U.S. four-year interest rate = $(1+.07)^4$ = 131.08% or 1.3108. Mexican four-year interest rate = $(1+.20)^4$ = 207.36% or 2.0736.

$$p = \frac{(1+i_b)}{(1+i_f)} - 1 = \frac{1.3108}{2.0736} - 1$$

$$= -.3679 \text{ or } -36.79\%.$$

Canadian dollar $\dfrac{|\$.80-\$.82|}{\$.82} = 2.44\%$

Japanese yen $\dfrac{|\$.012-\$.011|}{\$.011} = 9.09\%$

The forecast error was larger for the Japanese yen.

3. The forward rate of the peso would have overestimated the future spot rate because the spot rate would have declined by the end of each month.

4. Semistrong-form efficiency would be refuted since the currency values do not adjust immediately to useful public information.

5. The peso would be expected to depreciate because the forward rate of the peso would exhibit a discount (be less than the spot rate). Thus, the forecast derived from the forward rate is less than the spot rate, which implies anticipated depreciation of the peso.

6. As the chapter suggests, forecasts of currencies are subject to a high degree of error. Thus, if a project's success is very sensitive to the future value of the bolivar, there is much uncertainty. This project could easily backfire, because the future value of the bolivar is very uncertain.

ANSWERS TO SELF-TEST QUESTIONS FOR CHAPTER 10

1. Managers have more information about the firm's exposure to exchange rate risk than do shareholders and may be able to hedge it more easily than shareholders could. Shareholders may prefer that the managers hedge for them. Also, cash flows may be stabilized as a result of hedging, which can reduce the firm's cost of financing.

2. The Canadian supplies would have less exposure to exchange rate risk because the Canadian dollar is less volatile than the Mexican peso.

3. The Mexican source would be preferable because the firm could use peso inflows to make payments for material that is imported.

4. No. If exports are priced in dollars, the dollar cash flows received from exporting will depend on Mexico's demand, which will be influenced by the peso's value. If the peso depreciates, Mexican demand for the exports would likely decrease.

5. The earnings generated by the European subsidiaries will be translated to a smaller amount in dollar earnings if the dollar strengthens. Thus, the consolidated earnings of the U.S.-based MNCs will be reduced.

ANSWERS TO SELF-TEST QUESTIONS FOR CHAPTER 11

1. Amount of A$ to be invested today   = A\$3,000,000/(1+.12)
   = A\$2,678,571

   Amount of U.S. \$ to be borrowed to convert to A$ = A\$2,678,571 × \$.85
   = \$2,276,785

   Amount of U.S. \$ needed in one year to pay off loan = \$2,276,785 × (1+.07)
   = \$2,436,160

2. The forward hedge would be more appropriate. Given a forward rate of \$.81, Montclair would need \$2,430,000 in one year (computed as A\$3,000,000 × \$.81) when using a forward hedge.

3. Montclair could purchase currency call options in Australian dollars. The option could hedge against the possible appreciation of the Australian dollar. Yet, if the Australian dollar depreciates, Montclair could let the option expire and purchase the Australian dollars at the spot rate at the time it needs to send payment. A disadvantage of the currency call option is that a premium must be paid for it. Thus, if Montclair expects the Australian dollar to appreciate over the year, the money market hedge would probably be a better choice, since the flexibility provided by the option would not be useful in this case.

4. Even though Sanibel Co. is insulated from the beginning of a month to the end of the month the forward rate will become higher each month, because the forward rate moves with the spot rate. Thus, the firm will pay more dollars each month, even though it is hedged during the month. Sanibel will be adversely affected by the consistent appreciation of the pound.

5. Sanibel Co. could engage in a series of forward contracts today to cover the payments in each successive month. In this way, it locks in the future payments today and does not have to agree to the higher forward rates that may exist in future months.

6. A put option on SF2,000,000 would cost \$60,000. If the spot rate of the SF reached \$.68 as expected, the put option would be exercised, which would yield \$1,380,000 (computed as SF2,000,000 × \$.69). Accounting for the pre-

mium costs of $60,000, the receivables amount would convert to $1,320,000. If Hopkins remains unhedged, it expects to receive $1,360,000 (computed as SF2,000,000 × $.68). Thus, the unhedged strategy is preferable.

ANSWERS TO SELF-TEST QUESTIONS FOR CHAPTER 12

1. Salem could attempt to purchase its chemicals from Canadian sources. Then, if the C$ depreciates, the reduction in dollar inflows resulting from its exports to Canada will be partially offset by a reduction in dollar outflows needed to pay for the Canadian imports.

   An alternative possibility for Salem is to finance its business with Canadian dollars, but this would probably be a less efficient solution.

2. A possible disadvantage is that Salem would forego some of the benefits if the C$ appreciated over time.

3. The consolidated earnings of Coastal Corp. will be adversely affected if the pound depreciates because the British earnings will be translated into euro earnings for the consolidated income statement at a lower exchange rate. Coastal could attempt to hedge its translation exposure by selling pounds forward. If the pound depreciates, it will benefit from its forward position, which could help offset the translation effect.

4. This argument has no perfect solution. It appears that shareholders penalize the firm for poor earnings even when the reason for poor earnings is a weak euro that has adverse translation effects. It is possible that translation effects could be hedged to stabilize earnings, but Arlington may consider informing the shareholders that the major earnings changes have been due to translation effects and not to changes in consumer demand or other factors. Perhaps shareholders would not respond so strongly to earnings changes if they were well aware that the changes were primarily caused by translation effects.

5. Lincolnshire has no translation exposure since it has no foreign subsidiaries. Kalafa has translation exposure resulting from its subsidiary in Spain.

ANSWERS TO SELF-TEST QUESTIONS FOR CHAPTER 13

1. Possible reasons may include
   more demand for the product (depending on the product)
   better technology in Canada
   fewer restrictions (less political interference)

2. Possible reasons may include
   more demand for the product (depending on the product)
   greater probability to earn superior profits (since many goods have not been marketed in Mexico in the past)
   cheaper factors of production (such as land and labor)
   possible exploitation of monopolistic advantages

3. U.S. firms prefer to enter a country when the foreign country's currency is weak. U.S. firms normally would prefer that the foreign currency appreciate after they invest their dollars to develop the subsidiary. The executive's comment suggests that the euro is too strong, so any U.S. investment of dollars into Europe will not convert into enough euros to make the investment worthwhile.

4. It may be easier to engage in a joint venture with a Chinese firm, which is already well established in China, to circumvent barriers.

5. The government may attempt to stimulate the economy in this way.

ANSWERS TO SELF-TEST QUESTIONS FOR CHAPTER 14

1. In addition to earnings generated in Jamaica, the NPV is based on some factors not controlled by the firm, such as the expected host government tax on profits, the withholding tax imposed by the host government, and the salvage value to be received when the project is terminated. Furthermore, the exchange rate projections will affect the estimates of dollar cash flows received by the parent as earnings are remitted.

2. The most obvious effect is on the cash flows that will be generated by the sales distribution center in Ireland. These cash flow estimates will likely be revised downward (due to lower sales estimates). It is also possible that the estimated salvage value could be reduced. Exchange rate estimates could be revised as a result of revised economic conditions. Estimated tax rates imposed on the center by the Irish government could also be affected by the revised economic conditions.

3. New Orleans Exporting Co. must account for the cash flows that will be forgone as a result of the plant, because some of the cash flows that used to be received by the parent through its exporting operation will be eliminated. The NPV estimate will be reduced after this factor is accounted for.

4. (a) An increase in the risk will cause an increase in the required rate of return on the subsidiary, which results in a lower discounted value of the subsidiary's salvage value.

   (b) If the rupiah depreciates over time, the subsidiary's salvage value will be reduced because the proceeds will convert to fewer dollars.

5. The dollar cash flows of Wilmette Co. would be affected more because the periodic remitted earnings from Thailand to be converted to dollars would be larger. The dollar cash flows of Niles would not be affected so much because interest payments would be made on the Thai loans before earnings could be remitted to the United States. Thus, a smaller amount in earnings would be remitted.

6. The demand for the product in the foreign country may be very uncertain, causing the total revenue to be uncertain. The exchange rates can be very uncertain, creating uncertainty about the dollar cash flows received by the U.S. parent. The salvage value may be very uncertain; this will have a larger effect if the lifetime of the project is short (for projects with a very long life, the discounted value of the salvage value is small anyway).

ANSWERS TO SELF-TEST QUESTIONS FOR CHAPTER 15

1. Acquisitions have increased in Europe to capitalize on the inception of the euro, which creates a single European currency for many European countries. This not only eliminates the exchange rate risk on transactions between the participating European countries, but it also enables one to more easily compare valuations among European countries to determine where targets are undervalued.

2. Common restrictions include government regulations, such as antitrust restrictions, environmental restrictions, and red tape.
3. The establishment of a new subsidiary allows an MNC to create the subsidiary it desires without assuming existing facilities or employees. However, the process of building a new subsidiary and hiring employees will normally take longer than the process of acquiring an existing foreign firm.
4. The divestiture is now more feasible because the dollar cash flows to be received by the U.S. parent are reduced as a result of the revised projections of the krona's value.

ANSWERS TO SELF-TEST QUESTIONS FOR CHAPTER 16

1. First, consumers on the islands could develop a philosophy of purchasing homemade goods. Second, they could discontinue their purchases of exports by Key West Co. as a form of protest against specific U.S. government actions. Third, the host governments could impose severe restrictions on the subsidiary shops owned by Key West Co. (including the blockage of funds to be remitted to the U.S. parent).
2. First, the islands could experience poor economic conditions, which would cause lower income for some residents. Second, residents could be subject to higher inflation or higher interest rates, which would reduce the income that they could allocate toward exports. Depreciation of the local currencies could also raise the local prices to be paid for goods exported from the United States. All factors described here could reduce the demand for goods exported by Key West Co.
3. Financial risk is probably a bigger concern. The political risk factors are unlikely, based on the product produced by Key West Co. and the absence of substitute products available in other countries. The financial risk factors deserve serious consideration.
4. This event heightens the perceived country risk for any firms that have offices in populated areas (especially next to government or military offices). It also heightens the risk for firms whose employees commonly travel to other countries and for firms that provide office services or travel services.
5. Rockford Co. could estimate the net present value (*NPV*) of the project under three scenarios: (1) include a special tax when estimating cash flows back to the parent (probability of scenario = 15%), (2) assume the project ends in 2 years and include a salvage value when estimating the *NPV* (probability of scenario = 15%), and (3) assume no Canadian government intervention (probability = 70%). This results in three estimates of *NPV*, one for each scenario. This method is less arbitrary than the one considered by Rockford's executives.

ANSWERS TO SELF-TEST QUESTIONS FOR CHAPTER 17

1. Growth may have caused Goshen to require a large amount for financing that could not be completely provided by retained earnings. In addition, the interest rates may have been low in these foreign countries to make debt financing an attractive alternative. Finally, the use of foreign debt can reduce the exchange rate risk since the amount in periodic remitted earnings is reduced when interest payments are required on foreign debt.

2. If country risk has increased, Lynde can attempt to reduce its exposure to that risk by removing its equity investment from the subsidiary. When the subsidiary is financed with local funds, the local creditors have more to lose than the parent if the host government imposes any severe restrictions on the subsidiary.

3. Not necessarily. German and Japanese firms tend to have more support from other firms or from the government if they experience cash flow problems and can therefore afford to use a higher degree of financial leverage than firms from the same industry in the United States.

4. Local debt financing is favorable because it can reduce the MNC's exposure to country risk and exchange rate risk. However, the high interest rates will make the local debt very expensive. If the parent makes an equity investment in the subsidiary to avoid the high cost of local debt, it will be more exposed to country risk and exchange rate risk.

5. The answer to this question is dependent on whether you believe unsystematic risk is relevant. If the CAPM is used as a framework for measuring the risk of a project, the risk of the foreign project is determined to be low, because the systematic risk is low. That is, the risk is specific to the host country and is not related to U.S. market conditions. However, if the project's unsystematic risk is relevant, the project is considered to have a high degree of risk. The project's cash flows are very uncertain, even though the systematic risk is low.

ANSWERS TO SELF-TEST QUESTIONS FOR CHAPTER 18

1. A firm may be able to obtain a lower coupon rate by issuing bonds denominated in a different currency. The firm converts the proceeds from issuing the bond to its local currency to finance local operations. Yet, there is exchange rate risk because the firm will need to make coupon payments and the principal payment in the currency denominating the bond. If that currency appreciates against the firm's local currency, the financing costs could become larger than expected.

2. The risk is that the Swiss franc would appreciate against the pound over time since the British subsidiary will periodically convert some of its pound cash flows to francs to make the coupon payments.

   The risk here is less than it would be if the proceeds were used to finance U.S. operations. The Swiss franc's movement against the dollar is much more volatile than the Swiss franc's movement against the pound. The Swiss franc and the pound have historically moved in tandem to some degree against the dollar, which means that there is a somewhat stable exchange rate between the two currencies.

3. If these firms borrow U.S. dollars and convert them to finance local projects, they will need to use their own currencies to obtain dollars and make coupon payments. These firms would be highly exposed to exchange rate risk.

4. Paxson Co. is exposed to exchange rate risk. If the yen appreciates, the number of dollars needed for conversion into yen will increase. To the extent that the yen strengthens, Paxson's cost of financing when financing with yen could be higher than when financing with dollars.

5. The nominal interest rate incorporates expected inflation (according to the so-called Fisher effect). Therefore, the high interest rates reflect high expected inflation. Cash flows can be enhanced by inflation because a given profit margin converts into larger profits as a result of inflation, even if costs increase at the same rate as revenues.

ANSWERS TO SELF-TEST QUESTIONS FOR CHAPTER 19

1. The exporter may not trust the importer or may be concerned that the government will impose exchange controls that prevent payment to the exporter. Meanwhile, the importer may not trust that the exporter will ship the goods ordered and therefore may not pay until the goods are received. Commercial banks can help by providing guarantees to the exporter in case the importer does not pay.

2. In accounts receivable financing, the bank provides a loan to the exporter secured by the accounts receivable. If the importer fails to pay the exporter, the exporter is still responsible to repay the bank. Factoring involves the sales of accounts receivable by the exporter to a so-called "factor," so that the exporter is no longer responsible for the importer's payment.

3. The guarantee programs of the Export-Import Bank provide medium-term protection against the risk of nonpayment by the foreign buyer due to political risk.

ANSWERS TO SELF-TEST QUESTIONS FOR CHAPTER 20

1. $r_f = (1 + i_f)(1 + e_f) - 1$
   If $e_f = -6\%$, $r_f = (1 + .09)[1 + (-.06)] - 1$
   $= .0246$, or 2.46%
   If $e_f = 3\%$, $r_f = (1 + .09)(1 + .03) - 1$
   $= .1227$, or 12.27%

2. $E(r_f) = 50\%(2.46\%) + 50\%(12.27\%)$
   $= 1.23\% + 6.135\%$
   $= 7.365\%$

3. $e_f = \dfrac{(1 + r_f)}{(1 + i)} - 1$
   $= \dfrac{(1 + .08)}{(1 + .05)} - 1$
   $= .0286$, or 2.86%

4. $E(e_f) = $ (Forward rate – Spot rate)/Spot rate
   $= (\$.60 - \$.62)/\$.62$
   $= -.0322$, or 3.22%
   $E(r_f) = (1 + i_f)[1 + E(e_f)] - 1$
   $= (1 + .09)[1 + (-.0322)] - 1$
   $= .0548$, or 5.48%

5. The two-currency portfolio will not exhibit much lower variance than either individual currency because the currencies tend to move together. Thus, the diversification effect is limited.

ANSWERS TO SELF-TEST QUESTIONS FOR CHAPTER 21

1. The subsidiary in Country Y should be more adversely affected because the blocked funds will not earn as much interest over time. In addition, the funds will likely be converted to dollars at an unfavorable exchange rate because the currency is expected to weaken over time.

2. $E(r) = (1 + i_f)[1 + E(e_f)] - 1$
   $= (1 + .14)(1 + .08) - 1$
   $= .2312$, or 23.12%

3. $E(e_f) = $ (Forward rate – Spot rate)/Spot rate
   $= (\$.19 - \$.20)/\$.20$
   $= -.05$, or -5%
   $E(r) = (1 + i_f)[1 + E(e_f)] - 1$
   $= (1 + .11)[1 + (-.05)] - 1$
   $= .0545$, or 5.45%

4. $e_f = \dfrac{(1+r)}{(1+i_f)} - 1$

   $= \dfrac{(1+.06)}{(1+.90)} - 1$

   $= -.4421$, or -44.21%

   If the bolivar depreciates by less than 44.21 percent against the dollar over the one-year period, a one-year deposit in Venezuela will generate a higher effective yield than a one-year U.S. deposit.

5. Yes. Interest rate parity would discourage U.S. firms only from covering their investments in foreign deposits by using forward contracts. As long as the firms believe that the currency will not depreciate to offset the interest rate advantage, they may consider investing in countries with high interest rates.

index

index

index

index